INTERNATIONAL ECONOMIC LAW AS SYMPHONY

This open access book brings together some of the most eminent scholars of international trade to celebrate the scholarly, diplomatic, and institution-building achievements of Thomas Cottier, Professor Emeritus of International Economic Law at the University of Bern and founder of the World Trade Institute.

Over his half-century career, Thomas Cottier has promoted the development of international trade law by shaping our understanding of how multiple layers of law interact to form a global legal system. While multilateral trade law is the 'melody' of the system, it is made fuller by a host of regional and national layers of harmonising – and sometimes discordant – legal rules.

Covering both general trade policy and the economic relations between Switzerland and the EU, the chapters examine Thomas Cottier's fundamental belief in the necessity of studying the interaction of every level of governance – local, national, and international – when considering the policies of economic exchange between countries, as well as his cosmopolitan belief in the need to foster a global community dedicated to bettering the lives of individuals around the world. The special relationship between the EU and Switzerland is addressed, honouring Professor Cottier's dedication to the political debates within Switzerland on the extent to which the country should participate in the European project, exemplifying the themes of multilayered governance and the common concerns of all people.

The book's contributors comprise leading scholars and practitioners who have worked closely with, or whose work and professional journeys have been largely influenced by, Thomas Cottier.

International Economic Law as Symphony

Thomas Cottier and the Harmonies of Trade

Edited by
Krista Nadakavukaren Schefer
Rodrigo Polanco
and
Pierre Sauvé

•HART•
OXFORD • LONDON • NEW YORK • NEW DELHI • SYDNEY

HART PUBLISHING

Bloomsbury Publishing Plc

Kemp House, Chawley Park, Cumnor Hill, Oxford, OX2 9PH, UK

1385 Broadway, New York, NY 10018, USA

Bloomsbury Publishing Ireland Limited, 29 Earlsfort Terrace, Dublin 2, D02 AY28, Ireland

HART PUBLISHING, the Hart/Stag logo, BLOOMSBURY and the Diana logo are trademarks of Bloomsbury Publishing Plc

First published in Great Britain 2025

Open access was funded by the Swiss National Science Foundation.

A catalogue record for this book is available from the British Library.

A catalogue record for this book is available from the Library of Congress.

Library of Congress Control Number: 2025930487

ISBN: HB: 978-1-50998-078-9
ePDF: 978-1-50998-076-5
ePub: 978-1-50998-077-2

Typeset by Compuscript Ltd, Shannon

For product safety related questions contact productsafety@bloomsbury.com

To find out more about our authors and books visit www.hartpublishing.co.uk. Here you will find extracts, author information, details of forthcoming events and the option to sign up for our newsletters.

TURNING THE TIDES OF TRADE

MARION PANIZZON

There was a gap at Berne law school
Something was amiss, a hole in our midst
The law in the books had not yet understood
How taxes, customs, duties were
Penalizing Swiss watches, metals, drugs and other goodies

When exported to more advantageous production hubs
Students had to grasp how global commerce works
That consumer protection and clinical tests
Means hell for export industries' perks

Thomas took the plunge to carefully, and sometimes less
Assess, whether the capacities of Swiss legal nerds
Were ready to absorb the learnings on the WTO
Necessity test and the Chapeau, to many sounded absurd

At Fribourg's faculty the enthusiasm was more reserved
Yet, the tale of GATT had spread like fire
Word was that Thomas coursework was real bliss
Compared to other classes that were more hit and miss

With Neuchatel an ally, BENEFRI in tow
Such solid foundation for an academic sisterhood was a gain
Doctoral candidates formerly taught in divorce and debts
Were now imbibing an education in production chains

With foresight Thomas and his crew of scholars
Paved the way for the World Trade Institute, a bustling center
As one could see from offices illuminated at night
Announcing the rise of a new working class, so please enter

A map producing factory site, proved for the WTI just right
Located on a side-street named for Albert Haller, a man of more than one identity
Physician, botanist and poet lore of Bernese bourgeoisie
For the WTI, Haller's career was to provide visitors with access to the IT

There was nothing to hide in that new building
Fashioned and financed by Berne's feminist pioneers
Glass was to pierce the ceilings without pain
Transparency prevailed without recourse to veneer

In those see-thru office spheres, known as the aquarium
Neither a secret lover nor the chocolate bar, could hide
As everyone would fear Thomas' nightly raids
Destined at desks turning into snacking fests; disorder, was against his pride

On the lake of Thun, to keep afloat
Exchanging his life vest for a ski dress
Thomas keeps Buddy on course, his beloved sailing boat
It takes progressive Swissness, to raid for progress

A member-driven organization with a centre that often does not hold?,[1]
Such governing under duress leads sometimes to a mess
Take trade and human rights instead, we're told
To remove protectionist excess

Suffering from tidal waves of sovereign 'old'
Leads nations to renounce to the most-favoured nation fest
Yet, despite the fate of mercantile recess – the WTO will not fold
For the guardian of the World Trade Institute, there is no idle rest

Who's afraid of equity? A balancing act bespoke
To estop the angry Eurocentric mould,
Conversely, if the legal texts would soak estoppel
They'd mount like that Appellate Body's case load

As if Jupiter himself had multilateralism divided
Pitting Olympians against the Titans' trumping load
Who put an end to trade disputes revived?
For this civil servant, there was one thing he never traded, nor he sold

[1] WB Yeats, 'The Second Coming' (1919).

Which is to keep generations of MILEs, faculty and staff engaged and bold
To regroup, team up and to reset an isolated single-mind
Sharks were nurtured bait, while whales were told to wait
His finest quality was to turn a green room color-blind

Trade 2.0 gave the quotas a final blow
And TRIPS received a mailbox rule
For Thomas, India was not to wait
The rule of law is not for a fool

When the WTO escaped a wedlock fate
Doha went on linking South to North in haste
The TRIPS accumulated patent filings
Yet, patent overgreening was not on its plate

Thomas's visions, for sure, were not putting his mind at ease:
To affirm a trader's human rights
To attenuate the plights of humankind
To debate federalism, Thomas went straight into a fight

Once the USA amputated the WTO dispute bodies
Time was ripe to criticize the judges' disregard
For commonsensicals like trade defense and remedies
The rule of law evaporated into a nirvana, and hit traders hard

To take the 'road less travelled',[2] Thomas
For his Walden had found Silvia, and softer peace
Her companionship was vital for his scholarship
Family at home and another one at work, a lot to shoulder
When one does not have the golden fleece

Together with his teachers, friends and students around the world
Many occasions to give apology or to receive utopia
Those who had committed to work with him, learned from his skills
Yet, we all had to walk the line to avoid dystopia

If Thoreau went back to nature, and Yeats rejoiced in golden apples,
Cottier let his kite fly high into blue skies, and not in vain
Kipling-like, to get the East to talk to West and the South to North
To keep the conversation going, running in his veins … since:

'Never the twain shall meet', no option for this staunch believer in humanity.[3]

[2] Henry David Thoreau, *Walden or Life in the Woods* (Ticknor and Fields, 1854).
[3] A line from Rudyard Kipling, 'The Ballad of East and West' (1989).

PREFACE

Thomas Cottier, to whom this volume is dedicated as a Festschrift, has been a leading figure in the creation of a scholarly and intellectual community surrounding world trade law, especially the law of the World Trade Organization (WTO). The WTO was a major transformation of the multilateral trade order represented by the General Agreement on Tariffs and Trade (GATT). One aspect of that transformation was the creation of a dispute settlement system based upon law, not diplomacy – with a form of compulsory jurisdiction, binding dispute rulings that did not require political acquiescence, and an appellate tribunal, the Appellate Body.

In the GATT era, where dispute panels existed but reflected more a form of diplomatic mediation than judicial rigour, there were only a few scholars who treated world trade law as a serious branch of jurisprudence. Thomas Cottier was among these, and the conferences and collaborations that he put together in the early years of the WTO (especially the World Trade Forum, which Cottier co-convened with Petros Mavroidis) were indispensable in bringing together – as well as forming a group of – outstanding legal scholars who could provide serious analysis and critique of the emerging case law of the Appellate Body.

Many of these scholars have provided original contributions to this volume. The current moment, unlike when Cottier was beginning his annual World Trade Forum conferences in the late 1990s, is one much more of anxiety than hope for the fate of the rule of law in international trade relations. Nevertheless, the WTO jurisprudence, and perspectives of scholars such as Cottier and his colleagues and former students represented in this book, have shaped discourse about trade law and policy in a way that, I believe, is largely irreversible.

Politics may in the end prevail, but the law as it has evolved will still shape political debate and conflict over trade. The blockage of the Appellate Body has nevertheless not prevented a significant number of disputes from being decided by panels, which have largely followed the lines of jurisprudence developed over two decades by the Appellate Body. Some of these post-AB panel rulings have been ignored, some implemented, a few have been appealed to an ad hoc mechanism established by a subset of WTO Members (the 10-person Multi-Party Interim Appeal Arbitration Arrangement, or MPIA, one of whom is Cottier). Other post-AB panel rulings have shaped or instigated particular political settlements. But all remain part of the normative landscape. To the extent that justice, or fairness, plays a large role, explicit or implicit, in trade disputes, legal standards and concepts inevitably shape how these conflicts play out.

As a pioneering scholar in world trade law, Cottier had a range of strengths that have been discussed in the introduction to this volume as well as by a number of the contributors.

First of all, he was a real scholar. Although an insider in the sense that he participated as a panelist in disputes and was a negotiator for the Swiss government at times, he was always more interested in the ideas and the deep structural questions of the legal system of trade than in gossip around the Secretariat, or hobnobbing with notables in politics or business. In the GATT era, this profile of academic seriousness in the field was highly unusual.

Again, unusually, he had a strong background and scholarly record in public law, Swiss and comparative. I came to the international trade field from (in my case Canadian) constitutional and administrative law and I felt that always with Cottier we were talking the same language in probing issues of legitimacy where trade dispute authorities were grappling with the review of complex domestic regulatory schemes, particularly those that were the product of pluralist democracies. By contrast, many of those writing in the field in the relatively early days were either commercial lawyers, anti-dumping attorneys, or dilettantes in law whose main background was in economics. The latter group was ill at ease in dealing with, for instance, trade and environment or trade and health controversies, indeed often hostile to broad public policy concerns being brought within the GATT/WTO house, as it were, although this was inevitable given the sweep of the WTO agreements in areas such as intellectual property or technical regulations.

Also, in the early days the trade law intellectual community was heavily male-dominated, and its inner circles had few scholars from emerging economies or the developing world. Cottier's own mentorship contributed a great deal to redressing the gender imbalance. Under Cottier's leadership and thanks to his vision, the World Trade Institute (WTI) ended up forming generations of trade law scholars and practitioners from throughout the global South.

Cottier also sought to introduce concepts and approaches from non-trade areas of international law into the jurisprudence of the WTO, again in contrast to a certain narrowness in the early generation of international economic lawyers who (ironically, given the system's trajectory) sometimes displayed a certain arrogance that trade law was serious 'law' while public international law, especially in areas such as human rights and environment, was mostly hot air.

A final, personal note. I had hoped to contribute an essay to this volume but was prevented by a fluke health issue that preoccupied me for some months (and thankfully is resolved). I am sure in my future scholarship I will come to engage again with Thomas's immense contribution to these debates as well as others in the intellectual community he developed and nourished, which is ably represented in these pages. In our discussions and debates, I often came to different conclusions from Cottier, on issues such as policy space for domestic regulatory diversity and the role of science in trade law, but I always had the sense of being in dialogue with someone who fully understood what was at stake in these controversies and who always addressed them with scholarly rigour and without ideological rancour.

I salute Thomas on the happy occasion of this Festschrift, which also coincides with what I hope will be a very happy 75th birthday.

Robert Howse
Professor, New York University School of Law, USA

ACKNOWLEDGEMENTS

The editors and authors of this book would like to express their gratitude for the generous financial support of the Swiss National Science Foundation, which has made this publication available in open access.

TABLE OF CONTENTS

PART II
REGIONAL TRADE RELATIONS BETWEEN UNEQUALS: SWITZERLAND, THE EU AND BEYOND

PART III
ADDRESSING COMMON CONCERNS AND THE FUTURE CHALLENGES TO TRADE LAW

PART IV
THE LIVING LEGACY OF THOMAS COTTIER

LIST OF CONTRIBUTORS

Frederick M Abbott, Edward Ball Eminent Scholar Professor of Law, Florida State University (FSU) College of Law

Zaker Ahmad, Georg Forster Postdoctoral Fellow, University of Göttingen; Associate Professor of Law, University of Chittagong, Bangladesh

Arthur Appleton, Appleton Luff – International Lawyers, Senior Adjunct Professor at Johns Hopkins School of Advanced International Studies (SAIS Europe)

Iryna Bogdanova, Postdoctoral Researcher, University of Luxembourg

William J Davey, Guy Raymond Jones Chair in Law Emeritus, University of Illinois College of Law (Director, Legal Affairs Division, WTO – 1995–99)

Panagiotis Delimatsis, Professor of EU and International Economic Law, Tilburg University

Roberto Echandi, Global Trade Specialist, World Bank, Non-Resident Fellow World Trade Institute, University of Bern

Malebakeng Agnes Forere, Associate Professor in Law, University of the Witwatersrand (WITS), South Africa

Maria George, PhD candidate at the Graduate Institute, Geneva (IHEID)

Christian Häberli, Senior Research Fellow, World Trade Institute (WTI), University of Bern

Michael Hahn, Professor of European and International Economic Law, Managing Director of the Institute of European and International Economic Law, Director, World Trade Institute (WTI), Faculty of Law, University of Bern

Gary Horlick, Visiting Lecturer, Yale Law School; Law Offices of Gary N Horlick

Robert Howse, Professor, New York University

Sufian Jusoh, Director and Professor of International Trade and Investment, Institute of Malaysian and International Studies (IKMAS UKM), National University of Malaysia

Christine Kaufmann, Professor of Public Law, Public International and European Law, University of Zurich

Elisa Lunardon, Legal Trainee, Noyb – European Center for Digital Rights

Gabrielle Marceau, Associate Professor at the University of Geneva and Senior Counsellor in Research at the Economic Research and Statistics Division, WTO Secretariat

Petros C Mavroidis, Edwin B Parker Professor of Foreign & Comparative Law, Columbia Law School

Krista Nadakavukaren Schefer, Vice-Director, Swiss Institute of Comparative Law; Senior Fellow, World Trade Institute (WTI), University of Bern

James J Nedumpara, Professor and Head, Centre for Trade and Investment Law & India Chair, WTO Chairs Program

Matthias Oesch, Professor and Chair for Public Law, European Law and International Economic Law, University of Zurich

Marion Panizzon, Senior Research Fellow, World Trade Institute (WTI), University of Bern

Ernst-Ulrich Petersmann, Professor Emeritus, European University Institute (EUI)

Rodrigo Polanco, Senior Lecturer and Researcher, World Trade Institute (WTI), University of Bern; Legal Adviser, Swiss Institute of Comparative Law

Intan Murnira Ramli, Senior Policy Fellow, Policy Design Department, Economic Research Institute for ASEAN and East Asia (ERIA)

Pierre Sauvé, Senior Trade Specialist, World Bank (Director of Studies, World Trade Institute (WTI)–2008–14; Director of External Programs and Academic Partnerships, WTI - 2014–17)

Ana Sijakovic Kressner, Research Fellow, Institute of European and International Economic Law, Faculty of Law, University of Bern

Peter Van den Bossche, Chair Professor of International Economic Law, Xi'an Jiaotong University, China; Fellow Emeritus, World Trade Institute, Bern, Switzerland; Professor Emeritus of International Economic Law, University of Bern, Switzerland, and Maastricht University, The Netherlands; and former Member and Chair of the Appellate Body of the World Trade Organization.

1

Introduction

KRISTA NADAKAVUKAREN SCHEFER,
RODRIGO POLANCO AND PIERRE SAUVÉ

It is no exaggeration to say that Thomas Cottier is one of the founding fathers of modern international economic law (IEL). He is also the founding father of the study of international economic law in Switzerland. Thomas was not the first scholar in Switzerland to recognise the importance of international exchange to the country's well-being,[1] but he was the first to clothe a professorship solely focused on the rules governing such exchanges and the first to establish a globally focused academic programme dedicated to educating young professionals in the economics, politics and law of international trade.

He did this, moreover, not with a mindset of lecturing about the technical rules (of which there are plenty – and about which he knows an enormous amount), but with one of gaining a deeper understanding of the interactions of multiple legal systems on trade law as a branch of general international law. Laws from different jurisdictions and laws from different legal regimes, as well as the foundational principles of international law itself, were the basic tools Thomas applied when addressing legal questions.

His earliest international law publications examined fundamental concepts such as 'estoppel' and 'acquiescence', and integrated constitutional law concepts into ideas such as 'legality'.[2] His writings on international trade rules began prior to the completion of the Uruguay Round of multilateral trade negotiations conducted within the framework of the General Agreement on Tariffs and Trade, and at a time during which intellectual property law was emerging as a new frontier of

[1] Arthur Dunkel (1932–2005), General Secretary of the GATT during the Uruguay Round, was also educated and a lecturer at Swiss universities (University of Lausanne and University of Fribourg, respectively).

[2] Jörg Paul Müller and Thomas Cottier, 'Stichworte "Acquiescence" und "Estoppel" in *Encyclopedia of Public International Law*, vol 7 (North Holland, 1982) 5–7 bzw, 78–81; Thomas Cottier, *Die Verfassung und das Erfordernis der gesetzlichen Grundlage. Eine Untersuchung zum Legalitätsprinzip und schweizerischen Gesetzesverständnis aus individualrechtlicher Sicht* (Rüegger, 1983); Thomas Cottier, *Die Verfassung und das Erfordernis der gesetzlichen Grundlage. Eine Untersuchung zum Legalitätsprinzip und schweizerischen Gesetzesverständnis aus individualrechtlicher Sicht*, 2nd extended edn (Rüegger, 1991).

trade governance. Intellectual property protection rules in the European integration context were topics of Thomas's writings in his pre-professorial period.[3] Far beyond his insightful depiction of a nascent trade rule-making field, these articles also explained why Thomas deemed it necessary to have international standards for protecting intellectual property rights – foremost among which was the belief that this would foster development.[4]

The early 1990s was also the time in which Thomas was developing his ideas about the relationship of constitutional structures, publishing an influential article on 'substance–structure pairing' in 1993.[5] These ideas continued to ripen, even

[3] Thomas Cottier, 'Die Bedeutung des GATT im Prozess der Europäischen Integration' in Olivier Jacot-Guillarmod, Dietrich Schindler and Thomas Cottier, *EG Recht und schweizerische Rechtsordnung: Föderalismus, Demokratie, Neutralität, GATT und europäische Integration* (Helbing & Lichtenhahn, 1990) 139–85; also in Hans-Joachim Meyer-Marsilius, Walter R Schluep and Werner Stauffacher (eds), *Beziehungen Schweiz – EG: Abkommen, Gesetze und Richtlinien, Kommentare*, vol 1 (Verlag Neue Zürcher Zeitung, 1989) 1.5; Thomas Cottier, 'The Prospects for Intellectual Property in GATT' (1991) 28(2) *CML Rev* 383; Thomas Cottier, 'Perspectives of Intellectual Property in the Triangle of GATT, EC and a European Economic Area' (1991) 5 *Entertainment Law Review* 147; Thomas Cottier, 'The Role of Intellectual Property in International Trade Law and Policy: Presentation to the Council of Presidents, and the Swiss Group, International Association for the Protection of Industrial Property (AIPPI), Lucerne, 19 September 1991' (1992) II *AIPPI Association Internationale pour la Protection de la Propriété Industrielle Annuaire* 197; also in (1992)1(1) *Schweizerische Mitteilungen über Immaterialgüterrecht (SMI)/Revue Suisse de la propriéteé intellectuelle (RSPI)* 11; Thomas Cottier, 'Intellectual Property in International Trade Law and Policy: The GATT Connection' (1992) 47(I) *Aussenwirtschaft. Schweizerische Zeitschrift für internationale Wirtschaftsbeziehungen* 79; Thomas Cottier, 'Der Schutz des geistigen Eigentums im Europäischen Wirtschaftsraum: eine Übersicht (Art 65 § 2 EWR-A)' in Olivier Jacot-Guillarmod (ed), *EWR-Abkommen: Erste Analysen. Schriften zum Europarecht*, vol 9 (Schulthess, 1992) 411–32; Thomas Cottier, 'Der Schutz des geistigen Eigentums' in Roger Zäch, Daniel Thürer and Rolf H Weber (eds), *Das Abkommen über den Europäischen Wirtschaftsraum. Eine Orientierung* (Schulthess, 1992) 23–50; Thomas Cottier and Thu-Lang Tran-Thi, 'Le GATT et l'Uruguay Round: l'importance du projet d'accord TRIPs et son impact sur le droit de la propriété intellectuelle en Suisse' (1993) 2(5) *Aktuelle Juristische Praxis* 632.

[4] Thomas Cottier, 'The Value and Effects of Protecting Intellectual Property Rights within the World Trade Organization/La valeur et les consequences économiques de la protection de la propriété intellectuelle dans le cadre du GATT' in ALAI Association Littéraire et Artistique Internationale: Economie et les droits d'auteur dans les conventions internationales. Journées d'études à Genève, 27/28 juin 1994/ Economy and Authors' Rights in the International Conventions Geneva Study Session, 27/28 June 1994 (Bern, 1994) 13–22, 23–32, 70–89; Thomas Cottier, 'Die völkerrechtlichen Rahmenbedingungen der Filmförderung in der neuen Welthandelsorganisation WTO-GATT' (1994) 38 *Zeitschrift für Urheber- und Medienrecht (ZUM)* 749; Thomas Cottier, 'Das Problem der Parallelimporte im Freihandelsabkommen Schweiz-EG und im Recht der WTO-GATT' in (1995) 1 *Schweizerische Mitteilungen über Immaterialgüterrecht (SMI)/Revue suisse de la propriété intellectuelle (RSPI)* 37; Thomas Cottier, 'The Protection of Intellectual Property Rights: A Requirement for Technology Cooperation, Foreign Investment and Equitable Returns in Biotechnology Prospecting' in Schweizerisches Zentrum für internationale Landwirtschaft ZIL (eds), *Biotechnologie für Entwicklungsländer? Chancen und Risiken der Biotechnologie bei landwirtschaftlichen Nutzpflanzen. Eine Zusammenstellung der Vorträge des SVIAL/ZIL-Symposiums an der ETH Zürich, 8.-9. Juli 1994* (Vdf, 1995) 65–72; Thomas Cottier, 'Current and Future Issues Related to the TRIPS Agreement – A European Perspective' (1995) IX *AIPPI Annuaire*; XXXVIe Congrès de Montréal 1995 (25–30 juin 1995) Workshops I–X, Panel d'information (AIPPI, 1995) 83–93.

[5] Thomas Cottier, 'Constitutional Trade Regulation in National and International Law: Structure-Substance Pairings in the EFTA Experience' in Meinhard Hilf and Ernst-Ulrich Petersmann (eds), *National Constitutions and International Economic Law* (Deventer, 1993) 409–42.

as he continued producing multiple articles to explain the rules of the then-new World Trade Organization (WTO).[6]

Thomas never let his interest in multilateralism overshadow his conviction that national law needed to recognise the central importance of preferential (and regional) trade partnerships. His contribution to the Swiss debate on European relations was consistently forceful.[7] Questions about the Swiss and European markets' deepening integration, in the area of competition law and policy, for example, were also taken up by Thomas, including in areas beyond those covered by the WTO.[8]

The Cottier opus continued to expand, with Switzerland's obligations and opportunities in the context of the WTO and the ever-deepening European project the main focus of his scholarship.[9] The outlines of future projects were also

[6] Thomas Cottier, Serge Pannatier and Manfred Wagner, 'Les accords du GATT/OMC et la construction' in Baurecht vol 1 (1995) 27–32; Thomas Cottier (with Benoît Merkt), 'Die Auswirkungen des Welthandelsrechts der WTO und des Bundesgesetzes über den Binnenmarkt auf das Submissionsrecht der Schweiz' in Roland von Büren and Thomas Cottier (eds), *Berner Tage für juristische Praxis BTJP 1996: Die neue schweizerische Wettbewerbsordnung im internationalen Umfeld: Globalisierung, Wettbewerbsrecht, öffentliches Beschaffungswesen* (Stämpfli Verlag, 1997) 35–86.

[7] Thomas Cottier and Manfred Wagner, 'Auf dem Weg zum Binnenmarkt Schweiz. Kommentar' in Hans-Joachim Meyer-Marsilius, Walter R Schluep and Werner Stauffacher (eds), *Beziehungen Schweiz – EG: Abkommen, Gesetze und Richtlinien, Kommentare*, vol 3 (Orell Füssli Verlag, 1995) Ziff 3.6.1, VIII: Kommentar 1–13; reprinted as 'Auf dem Weg zum Binnenmarkt Schweiz' in Euro Info Center Schweiz OSEC. Information und Dokumentation zu EU und EWR, April 1995, 1–4/'Vers un marché intérieur suisse' in Euro Info Centre Suisse OSEC. Information sur l'UE et l'EEE, Avril 1995, 1–4; Thomas Cottier and Manfred Wagner, 'Das neue Bundesgesetz über den Binnenmarkt (BGBM): Übersicht und kurzer Kommentar' (1995) 4(12) *Aktuelle Juristische Praxis* 1582.

[8] Thomas Cottier and Philipp Probst, 'Die Extraterritorialität des Wettbewerbsrechts der Europäischen Union. Kommentar' in Hans-Joachim Meyer-Marsilius, Walter R Schluep and Werner Stauffacher (eds), *Beziehungen Schweiz – EG: Abkommen, Gesetze und Richtlinien, Kommentare*, vol 5 (Orell Füssli Verlag, 1996) Ziff 10.1, VIII: Kommentar 53 bis 67; Thomas Cottier and Benoit Merkt, 'La fonction fédérative de la liberté du commerce et de l'industrie et la loi sur le marché intérieur suisse: l'influence du droit européen et du droit international économique' in Piermarco Zen-Ruffinen and Andreas Auer (eds), *De la constitution. Etudes en l'honneur de Jean-François Aubert* (Helbing & Lichtenhahn, 1996) 449–71.

[9] Thomas Cottier, 'Zwischen Integration und Weltwirtschaft: rechtliche Spielräume der Schweiz nach der Uruguay- Runde des GATT' in Wolf Linder, Prisca Lanfranchi and Ewald R Weibel (eds), *Schweizer Eigenart – eigenartige Schweiz* (Paul Haupt, 1996) 231–44; Thomas Cottier, 'Handlungsspielräume und Zwangslagen der Schweiz in den internationalen Handelsbeziehungen' in Klaus Armingeon (ed), *Der Nationalstaat am Ende des 20. Jahrhunderts. Beiträge im Rahmen der Berner Vortragsreihe: 'Die Schweiz im Prozess der Globalisierung'* (Paul Haupt, 1996) 181–99; Thomas Cottier, 'Die Globalisierung des Rechts – Herausforderungen für die Praxis, Ausbildung und Forschung. Vortrag anlässlich der Hauptversammlung des Bernischen Juristenvereins, Burgdorf, vom 2. November 1996' (1997) 133(4) *Zeitschrift des Bernischen Juristenvereins* 217; Thomas Cottier, 'Das Ende der bilateralen Ära: Rechtliche Auswirkungen der WTO auf die Integrationspolitik der Schweiz' in Thomas Cottier and Alwin R Kopše (eds), *Der Beitritt der Schweiz zur Europäischen Union/L'adhésion de la Suisse à l'Union européenne* (Schulthess Juristische Medien, 1998) 87–112; Thomas Cottier and Krista Nadakvukaren Schefer, 'The Relationship Between World Trade Organization Law, National and Regional Law' (1998) 1(1) *Journal of International Economic Law* 83; Thomas Cottier and Daniel Wüger, 'Der schweizerische Föderalismus aus der Sicht von Globalisierung und europäischer Integration' (1999) *Rote Revue* No 2, 12; Thomas Cottier and Daniel Wüger, 'Auswirkungen der Globalisierung auf das Verfassungsrecht: Eine Diskussionsgrundlage' in Beat Sitter-Liver (ed), *Herausgeforderte Verfassung: Die Schweiz im globalen Kontext, 16. Kolloquium (1997) der Schweizerischen Akademie der Geistes- und Sozialwissenschaften*

apparent in Thomas's work: questions of how to ensure the enforcement of international law, given state sovereignty and the demands of national constitutions;[10] the reconciliation of trade liberalisation with other social values;[11] and eventually, reforming the institutional (and constitutional) weaknesses of the WTO.[12]

(Academic Press Fribourg, 1999) 241–81; Thomas Cottier, 'Die Auswirkungen der Uruguay-Runde auf die internen Entscheidungsprozesse der Schweiz: ein Rückblick' (1999) 10(3) *LeGes* 39; Thomas Cottier and Rachel Liechti-McKee, 'Schweizer Spezifika: Direkte Demokratie, Konkordanz, Föderalismus und Neutralität als politische Gestaltungsfaktoren' in Fritz Breuss, Thomas Cottier and Peter-Christian Müller-Graff (eds), *Die Schweiz im europäischen Integrationsprozess* (Nomos, 2008) 39–61.

[10] Thomas Cottier and Krista Nadakvukaren Schefer, 'Non-violation Complaints in WTO/GATT Dispute Settlement: Past, Present and Future' in Ernst-Ulrich Petersmann (ed), *International Trade Law and the GATT/WTO Dispute Settlement System* (Kluwer Law International, 1997) 145–83; Thomas Cottier and Krista Nadakavukaren Schefer, 'Switzerland: The Challenge of Direct Democracy' in John J Jackson and A Sykes (eds), *Implementing the Uruguay Round* (Clarendon Press, 1997) 333–63; Thomas Cottier, 'Die Durchsetzung der Prinzipien und Beschlüsse der WTO: Das Streitbeilegungsverfahren und seine Auswirkungen' in *Die Bedeutung der WTO für die europäische Wirtschaft. Referate des XXX. FIW-Symposiums* (Carl Heymanns, 1997) 121–37; Thomas Cottier, 'Dispute Settlement in the World Trade Organization: Characteristics and Structural Implications for the European Union' (1998) 35(2) *CML Rev* 325; Thomas Cottier, 'The WTO Dispute Settlement System: New Horizons' in American Society of International Law (ed), *The Challenge of Non-State Actors. Proceedings of the 92nd Annual Meeting, April 1–4, 1998* (American Society of International Law, 1998) 86–91; Thomas Cottier, 'Das Streitschlichtungsverfahren in der Welthandelsorganisation: Wesenszüge und Herausforderungen' in Peter-Christian Müller-Graff (ed), *Die Europäische Gemeinschaft in der Welthandelsorganisation. Globalisierung und Weltmarktrecht als Herausforderung für Europa* (Nomos, 1999/2000) 179–88.

[11] Thomas Cottier, 'The WTO and Environmental Law: Three Points for Discussion' in Agata Fijalkowski and James Cameron (eds), *Trade and the Environment: Bridging the Gap* (Cameron May, 1998) 56–64, revised as 'The WTO and Environmental Law: Some Issues and Ideas' (2005) 4(2) *ICFAI Journal of Environmental Law* 47; Thomas Cottier, 'The Protection of Genetic Resources and Traditional Knowledge: Towards More Specific Rights and Obligations in World Trade Law' (1998) 1(4) *Journal of International Economic Law* 555; Thomas Cottier and Alexandra Caplazi, 'Labour Standards and World Trade Law: Interfacing Legitimate Concerns' in Thomas Geiser, Hans Schmid and Emil Walter-Busch (eds), *Arbeit in der Schweiz des 20. Jahrhunderts. Wirtschaftliche, rechtliche und soziale Perspektiven* (Paul Haupt, 1998) 469–508; Thomas Cottier and Alexandra Caplazi, 'Marktzugang, Strukturerhaltung und Sozialdumping: Ungelöste Spannungsfelder im öffentlichen Beschaffungswesen' in Peter Forstmoser et al (eds), *Der Einfluss des europäischen Rechts auf die Schweiz, Festschrift zum 60. Geburtstag von Roger Zäch* (Schulthess Polygraphischer Verlag, 1999) 257–79; Thomas Cottier, 'Trade and Human Rights: A Relationship to Discover' (2002) 5(1) *Journal of International Economic Law* 111; Thomas Cottier, 'TRIPS, the Doha Declaration and Public Health' in (2003) 6(2) *Journal of World Intellectual Property* 385; Thomas Cottier, Elisabeth Tuerk and Marion Panizzon, 'Handel und Umwelt im Recht der WTO: Auf dem Weg zur praktischen Konkordanz' (2003) 14 (special issue) *Zeitschrift für Umweltrecht ZUR* 155.

[12] Thomas Cottier and Krista Nadakavukaren Schefer, 'Conflict Resolution in the World Trade Organization. Assessing the Story so far: Hope on the Horizon?' in Halina Ward and Duncan Brack (eds), *Trade, Investment and the Environment. Proceedings of the Royal Institute of International Affairs Conference, Chatham House, London, October 1998* (Taylor & Francis, 2000) 187–202; Thomas Cottier, 'Proposals for Moving from Ad hoc Panels to Permanent WTO Panelists' in Federico Ortino and Ernst-Ulrich Petersmann (eds), *The WTO Dispute Settlement System 1995–2003* (Kluwer Law International, 2004) 31–39 (first published in Ernst-Ulrich Petersmann (ed), *Preparing the Doha Development Round: Improvements and Clarifications of the WTO Dispute Settlement Understanding. Conference Report* (Florence, 13–14 September 2002) 40–52); Thomas Cottier and Satoko Takenoshita, 'The Balance of Power in WTO Decision-Making: Towards Weighted Voting in Legislative Response' (2003) 58(II) *Aussenwirtschaft* 171; reprinted in Mitsuo Matsushita and Dukgeun Ahn (eds), *WTO and East Asia. New Perspectives* (London, 2004) 51–89; Thomas Cottier, 'Zehn Jahre WTO: Eine Standortbestimmung' (2005) 85(2) *Wirtschaftsdienst. Zeitschrift für Wirtschaftspolitik* 67;

By the early 2010s, Thomas's attention to climate change and IEL's responses to it were firmly developing. His approach to the question took a concept from environmental policymaking – 'common concern of mankind' – and suggested it as a principle of law to not only guide, but to authoritatively define states' obligations to the global order. A 2012 paper,[13] enhanced by an article situating the notion of common concern as a concept containing another borrowed legal construct, this time from humanitarian law – responsibility to protect[14] – formed a basis for numerous further works on this topic taken up by Thomas and his students.[15] His theory on multilayered governance was also developing at this time.[16]

Post-retirement, Thomas's work to promote a rules-based international trading system and Switzerland's active participation in it continued. His work on these questions became ones with more obviously high political relevance (those, for example, of Switzerland's relationship with the EU[17] and of the possibilities for neutral states to use economic sanctions in the context of the war in Ukraine). Thomas's grasp of philosophy and history began to flow more visibly into his work. His writings in these areas are directed not only at scholarly communities, but also at policy-makers and the public at large. It is for this reason that Thomas Cottier deserves recognition for his lifelong work in the area of international law in the

Thomas Cottier, 'The Erosion of Non-Discrimination: Stern Warning Without True Remedies' (2005) 8(3) *Journal of International Economic Law* 595; Thomas Cottier, 'DSU Reform: Resolving Underlying Balance-of-Power Issues' in Giorgio Sacerdoti, Alan Yanovich and Jan Bohanes (eds), *The WTO at Ten. The Contribution of the Dispute Settlement System* (Cambridge University Press, 2006) 259–65; Thomas Cottier, 'Mini-symposium: The Future of Geometry of WTO Law' (2006) 9(4) *Journal of International Economic Law* 775; Thomas Cottier, 'Das internationale Handelssystem hinkt der Globalisierung hinterher. Ein Schweizer Forschungsprojekt erarbeitet die Grundlagen für die Überarbeitung des Welthandelssystems' (2007) *IO new management. Zeitschrift für Unternehmenswissenschaften und Führungspraxis* No 4, 8–11, minimally modified in UniPress (Universität Bern) 136/April 2008 (Welten im Handel) 5–7; Thomas Cottier, 'Preparing for Structural Reform in the WTO' (2007) 10(3) *Journal of International Economic Law* 497, also in William J Davey and John Jackson (eds), *The Future of International Economic Law* (Oxford University Press, 2008) 59–70; Thomas Cottier and Satako Takenoshita, 'Decision-Making and the Balance of Powers in WTO Negotiations: Towards Supplementary Weighted Voting' in Stefan Griller (ed), *At the Crossroads: The World Trading System and the Doha Round* (Oxford University Press, 2008) 181–229; Thomas Cottier, 'Der Strukturwandel des Aussenwirtschaftsrechts' (2019) *Swiss Review of International and European Law* No 2, 203.

[13] Thomas Cottier, 'The Emerging Principle of Common Concern: A Brief Outline' in Ernst-Ulrich Petersmann (ed), *Multilevel Governance of Interdependent Public Goods: Theories, Rules and Institutions for the Central Policy Challenge in the 21st Century* (Cadmus at EUI, 2012) 185–93.

[14] Krista Nadakavukaren Schefer and Thomas Cottier, 'Responsibility to Protect (R2P) and the Emerging Principle of Common Concern' in Peter Hilpold (ed), *Die Schutzverantwortung (R2P). Ein Paradigmenwechsel in der Entwicklung des internationalen Rechts?* (Brill, 2013) 123–42; republished in Peter Hilpold (ed), *Responsibility to Protect (R2P). A New Paradigm of International Law?* (Brill Nijhoff, 2015) 123–42.

[15] Thomas Cottier and Zaker Ahmad (eds), *The Prospects of Common Concern of Humankind in International Law* (Cambridge University Press, 2021).

[16] Thomas Cottier, 'Multilayered Governance, Pluralism, and Moral Conflict' (2009) 16(2) *Indiana Journal of Global Legal Studies* 647; 'Multilayered Governance und Verfassungstheorie im Völkerrecht. Vortrag im Rahmen des C[enter for] G[lobal] S[tudies]-Forum 2012 Top Down – Bottom Up? Globalisierung und Gerechtigkeit' (University of Bern, 20 February 2012).

[17] Thomas Cottier, 'Die Souveränität und das institutionelle Rahmenabkommen' (2019) 115(11) *Schweizerische Juristen-Zeitung* 345.

form of a Liber Amicorum (or, as it would be called in Switzerland, a *Festschrift*). The occasion of Thomas's 75th birthday offers an opportunity to those who have journeyed with him to celebrate a career spanning 50 years of thinking about the law, from his training in constitutional and international law under Professor Jörg Paul Müller to his work with the Swiss delegation negotiating the Uruguay Round and the European Economic Area, to his work on General Agreement on Tariffs and Trade (GATT) and WTO dispute settlement panels, his teaching and his writing, and to his recent appointment as a member of the Multi-Party Interim Appeal Arbitration Arrangement.

The three editors decided to work together on this volume because we are each tied to a different aspect of Thomas's career.

Krista met Thomas when she, freshly arrived in Bern after completing her legal degree in the USA, sat in on his courses on European Community (EC, as it was then) law and EC external economic relations law. Already familiar with international trade law from a course with John H Jackson – also a former professor of Thomas's – she joined Thomas's first team of assistants at the University of Bern's newly founded Institute of European and International Economic Law (IEW), of which Thomas was the first director. Their first research collaborations took up topics that reflected Thomas's belief in the need for rigorous analysis of trade law as a field of international law – for example, the question of what is the fundamental role of non-violation complaints in the World Trade Organization (WTO). They also wrote about the arguments for and against permitting an individual to invoke WTO provisions against its government in domestic courts. This question of the 'direct effect' of international rules was just one of many pieces in which Thomas set forth ideas about the relationship between national and international law, and it helped form a basis for his later ideas about multilayered governance. Other questions that were early indications of Thomas's imaginative capacities were behind our combined work on the definition of 'full autonomy in trade relations' as regards the WTO membership qualifications and the efforts we put into the early review of the then-still-new Dispute Settlement Understanding. Krista's views on what she considered 'trade sanctions' were challenged when Thomas, as her habilitation supervisor, pointed out the technical difference between the terms 'sanctions' and 'measures'. While the former was a common-usage term for the latter, Thomas's demand for legal precision forced her to reconsider the title of the work and left a lasting impression on the value of legal accuracy (even if at the cost of marketability).

Krista also witnessed the significant expansion of Thomas's impacts on the international academic and policy-making landscapes when, in 1999, he joined with Petros Mavroidis (also a contributor to this volume) and Damien Neven to form the World Trade Institute (WTI). Moving from the University of Bern's main building to the new premises on Hallerstrasse, the combined office space of the IEW and the WTI signalled a significant new chapter in Thomas's career.

The WTI and its flagship Master of International Law and Economics (otherwise known as the MILE programme) was an unabashedly ambitious project. Outwardly oriented, the establishment of a multidisciplinary graduate programme of study in the law, economics and political economy of trade governance found its root in Thomas's experience as a Swiss negotiator in the Uruguay Round of GATT negotiations and translated his belief that better and more broadly trained officials, particularly from developing countries, stood a better chance of producing better – and reciprocally beneficial – trade outcomes. The idea of promoting the pursuit of applied policy research and training against an enlarged multidisciplinary canvas was and remains unique. The prescience of Thomas's focus on scaling up the capacity of promising cohorts of trade policy officials and experts can be seen from the fact that the WTI came into being a full seven years before the multilateral trade community launched its Aid for Trade initiative aimed at building up the capacity of developing countries to design and implement sounder trade policies and addressing the key supply-side constraints holding back their fuller participation in world trade.

The institution-building phase of Thomas's career at the WTI saw him collaborate closely with Pierre Sauvé. Having already got to know each other as members of the Evian Group, an informal trade-focused think tank led by the International Institute for Management Development (IMD)'s Jean-Pierre Lehmann in Lausanne, Thomas invited Pierre to join the MILE faculty to teach a module on trade in services. Trade in services is a field of trade governance characterised, then and now, by considerable sectoral and regulatory heterogeneity that has long pointed to the need for multilayered policy approaches dear and central to Thomas's scholarship. Starting in 2005, Pierre deepened his WTI ties by co-leading, at Thomas's behest, the National Centre of Competence for Research (NCCR) Trade Regulation research team on trade in services, whose work paid particular attention to comparative regional dynamics in services trade. His ties to the Institute's expanding training and research portfolio would deepen further when joining the WTI staff in 2008, first as Director of Studies overseeing the MILE programme, a role he assumed from 2008 to 2014. This period witnessed a significant expansion of the Institute's international outreach portfolio, with Pierre serving as Director of External Programs and Academic Partnerships. This included a major, seven-year project funded by the Swiss State Secretariat for Economic Affairs (SECO), which Thomas initiated with a view to building WTI-like capacity in partner universities in five developing countries – Chile, Indonesia, Peru, South Africa and Vietnam. Since joining the Geneva office of the World Bank in 2017, Pierre has continued to cooperate closely with the Institute, maintaining his faculty affiliation and contributing to a range of WTI-led training programmes, a number of which are associated with his new employer.

Rodrigo Polanco Lazo met Thomas later in his career as one of a batch of PhD students Thomas supervised who were sponsored to complete their doctoral studies thanks to a scholarship funded by SECO. This scholarship was part of a Program on the Promotion of Human Capacities in Trade Law and Policy – for which the WTI was the implementing agency between 2010 and 2017. Together with Pierre, Rodrigo played a key role in implementing the SECO/WTI Academic Cooperation Project depicted above, an initiative in which Thomas also played a prominent role during the final part of his tenure as WTI Managing Director.

I. The Volume

Thomas Cottier's love of music may not be expressed explicitly in his work, but his highly developed sense of composing grand themes, enriching those melodies with harmonising strands, and orchestrating the interaction of multiple players characterises his career. This volume seeks to capture Thomas's understanding of the complex symphony that the reality of international economic law in practice is. This volume emphasises Thomas's abilities as a composer of IEL, as a masterful instrumentalist, and as a conductor of the score. His attention to detail while not forgetting the emotional impact of the whole on the audience is what characterises Thomas's approach to IEL. We have done our best to capture these multiple, harmonising roles in the following pages.

A Swiss through and through, Thomas is a skier, a hiker and a sailor; he is multi-lingual; and he is a believer in both defensive military and international peace processes. He has led the charge to establish the study of cross-border flows of goods and services as an element of legal training in Switzerland. With convictions supported by the principles of liberal trade, Thomas has devoted much of his energy to ensuring that Switzerland's negotiating position towards the EU maintains a focus on the economic benefits of free exchange. His academic pursuits parallel these efforts, but the programmes he has established in Bern are only partly motivated by the desire to support the Swiss trade negotiating teams with a solid understanding of the instruments of trade law policy-making, for Thomas is also a student of the world. He spent several years abroad, attending kindergarten in Ann Arbor, Michigan, studying at the University of Cambridge and returning to Ann Arbor (this time to the University of Michigan) after his thesis, and has taught at universities around the globe. He has pushed for a better understanding of international legal processes, viewing international law as a pendant to domestic law, and looking at international trade law as a tool for improving the conditions of life for individuals. Thomas's concern for the human condition only increased over the years, with his newest theoretical efforts placed on the truly global questions of how to adapt the international legal system to the challenges of a changing climate. In the spirit of 'differential geometries', the contributors, too, cover a wide scope of Thomas's interests and influences. They include contemporaries as well as students, all persons who have been close to Thomas and who have influenced or have been influenced by him.

The authors write on one of three general topics that underlie much of Thomas's work: WTO policy (Part I), regionalism as an aspect of multilayered governance (Part II) and common concern (Part III). While these are by far not the only themes in Thomas's repertoire (or in the authors' own), they capture much of his particular contribution to IEL literature. Thomas's work on these topics was simultaneously foundational, detailed and thought-provoking, and the authors' chapters are equally so.

A. Prelude

A poem by Marion Panizzon opens the book. Marion is a former assistant, doctoral student and habilitation advisee of Thomas's, as well as a published poet. Her heartfelt contribution summarises in poetry what is hard to capture in prose: Thomas's value to the discipline, his colleagues and his country as an idealistic but nevertheless determined thinker. Her words are a fitting introduction to a work dedicated to the 'experimental kite'-flying, 'deep believer in humanity' that Thomas Cottier is. The poem is followed by an introductory note by Robert Howse, a long-time colleague of Thomas's who now is at New York University. Rob's Preface eloquently captures Thomas's overall contributions to the field of international economic law and points to both Thomas's personal and intellectual powers as reasons for his tremendous imprint on those of us working on the larger questions of international interactions.

B. Part I: Trade Policy from GATT to Today's WTO

The first chapter in Part I starts with a contribution by **Frederick M (Fred) Abbott**, one of Thomas's closest friends and an active advocate for ensuring that intellectual property rights serve the needs of disadvantaged individuals as well as inventors. His piece, fittingly, looks at the Agreement on Trade-Related Aspects of Intellectual Property Rights (TRIPS Agreement), both its negotiation phase, of which Thomas was an integral part, and its continuing development.

Chapter two is by another long-time friend and colleague of Thomas and a former director of the Legal Affairs Division of the World Trade Organization. **William (Bill) Davey**'s chapter looks at WTO dispute settlement in the context of the current breakdown of the appellate mechanism. The candid views Davey reveals in his explanation about the reasons behind this failure (largely stemming from the consensus decision-making procedures and the possibility of third-party interventions in the dispute resolution proceedings) make this chapter particularly interesting.

Peter Van den Bossche, who assumed until recently the role of Director of Studies at the WTI and who, like Thomas, studied under John H Jackson at the University of Michigan, critically explores how discussions on the reform of the WTO's dispute settlement system were conducted in 2023 and early 2024. These discussions were held in the run-up of the 13th WTO Ministerial Conference in February/March 2024 under the so-called 'Molina Process' led by Guatemala's

Deputy Permanent Representative to the WTO, Marco Molina. Peter's contribution further assesses the proposed changes to the WTO dispute settlement system reflected in the Consolidated Text of a draft Ministerial Decision on Dispute Settlement, submitted to the General Council on 14 February 2024, focusing in particular on proposed changes to panel proceedings, compliance, guidelines for adjudicators, procedures to discuss legal interpretations, Secretariat support, transparency and the periodic review of the implementation of the reform agenda. The author pulls no punches in depicting the proposed changes as a mixed bag of good, ill-conceived, futile and unnecessary changes. Despite its gaps and imperfections, the draft consolidated text is nevertheless depicted as a 'tour de force'.

James Nedumpara from the Centre for Trade Law and Investment at the Indian Institute of Foreign Trade, with whom the WTI has for close to a decade held a joint Summer Academy programme in New Delhi targeting Indian law students and officials, explores Thomas Cottier's contribution to our evolving understanding of subsidy disciplines. This is done, in part, through a review of major WTO dispute panel decisions dealing with subsidy-related matters. Nedumpara further recalls the multiple scholarly channels through which Thomas has long suggested the need for fresh thinking on the design and implementation of subsidy disciplines.[18]

Petros Mavroidis is another of the WTI's founders and, like Thomas, an eminent scholar in international trade law. In his chapter, Petros writes about the very topical issue of the questions arising around national security in WTO dispute settlement. WTO adjudicating bodies have had to entertain several national security disputes recently. His chapter argues that, judging by the record so far, one cannot rejoice at the outcome. More importantly, the nature of similar disputes makes them unsuitable candidates for adjudication. According to Mavroidis, the world trading community would be better served subjecting them to a consultation/conciliation process.

Gabrielle Marceau, a shaper of the WTO dispute settlement system from within the Organisation, also pays tribute to Thomas's involvement in the dispute settlement system. Her piece, co-authored with **Maria George**, looks at four institutional functions of the WTO and how they have evolved in the context of the emerging climate crisis. Their chapter provides the substantive content of the WTO's 'new' role beyond its traditional mandate, representing a concerted effort to bring the trade and climate regimes closer together and into congruence. To understand the origins and potential of this new role, the chapter then examines the evolving priorities of WTO members, starting with the Twelfth Ministerial Conference (MC12) outcome document and specific proposals from members dealing with climate change. Finally, the chapter looks at three ways in which the

[18] See, eg his interview in the Neue Zürcher Zeitung on 30 July 2018, www.nzz.ch/schweiz/wir-werden-uns-zwangslaeufig-staerker-an-die-eu-anlehnen-muessen-ld.1407586. See also Thomas Cottier, Garba Malumfashi, Sofya Matteotti, Olga Nartova and Joelle de Sepibus, 'Energy in WTO Law and Policy. The Prospects of International Trade Regulation: From Fragmentation to Coherence' (2011) 10.1017/CBO9780511792496.007.

potential of this new role may manifest itself in the WTO's future work: in promoting coherence between trade-related climate action and environmental principles; in filling the gap in trade rules to deal with the challenges posed by climate change; and in addressing the climate finance gap.

Christian Häberli is, like Thomas, a frequent panelist in WTO Dispute Settlement Understanding proceedings. He also works with the WTI and shares Thomas's broad vision of law and legal systems. His chapter in this book is dedicated to the role that panels play in the dispute resolution system. At a time when the failure of the appellate body is seen as the potential end of the WTO system, Haeberli's piece provides a chance to step back and consider the fundamental role of the first instance decision-makers.

C. Part II: Regional Trade Relations between Unequals: Switzerland, the EU and Beyond

Christine Kaufmann has worked with Thomas for years, as a project leader at the WTI, as a professor of trade and leader of an institute on the social responsibility of businesses, and as a collaborator on Thomas's project to promote the study and political awareness of international economic law in Switzerland. Her chapter draws parallels between Schuman's European integration project and Thomas's efforts to create an international economic law-based ecosystem to promote Switzerland as an active participant in Europe's liberal project. She points to the importance of the planning and political acumen of the creators, as well as to the institution-building that was common to these efforts.

Matthias Oesch, one of Thomas's early graduate students and currently also a professor of international economic law, has written, together with **Elisa Lunardon**, a chapter showcasing Cottier's work on multilayered governance. In their contribution, they take up his idea of examining the various layers of government not individually but instead holistically, taking the case study of another of Thomas's concerns: Switzerland's integration into the EU legal area through a plethora of bilateral agreements, and the role that the Swiss Federal Supreme Court has in their interpretation, without having the right to refer questions to the European Court of Justice (ECJ).

Along the same line, Thomas's successor as managing director of the IEW, **Michael Hahn**, together with **Ana Sijakovic Kressner**, examine the role of the Court of Justice of the EU (CJEU) with regard to Switzerland and Swiss operators. In their chapter, they conclude that the current impact of the ECJ/CJEU – as well as EU law – on the Swiss legal order is far from negligible. Switzerland's decision to remain outside the EU while simultaneously wishing to participate in the EU's internal market has created a situation in which Switzerland, although nominally unburdened by the obligations of an EU Member State, implements most of the 'laws' of the internal market. At the same time, its interests are not projected into the Union's decision-making process. Thus, even if the ECJ's decisions are not technically binding, whatever that court says about EU law inevitably serves as a contextual reference for Swiss decision-makers.

Panagiotis Delimatsis joined the WTI under the NCCR Trade Regulation project, which Thomas co-led, working on issues linked to trade, investment and the movement of labour in services alongside Pierre Sauvé and Marion Panizzon. Recalling the extraordinary depth of the relationship between Switzerland and the EU, Delimatsis's contribution recalls how the fate of the two partners is inextricably intertwined, characterised by the high degree of interdependence implicit in geographical proximity. While the EU–Swiss bilateral relationship has been long-standing and dynamic, displaying a gradual but unmistakenly discernible deepening of economic integration, the paradox is that it does not extend deeply to services despite the sector's predominance in both partners' economies. Important consequences flow from such a gap. Absent a comprehensive institutional framework governing services trade issues, Delimatsis observes that updates of the Swiss–EU sectoral agreements only take place when they are in the interests of the EU. His chapter focuses on the Agreement on the Free Movement of Persons (AFMP) tying the two trading partners. It reviews a range of systemic issues linked to the supply of services in the bilateral context with a particular focus placed on the issue of recognition of professional qualifications of service providers governed by the AFMP.

Borrowing on a central theme of Thomas Cottier's scholarship, **Sufian Jusoh**, who completed his PhD in law under Thomas at the WTI, and his co-author (and wife) **Intan Murnira Ramli** analyse the role of multilayered governance in the integration process of the Association of Southeast Asian Nations (ASEAN), a process both have been closely involved with in recent years through applied policy research. Their contribution recalls how multilayered governance has proven crucial to ASEAN's integration journey, providing opportunities for more inclusive and participatory governance and for the sharing of best practices and resources among Member States. Such an approach points to the need for ASEAN Member States to maintain a balance between different layers of governance whilst ensuring that they work together effectively to achieve the regional compact's goals through effective communication, close coordination and cooperation among all stakeholders. Doing so can ensure that policies and decisions are aligned and cohesive within a regional grouping marked by considerable diversity in development levels and collective preferences.

D. Part III: Old and New Challenges to International Trade Relations: From the WTI's Inception to Common Concern

Some of Thomas Cottier's most recent doctoral students have also contributed to this volume. **Iryna Bogdanova** and **Zaker Ahmad**, part of the last research project that Cottier undertook before his retirement (the Swiss National Science

Foundation-funded 'Towards a Principle of Common Concern in Global Law: Foundations and Case Studies'), examine the role of the emerging principle of 'Common Concern of Humankind' (CCH) as a qualified reading of state sovereignty. Their chapter studies whether there is room for deference to a rules-based global order when, in recent years, countries have taken a turn away from rules-based interactions between states and embarked on aggression in the name of security and the race for subsidies in the name of climate protection, among other things. They conclude that the doctrine remains more relevant than ever, particularly in the move towards the rule of law rather than the rule of power.

In her chapter, **Malebakeng Agnes Forere**, whose PhD work at the WTI was funded by the SECO/WTI project, uses CCH to examine the phenomenon of 'land investment' or 'landgrabs' in Africa, which has caught the attention not only of local governments, but also of civil society, international organisations and intergovernmental fora. Using that framework, she suggests the various roles that communities, investors, states and international bodies can play in curbing landgrabs.

Ernst-Ulrich Petersmann, another important international economic law scholar and frequent collaborator of Thomas Cottier, has written a chapter highlighting Thomas's contribution to European Economic Integration Law, WTO dispute settlement reform, and human and constitutional rights in international economic law. He frames Cottier's contribution to the analysis of Europe's ordoliberal constitutionalism, detailing the principles and methodologies used in Europe as drivers for sustainable development reforms in a multipolar world.

E. Part IV: The Living Legacy of Thomas Cottier

The final section of the book looks more personally at Thomas Cottier as a shaper of international economic law's landscape, emphasising his personality as core to his influence. **Arthur Appleton**, a long-standing WTI lecturer and member of its Advisory Board, tells the history of the development of the WTI's flagship MILE programme. He sees the programme, as well as the research and outreach activities undertaken at the WTI, as a manifestation of Swiss soft power at its best, linking academia, international organisations and government officials.

The next chapter is a broad look at international economic law by **Gary Horlick**, long a MILE faculty member and one of the world's leading trade lawyers in the areas of subsidies and contingent protection. For that reason, his contribution to the volume focuses not only on Thomas's academic production (either directly or indirectly, as PhD supervisor and organiser of conferences – notably the flagship World Trade Forum), but also on his contribution as a panelist in GATT and WTO disputes.

Roberto Echandi's mythical musings round off the volume. As someone working with governments to urge developmental progress through international economic activities and a Senior Fellow of the WTI, Roberto has a deep appreciation for Thomas's contributions to the field. His admonishment to all of us to keep in mind the need to remain true to moving forward despite the pull of politics is thought-provoking. His reference to Thomas as a *Leitbild* for such dedication to the cause of promoting international economic relations perfectly captures our mutual appreciation for the man to whom this volume is dedicated.

Thomas, we hope you enjoy the following pages and we all wish you many more happy years to come!

PART I

Trade Policy from GATT to Today's WTO

2

Our Life in TRIPS

FREDERICK M ABBOTT

I met Thomas 35 years ago at a meeting of the American Society of International Law in Washington, DC. We happened to be sitting next to each other in a session, and I noticed that his name tag indicated an affiliation with the Swiss Federal IP Office. We began conversing about the ongoing Agreement on Trade-Related Aspects of Intellectual Property Rights (TRIPS Agreement) negotiations, and I ventured that the Swiss had put forward an innovative proposal that I found quite interesting. He replied to the effect that he was the drafter of that proposal. Thus began our friendship and collaboration. Bringing things full circle, on 25 April 2024, Thomas and I participated in the World Trade Organization's (WTO) "30 Years of TRIPS – High Level Dialogue'.[1] Both of us, it seems, have stayed involved with this unique legal creation.

Over the course of the past few decades, Thomas and I each have expended many thousands of words on the TRIPS Agreement. We have just published the fifth edition of our course book on international IP law, adding junior talent to the original three authors. We have witnessed the evolution of the international IP system, including its struggle to achieve an appropriate balance between the rights of innovators and creators and the interests of the wider public. We do not always agree on where the balancing line should be drawn, but our differences are nuanced.

On this important occasion, I begin by revisiting the innovative 1988 Uruguay Round proposal put forward by Thomas and the Swiss delegation. Quoted below are some paragraphs from 1989 in which I described the Swiss proposal and the reaction to it:

> In late June 1988 the Swiss presented a proposal to the TRIPs working group (fn 88) that called for adoption of an amendment to the General Agreement. (fn 89) Under the proposed amendment GATT benefits may be nullified or impaired by the under-protection, over-protection, or absence of protection of intellectual property. GATT states would undertake to eliminate trade distortions resulting from derogations.

[1] WTO, '30 Years of TRIPS – High Level Dialogue: Charting the Way Ahead', www.wto.org/english/tratop_e/trips_e/trip_2503202415_e/trip_2503202415_e.htm.

> Assurances would be given for prompt, effective, and non-discriminatory administrative and judicial procedures and enforcement. 'Indicative lists' would be established to describe trade distortions resulting from under-protection, overprotection, or lack of protection of intellectual property, and from practices constituting inadequate procedures. Listed items would be presumed to nullify or impair GATT benefits. These lists would be evolutionary, and a committee would be established to offer proposals for adoption by the GATT. The parties would notify each other (through the GATT Secretariat) regarding proposed changes in intellectual property laws and would consult as requested prior to making such changes. Disputes would be settled in accordance with the procedures set forth in the General Agreement.
>
> United States negotiators greeted the Swiss proposal unenthusiastically. (fn 90) The United States took the view that an unacceptable level of compromise on substantive standards would be necessary to achieve the level of consensus required to amend the General Agreement.
>
> 88. Proposition de la Suisse, GATT TRIPs Doc. MTN.GNG/NG11/W/25 (June 29, 1988).
>
> 89. As opposed to a limited code. See infra [discussion on institutional arrangements].
>
> 90. According to industry sources close to the intellectual property negotiations, United States negotiators viewed the Swiss proposal as an unacceptable compromise because of its apparent lack of attention to elaborating specific substantive norms. This initial adverse reaction was probably due in part to a certain (seemingly deliberate) ambiguity in the Swiss proposal regarding the level of detail to be achieved by the indicative lists.[2]

While the Swiss proposal did not gain traction in the Uruguay Round negotiations, Thomas continued to develop the idea of 'variable geometries' in terms of differentiating standards of IP to be expected from countries at different levels of development.[3] He has argued that one size does not fit all – either with respect to the level of economic development or the specific IP subject matter. Thus, he argues, the level of compliance a country should be expected to achieve in relationship to the TRIPS standard should not be static, but should change as the country makes progress in its level of economic development and its corresponding technological capacity. Standards might vary in relation to the field of application, whether the arts or sciences, or along some other lines.

I. Development and IP

Thomas sees IP rights as making a significant contribution to technological progress.[4] Perhaps Thomas's view is at least in part shaped by his lifetime centred

[2] Frederick Abbott, 'Protecting First World Assets in the Third World: Intellectual Property Negotiations in the GATT Multilateral Framework' (1989) 22 *Vanderbilt Journal of Transnational Law* 689.

[3] See, eg Thomas Cottier, 'Inequality and Intellectual Property: Equity, Innovation and Creative Imitation' in Daniel Benoliel et al (eds), *Intellectual Property, Innovation and Economic Inequality* (Cambridge University Press, 2024). Excerpted in Frederick M Abbott et al, *International Intellectual Property in an Integrated World Economy* (Aspen Publishing, 2024) 166ff.

[4] See WTO, '30 Years of TRIPS' (n 1).

in Switzerland, where technological progress is evident almost everywhere and where there is limited reason to be sceptical of the role that IP may play. Going along with this, he believes that the TRIPS Agreement is a major accomplishment of the General Agreement on Tariffs and Trade (GATT) and the WTO legal systems. This is worth mentioning because there yet remains scepticism, particularly in parts of the developing world and among non-governmental organisations, about the value of IP. In some sense, among academics, it is not the common position that IP has played a net positive role.

Thomas, however, has maintained an abiding interest in the circumstances of developing countries throughout the past 30 years of the TRIPS Agreement. A good deal of his scholarly attention has been directed towards acknowledging property rights in traditional knowledge. Confirming his foresight, in May 2024 we witnessed adoption of the WIPO Treaty on Intellectual Property, Genetic Resources and Associated Traditional Knowledge.[5]

Permeating Thomas's work on IP has been a dual interest in equity and human rights.[6] Perhaps as an outgrowth of that, he has most recently turned attention to developing what he refers to as an emerging doctrine of international law, the 'common concern of humankind'.[7] The theorem behind that, it seems to me, is that there are issues confronting humankind that transcend individual regional, national and/or private civil interests, and where individualised interests should give way to the preferred outcome for the planet as a whole. His theorem is not directed solely or even preponderantly towards IP, but extends to subject matter such as the use of subsidies to promote development of sustainable energy sources and mitigation of climate change. Thomas has evidenced particular concern with regard to achieving the goals of sustainable development with respect to the environment.[8]

II. TRIPS at 30

As noted at the outset of this contribution, on 25 April 2024, Thomas and I participated on a High-Level Panel at the WTO, reflecting on the experience of the

[5] WIPO Treaty on Intellectual Property, Genetic Resources and Associated Traditional Knowledge, adopted 24 May 2024.

[6] See, eg Cottier (n 3); Thomas Cottier, 'Embedding Intellectual Property in International Law' in Pedro Roffe and Xavier Seuba (eds), *Current Alliances in International Intellectual Property Lawmaking: The Emergence and Impact of Mega-Regionals*, Global Perspectives and Challenges for the International Intellectual Property System Number 4 (ICTSD-CEIPI, 2017) 15–44; Thomas Cottier, 'Copyright and the Human Right to Property: A European and International Law Approach' in Christophe Geiger, Craig Nard and Xavier Seuba (eds), *Intellectual Property and the Judiciary* (Edward Elgar, 2018) 116–43; also excerpted in Abbott et al (n 3).

[7] Thomas Cottier, 'The Principle of Common Concern of Humankind' in Thomas Cottier (ed), *The Prospects of Common Concern of Humankind in International Law* (Cambridge University Press, 2021) 3–91.

[8] See, eg ibid 11–16; Cottier, 'Embedding Intellectual Property' (n 6).

TRIPS Agreement and prospects for the future. The following discussion reflects the remarks I made at that session.

A. Protecting First World Assets

The panel organisers posed the question of whether the TRIPS Agreement has succeeded in providing the framework for building a diverse knowledge economy. First, it should be acknowledged that building a diverse knowledge economy was not the objective of the developed country architects of the Uruguay Round. The TRIPS negotiations were designed to prevent perceived misappropriation of IP; that is, US, European and Japanese IP owners considered that they had been prevented from securing anticipated rates of return in markets, largely in developing countries, where IP was used without compensation by third parties. The negotiations were a matter of 'protecting first world assets'.[9]

Pro-innovation aspects of IP and IP protection's potential for improving the economies of developing countries were used modestly as selling points to encourage a consensus. This was viewed as necessary because the Uruguay Round negotiators recognised that developing countries, on the whole, viewed the TRIPS negotiations as an exercise in compelled rent transfer.

Has the TRIPS Agreement fulfilled its purpose in encouraging the protection of patented technologies and other IP in the developing world? I think the evidence supports that patent subject matter has been extended and that in the larger developing country markets, such as Brazil, India, South Africa and China, there is substantially less misappropriation of IP than would have been the case without the TRIPS Agreement. This is true even taking account of imperfect records, for example for China.

In the meantime, over the past 30 years, the world has witnessed extraordinary accomplishments in the evolution of technologies, even if some of those accomplishments leave us wondering whether, as a human race, we are actually better off. What we do not know is whether there is a correlation between the increased prevalence of IP rights and enforcement on the one hand and a societal increase in innovation on the other. It takes us back to the 1950s and the work of Fritz Machlup, who, when asked whether the USA should retain a patent system, said that it was difficult to justify with empirical data, but given that the USA seemed to be succeeding economically, he could not recommend getting rid of it.[10]

[9] See Abbott (n 2).

[10] Fritz Machlup, 'An Economic Review of the Patent System' (Subcommittee on Patents, Trademarks and Copyrights, of the Committee on the Judiciary, 85th Congress, 2nd session, 1958) ('If we did not have a patent system, it would be irresponsible, on the basis of our present knowledge of its economic consequences, to recommend instituting one. But since we have had a patent system for a long time it would be irresponsible, on the basis of our present knowledge, to recommend abolishing it. This last statement refers to a country such as the United States of America – not to a small country and not a predominantly nonindustrial country, where a different weight of argument might well suggest another conclusion').

Machlup's was hardly a ringing endorsement, but perhaps we might say the same about the TRIPS Agreement. I doubt we have empirically established a causal relationship between its entry to force and technological progress, but we have had technological progress.

This still leaves the issues of distributional effect, which were discussed during the Uruguay Round negotiations. With exceptions, the economic situation of individuals living in developing countries has improved since the conclusion of the Uruguay Round, but inequality in the sense of technological capacity across countries and regions persists. Thus, arguably one of the perceived threats of the TRIPS Agreement has been realised; that is, it has embedded technological advantage in certain countries and regions.[11] There are exceptions, however, as the example of China highlights. What accounts for the exceptions? It is complicated, but a simplified explanation is that China took a soft approach to the implementation of the TRIPS Agreement.[12]

B. Law and its Limitations

We have entered a period of delegalisation within and outside the WTO. When it entered into force in 1995, the WTO Agreement and its embedded multilateral trade agreements, including the TRIPS Agreement, were an experiment in deep legalisation of the international trading system. Since 1995, there has been a lot of pushback on this experiment. The WTO is not alone in experiencing this. The broader treaty-based system of international relations, whether at the United Nations, the World Health Organization (WHO) or other multilateral institutions, faces challenges in governance reflective of a divisive environment among nations. It is difficult to reach agreement on almost anything. And in this environment, countries are reluctant to cede control over the outcome of disputes to international judicial or arbitral bodies.

A case in point is the so-called 'Phase 1' agreement between the USA and China of 2020 that sought to address a number of outstanding trade and investment issues between the countries. These notably include important IP and technology transfer-related issues.[13] If you look at how disputes are resolved under that agreement, there is no judicial or arbitral dispute settlement mechanism. In the event of disagreement, the parties ultimately refer the matter to their senior trade officials. If those trade officials cannot agree on an appropriate resolution, the remedy of

[11] See Frederick Abbott, 'Managed Trade and Technology Protectionism: A Formula for Perpetuating Inequality?' in Benoliel et al (n 3).

[12] See Frederick M Abbott, 'Technology Governance in a Devolved Global Legal Order: Lessons from the China–USA Strategic Conflict' in Chia-Jui Cheng (ed), *A New Global Economic Order* (Brill Nijhoff, 2021).

[13] Economic and Trade Agreement between the Government of the United States of America and the Government of the People's Republic of China', dated 15 January 2020.

either party is to withdraw from the agreement.[14] It is effectively a return to power-based trade relations in which the outcome of the dispute is dependent on the relative strength of the parties.

Technology-related disputes have become so intense that they are difficult to resolve through negotiation or legal dispute settlement, particularly as they relate to military technology and cyber security. There is increasing recourse to the exercise of governmental powers to block transactions with disfavoured countries and/or entities, or to require divestments.[15] One cannot help but be reminded of Olivier Long's 'Law and Its Limitations in the GATT Multilateral Trading System'[16] and his reminder that not every trade dispute among nations can be settled by lawyers.

Dispute settlement is not alone in being broken. Embedded in the WTO, the TRIPS Agreement is also subject to the Organization's dysfunction at the negotiating table. Developments regarding the agreement in terms of negotiating new commitments and addressing ongoing concerns of WTO members regarding implementation are subject to the forces generally at work in the sphere of international political relations. At present, there is limited reason for optimism concerning forward-looking negotiations at the WTO.

C. Trilateralism

When the TRIPS Agreement was being negotiated in the late 1980s and early 1990s, it was anticipated that the centre of gravity regarding IP negotiations and oversight of implementation would shift from WIPO to the WTO. Perhaps for the 15 or 20 years following the entry into force of the TRIPS Agreement, the gravitational pull of the WTO was powerful. In those years, most discussions of IP matters at the international level tended to focus on what was happening at the WTO, even as WIPO continued its role in managing the Patent Cooperation Treaty and Madrid Systems. However, at least three phenomena combined to reduce the influence of the WTO in today's world.

First, various efforts at adopting new rules in the WTO stalled. With consensus decision-making at WTO making it exceedingly difficult to reach agreements, negotiations regarding the source and origin of genetic resources, geographical indications and non-violation nullification or impairment remained unresolved.

Second, the ill-advised effort to penalise South Africa for authorising parallel importation of patented pharmaceutical products undermined the credibility of the WTO as an organisation in balancing producer and consumer interests.[17]

[14] See Abbott, 'Technology Governance' (n 12).

[15] See, eg The Committee on Foreign Investment in the United States (CFIUS), https://home.treasury.gov/policy-issues/international/the-committee-on-foreign-investment-in-the-united-states-cfius.

[16] Olivier Long, *Law and Its Limitations in the GATT Multilateral Trade System* (Martinus Nijhoff Publishers, 1985).

[17] See Frederick M Abbott, 'The Doha Declaration on the TRIPS Agreement and Public Health: Lighting a Dark Corner at the WTO' (2002) 5 *Journal of International Economic Law* 469.

Diplomatic pressure on South Africa from the USA and the EU, accompanied by civil litigation initiated by major multinational pharmaceutical companies challenging a 1997 South African legislative measure, was intended to block importation of medicines placed by the same pharmaceutical companies at lower prices on markets outside South Africa. The practice of so-called 'parallel importation' was not prohibited by the TRIPS Agreement, yet the TRIPS Agreement was invoked as if it was. The South Africa 'Medicines Act' case was the subject of wide international attention and concern. While South Africa ultimately prevailed, the unwarranted episode generated a legacy of distrust.

Third, the WTO began to lose its status as the premier trade organisation. At least in part reflecting the first two phenomena, the high-income countries shifted their negotiations on IP protections to bilateral and regional fora, effectively bypassing the WTO.[18]

In the meantime, the WHO became increasingly concerned about the role that IP rights play in influencing the availability of pharmaceutical and other medical therapies. The WHO Global Strategy and Plan of Action, adopted in 2008, reflected these concerns.[19] WHO members began to spend considerable time negotiating about IP, including in the context of what became the Pandemic Influenza Preparedness Framework. The COVID-19 pandemic accentuated the IP-related conversations, and discussions regarding the transfer of technology took centre stage.[20]

Third, WIPO took on a more active role in terms of negotiating new agreements, such as the Treaty for the Visually Impaired,[21] and a WIPO Treaty on Intellectual Property, Genetic Resources and Associated Traditional Knowledge was recently adopted.[22] And while a practical matter, the EU's successful conclusion of the Geneva Act (2015) of the Lisbon Agreement on Appellations of Origin,[23] may not have had much effect, the effort demonstrated the possibility of bypassing the USA and other opposing members, and in that sense demonstrated that consensus is not needed to conclude an agreement at WIPO. On top of this, WIPO has assumed an active role in discussions on the relationship between IP rights and public health in the context of the WHO–WIPO–WTO trilateral group, evidencing a balanced perspective on social concerns arising out of IP protections. WIPO is also pursuing a green agenda.[24]

[18] See, eg Frederick Abbott, 'The Evolution of Public Health Provisions in Preferential Trade and Investment Agreements of the United States' in Roffe and Seuba (n 6) 45–63.

[19] The Global Strategy and Plan of Action on Public Health, Innovation and Intellectual Property (GSPA-PHI) adopted in May 2008 (WHA 61.21).

[20] See Frederick Abbott, *Intellectual Property and Technology Transfer for COVID-19 Vaccines: Assessment of the Record* (WIPO, 2023) www.wipo.int/publications/en/details.jsp?id=4684.

[21] Marrakesh Treaty to Facilitate Access to Published Works for Persons Who Are Blind, Visually Impaired or Otherwise Print Disabled, adopted 27 June 2013, www.wipo.int/treaties/en/ip/marrakesh/.

[22] See n 5.

[23] Geneva Act of the Lisbon Agreement on Appellations of Origin and Geographical Indications, adopted 20 May 2015, www.wipo.int/wipolex/en/treaties/textdetails/15625.

[24] See, eg WIPO Green, www3.wipo.int/wipogreen/en/.

The net of all of this is that the TRIPS Agreement did not take over the IP space at the multilateral level. IP rights are only partially TRIPS-based rights. IP treaties existed long before the TRIPS Agreement, the IP flexibilities in the TRIPS Agreement were flexibilities that existed before the TRIPS Agreement was negotiated, and enforcement predominantly takes place in national legal systems. The WTO is a presence that exercises a remote effect; it remains for countries to make decisions and act. These decisions are not controlled from Geneva, whether from the WTO, WIPO or elsewhere, and they are increasingly less influenced by the Geneva-based institutions.

D. The Waiver Debate

The decision by the governments of India and South Africa to request a broad TRIPS waiver from WTO members in reaction to the COVID-19 outbreak was disappointing. A great deal of effort had gone into affirming the right of WTO members to take measures to protect public health by using TRIPS flexibilities, and responding to COVID-19 seemed an obvious point at which to exercise those flexibilities. It is hard to understand what prompted a decision to 'request permission' from WTO members to take necessary actions to overcome obstacles presented by IP rights, particularly given that resistance to such a request seemed inevitable based on historical precedent. Both Carlos Correa and I pointed out early on in the pandemic that if countries somehow found WTO processes too cumbersome to deal with, the COVID-19 pandemic was a public health emergency of international concern that justified the invocation of national security interest to override potential IP barriers pursuant to Article 73 of the TRIPS Agreement.[25]

What would a claim look like for a TRIPS violation at the WTO if a member had taken steps to develop and produce a vaccine that was used to inoculate its citizens and prevent a substantial number of deaths? Would any WTO dispute settlement panel find a violation? What would be the remedy? And the decision to request the waiver was not without possible longer-term consequences, as there is now some suggestion that a form of WTO permission may be needed to address urgent public health interests, though I would caution against making too much of that.

Not all WTO members are yet mindful of the fact that actions to override IP rights need to be undertaken pursuant to national law. A waiver at the WTO does not change national law. It does not grant a compulsory licence.

As governments consider preparation for future pandemics, it is important that they focus on creating the rules and regulations within their national legal systems that will allow them to take urgent measures as necessary to address potential IP

[25] See, Frederick Abbott, 'The TRIPS Agreement Article 73 Security Exceptions and the COVID-19 Pandemic' (South Centre (Geneva), August 2020), Research Paper No 116.

barriers. This might be as simple as adopting a provision in national law that says that, in the event of a declared national emergency regarding public health, the government is empowered to use any and all IP as necessary or useful in confronting the emergency.

E. Article 66.2 and the LDCs

Article 66.2 of the TRIPS Agreement incorporates an obligation on the developed countries to provide ('shall provide') incentives to their enterprises and institutions to transfer technology to least-developed countries (LDCs) to enable the creation of a sound and viable technology base. There is minimal negotiating history regarding this provision.[26] Presumably, it was incorporated as a means to persuade LDCs to join the Uruguay Round consensus on TRIPS.

In 2001, there was an agreement on an annual reporting mechanism for the developed countries regarding the steps that had been taken to implement the Article 66.2 obligation.[27] The WTO has instituted an annual workshop at which the developed countries and LDCs discuss these reports.

The high-income developed countries have complied with the annual reporting mechanism, even though the reports have tended to combine a range of foreign aid-directed programmes that incorporate various elements that might not ordinarily be considered 'technology transfer' understood in an industrial policy sense.[28] And, because developed country programmes may not internally distinguish between LDCs and developing countries more broadly, it can be difficult to disaggregate the data and identify precisely what programmes have benefited the LDCs in terms of technology transfer. A review of the submissions by the developed countries indicates that most of the programmes reference government-funded activities in the nature of foreign aid. Few incentives directed towards encouraging private sector transfer of technology are described. One recurring theme from the developed country side has been that to better address the interests of the LDCs, what is needed is more precise identification by the LDCs of what types of technology transfer they require.

In April 2024, I participated in the WTO annual workshop. There appeared to be a general consensus among both developed and LDC participants that the LDCs devoted considerable attention to the precise identification of needs and that the presentations by the LDC delegations were substantially more detailed and specific than in previous years. From the developed country side, there was an acknowledgement that most of their programmes were not directed towards

[26] See UNCTAD-ICTSD, *Resource Book on TRIPS and Development* (2005) 725ff.

[27] See Jessyca van Weelde et al, 'Reflection on the Implementation of Decision on Implementation of Article 66.2 of the TRIPS Agreement: Incentive for Technology Transfer to Least-Developed Countries' (WTO, 2023) Staff Working Paper ERSD-2023-12 3, www.econstor.eu/handle/10419/280935.

[28] See generally ibid.

providing incentives to private sector enterprises specifically aimed at promoting technology transfer to LDCs. Still, the developed country side was receptive to suggestions about what types of changes might be made.

A few points are deserved here. First, a significant part of LDC concerns is in the area of agriculture. This reflects their interest in technology transfer that addresses issues such as improved irrigation systems, greater access to tractors and other farm equipment, and related technologies. Second, the LDCs raised concerns about being able to identify and apply for the types of assistance they may be seeking and avoiding bureaucratic entanglements. Finally, there were some concerns raised about the linking of assistance to politics, although this is perhaps from a small number of LDC delegations.

The developed countries had an interest in exploring what types of incentives might be available to encourage the private sector to participate in technology transfer. The possibilities for direct subsidies, loan guarantees and tax incentives were discussed. The point was made by one developed country delegation that it might be helpful not to focus solely on large multinational corporations, but also to consider whether small and medium-sized enterprises in the developed countries might be encouraged to transfer technology and by what types of incentives.

The annual review concluded on a relatively optimistic note. It appears at least that progress is being made towards more effective technology transfer, though, of course, the proof will be in the pudding. That is, the real result will depend on what will be the follow up.

Of particular interest for this contribution is that Thomas Cottier had recently produced a paper on the subject of potential tax incentives to encourage the transfer of technology from developed to developing countries, which he then discussed and made available at a session addressing 30 years of TRIPS implementation shortly following the LDC workshop.[29] Perhaps unsurprisingly, tax incentives are a complicated matter and run into controls exercised by regional tax authorities and by the WTO subsidies agreement, among others. None of these complications would seem to stand in the way of providing incentives to benefit LDCs, but the area appears to require some careful planning.

We must acknowledge that the TRIPS Agreement has been in force for 30 years and that now 'getting serious' about providing incentives for the transfer of technology to LDCs is a little late in coming. Yet better this than the alternative.

III. Remarks on Implementation

We now have 30 years of TRIPS implementation. As our recently deceased colleague Pedro Roffe observed, the basic agreement 'as such' is no longer the

[29] Thomas Cottier, 'Tax Incentives for Technology Dissemination in Trade and Investment by Exporting and Home States' (27 April 2023) Working Paper.

source of much political debate. It has largely been accepted as an international baseline. But, as noted above, given the fractious nature of the international environment today, it seems unlikely that there is much that will be done in terms of updating or modifying the scope of the agreement anytime soon. This is, of course, acknowledging that the future is notoriously difficult to predict.

The most significant events in the history of the implementation of the TRIPS Agreement have surrounded the relationship between IP rights and public health. But those controversies have largely arisen not because of anything written into the TRIPS Agreement, but because of efforts at over-enforcement by some industry interests.

There remains a strong interest in better balancing the technological capacities of developed and developing countries, now better categorised more narrowly into high-income, high middle-income, low middle-income and least developed countries. Even then, these categorisations may need to be more country specific. The interest is reflected in discussions regarding the transfer of technology and whether there is some obligation on the part of the more technologically advanced to assist in bringing up the capacity of the less technologically advanced. This is a discussion that goes back more than 50 years, and there is no obvious end in sight. One thing that appears to be at least somewhat clear is that IP in and of itself does not constitute 'technology transfer', which is instead a broader concept that involves everything from financing to the training of human resources. IP is a 'necessary but insufficient' element.

Thomas Cottier has stepped into the fray with a major new conceptual framework he refers to as a 'common concern of humankind', suggesting that we consider certain categories of technological development should be made more openly available to benefit everyone. Perhaps this concept can be used to encourage a wider sharing of technology that is fundamentally necessary to maintain the health of the planet and its population. It is certainly an optimistic concept, particularly given the current penchant for zero-sum game politics. But we should be entitled to entertain an optimistic note given that we collectively have nowhere else to go, at least until our Martian colonies bloom.

I observed in concluding my presentation at the High-Level Panel that IP is neither inherently good nor bad. It is what people do with IP that can be either good or bad. These are conscious choices made by people.

3

WTO Dispute Settlement: What Went Wrong? What Might be Done?

WILLIAM J DAVEY

It is a distinct honour to contribute to this volume lauding the career of Thomas Cottier, one of the leading General Agreement on Tariffs and Trade (GATT) and World Trade Organization (WTO) thinkers of his generation. He was instrumental in the establishment and operation of the University of Bern's World Trade Institute, which has nurtured a new generation of WTO experts and scholars. In his own scholarship, Thomas has written extensively and insightfully on various international trade and intellectual property law issues, including thoughtful consideration of decision-making in the WTO.

In this short piece, I focus on a field in which Thomas was particularly involved – the GATT and WTO dispute settlement system. Thomas served as a Swiss negotiator on dispute settlement in the GATT Uruguay Round and served many times as a panelist and panel chair in the heyday of that system when it was considered to be the crown jewel of the WTO. Following the demise of the WTO Appellate Body, Thomas was appointed as one of 10 arbitrators under the Multiparty Interim Appeal Arbitration Arrangement (MPIA), pursuant to which a number of WTO members have agreed to an appellate procedure based on Article 25 of the WTO Dispute Settlement Understanding (DSU). Since Thomas's career has been so intimately involved with the GATT/WTO dispute settlement system, it is appropriate to consider that system and its recent problems in this tribute volume.

The Uruguay Round's grand innovations in dispute settlement were: (i) the adoption of compulsory dispute settlement of WTO matters in the WTO dispute settlement system, with automatic adoption of the results and potential retaliatory measures, in each case absent a consensus to the contrary; and (ii) the creation of the Appellate Body. Since 2019, the USA has blocked consensus on the appointment of new members of the Appellate Body, and, as a consequence, the Appellate Body ceased to function as the terms of its members expired. Since the DSU provides that automatic adoption of panel reports is postponed during the pendency of an appeal,[1] current practice allows adoption to be blocked for an unlimited period

[1] DSU, Art 16(4).

of time by an appeal to the non-functioning Appellate Body.[2] Thus, the principal dispute settlement innovations of the Uruguay Round have been effectively nullified.[3] In this chapter, I consider why the WTO dispute settlement system has failed to function as envisaged. In particular, I evaluate two possible reasons for its failure: (i) the structure of the WTO, with its consensus-based decision-making system; and (ii) the very nature of third-party dispute settlement involving sovereign states.

I. WTO Structure: The Effect of Consensus Decision-Making on Dispute Settlement

The role of consensus decision-making in the demise of the WTO dispute settlement system can be examined from two perspectives: first, the effect of the consensus requirement on the operation of the WTO Dispute Settlement Body (DSB); and second, the effect of the consensus requirement on amending or interpreting the WTO agreements so as to modify decisions of panels or the Appellate Body that most of the WTO membership disagrees with.

A. The Effect of the Consensus Requirement on the DSB's Operation

As noted earlier, one of the two major changes to GATT dispute settlement coming out of the Uruguay Round was the decision that the authorisation for the establishment of panels, adoption of their reports and suspension of concessions would be automatic. The DSU provides that the DSB has to authorise those actions, absent a consensus to the contrary.[4] All other DSB decisions provided for in the DSU are

[2] The WTO website listed over 30 cases in this status as of 22 April 2024 (with cases dating back to September 2018), although some of those cases have probably become moot or have otherwise been settled.

[3] For an overview of the factors leading to the demise of the Appellate Body and attempts to revise and resurrect the dispute settlement system, see William J Davey, 'WTO Dispute Settlement: Crown Jewel or Costume Jewelry' (2022) 21 (special issue 3) *World Trade Review* 291. As of 1 May 2024, the system has continued to function in the sense that consultations are requested, panels established and composed, and reports circulated, but only six reports have been adopted by the WTO Dispute Settlement Body since 1 January 2021, while 14 panel decisions (in 19 reports) have been consigned to limbo by an appeal to the non-functioning Appellate Body. Two reports were effectively 'adopted' for certain DSU purposes (ie DSU, Arts 21–22) as a result of completed appeals under the MPIA or equivalent procedure. While negotiators have recently committed to 'having a fully and well-functioning dispute settlement system accessible to all Members by 2024' (Ministerial Decision of 2 March 2024 on Dispute Settlement Reform, WTO Doc WT/L/1192 (4 March 2024)), it does not appear much progress has been made on the fundamental issues as of mid-2024.

[4] DSU, Arts 6.1, 16.4, 17.14, 22.6 and 22.7.

required to be taken by consensus.[5] The consensus requirement for 'other' decisions has been problematic in two respects.[6]

First, the rules for DSB meetings require that the meeting's agenda be adopted at the beginning of the meeting. It has been argued that a meeting can be blocked if a member refuses to join a consensus to adopt the agenda. When this was attempted in the *EC Bananas III* (DS27) case in respect of a request to suspend concessions pursuant to DSU, Article 22,[7] the DSB chair essentially ruled that a failure to adopt the agenda could not prevent the meeting from going forward with respect to items that were subject to automatic approval absent consensus to the contrary. The rationale was not explicitly set out. The chair's ruling was challenged, but the chair ruled that there was not a consensus to overrule his decision. A vote to override his ruling was then requested by the EU, but after a long recess, the chair ruled that there would be no vote and that the meeting would go forward. It was not clear at that point what was going to happen, but the EU then requested arbitration of the level of suspension pursuant to DSU, Article 22.6, which had the effect of removing the contested item from the agenda, and the meeting later went forward with the rest of the agenda.[8] The problem has not arisen again, but it is lurking in the shadows, as I do not think there is agreement on how to handle it if a member persists in its objection and has the support of other members.

Second, the DSU requires that the DSB appoint members of the Appellate Body. Since this action is provided for in the DSU, it requires consensus under DSU, Article 2.4, and a recalcitrant member can prevent such appointments. As the USA has shown, one member can, and has, effectively eliminated the Appellate Body from the WTO dispute settlement system.

These two examples demonstrate that the WTO dispute settlement system, as initially structured, depended on the good faith of all members in order to function

[5] DSU, Art 2.4. Under DSB procedural rules, decisions can be taken by voting if consensus cannot be reached, but, pursuant to Art 2.4, those rules are trumped for decisions provided for in the DSU.

[6] There is also a potential problem where the DSU conditions the automaticity requirement. See, eg DSU, Art 4.8 (shorter consultation period for cases involving perishable goods, but no mechanism for resolving disputes over perishability), Arts 21.7 and 21.8 (DSU shall take certain matters into consideration in cases involving developing countries, but no mechanism for ensuring that happens) and Art 24.2 (provides for the possibility of invoking the good offices of the Director-General before a panel request is made in a case involving a least-developed member, but does not specify for how long the request must be delayed). A DSB meeting can potentially be disrupted if one of these issues is raised and the argument is made that automaticity does not apply. This sort of problem has not caused serious problems to date, although brief disruptions of individual meetings have occurred.

[7] The underlying issue was an attempt by the EU and others to block a request by a successful complainant (the US) for authority to suspend concessions under DSU, Art 22.2 in light of the EU's failure to implement DSB recommendations in the *EC – Bananas III* case by the end of the reasonable period of time set for implementation. The EU objected to the appropriateness of this request on the grounds that: (i) it had in fact implemented the recommendations by the deadline and thus there was a dispute over whether there had been implementation; and (ii) the dispute had to be resolved pursuant to DSU, Art 21.5 before authority to suspend concessions could be considered by the DSB.

[8] For a fuller discussion of the issue, see John H Jackson, William J Davey and Alan O Sykes, *Legal Problems of International Economic Relations*, 7th edn (West Academic Publishing, 2021) 273–75. The refusal to agree to an agenda has occasionally been invoked to block other WTO meetings.

effectively. By and large, the membership did, in fact, allow the system to operate as envisaged for over two decades. To me, that indicates that these structural issues did not inherently cause the downfall of the system, but rather only facilitated it. There were other, more serious problems in the system. It is important to bear in mind, however, that if these structural issues are not addressed, the system will remain at risk even if other changes to reform it are agreed upon.

B. The Effect of the Consensus Requirement on the WTO's Supervision of Dispute Settlement

It has been argued that a second structural aspect of the WTO has created problems for the operation of the dispute settlement system in that it is practically impossible for the membership to supervise the system because they can only change the results of the system by consensus.[9] That there is great difficulty in achieving consensus in the WTO is certainly true -on both procedural and substantive issues. For example, probably the first major member complaint about the operation of the dispute settlement system involved a procedural question - could/should panels and the Appellate Body accept unsolicited submissions from non-governmental organisations or individuals (NGOs). The controversy arose when a panel declined to consider unsolicited submissions from NGOs in the *USA - Shrimp* (DS58) case, stating that while it could seek information from non-parties under DSU, Article 13.1, it could not accept submissions that it had not sought. On appeal, the Appellate Body ruled that the panel had read Article 13.1 'in too literal a manner' and that a panel could accept unsolicited submissions, although it was not required to do so. Despite criticism of its decision, the Appellate Body later ruled that it also could accept and consider unsolicited submissions, and in the *EC - Asbestos* (DS135) case, it established procedures to be followed in that case in connection with such submissions. That decision generated a storm of controversy. At a special WTO General Council meeting called to discuss the matter, only the USA defended the Appellate Body decision without qualification. Some other members expressed the view that while unsolicited submissions should perhaps be permitted, WTO members should be the ones to establish procedures to do so, not the Appellate Body. The clear majority of those who spoke opposed the whole idea that WTO dispute settlement organs should consider unsolicited submissions from non-parties. Notwithstanding this widespread view, there was nothing the General Council could do to restrict the use of such submissions so long as one member - in this case, the USA - was prepared to block the consensus.[10]

[9] Claus-Dieter Ehlermann, 'Some Personal Experiences as Member of the Appellate Body of the WTO' (European University Institute, 2002) Policy Papers, RSC No 02/9, para 124.

[10] For a fuller discussion of this matter, see Jackson et al (n 8) 258–60. It appears that the Appellate Body thereafter curtailed its consideration of such submissions. In any event, it has never again established procedures for receiving them.

More generally, the WTO's record in negotiating anything on substance is rather dismal.[11]

While the lack of a working WTO negotiating function is a serious problem for the organisation and its credibility,[12] I do not think that this was the major cause of the failure of the WTO dispute settlement system. I think that the amicus controversy was an exception, and that in almost all cases where parties have disagreed with panel or Appellate Body decisions, there was no majority, let alone a supermajority, of WTO members that would have reversed the decisions by interpreting or amending the underlying treaty provisions at issue. The problem rather is that there are provisions in the WTO agreements that are unclear as to their meaning or incomplete in dealing with an issue. In some cases, those issues were raised but not resolved in the Uruguay Round negotiations. In other cases, I think it is safe to say that if they had been raised in negotiations, they would not have been resolved. The real issue for a dispute settlement system is to what extent the system should attempt to resolve those unsettled issues where the parties are sovereign states.

II. The Problem of Third-Party Adjudication of Sovereign State Disputes

There will always be difficulties with third-party adjudication of disputes between sovereign states. Fundamentally, the problems arise from the fact that sovereignty, by definition, means that a state has the power to ignore a decision by third-party adjudicators. That power exists even if a state has accepted to submit a dispute to the third-party adjudicators, absent some sort of enforcement mechanism. This situation is demonstrated by looking outside the WTO. The premiere system of third-party adjudication in the international arena is the International Court of Justice (ICJ). Yet that body has no power to enforce its decisions, and it suffers from the fact that not all major powers accept its compulsory jurisdiction. The same problem exists for the International Criminal Court. For example, among the major users of the WTO dispute settlement system, China, Indonesia, South Korea and the USA have not agreed to submit to the jurisdiction of either of those

[11] While there were some successes in the late 1990s – the Information Technology Agreement and the completion of the negotiations on financial and telecommunications services – the record over the last quarter century does not show many. Basically, the only agreements reached have been the 2013 Trade Facilitation Agreement (mainly concerned with technical assistance in the customs area) and the 2022 limited agreement on fisheries subsidies that is not yet in force. To the extent that there have been controversial decisions on substantive issues in dispute settlement, it would seem that there is no hope of changing outcomes through negotiations, absent, perhaps, as one part of a comprehensive package deal, such as the Uruguay Round. No one thinks such a deal could be reached in the foreseeable future.

[12] The failure of the WTO ministerial conferences to produce meaningful results undermines the organisation's claim to be the pre-eminent forum for multilateral trade negotiations.

bodies; and Argentina, Brazil and France do not accept the compulsory jurisdiction of the ICJ.[13]

Initially, it appeared to me that the WTO might avoid these problems because its members had only recently agreed to its rules, and those rules tended to be in their overall economic interest. Moreover, the fact that they were granted a reasonable period of time to comply with decisions and faced no claim for damages, but only prospective remedies, seemed to make the system more likely to be accepted. And, indeed, the WTO dispute settlement system was viewed as a success in its early years.[14] What changed? I think that there were two fundamental changes affecting the system over time. First, the world changed; second, the dispute settlement system was faced with some cases where the parties had fundamentally different views of what the WTO rules provided.

A. A Changing World Order Challenges Dispute Settlement Systems

First, how did the world change? While the WTO was being negotiated, it appeared that the WTO's promotion of liberalised trade based on market principles through a rules-based multilateral trading system was the way of the future. The Cold War had just ended, and the former Communist countries of Eastern Europe were transitioning towards market economies. Likewise, China was becoming more market-oriented and involved in the world trading system, culminating with its accession to the WTO in 2001. But soon after the WTO agreements came into force, the world started to change. First, trade liberalisation as a policy became more controversial as anti-globalisation protests focusing on labour and environmental issues multiplied, as epitomised by the riotous protests at the WTO's Ministerial Conference in Seattle in 1999.[15] While those protests attracted those on the left of the political spectrum, there followed a rise in right-wing opposition to economic integration, culminating in Brexit and the election of Donald Trump as US President in 2016, but seen in political developments in other countries as well.[16] After the ascension of Xi Jinping in 2012, China's move towards more market-oriented economic policies seemed to reverse, and its large,

[13] Declarations Recognizing the Jurisdiction of the Court as Compulsory, www.icj-cij.org/declarations; The States Parties to the Rome Statute, https://asp.icc-cpi.int/states-parties.

[14] William J Davey, 'The WTO Dispute Settlement System: The First Decade' [2005] *Journal of International Economic Law* 17; William J Davey, 'The WTO Dispute Settlement System: Dealing with Success' in Julien Chaisse and Tsai-yu Lin (eds), *International Economic Law and Governance: Essays in Honour of Mitsuo Matsushita* (Oxford University Press, 2016).

[15] Joseph Kahn and David E Sanger, 'Trade Obstacles Unmoved, Seattle Talks End in Failure' *New York Times* (4 December 1999) https://archive.nytimes.com/www.nytimes.com/library/world/global/120499wto-talks.html.

[16] Peter S Goodman, 'Trump Just Pushed the World Trade Organization Toward Irrelevance' *New York Times* (23 March 2018) www.nytimes.com/2018/03/23/business/trump-world-trade-organization.html.

allegedly subsidised exports to the rest of the world expanded and became more controversial.[17]

Second, a type of Cold War situation effectively returned when Russia invaded Ukraine, and US–China relations became more contentious over dual-use technology and Taiwan.

Third, worries about the capability of far-flung supply chains to reliably deliver critical components and goods arose during the COVID pandemic and led to additional concerns about national security and the promotion of 'onshoring', which reduces trade.[18]

All of this undermined the WTO because it meant that there was no longer widespread agreement on the basic tenets of the rules-based WTO trading system. As such, one could expect that resolving disputes in the WTO would become more difficult. A prime example is the problem the WTO has had in satisfactorily dealing with cases involving restrictions imposed for national security reasons.[19] It will probably have similar problems with economic policy measures that, for some of the reasons noted above, emphasise local manufacturing in ways arguably inconsistent with the WTO's national treatment and subsidy rules.

B. Controversial Decisions Undermine Acceptance of Dispute Settlement Results

Second, compared to its initial years, the WTO dispute settlement system began to issue decisions that were more controversial, particularly in cases involving trade remedies – dumping, subsidies and safeguards. That is not to say that the early years of WTO dispute settlement did not involve controversial cases: *USA – Gasoline* (DS2), *EC – Bananas III* (DS27), *EC – Hormones* (DS26), *USA – Shrimp* (DS58), *Japan – Film* (DS44) come immediately to mind, but there were others.[20] However, these cases involved specific measures and were resolved over time in ways that the losing party could accept; and the Appellate Body stressed in a number of them that the policy goals embodied in the underlying measures were not in question, but rather only the specific means that been applied to achieve them. In contrast, the controversial trade remedy cases: (i) concerned frequently used laws, which meant that the decisions would impact many individual cases, both then pending and to come in the future; and (ii) involved issues where the parties had strikingly different views of what the agreements provided. The Appellate Body did not seem

[17] Nicholas R Lardy, *The State Strikes Back: The End of Economic Reform in China?* (Peterson Institute for International Economics, 2019).

[18] By Nelson D Schwartz, 'Supply Chain Woes Prompt a New Push to Revive US Factories' *New York Times* (5 January 2022) www.nytimes.com/2022/01/05/business/economy/supply-chain-reshoring-us-manufacturing.html.

[19] Warren Maruyama and Alan Wm Wolff, 'Saving the WTO from the National Security Exception' (Peterson Institute for International Economics, 2023) Working Paper 23-2.

[20] See Davey (2005) (n 14) 18–21.

to accord the deference to government action in the trade remedy field as it did in health and environmental cases.[21]

In this regard, it must be said that the parties to a dispute often seem to view all adverse rulings as controversial, which is hardly the case, but I think it can be said that there are a few WTO decisions that can be properly labelled controversial because they touched on important issues where there had been extensive negotiations in the Uruguay Round and where one or more WTO members are convinced that the Appellate Body decisions did not reflect the results of the negotiations. While I think that the number of such controversial decisions, as I have defined them, is small, the existence of only a few such decisions has served as a basis to attack the system as a whole, particularly in the USA.[22] And, unfortunately, to the extent that there is some justification for these criticisms, it makes the WTO dispute settlement as a whole more difficult to defend.

This sort of problem tended not to arise in the GATT dispute settlement system, which was generally viewed as a success.[23] If a party felt strongly that the decision was wrong because it did not reflect what had been negotiated, it could block the adoption of the panel report. That created an incentive for panels to resolve disputes in a way that the parties could accept. This meant that decisions were briefer and tended to avoid controversial issues where possible. This changed with the advent of the WTO dispute settlement system. Panels and the Appellate Body became empowered to operate more freely and independently since their reports could not be blocked except by consensus, a very unlikely result. This led complaining parties to bring more and more controversial claims. With the breakdown of the WTO's negotiating function, there seemed to be efforts by some members to achieve through litigation in dispute settlement what could not be achieved in negotiations. To an extent, I think that the Appellate Body's mere existence and its decisions encouraged this outcome. Panels felt the need to consider more claims and issues so that more of their findings would remain intact, even if the Appellate Body reversed parts of their decisions. The Appellate Body itself felt it had to decide all issues appealed. All of this encouraged complaining parties to be more aggressive in their claims.

[21] ibid 22–23.

[22] The four most criticised Appellate Body decisions in the USA are: (i) the decisions disallowing the use of 'zeroing' as a dumping calculation method in reviews conducted in antidumping cases; (ii) a related complaint that the Appellate Body effectively refused to apply Art 17.6(ii) of the WTO Antidumping Agreement (relating to permissible interpretations); (iii) the decisions requiring 'unforeseen developments' to be shown in safeguard cases; and (iv) the decisions defining the term 'public body' under the WTO Subsidies Agreement. The USA has also expressed concerns over the Appellate Body's interpretation of Art 2.1 of the TBT Agreement. US Trade Representative, 'Report on the Appellate Body of the World Trade Organization' (February 2020).

[23] Robert E Hudec, *Enforcing International Trade Law* (Butterworth Legal Publishers, 1993) 353; William J Davey, 'Dispute Settlement in GATT' [1987] *Fordham International Law Journal* 51. The fact that the loser could ultimately block adoption of the panel report by the GATT Council did mean, however, that controversial cases were either not commenced or not resolved.

Moreover, the Appellate Body seemed to believe that it had a mandate to clarify the meanings of WTO provisions even if that required it to resolve ambiguities in the agreements, as opposed to avoiding them.[24] This position could certainly be justified by DSU, Article 3.2, which provides that 'Members recognize that [the WTO dispute settlement system] serves … to clarify the existing provisions of [the WTO agreements] in accordance with the customary rules of interpretation of public international law'. But the same article also provides that the system serves 'to preserve the rights and obligations' of WTO members, a task in no little tension with an aim to resolve ambiguities. After all, did the negotiators of the WTO agreements, who deliberately fudged some issues in order to conclude the negotiations, really expect that the dispute settlement system would issue definitive rulings resolving them? I doubt it. Indeed, this use of the dispute settlement system in lieu of negotiations was criticised early on by the then-three living former Directors-General.[25]

In any event, these two changes – in the world at large and in the unwillingness of some WTO members (in particular, the USA) to accept certain controversial decisions of the current WTO dispute settlement system – suggest that that system is no long viable, as discussed below.

III. What Can be Done?

In considering what might be done now to resolve the crisis in WTO dispute settlement, I note that there is a divide between those who want a stricter dispute settlement mechanism (including the possibility of an appeal) and those (principally the USA) who seem to want a looser system (with no or limited appeal). Those who prefer the first alternative have created their own workaround to the US intransigence on Appellate Body appointments through the MPIA. That system could continue and satisfy its adherents, at least to disputes among themselves. But some other approach must be followed to convince the USA and non-MPIA participants to accept a more binding dispute settlement system than what exists in practice currently (ie the possibility of consigning panel reports to oblivion by appealing them to the non-functioning Appellate Body). I think it is accepted that the current bifurcated system, in which some accept binding dispute settlement and others do not, is inherently unstable and cannot last forever, but it could exist for a long time if no compromise can be reached. In this section, I consider several alternatives to address this problem and some of the others that I raised earlier.

[24] Peter van den Bossche, 'The Demise of the WTO Appellate Body: Lessons for Governance of International Adjudication?' (WTI, 2021) Working Paper No 02/2021, sec 4.2.1, www.wti.org/media/filer_public/c2/ef/c2efc2de-ce85-45c7-9512-9286e14fca47/wti_working_paper_02_2021.pdf.

[25] Jackson et al (n 8) 189 (quoting 2001 statement by Arthur Dunkel, Peter Sutherland and Renato Ruggiero).

A. Structural Issues

As to the structural problems, it would be useful to agree that any WTO member can place an item on the DSB's agenda and remove the requirement that the agenda be approved at the beginning of a DSB meeting. Second, to the extent that individuals need to be appointed to positions by the DSB, there should be an accepted procedure for dealing with a lack of consensus. While I offer these as desirable changes, they are probably not essential, although if nothing is done, the possibility of blockage in the system remains.

B. National Security

As to the problems arising from a changing world order and an increase in armed conflict, I think that national security issues need to be removed from consideration by the dispute settlement system. As currently worded, GATT, Article XXI seems open to dispute settlement review in respect of determining whether a precondition for its invocation exists, such as an 'emergency in international relations'. But trying to resolve such disputes in a judicial process is a hopeless task. That has always been the view of the major parties in GATT and was, in fact, GATT practice after the Czech–US dispute over export controls in the late 1940s.[26] Preferably, in return for removing such cases from the dispute settlement system, WTO members could agree that a member adversely affected by a measure justified under Article XXI could suspend equivalent concessions, with the role of dispute settlement being limited to determining equivalence, as now done under DSU, Article 22.[27]

C. A New Dispute Settlement Approach

Essentially, the WTO dispute settlement system now faces an existential crisis because of what might be called judicial overreach. As noted, the system seemed to become intent on making law, rather than resolving disputes. Thus, any reform must return the system to its initial purpose of resolving disputes, not making law. As far as appeals are concerned generally, it appears that WTO members seemed to have believed at the end of the Uruguay Round that they had created a right to a limited appeal – one that was intended to correct obviously 'bad' panel reports.[28]

[26] ibid 658–60.

[27] See also Maruyama and Wolff (n 19).

[28] Bruce Hirsh, 'Resolving the WTO Appellate Body Crisis: Proposals on Overreach' (December 2019) 3–4. Indeed, the fact that the initial make-up of the Appellate Body did not include many trade law specialists suggests that the Appellate Body was not intended to delve into the intricacies of WTO rules; see also Joseph Weiler, 'The Rule of Lawyers and the Ethos of Diplomats Reflections on the Internal and External Legitimacy of WTO Dispute Settlement' (2001) 35(2) *Journal of World Trade*

It follows that the prime goal of reforms must be to simplify the dispute settlement system overall. This would have the side effect of reducing delays and making the system more useful for quickly resolving trade disputes.

What would be the prime components of a reformed dispute settlement system? While I cannot, in this brief chapter, go into great detail and evaluate these suggestions, I think that there should be a focus on simplification and restraint. I would suggest the following four components of reform:

1. In order to reduce the number of disputes reaching the panel stage, I would make mediation mandatory after consultations have failed to resolve a dispute. In other words, before a panel could be requested, the parties would have to meet with a mediator, whose charge would be to settle or narrow the dispute. The possibility of mediation is provided for in DSU, Article 5, but it has never been much used despite attempts by the Directors-General to promote it.[29] The WTO would have to have a group of individuals charged with carrying out this task or a procedure for selecting individuals to do so. They could be trade diplomats from neutral countries or independent individuals with international trade law expertise. A mix of possibilities probably would be the best starting point. While I have some doubts about the efficacy of mediation, it is noteworthy that courts, at least in the USA, make extensive use of pretrial and settlement conferences, which suggests that they can be useful.
2. In order to focus disputes that are considered by panels, word lengths should be placed on submissions. I have had some doubts in the past about the appropriateness of this, but I now think it would be worthwhile. At a minimum, it would cause parties to drop arguments that are of little consequence to the main issues in a case. In that regard, I think, in particular, of claims that DSU, Article 6.2 was violated because the panel request failed to adequately summarise the legal basis of the complaint, which virtually never succeeded, and claims that are duplicative. At its best, it could cause parties to focus on their primary claims and best arguments. Setting the precise word limits would be difficult. The limits could be phased in over the course of several years. Unfortunately, there would probably have to be a procedure allowing requests for increased word limits in specific cases, but such requests should be granted only sparingly. Once word limits are put in place, consideration should be given to normally holding only one panel meeting with the parties, with the possibility of a second meeting being up to the panel. This, too, would serve to get the parties to focus on their key claims and arguments.

191, 199–200, www.nftc.org/default/trade/WTO/Resolving%20the%20WTO%20Appellate%20Body%20Crisis_Proposals%20on%20Overreach.pdf.

[29] Consideration should also be given to requiring a second mediation session following the first panel meeting, although I would not suggest doing that until the effectiveness of the initial mediation session is demonstrated. Although such a process during the dispute is foreseen as part of a panel's function by DSU, Art 11, I think it would be preferable for an independent third party to perform it lest the panel's objectivity be put in question.

3. Panelists must adopt a new ethos recognising that their role is to resolve disputes, not make law. This may require panels to invoke the principle of *non liquet*. A *non liquet* occurs when a judicial body decides not to rule on a case because the law is not clear or, put another way, there is a gap in the law. In the past, I have felt that the WTO system should avoid invoking this principle, but given that experience has now shown the number of ambiguities in the WTO agreements and the potential negative consequences to the organisation of trying to resolve them through dispute settlement, I think that this technique must form part of reforming how panelists should view their role. Similarly, panels should be encouraged to exercise judicial economy where possible. This should be easier in the absence of broad appeals.[30]
4. The right to appeal should be strictly limited. For example, it could be provided that to obtain an appellate review, a party would first have to convince a reconstituted appellate entity that the panel report conflicted with another panel report or reached an implausible interpretation of an agreement. The presumption would be that appeals would be rare and, where they occurred, would be limited to the narrow issues mentioned.[31] To the extent that appeals were limited, one could consider having the appellate function conducted on a more ad hoc basis.[32]

The foregoing reforms would likely lead to shorter panel reports. It would reverse the process described at the end of section II.B above, which detailed how the prior system encouraged more claims and arguments, and led to longer and longer panel and Appellate Body reports. Panel reports: (i) would be written with the aim of settling a dispute, not proofing themselves against an appeal; and (ii) would consider fewer claims and arguments because of word limits on submissions, *non liquet* and judicial economy. Shorter reports could be drafted more quickly. With the limits on appeals, the overall process would be much faster than at present.

If the foregoing reforms were adopted, one question would remain: would the changes be sufficient for the USA and others who have grown used to appealing into the void to be willing to accept the automatic adoption of panel (and appellate) reports as the rule? It would be extremely unfortunate if they did not. That would effectively mean a return to the GATT system, where the adoption of a report could be blocked by the losing party. The system could still work in a useful way if the GATT ethos of accepting most panel reports were followed, but the shortcomings of the GATT system would reappear, notably the inability to resolve

[30] William J Davey, 'Has the WTO Dispute Settlement System Exceeded Its Authority' [2001] *Journal of International Economic Law* 79, 106, 108–10.

[31] There would, of course, be many requests for review and much time would be spent on arguments over whether the conditions for appeal had been met. But over time, one could expect standards to develop that would reduce appeal attempts.

[32] For example, this limited appellate review could be conducted by the most experienced panelists sitting as an ad hoc body to resolve conflicts or correct truly bad decisions. I develop the idea of limited appeals in more detail in Davey (2022) (n 3) 297.

controversial cases.[33] In such a circumstance, the many WTO members, and particularly those that created the MPIA, who were happy with Uruguay Round changes and the role played by the Appellate Body would be faced with the question of whether they wanted to continue to use the MPIA. I see no reason why they could not do so if they were willing to have a binding dispute settlement amongst themselves. Hopefully, others would join the MPIA or agree to use similar procedures on an ad hoc basis, as has already occurred.

All of this represents a change in thinking for me. When the WTO was created, I was a firm supporter of a strict dispute settlement system, and I think that system, by and large, worked in the first years. Thus, I worry that extensive reforms to curtail its role may be an unjustified overreaction to the current crisis, which, after all, is mainly due to one member – the USA. However, in the future, I think that the WTO dispute settlement system will be sorely tested due to the changes in the world outlined above. It seems to me that disputes arising from measures taken in light of the renewal of the Cold War and the desire of members to promote, subsidise and protect their critical industries will tax the system. Thus, the reforms outlined above may be useful to help the system weather the coming disputes.

I would have preferred to continue the Uruguay Round system, but ultimately, the judicial independence allowed in that system led to decisions that were unacceptable to some members (particularly the USA), and that led to its demise. In retrospect, Bob Hudec – the leading authority on GATT dispute settlement – was probably right when he noted at the end of the Uruguay Round that the system would work only if the membership were ready for strict dispute settlement.[34] In the end, at least one of them was not. One can speculate about whether this failure would not have occurred but for a US President like Trump and his anti-WTO trade advisors. But, given the growth over the years of increased questioning of multilateralism in trade matters, a trend that has continued under the Biden Administration and that is not unique to the USA, I am not sure that this can all be blamed on Trump. In any event, what remains imperative now is to recreate a dispute settlement system that all WTO members can live with. Hopefully, one that Thomas Cottier could accept.[35]

[33] See Davey (1987) (n 23).

[34] Hudec (n 23) 364. Hudec had doubts that the USA was.

[35] For some of Thomas's ideas on improving the WTO dispute settlement system through strengthening the panel process and limiting appeals, see Thomas Cottier, 'Recalibrating the WTO Dispute Settlement System: Strengthening the Panel Stage' (Centre for International Governance Innovation, 20 April 2020) www.cigionline.org/Articles/recalibrating-wto-dispute-settlement-system-strengthening-panel-stage/?utm_source=google_ads&utm_medium=grant&gad_source=1&gclid=EAIaIQobChMIt-vssd3xhQMVAxatBh1yFwTkEAMYASAAEgItjfD_BwE.

4

The Uncertain Future of WTO Dispute Settlement: An Appraisal of the February 2024 Consolidated Text Resulting from the Molina Process

PETER VAN DEN BOSSCHE*

I. Introduction

Thomas Cottier is very much part of the successful past, the troubled present and the uncertain future of the dispute settlement system of the World Trade Organization (WTO). He served between 1997 and 2021 as a panellist in seven WTO disputes, including the groundbreaking cases *EC – Hormones* (DS 26, DS48) and *Canada – Renewable Energy/Canada – Feed-In Tariff Program* (DS412, DS426).[1] Since 2020, he has been the *éminence grise* in the formidable group of Multi-Party Interim Appeal Arbitration Arrangement (MPIA) arbitrators, who stand ready to hear and decide appeals from panel reports now that the Appellate Body can no longer do so. His 2021 seminal article in the *Journal of International Economic Law*, 'Recalibrating the WTO Dispute Settlement System: Towards New Standards of Appellate Review', may well offer a way out of the current crisis by redefining the role of the Appellate Body in the WTO dispute settlement system of tomorrow.[2] I have known and admired Thomas for over 30 years, which is probably

* A longer version of this contribution was published as WTI Working Paper No 2/2024. A shorter version will be published as Peter Van den Bossche, 'WTO Dispute Settlement Reform: A Critical Assessment of the February 2024 Consolidated Text of a Draft Ministerial Decision on Dispute Settlement' in Valentina Vadi and David Collins (eds), *Routledge Handbook on International Economic Law* (Routledge, forthcoming) ch 8. The author would like to thank Triplicane Satish for his excellent research assistance.

[1] *EC – Hormones* (DS26, DS48) (1997); *India – Patents* (DS50, DS79) (1997); *Canada – Renewable Energy/Canada – Feed-In Tariff Program* (DS412, DS426) (2012); *China – Cellulose Pulp* (DS483) (2017); *Thailand – Cigarettes (Philippines) (Art 21.5)* (DS371) (2018); *Thailand – Cigarettes (Philippines) (Art 21.5) II* (DS371) (2019); and *India – Sugar and Sugarcane* (DS580) (2021).

[2] Thomas Cottier, 'Recalibrating the WTO Dispute Settlement System: Towards New Standards of Appellate Review' (2021) 24 *Journal of International Economic Law* 515.

less than other contributors to this Festschrift. I did, however, have the privilege of frequent interaction with him after I joined his academic home, the World Trade Institute, in 2016. Many of our discussions related to the WTO dispute settlement system, and while we sometimes disagreed, his belief in rules-based dispute resolution always inspired me. Hence, I have decided to write this contribution to the Festschrift on the most recent developments in the attempt of WTO members to 'revive' the WTO dispute settlement system.

This contribution will not look back on the past success of the WTO dispute settlement system, nor will it discuss old efforts, which started as early as 1998, to further improve it.[3] This contribution will also not dwell on the causes and the severity of the current crisis, nor on the EU initiative to limit the damage and secure rules-based WTO dispute settlement among willing members.[4] Rather, it first deals with how the discussions on the reform of the WTO dispute settlement system were conducted in 2023 and early 2024 in the run-up of the 13th WTO Ministerial Conference in February/March 2024, and then critically assesses the proposed changes to the WTO dispute settlement system reflected in the Consolidated Text of a draft Ministerial Decision on Dispute Settlement, submitted to the General Council on 14 February 2024.[5] The chapter focuses, in particular, on the proposed changes to panel proceedings, compliance, guidelines for adjudicators, procedures to discuss legal interpretations, Secretariat support, transparency and the periodic review of the implementation of the reform agenda.[6]

II. The Molina Process

In June 2022, 30 months after the crisis of the WTO dispute settlement system became acute, the Ministerial Conference of the WTO 'recognize[d] the importance and urgency of addressing' the 'challenges and concerns with respect to the dispute settlement system' and 'commit[ted] to conduct discussions with the view of having a fully and well-functioning dispute settlement system accessible to all Members by 2024'.[7] In the months immediately preceding and following the

[3] 'Marrakesh Ministerial Decision on the Application and Review of the Understanding on Rules and Procedures Governing the Settlement of Disputes, Adopted on 15 April 1994'; WTO Ministerial Conference, 'Ministerial Declaration Adopted on 14 November 2001, WT/MIN(01)/DEC/1' (20 November 2001) para 30.

[4] WTO, 'Multi-Party Interim Appeal Arbitration Arrangement Pursuant to Article 25 of the DSU, JOB/DSB/1/Add.12' (30 April 2020).

[5] WTO General Council, 'Special Meeting of the General Council on 14 February 2024, Report by HE Mr Petter Ølberg, Chairman of the DSB, JOB/GC/385' Annex 1.

[6] Due to restrictions on the length of this contribution, the proposed changes regarding alternative dispute resolution and arbitration (set out in Title I of the Consolidated Text) and on the accessibility, technical assistance, capacity building and legal advice (set out in Title VIII of the Consolidated Text), while worthy of careful attention, will not be discussed. For a discussion of these proposed changes, see Peter Van den Bossche, 'WTO Dispute Settlement Reform: An Assessment of the February 2024 Consolidated Text' (WTI, 2024) WTI Working Paper No 2/2024.

[7] WTO Ministerial Conference, Twelfth Session, 'MC 12 Outcome Document, Adopted 17 June 2022, WT/MIN(22)/24 Dated 22 June 2022' para 4.

latter commitment, the USA, which had previously shown no interest in reviving the WTO dispute settlement system, convened a number of mostly bilateral meetings 'to understand Members' expectations regarding the operation of the dispute settlement system'.[8] During these meetings, members reportedly 'identified and discussed more than 230 interests'.[9] With these expressed interests as a starting point, Mr Marco Molina, the then Deputy Permanent Representative of Guatemala to the WTO, initiated in February 2023, at the request of a number of key WTO members, informal discussions on dispute settlement reform (hereinafter the Molina Process). Note that Molina never got an official mandate from the WTO Dispute Settlement Body (DSB) to serve as facilitator of the reform discussions or convener of the related meetings.[10] Molina did, however, report on the ongoing discussions to the DSB every two months, and at these DSB meetings, many members stated that 'they saw great value in this process', 'recognized that the informal process has achieved significant progress so far' and 'commended Mr Marco Molina for his outstanding leadership in this informal process'.[11]

In response to Molina's invitation 'to propose ideas and conceptual approaches that could potentially address the interests identified', members tabled more than 70 proposals on which 'interest-based conversations' were started among the Geneva-based dispute settlement experts of members.[12] Between February 2023 and February 2024, Molina convened 'more than 350 meetings, including 110 plenary sessions open to all WTO Members, as well as numerous small-group and bilateral meetings'.[13] In total, 145 of the then 164 WTO members participated in these meetings.[14] While Molina confidently stated that 'Members have had ample opportunities to share their views',[15] not all members agreed. In July 2023,

[8] 'Report by the Convener of the Informal Reform Discussions – Mr Marco Molina of Guatemala' (2024 Molina Report) para 1.13. This report was included in the report by the Chairperson of the DSB to the WTO General Council on 14 February 2024, referred to in n 5.

[9] ibid.

[10] Also note that the WTO Secretariat was not directly involved in the Molina Process.

[11] WTO General Council (n 5) para 1.6. Note that shortly after presenting his report to the General Council on 14 February 2024 and a few days before the start of the Ministerial Conference meeting in Abu Dhabi on 26 February 2024, Molina was summarily fired by his government. No reason was given for his removal, but professional jealousy was reportedly what motivated this most unfortunate and unwarranted action.

[12] 2024 Molina Report (n 8) paras 1.14, 1.15 and 1.22. For an explanation of the 'interest-based approach' to the dispute settlement reform discussions adopted by Molina, see paras 1.15–1.20. Note, in particular, that according to Molina, 'an interest-based approach offers the key advantage of reducing power imbalances and fostering inclusive dynamics, allowing every Member to contribute meaningfully. By centring discussions around interests and concerns rather than leverage, this approach ensures fairness and equality for all Members, regardless of their size or status. This commitment to valuing every perspective equally ensures that our collective pursuit of optimal solutions remains untainted by external factors' (para 1.19).

[13] ibid 1.29. Molina also had bilateral meetings with members whenever requested (ibid).

[14] ibid 1.30.

[15] ibid 1.29. Note in this regard that 'each iteration of the text reflects feedback received from the plenary sessions, to which all Members are invited to participate' and that 'the changes introduced into each iteration resulted from conversations and understandings reached during those plenary sessions'. See ibid para 1.25. Note also that 'if delegates are unsure about certain aspects of the text or they need to consult with their Capitals, we leave the discussion and revisit issues at the following plenary session'. See ibid para 1.28.

the African Group signalled unease with the Molina Process and called for 'the commencement of an effective and inclusive multilateral process on dispute settlement reform', which would 'facilitate the participation of developing and least-developed countries (LDCs), including delegations with limited resources'.[16] The African Group voiced concerns regarding, in particular, the pace of the scheduled meetings and the limited time to consult with capitals and regional groupings.[17] In September 2023, Indonesia voiced similar concerns when it observed that

> many Members from developing countries and LDCs, who inherently do not have a dedicated delegate for the dispute settlement reform issue, experience difficulties in fully and effectively participating in the informal discussion due to scheduling conflicts between such discussion and other formal meetings or negotiations.[18]

In November 2023, Egypt, India and South Africa also voiced concerns regarding the pace and format of the Molina Process.[19] These are, unfortunately, concerns that especially the least-developed country members have repeatedly and rightly expressed in the context of many WTO discussions or negotiations.

Attached to the report that Molina presented at the General Council meeting on 14 February 2024, ie two weeks before the Ministerial Conference in Abu Dhabi (MC13), was the seventh revision of the Consolidated Text of a draft Ministerial Decision on Dispute Settlement (hereinafter the Consolidated Text). In his report to the General Council, Molina noted that in the reform discussions, 'significant progress has been achieved' and that the seventh revision 'reflects Members' collective understandings and expectations regarding the system's operation'. The latter statement creates the impression that this latest version of the Consolidated Text has consensus support. This is, however, not the case. Two days before Molina presented his report, Bangladesh, Egypt, India, Indonesia and South Africa (hereinafter the BEIIS Group) voiced their concern that the 'far-reaching changes' proposed in the reform process 'would fundamentally alter the nature of the dispute settlement system of the WTO' and 'undermine interests that we, as developing countries, including LDCs, have identified as essential in a reformed WTO dispute settlement system'.[20] The BEIIS Group noted that 'concerns and

[16] 'Communication from the African Group on Dispute Settlement Reform, JOB/DSB/5' 2.

[17] ibid 2.

[18] 'Communication from Indonesia, Dispute Settlement Reform Discussion: A Thought on the Process, JOB/DSB/6 Dated 19 September 2023' para 2.3.

[19] 'Joint Communication from Egypt, India, and South Africa, Reflections on the Reform of the WTO Dispute Settlement System, JOB/DSB/7 Dated 24 November 2023' para 5. This communication includes additional critical comments that the informal process allowed for in-person participation in Geneva, but not for online participation by capital-based experts, and that the composition of the drafting groups had not been made public.

[20] 'Joint Communication from Bangladesh, Egypt, India, Indonesia, and South Africa, Dispute Settlement Reform: Reflections on Substantive Issues, JOB/DSB/8, dated 12 February 2024' (BEIIS Group Communication) para 2. Note that in para 1.50 of his report to the General Council on 14 February 2024, the DSB Chairperson referred to this Communication, but merely to note that it contained the 'reflections on some substantive issues' of five members.

reservations that have been raised by us in the course of the ongoing discussions have not been recorded' and that the Consolidated Text 'presents a misleading view and suggests that there is convergence on the majority of the issues in the text'.[21]

While the Consolidated Text does not (yet) reflect a consensus among members regarding WTO dispute settlement reform, its most important shortcoming is that it does not even address the issue that triggered the current crisis, namely the functioning of the Appellate Body. While Molina stated that 'significant progress has been made', there were 'conceptual differences among members regarding the operation' of the 'appeal or review' mechanism and, therefore, work on other issues was 'prioritized'.[22] The Consolidated Text contains a placeholder title, 'Appeal/Review Mechanism', with the text '[Work in Progress]'. As the BEIIS Group stated, 'the central interest that motivated Members to engage in this informal exercise, ie the restoration of the Appellate Body, has not been addressed'.[23] Be this as it may, the Consolidated Text arguably represents, as Molina reported to the General Council on 16 February 2024, 'the most optimal calibration' of interests 'achievable until today in most of the areas under consideration'.[24] At its session in Abu Dhabi in February/March 2024, the Ministerial Conference recognised 'the progress made' through the Molina Process 'as a valuable contribution to fulfilling our commitment' of 'having a fully and well-functioning dispute settlement system accessible to all Members by 2024'.[25] One may expect that, notwithstanding the lack of consensus support, the ongoing WTO dispute settlement reform process will build on the proposed changes reflected in the Consolidated Text. These proposed changes, therefore, deserve and require careful attention and critical assessment, as do the objections and concerns expressed by the BEIIS Group.

III. Panel Proceedings

Title II of the Consolidated Text deals with panel proceedings. It introduces changes regarding the establishment of panels (chapter I) and the composition of panels (chapter II), as well as changes to streamline the panel process (chapter III) and ensure the conciseness of panel reports and adherence to the time frame (chapter IV).

[21] ibid 3.
[22] 2024 Molina Report (n 8) para 1.37.
[23] BEIIS Group Communication (n 20) para 4. As the BEIIS Group stated: 'we believe that the central focus of the reform efforts should be aimed at prioritizing the restoration of the Appellate Body. The discussion on the intricacies of the review standards should be considered once there is consensus on the structure of the two-tier system, with the Appellate Body at the core'. See ibid para 6.
[24] 2024 Molina Report (n 8) para 1.21.
[25] WTO Ministerial Conference, Thirteenth Session, 'Ministerial Decision on Dispute Settlement Reform, Adopted 2 March 2024, WT/MIN(24)/37, Dated 4 March 2024'.

A. Establishment of Panels

Regarding the establishment of panels, Article 6.1 of the Dispute Settlement Understanding (DSU) currently allows the respondent in a dispute to prevent the establishment of a panel when the request for that establishment is discussed for the first time in the DSB as a decision on panel establishment then still requires consensus among members. It is only when the request for a panel is on the agenda of the DSB for the second time that the decision on the establishment is taken by reverse consensus and thus cannot be blocked by the respondent. In almost all disputes to date, respondents have prevented a panel from being established when the request for establishment is on the agenda of the DSB for the first time, thus prolonging the time it takes to settle a dispute. Pursuant to chapter I of the Consolidated Text, members would agree not to exercise their right under Article 6.1 of the DSU to prevent the establishment of a panel when the request for establishment first appears on the agenda of the DSB.[26] This is not a new idea; panel establishment by reverse consensus at the first DSB meeting has been proposed before.[27] But, as in the past, it is objected to by some members, and now by the BEIIS Group, because: (i) such 'expedited' establishment would 'constrain the flexibility of Members to explore potential amicable solutions to resolve their disputes'; and (ii) it would 'effectively reduce the time available, particularly for the responding party' and thus 'adversely impact the ability of developing countries including LDCs to access the dispute resolution system'.[28] Regarding (i), there is little evidence that members have indeed used – with any success – the period between the first and the second DSB meeting to reach a mutually agreed solution. Regarding (ii), it is clear that preventing the establishment of a panel allows the respondent additional time to prepare its defence. Such additional time is always welcome, especially for developing country members, but it could also be provided during the panel process.

B. Panel Composition

Chapter II of Title II concerns the panel composition, and in particular who can be panellists and how panellists are appointed. Pursuant to Article 8.3 of the DSU, citizens of the parties or third parties to a dispute can only serve as panellists when the parties agree to this. Under chapter II, members would agree that citizens of a third party who are not (or have not been in the past two years) affiliated with the government of any party or a third party may be nominated by the WTO Secretariat to serve as panellists.[29] However, parties may oppose such

[26] Consolidated Text, Title II, ch I.

[27] Peter Van den Bossche and Werner Zdouc, *The Law and Policy of the World Trade Organization: Text, Cases, and Materials*, 5th edn (Cambridge University Press, 2021) 316.

[28] BEIIS Group Communication (n 20) para 4.

[29] Consolidated Text, Title II, ch II, I.1 and fn 19.

nominations.[30] When the WTO Director-General is requested to appoint the panellists, members may object to the appointment of a citizen of a third party as a panellist.[31] It appears that the proposed change hardly alters the current state of play. Also, as stated by the BEIIS Group, this proposed change is among those changes that are not really required as the existing provisions of the DSU 'can adequately address Members' interests'.[32]

Of more importance is the proposed 'upgrading' of the WTO Secretariat's 'indicative list' of individuals that may serve as WTO panellists. Pursuant to Article 8.4 of the DSU, members may periodically suggest names of individuals for inclusion on this list and, upon approval by the DSB, those names shall be added to the list. The purpose of the indicative list is to assist in the selection of panellists, but it is generally recognised that this list has been of limited usefulness, arguably because members have not been sufficiently selective in suggesting potential panellists, nor has the DSB in approving them. In order to support the maintenance of a 'meaningful' indicative list, a member would, as proposed by the Consolidated Text, be 'encouraged to nominate' for inclusion in the indicative list up to three citizens and one non-citizen possessing 'significant relevant experience'.[33] In addition, individuals nominated to the indicative list must possess high ethical standards and the ability to communicate effectively, both orally and in writing in English, French or Spanish.[34] Interestingly, the Chairperson of the DSB, with the support of the WTO Secretariat, is mandated to check nominations made by members to ensure that nominated individuals meet the qualification requirements referred to above.[35] If the Chairperson would be of the opinion that the nominated individual does not meet these requirements, the Chairperson may recommend the nominating member not to nominate that individual.[36] The nominating member may decide to proceed with the nomination, but in that case, any member, at their request, may be informed by the Chairperson, in confidential consultations, which nominated individual the Chairperson recommended not to be nominated.[37] Note that the DSB is to approve the inclusion of an individual on the indicative list by consensus. To keep the indicative list updated, it will be recomposed every

[30] Consolidated Text, Title II, ch II, fn 20. This right of a party to oppose nominations by the WTO Secretariat is stated in Art 8.6 of the DSU, albeit that a party should only oppose nominations 'for compelling reasons'.

[31] Consolidated Text, Title II, ch II, para I.2.

[32] BEIIS Group Communication (n 20) para 4.

[33] Consolidated Text, Title II, ch II, paras II.1 and II.3. Para II.4 explains what constitutes 'relevant experience', ie experience as a legal practitioner in the field of international economic law or experience (presumably as a non-lawyer) relating to the subject matter of the WTO agreements. Academics in the field of international economic law and policy are only to be considered if they have the relevant experience described in para II.4 (see ibid para II.5). For further details on the experience required, see ibid fns 23–27.

[34] ibid para II.6.

[35] Consolidated Text, Title II, ch II, Appendix I, para 2.

[36] ibid para 4.

[37] ibid paras 4 and 5.

four years.[38] As to the use of the indicative list, the Consolidated Text states that the WTO Secretariat is 'encouraged to use the indicative list in proposing nominations for the panel'.[39] If the WTO Director-General is requested to compose a panel, the parties may agree that they each submit to the Director-General a list of at least 30 individuals on the indicative list. The Director-General is to appoint the panellists based on the overlap between the two lists.[40]

The BEIIS Group has criticised the changes proposed regarding the panel composition, particularly those relating to the qualifications of individuals nominated to the indicative list and the nomination of non-citizens to the indicative list. According to the BEIIS Group, these changes 'upset' 'the delicate balance between "the independence of the members, a sufficiently diverse background and a wide spectrum of experience", as specified in Article 8.2 of the DSU'.[41] The BEIIS Group notes that the Consolidated Text does not address concerns raised by developing countries, including the concern that the indicative list must be representative of the WTO membership in terms of geography, levels of development and legal systems, and the concern that the qualification criteria should be sufficiently flexible to enable capacity constrained developing country members to make nominations for inclusion to the indicative list.[42] The BEIIS Group objects to the emphasis on technical expertise in the qualification requirements. Although it may indeed be a challenge for developing country members to nominate citizens with the required technical expertise, it is unclear how they would benefit from nominating citizens who do not have technical expertise. Also note that, while they were perhaps speaking for all developing countries, the members of the BEIIS Group definitely have many citizens with the required technical expertise.

C. Streamlining the Panel Process

Chapter III of Title II concerns the streamlining of the panel process, particularly the submission of evidence, the timing of the filing of submissions and the meetings with the panel. The Consolidated Text proposes that a panel shall require, as part of its working procedures, the parties 'to submit all evidence, except evidence for the purpose of rebuttal, in their first written submission'.[43] This has long been a requirement set out in the working procedures of most, if not all, panels, and therefore it does not amount to much of a change. Regarding the timing of submissions, Article 12.6 of the DSU currently provides for sequential filing of

[38] Consolidated Text, Title II, ch II, para II.9.

[39] ibid para II.15.

[40] ibid paras III.1 and III.2. If the overlap provides less than three individuals, the Director-General shall complete the panel composition.

[41] BEIIS Group Communication (n 20) para 12.

[42] ibid 13.

[43] Consolidated Text, Title II, ch III, para 2. Note that the panel may grant an exception if a party shows good cause. See ibid.

the first written submissions and simultaneous filing of rebuttal submissions. The Consolidated Text proposes that both the first and the rebuttal submissions be filed sequentially.[44] As this allows the respondent an opportunity to respond more adequately to the arguments of the complainant as they evolve in the course of the proceedings, this change should be welcomed. With regard to the meetings of the parties with the panel, the Working Procedures, as set out in Appendix 3 of the DSU, currently provide for two substantive meetings of the panel with the parties. The Consolidated Text proposes that, unless one of the parties requests otherwise, only one substantive meeting shall be held.[45] One wonders how likely it is that a party will forgo the opportunity to make its case to the panel a second time. Lastly, in order to improve the efficiency of the panel proceedings, the Consolidated Text proposes that a panel shall send written questions to the parties and third parties in advance of the meeting(s) with them.[46] It shall do so at least 10 days before the relevant meeting, but with the understanding that the panel remains entitled to ask additional questions at any time.[47] Again, similar to the proposed change regarding the submission of evidence discussed above, the advance sending of written questions is already done by many panels. However, explicitly requiring panels to do so would nevertheless be useful.

While acknowledging the need to streamline panel proceedings, the BEIIS Group comments that one should evaluate whether the proposed changes do not make the panel proceedings more onerous for developing countries.[48] It notes that flexibility in the panel proceedings is 'of particular importance to developing countries' and that 'the changes proposed could be indicative, rather than mandatory'.[49]

D. Conciseness and Timeframe Adherence

Chapter IV of Title II deals with word limits for written submissions, time limits for oral submissions and a timetable for panel proceedings, taking into account the complexity of the dispute.[50] It is explicitly stated that a panel is expected to 'enforce' these word and time limits and 'ensure' strict adherence to time frames.[51] The Consolidated Text distinguishes between standard, complex and extraordinarily complex disputes, and sets out different word and time limits for each kind of dispute. For example, the parties' first written submission in a standard

[44] ibid para 3.
[45] ibid paras 4 and 6. Note that the party requesting a second meeting should explain the rationale behind its request and identify the selected issues on which the meeting should focus. The second meeting must be held no later than three weeks after the filing of the first written submission, and may be held in person, via a virtual platform or in a hybrid format. See ibid paras 6 and 7.
[46] Consolidated Text, Title II, ch III, Advance Written Questions by Panels, para 1.
[47] ibid paras 1 and 2.
[48] BEIIS Group Communication (n 20) para 8.
[49] ibid.
[50] Consolidated Text, Title II, ch IV, para 1.
[51] ibid.

dispute shall not exceed 30,000 words; in a complex dispute, 48,000 words; and in an extraordinarily complex case, 90,000 words.[52] The time limits for parties' oral submissions shall not exceed 60 minutes in standard disputes, 90 minutes in complex disputes and 120 minutes in extraordinarily complex disputes.[53] The Consolidated Text states explicitly that it is expected that 'the majority of disputes will normally fall into the standard category'.[54] It is for the panel to determine whether a dispute is complex or extraordinarily complex.[55] A panel will, however, only do so at the request of a party that successfully demonstrates that it is impossible to adequately present its case within the limits for standard disputes.[56] A dispute shall only be considered as extraordinarily complex in 'truly exceptional circumstances'.[57]

The Consolidated Text also provides for time frames within which a panel must issue its report in standard, complex and extraordinarily complex disputes. In standard disputes, the time frame shall not exceed nine months; in complex disputes, 12 months; and in extraordinarily complex disputes, 18 months.[58] To ensure compliance with applicable time frames, the panel and the parties shall follow the detailed, standardised timetable for standard and complex disputes set out in Appendix 1 to chapter IV of Title II.[59] Most interestingly and innovatively, in case a panel fails to meet the applicable time frames, the Chairperson of the DSB 'shall issue a public communication to the concerned panellists and Secretariat staff, reminding them about the critical importance of adhering strictly to timeframes'.[60] This amounts to public shaming and may well prove to be an effective way of ensuring compliance with the time frames. Moreover, panellists participating in multiple disputes showing a pattern of repeated delays shall be

[52] ibid para 2(a) for standard disputes, para 5(a) for complex disputes and para 6 for extraordinarily complex cases. For the word limits for rebuttal submissions and third-party subsidies, see ibid. Paras 8 and 9 set out word limits for requests for preliminary rulings and responses thereto, and parties' comments on the panel's interim report. Note that with regard to the word limits set out in para 2, the panel may apply flexibility by setting limits up to 35% higher. With regard to the word limits set out in paras 5, 8 and 9, this flexibility is limited to 25%. See ibid para 10. Where written submissions are provided in French or Spanish, the above word limits shall be increased by 15%. See ibid para 11.

[53] ibid para 2(b) for standard disputes, para 5(b) for complex disputes and para 6 for extraordinarily complex cases. For the time limits for third-party oral subsidies, see ibid. For oral submissions, panels enjoy the same flexibility as for written submissions. See ibid para 10.

[54] ibid fn 37.

[55] ibid para 3. In determining the complexity of a dispute, a panel shall take, inter alia, into account the complexity of the analysis required to determine a breach or a defence, the amount of expert and other complex evidence and the complexity of the measures at issue. See ibid.

[56] ibid fn 37.

[57] ibid.

[58] ibid paras 13, 14 and 16 respectively. Note that the time frame runs from the date of issuance of the working procedures following the organisational meeting to the date of issuance of the final report to the parties. See ibid.

[59] ibid para 15. In consultation with the parties, the panel may modify certain parts of these standardised timetables. See ibid. In case of *force majeure*, ie an unforeseen event beyond the control of the panel and the parties that prevents the conduct of panel work, the panel may, following consultations with the parties, suspend the proceedings as long as the unforeseen event continues to prevent the conduct of panel work. See ibid para 17.

[60] ibid para 21.

backlisted and no longer proposed as panellists by the WTO Secretariat.[61] Note, however, that the naming and shaming of panellists for failing to adhere to time frames could make it more difficult to find well-qualified adjudicators willing to accept an appointment as panellists.[62]

The BEIIS Group objects to giving panels the authority to determine the nature of a dispute (standard, complex or extraordinarily complex) and inviting parties to limit their claims as this 'shifts the locus of control over the panel process away from the disputing parties to the panel'.[63] Pursuant to the BEIIS Group, these changes dilute or render ineffective the 'Member-driven nature of the WTO'.[64] Also, the proposed changes make no attempt to accommodate the diversity of national circumstances, and in particular those of developing country members.[65] According to the BEIIS Group, 'when seen holistically', the changes proposed in the Consolidated Text 'make the dispute settlement process more onerous, complex, and difficult in actual practice for Members'.[66] It is not clear why this would be the case. The proposed changes regarding word and time limits for parties' submissions and the time frame for the panel proceedings should make disputes less complex and extensive, and, thus, the dispute settlement process less, not more, onerous. However, the categorisation of disputes as standard, complex or extraordinarily complex undoubtedly introduces a measure of 'subjectivity' into the panel proceedings,[67] and the word and time limits are, to a large degree, arbitrary. The latter is probably unavoidable and mitigated by the flexibility granted to a panel to adjust the limits.

IV. Compliance

Title IV of the Consolidated Text deals with the reasonable period of time (RPT) given to respondents to comply with the recommendations and rulings of an adjudicative report adopted by the DSB. Pursuant to Article 21.3 of the DSU, a member whose measure has been found inconsistent with its WTO obligations has, if it is impracticable to comply immediately, an RPT to do so. Article 21.3 does not define what an RPT is, but leaves it to the parties, to the DSB or to an arbitrator to agree on, or determine, what it is in a given dispute.[68] The Consolidated

[61] ibid.

[62] For non-governmental experts, the remuneration is modest, and the opportunity costs are often high. Government officials are not paid for panel work, which comes on top of an already demanding workload.

[63] BEIIS Group Communication (n 20) para 22.

[64] ibid 20.

[65] ibid 9.

[66] ibid 10.

[67] ibid 9.

[68] See Art 21.3(a), (b) or (c). An arbitrator determining the reasonable period of time under Art 21.3(c) is given as a guideline that this period should not exceed 15 months from the adoption of the report by the DSB.

Text, however, proposes a different approach.[69] First, to secure a mutually agreed solution to the dispute – which is, as stated in Article 3.7, clearly to be preferred – the Consolidated Text proposes that the parties, upon request of the complainant, shall engage regarding compliance in consultations 'at the level of ministers or designated senior officials' within 30 days following the adoption of the report.[70] If the respondent declines to engage in such consultations, the RPT shall be six months from the date of adoption of the report by the DSB.[71] Second, if the parties do not agree on the RPT within 45 days of the adoption of the report and if neither party requests arbitration to determine the RPT, the RPT shall be nine months from the date of adoption of the report.[72] Third, if a party requests arbitration on the RPT, the arbitrator shall determine the RPT within 90 days after the date of the request and shall, in determining the RPT, consider that the period 'may be shorter or longer than nine months, depending upon the particular circumstances in the Member concerned, but shall not exceed 15 months'.[73] The arbitrator is, however, explicitly reminded of the 'principle of prompt compliance as expressed in Article 21 of the DSU'.[74]

The BEIIS Group strongly objects to the proposed changes regarding the RPT, arguing that these changes would 'substantially shorten' the RPT and 'do not take into account the different legal and political systems of Members or provide sufficient S&DT [special and differential treatment] for developing countries, including LDCs'.[75] The latter criticism may appear, at first glance, unjustified since the Consolidated Text explicitly allows arbitrators to take 'the particular circumstances in the Member concerned' into consideration when determining the RPT.[76] However, as the BEIIS Group notes, 'historically, developing countries, including LDCs, have asked for a minimum RPT of 15 months'.[77] The Consolidated Text would cap the RPT at 15 months[78] and would thus restrict the flexibility currently available under Article 21.3 of the DSU. This is to the detriment of developing

[69] Note that Title IV does not apply to arbitration awards issued pursuant to Art 25 of the DSU. Parties, when entering into an arbitration agreement, may, however, agree to apply the provisions of this Title. See Consolidated Text, Title IV, para 7. This is surprising because, pursuant to Art 25.4 of the DSU, Art 21 of the DSU applies, mutatis mutandis, to arbitration awards.

[70] Consolidated Text, Title IV, para 2. Parties are also 'encouraged' to engage in alternative dispute settlement (ADR) procedures on compliance. See ibid para 3. These ADR procedures are the good offices, conciliation and mediation procedures provided for in Appendix 4, ch I, Title I of the Consolidated Text, 'Supplementary Rules for Procedures Undertaken Pursuant to Title IV (Compliance)'.

[71] ibid Title IV, para 4. The same is the case when the respondent declines to engage in ADR procedures. See ibid.

[72] ibid para 5.

[73] ibid paras 6, chapeau, and 6(a). The 'particular circumstances' referred to include the need for a legislative change and the special situation of developing or least-developed country members. See ibid para 6(b).

[74] ibid para 6(c).

[75] BEIIS Group Communication (n 20) para 25.

[76] See Consolidated Text, Title IV, para 6(a).

[77] BEIIS Group Communication (n 20) para 26.

[78] See Consolidated Text, Title IV, para 6(a).

country members in particular.[79] By penalising the refusal to engage in consultations in this way, the Consolidated Text does indeed break new ground. The question is, however, whether this strong 'encouragement' to engage in consultations is actually contrary to the interests of developing country members.

V. Guidelines for Adjudicators

Title V of the Consolidated Text sets out guidelines for adjudicators, particularly on treaty interpretation (chapter I), obiter dicta (chapter II) and the precedential value to be given to past reports (chapter III).

A. Treaty Interpretation

On first reading, the two-paragraph chapter on treaty interpretation appears to state the obvious, and would therefore appear to be totally unremarkable and harmless. This is, however, not the case. In the first four lines of the first paragraph, the Consolidated Text recalls that Article 3.2 of the DSU requires WTO adjudicators to interpret the covered agreements in accordance with customary rules of interpretation of public international law, and that Articles 31, 32 and 33 of the Vienna Convention on the Law of Treaties are to be applied.[80] This is obviously correct. What is interesting, however, is that in the following nine lines of this paragraph there is no further elaboration or clarification of the general rule of interpretation set out in Article 31; rather, the nine lines are about the supplementary means of interpretation.[81] The importance given to the supplementary means of interpretation, and in particular the preparatory work, ie the negotiating history of the WTO agreements, is a clear but misguided concession to the USA, which has often criticised the Appellate Body for not giving more importance to the negotiating history of agreements, and in particular the negotiating history of the agreements on trade remedies.[82] The problem is that there is no agreed negotiating history – no *travaux préparatoires* adopted by the parties to the negotiations – of the WTO agreements.[83] Those who wish to rely on the negotiating history usually rely on their own negotiating positions and papers. The invocation of the negotiating history then often becomes shamelessly self-serving. This disproportionate attention to supplementary means of interpretation of this first paragraph of chapter I is unfortunate.

[79] The BEIIS Group also objects to what it refers to as 'an element of mandatory Alternate Dispute Resolution (ADR) into the process, since refusal to engage in ADR would result in an RPT of 6 months'. See BEIIS Group Communication (n 20) para 25.
[80] Consolidated Text, Title V, ch I, para 1.
[81] ibid.
[82] ibid para 2.
[83] Van den Bossche and Zdouc (n 27) 209.

The second paragraph of the chapter on treaty interpretation has nothing to do with treaty interpretation, but with the burden of proof – or perhaps not really with that either. It starts by stating the obvious, namely that a complaining party bears the burden of establishing a prima facie case that another party has acted inconsistently with an obligation under the covered agreements.[84] It is only in the following sentences that it becomes clear why this paragraph is part of the Consolidated Text. Again, this reflects a misguided attempt to address a concern of the USA, namely that WTO adjudicators find inconsistencies with obligations not to be found in the covered agreements. To this end, this paragraph requires adjudicators to determine, first, whether the complainant has made a prima facie case of the existence of the obligation invoked, and only then, in the absence of an effective refutation by the other party, apply that obligation to the facts. Is this requirement, however, at all necessary? Does an adjudicator not always first establish whether the obligation invoked exists before applying it to the facts?

B. Obiter Dicta

The second chapter of Title V is entitled 'Focus on What is Necessary to Resolve the Dispute'. The first two paragraphs of the chapter primarily repeat language that was also used in the 2019 Draft General Council Decision on the Functioning of the Appellate Body and in the 2020 Multi-Party Interim Appeal Arbitration Arrangement.[85] Adjudicators should only make findings that will assist the DSB in making its recommendations and rulings, and should limit their reasoning to what is necessary to support their findings.[86] In other words, adjudicators should avoid obiter dicta, or, as the USA confusingly calls it, advisory opinions. While the Appellate Body occasionally said more than strictly speaking had to be said, the reality is that WTO adjudicators have been more than happy to exercise judicial economy and not rule on more than is needed. It is the complainants that bring a multitude of claims in what could often be a simpler case. The third paragraph of this chapter recognises this reality by authorising adjudicators to invite parties to focus on certain claims or even to exclude certain claims.[87] Such invitations are, however, not binding. It remains to be seen how many complainants will voluntarily give up on some of their claims. The BEIIS Group observes in this regard

[84] Consolidated Text, Title V, ch I, para 2.

[85] WTO General Council, 'Informal Process on Matters Related to the Functioning of the Appellate Body – Report by the Facilitator, HE Dr David Walker (New Zealand) on 15 October 2019, JOB/GC/222, Dated 15 October 2019, Annex with the Draft General Council Decision on the Functioning of the Appellate Body, under the Heading "Advisory Opinions"' 6; WTO (n 4) Annex 1, para 10.

[86] Consolidated Text, Title V, ch II, paras 1 and 2.

[87] ibid paras 3 and 4. Note para 4 explicitly states that 'the fact that a party to the dispute does not accept the invitation shall not prejudice the consideration of the case or the rights of the parties'.

that the Consolidated Text 'constrains the autonomy of disputing parties to fully explore all facets of their dispute'.[88]

C. Precedential Value of Past Reports

Finally, chapter III of Title V deals, in one, somewhat convoluted, paragraph, with the issue of precedent. As is well known, the USA has long been on a crusade against precedent in WTO dispute settlement, a stance that does not prevent it from invoking all the case law it agrees with and insisting that adjudicators follow that case law. The sole paragraph of this chapter starts out by stating what is undisputed, namely that WTO reports have no precedential value, meaning that they do not have binding force in a subsequent dispute.[89] What is problematic with the rest of this paragraph is, on the one hand, what it does not say, and, on the other hand, what it does say. What it does not say is that the ultimate purpose of WTO dispute settlement, as stated in Article 3.2 of the DSU, is to bring security and predictability to the international trading system, and that, therefore, there is a legitimate expectation of WTO members that the same legal issue will be decided in the same way in subsequent cases.[90] The omission of any reference to the ultimate purpose of the WTO dispute settlement system is undoubtedly deliberate and unfortunate. What the paragraph on precedent says is that while an adjudicator may refer to previous reports to the extent she/he considers the analysis in such reports 'persuasive', each adjudicator must in each dispute 'develop [her/his] own interpretation' of the WTO provisions at issue.[91] The paragraph concludes with the instruction to adjudicators that they 'may not presume that an interpretation of the covered agreements in a WTO dispute settlement report is persuasive'.[92] This is not how international adjudication – or, for that matter, any adjudication – works. Adjudicators build on the hard work done and lessons learned by previous generations of adjudicators. An adjudicator does not start afresh in each case with the interpretation of the relevant provisions. Also, the parties in a case will invoke the case law that supports their arguments and the adjudicator will thus start by considering the invoked case law. No adjudicator – except perhaps those with a dangerously big ego – will start out on a case with the presumption that her/his learned colleague adjudicators, who ruled on the interpretation of a provision earlier, got it wrong and that the work needs to be done all again. The instruction in the last sentence of this paragraph is thus misguided, if not outright foolish.

[88] BEIIS Group Communication (n 20) para 18.
[89] Consolidated Text, Title V, ch III, para 1.
[90] Note that the 2019 Draft General Council Decision of the Functioning of the Appellate Body, JOB/GC/222, dated 15 October 2019, 6 and the 2020 Multi-Party Interim Appeal Arbitration Arrangement, JOB/DSB/1/Add.12, dated 30 April 2020, 1 state that the 'consistency and predictability in the interpretation of rights and obligations under the covered agreements is of significant value to Members'.
[91] Consolidated Text, Title V, ch III, para 1.
[92] ibid.

VI. Procedures to Discuss Legal Interpretations

Title VI of the Consolidated Text deals with discussions among WTO members of legal interpretations adopted by WTO adjudicators, particularly in relevant WTO bodies (chapter I) and the discussion in the Advisory Working Group (chapter II).

A. Discussion in Relevant WTO Bodies

If the chairperson of a WTO body determines that an adjudicative report or arbitration award is relevant, or at the mere request of any member, this report or award will be put on the agenda of the next meeting of this body.[93] This will give members an opportunity to discuss 'at the expert level' 'the technical and policy implications' of the legal interpretations adopted.[94] Be that as it may, it is surprising that, to support this discussion 'at the expert level', it is considered necessary to instruct the Secretariat to circulate 'a summary document of the adjudicator's interpretive findings that should not exceed one page'.[95] One would expect that experts would need, if anything, more than a one-page summary. Also, when engaging in this discussion in the relevant WTO body, members are prohibited from discussing dispute-specific facts or the implementation of the DSB's recommendations.[96] One may expect that the parties to the dispute, and other members, will find it very challenging, if not impossible, to restrain themselves in this way. In any case, it is not clear whether this proposed change really adds something that is not yet possible under the current rules.

B. Advisory Working Group

Chapter II of Title VI provides for the establishment of an Advisory Working Group, which will be composed of all WTO members and operate under the auspices of the DSB.[97] The Advisory Working Group is to be a new mechanism for WTO members 'to discuss, build consensus and provide guidance on legal interpretations developed by adjudicators'.[98] Any member may request a discussion by the Advisory Working Group,[99] but, as explicitly stated, this mechanism 'is expected to be used rarely'.[100] The Advisory Working Group 'shall not relitigate disputes

[93] Consolidated Text, Title VI, ch I, para 1.
[94] ibid para 2, chapeau.
[95] ibid para 2(a).
[96] ibid para 2(c).
[97] Consolidated Text, Title VI, ch II, para 2.
[98] ibid paras 2 and 3.
[99] ibid para 6, chapeau. Such a request can, however, only be made after the RPT for implementation in the dispute concerned has expired. See ibid para 6(b).
[100] ibid para 4.

or function as an [appeal/review] mechanism'.[101] The outcome of the discussion in the Advisory Working Group may take the form of: (i) a draft recommendation, adopted by consensus, for the adoption of an authoritative interpretation by the Ministerial Conference or General Council; (ii) a recommendation, adopted by consensus, that the legal interpretation shall not be considered as persuasive and can therefore not be referred to by WTO adjudicators in support for their reasoning; or (iii) a record of members' diverging views about the interpretation.[102] It is important to note that the outcomes of discussions in the Advisory Working Group 'shall not have any retroactive effect' on the disputes in the context of which the legal interpretation at issue was adopted.[103]

Regarding this new mechanism to discuss legal interpretations adopted by adjudicators, the BEIIS Group expressed the concern that this change will 'have a far-reaching impact on the practice of the dispute resolution system' and is 'being proposed without rigorous, evidence-based analysis in the specific context of the WTO dispute settlement system'.[104] This is not the first time that a proposal to establish a political body or an expert group to assess legal interpretations adopted by WTO adjudicators is made. A similar proposal was already included in the 2005 Sutherland Report.[105] Unlike earlier proposals, the current proposal is more specific and detailed, particularly with regard to possible outcomes. However, it is not clear why there is a need for a new mechanism. Discussions on legal interpretations adopted by WTO adjudicators can already occur in the DSB or any other WTO body. What would the Advisory Working Group allow members to do that they currently cannot already do? Also, it is unlikely that, if established, such a mechanism shall be 'used rarely' and will not be used to 'relitigate' disputes. Members may be expected to use all means at their disposal to challenge any legal interpretation that is inimical to them. Finally, except in very unusual cases, the outcome of discussions in the Advisory Working Group will be a mere record of diverging views. How useful this is is open to debate.

VII. Secretariat Support

Title VII of the Consolidated Text deals with the WTO Secretariat staffing to support the work of WTO adjudicators (chapter I) and the responsibilities of these adjudicators in light of the support provided by the Secretariat (chapter II).

[101] ibid.

[102] ibid para 13. The outcomes shall be circulated as an unrestricted WTO document and included in the *WTO Analytical Index*. See ibid para 15. The record of diverging views shall include: '(i) the number of the Members that expressed the views during the discussion, (ii) the Members that supported or did not support the interpretation discussed and (iii) their reasonings'. See ibid para 13(c).

[103] ibid para 14. The validity or the implementation of the recommendations and rulings adopted in these disputes shall not be affected. See ibid.

[104] BEIIS Group Communication (n 20) para 4.

[105] WTO, *The Future of the WTO: Addressing Institutional Challenges in the New Millennium: Report by the Consultative Board to the Director-General Supachai Panitchpakdi* (2004) para 251.

A. Secretariat Staffing to Support Adjudicators' Work

Article 27.1 of the DSU states that the WTO Secretariat shall have 'the responsibility of assisting panels, especially on the legal, historical and procedural aspects of the matters dealt with, and of providing secretarial and technical support'. The WTO Secretariat plays a more important role in supporting WTO adjudicators than registries or legal secretariats of other international dispute resolution systems. The Consolidated Text states in this regard that in order 'to ensure high-quality support by the Secretariat',[106] members expect that the Secretariat staff has 'appropriate subject-matter expertise'.[107] As the footnote explains, this subject-matter expertise 'could be relevant committee experience, other experience drawn from the appropriate Secretariat Division, or other practical subject-matter expertise such as relevant government or private sector experience'.[108] The Secretariat lawyers assisting WTO adjudicators are among the very best WTO law experts, and one must therefore wonder why it was considered necessary to refer to members' expectation of subject-matter expertise of Secretariat staff. Perhaps some members wish to convey in this way their 'aversion' for lawyers with general international law expertise and/or an academic (rather than a government/private practice) background.

B. Responsibilities of Adjudicators and Scope of Support Provided by Secretariat Staff

Chapter II addresses an issue that has been the subject of considerable debate in recent years, namely the appropriate role of the Secretariat staff in WTO dispute settlement. In particular, with regard to panel proceedings, it has been suggested that it is the Secretariat staff, rather than the panellists, who decide cases.[109] As already stated above, the Secretariat undoubtedly plays a very important role in WTO dispute settlement. There is, however, an important, but often poorly understood, difference between 'holding the pen' in a case and 'deciding a case'. The Secretariat staff does the former; the latter is what the panellists do (or should do). This is an effective and appropriate division of responsibilities. Addressing concerns about the role of the Secretariat staff, the Consolidated Text finds it necessary to state explicitly that 'adjudicators shall have full responsibility for decision making';[110] that 'Members expect adjudicators to draft their reports with

[106] Consolidated Text, Title VII, ch I, para 1, chapeau.
[107] ibid para 1(a).
[108] ibid fn 68.
[109] Joost Pauwelyn and Krzysztof Pelc, 'Who Writes the Rulings of the World Trade Organization? A Critical Assessment of the Role of the Secretariat in WTO Dispute Settlement' (26 September 2019) https://papers.ssrn.com/abstract=3458872.
[110] Consolidated Text, Title VII, ch II, para 1(a).

the support of the Secretariat staff as appropriate';[111] and that 'adjudicators shall draft the conclusion section of their reports'.[112] If the Secretariat staff is requested to assist in drafting, they shall do so 'on the basis of written instructions by the adjudicators'.[113]

The BEIIS Group rightly comments on the proposed changes regarding the responsibilities of adjudicators and the role of the Secretariat that 'attempting to strictly delineate' the assistance provided by the Secretariat 'may have an impact that is opposite to the desired effect'.[114]

VIII. Transparency

Title VIII of the Consolidated Text deals with the transparency of WTO dispute settlement, which has long been a controversial issue. Transparency has two dimensions, namely transparency vis-à-vis WTO members (chapter I) and transparency vis-à-vis the general public (chapter II).

While there is now – at least in disputes between consenting developed country members – a high degree of transparency in WTO dispute settlement proceedings, this transparency is not provided for in the DSU. Regarding written submissions of the parties, Article 18.1 of the DSU states that these submissions 'shall be treated as confidential', albeit that a party is 'not precluded from disclosing statements of its own positions to the public'. Regarding meetings of WTO adjudicators with the parties, the Working Proceedings for Panels state that 'the panel shall meet in closed session',[115] and Article 17.10 of the DSU states that 'the proceedings of the Appellate Body shall be confidential'. For the BEIIS Group, the relevant changes proposed in the Consolidated Text 'completely inverted' 'the default positions on transparency' envisaged in the DSU and this thus 'raises grave concerns'.[116] However, since the BEIIS Group explicitly recognises that 'transparency is important in a member-driven organisation, especially for greater capacity building',[117] its opposition to greater transparency is presumably focused on transparency vis-à-vis the general public. Regarding the latter, the Consolidated Text proposes that

[111] ibid para 1(b). Secretariat staff is instructed to be 'responsive to (1) the parties' submissions and (2) specific requests of the adjudicators'. See ibid para 2(a). Also, to ensure that the Secretariat is responsive to the parties' submissions, the Consolidated Text requires that it shall not provide the panellists with issues papers before the first written submissions of the parties has been received. See ibid para 3. This is a somewhat bizarre requirement as one can hardly imagine that issues papers would ever be written before the first written submissions have been received.

[112] ibid para 1(c). Note, however, that the Secretariat staff is instructed to provide the necessary editorial support. See ibid para 2(c).

[113] ibid para 2(b).

[114] BEIIS Group Communication (n 20) para 32.

[115] DSU, Appendix 3, para 2.

[116] BEIIS Group Communication (n 20) para 16.

[117] ibid 15.

the Secretariat shall publish the non-confidential version of written submissions on the WTO website no later than seven days after the circulation of the report.[118] While this would indeed make available to the general public submissions that otherwise remain confidential, the executive summaries of the submissions attached to the publicly available report arguably already ensure sufficient transparency. The Consolidated Text also proposes that, if the parties to the dispute agree, the Secretariat shall make the substantive meetings with the parties accessible for observation by the public 'through live broadcasting or make a recording available a few days after the substantive meeting of the panel with the parties'.[119] If parties do not agree to this, the Secretariat shall make the substantive meetings with the parties accessible for observation by the general public 'via on-site viewing of an audio-visual recording or viewing of an audio-visual recording made available to the general public via an electronic system' no later than seven days after the date of circulation of the report.[120] As the BEIIS Group notes, developing country members 'had raised concerns about the asymmetrical ability of external stakeholders, particularly commercial interests, to influence or pressure the dispute proceedings'.[121] These concerns are not reflected in the Consolidated Text.

IX. Accountability Mechanism

Finally, Title X of the Consolidated Text provides for the establishment of an accountability mechanism, ie a mechanism for the periodic review by the DSB of the operation of the dispute settlement system and the implementation of the reforms set out in the Consolidated Text.[122] To the extent possible, such a review shall be based on factual and statistical information, compiled by the Secretariat.[123] In advance of the periodic review by the DSB, its Chairperson shall circulate a report setting out the factual and statistical information, along with any views expressed by members on the implementation of the reform elements listed in the Appendix to Title X.[124] The Chairperson's report 'may contain recommendations

[118] Consolidated Text, Title VIII, ch II, s I, para 1. At the request of a party, this may be delayed until after the adoption by the DSU of the report. See ibid.

[119] Consolidated Text, Title VIII, ch I, s II, para 1(a). Parties may also decide on any other modality, including in-person observation. See ibid.

[120] ibid para 1(b).

[121] BEIIS Group Communication (n 20) para 15.

[122] Consolidated Text, Title X, s I, para 1. The first Accountability Mechanisms Meeting of the DSB is scheduled for October 2026 and October of every second year thereafter. See ibid.

[123] ibid para 3.

[124] ibid para 10. The various steps in preparation of the report of the DSB Chairperson are set out in paras 5–9. Note that some of the reform elements have specific performance targets (eg establishment of panels at the first DSB meeting at which they are requested). In that case, the review is 'based on' the relevant factual and statistical information. Where a reform element does not have a performance target, the relevant factual and statistical information will merely 'assist' members to review the implementation of that reform element. See ibid para 14.

of action to be decided by the DSB'.[125] The proposed accountability mechanism will undoubtedly allow for a better-informed discussion on the operation of the WTO dispute settlement system and the reforms members would decide on.

X. Conclusion

The Molina Process and the Consolidated Text on the draft Ministerial Decision on Dispute Settlement which emerged from it were not successful in resolving the crisis of WTO dispute settlement. This is, first and above all, because no agreement could be reached on the issue of the nature and scope of appellate review, ie the issue that triggered the current crisis. Moreover, on many other issues, the proposed changes reflected in the Consolidated Text enjoy less support than the Molina Report may lead one to believe. A group of influential developing countries, referred to above as the BEIIS Group, have expressed their disagreement or voiced grave concerns regarding many of the proposed changes.

At the 13th WTO Ministerial Conference in Abu Dhabi in February/March 2024, WTO members took note of the work on dispute settlement reform done so far and instructed their officials 'to accelerate discussions in an inclusive and transparent manner, build on the progress already made, and work on unresolved issues', with a self-imposed deadline of the end of 2024 in mind.[126] At the DSB meeting of April 2024, the DSB formalised the dispute settlement reform process and appointed Ambassador Usha Dwarka-Canabady of Mauritius as the facilitator of this process. Six co-convenors were appointed to assist the facilitator on specific issues. Experts of members continue their technical work on the reform and, each month, members meet at the ambassador level to discuss the progress made. At the July 2024 meeting, the co-convenors dealing with the issue of appellate review announced that they intend to share with members in early September 2024 a draft document which they 'anticipate will be useful for structuring future discussions'.[127] Ambassador Dwarka-Canabady very diplomatically stated that the issue of appellate review 'might take a bit more time'.[128]

The proposed changes to WTO dispute settlement reflected in the Consolidated Text of February 2024 are a mixed bag of good, ill-conceived, futile and unnecessary changes. The good changes – many of which are long overdue – include the establishment of panels at the first DSB meeting, the upgrading of the indicative list, the sequential filing of rebuttal submissions, the furtherance of timely compliance, flexible word limits for written submissions, the strengthening of transparency and

[125] ibid para 11.
[126] WTO Ministerial Conference, Thirteenth Session (n 25).
[127] 'Facilitator, Co-Convenors Update Members on Dispute Settlement Reform Work, 18 July 2024' www.wto.org/english/news_e/news24_e/disp_18jul24_e.htm.
[128] ibid.

the establishment of an accountability mechanism. The ill-conceived changes – most of which address long-standing grievances of the USA and are potentially harmful – include the guidelines for adjudicators regarding treaty interpretation and the precedential value of past reports, as well as the delineation of the role of the WTO Secretariat and the naming and shaming of adjudicators for exceeding the time frames. The futile changes – which are unlikely to have much of an impact – include the possibility of having one rather than two meetings with the parties, the appointment of third-party nationals as panellists and the establishment of the Advisory Working Group. Finally, the unnecessary changes – which do not go (much) beyond what is already possible under existing rules or concern practices and features which are firmly established – include the timely submission of evidence, the time limits for oral submissions and the requirement of appropriate subject-matter expertise of the WTO staff. Having said that, the Consolidated Text, with its gaps and imperfections, is nevertheless a tour de force of, in particular, Molina, for which he deserves the greatest respect.

The (geo-)economic and (geo-)political realities of the twenty-first century are very different from those at the end of the twentieth century, when the current WTO dispute settlement system was conceived. The dispute settlement system of tomorrow may thus have to be different from the system that has served WTO members very well for many years. However, any dispute settlement system worth having should be a rigorously rules-based system, with compulsory jurisdiction, appellate review, impartial and independent adjudicators, and timely, legally binding and enforceable rulings, which provides security and predictability to the multilateral trading system. Unfortunately, assuming that the USA is willing to agree to any kind of binding international trade dispute resolution, this is not the system that it would want to see established. This makes resolving the current crisis very difficult. If no agreement on a 'fully and well-functioning dispute settlement system' can be reached, it is better to 'muddle on' with the current system supplemented with the MPIA than to accept a new system that is not worth having. I am confident that such an assertion would command Professor Cottier's approval.

5

Clarifying Subsidy Disciplines in the WTO: Thomas Cottier as an Adjudicator

JAMES J NEDUMPARA*

Thomas Cottier has donned many hats in his long and illustrious career – as a trade negotiator, an academic par excellence, an outstanding arbitrator and, most importantly, an institution builder. Cottier's range is outstanding and breathtaking. While his core expertise is in intellectual property rights and technology,[1] his contribution has profoundly impacted various branches of international economic law.

In the last few decades, especially until the Appellate Body crisis wrecked the system, World Trade Organization (WTO) litigation formed an active part of international dispute settlement. However, unlike other international law adjudicators, WTO panellists are not generally selected from the bar. Most of them are astute diplomats or accomplished trade professionals, but are seldom known outside their respective circles. Cottier is truly an exception to this rule. Cottier spearheaded the creation of an institution, the World Trade Institute, that is dedicated to mainstreaming and popularising the study of international trade law and economics. Cottier's students have gone on to serve several national governments, research institutions and international institutions, and are holding the mantle for the new generation of leadership in international trade and related disciplines.

Thomas Cottier is one of the few trade adjudicators who have dealt with consequential cases during both the General Agreement on Tariffs and Trade (GATT) and WTO eras. The Chilean challenge of certain EC measures on Dessert Apples evokes certain nostalgia for GATT law enthusiasts.[2] Cottier was the Chair of the

* The opinions expressed in this chapter are personal and should not be attributed to the author's organisation.

[1] Thomas Cottier, 'Working Together Towards TRIPS' in WTO (ed), *The Making of the TRIPS Agreement* (World Trade Organization, 2015), in which Cottier recounts his experience of participating in the TRIPS negotiations as a part of Switzerland's negotiating team.

[2] GATT Panel Report, *European Economic Community – Restrictions on Imports of Dessert Apples – Complaint by Chile*, L/6491, adopted 22 June 1989, BISD 36S/93.

GATT Panel in *USA – Automobiles*[3] – popularly known as the Gas Guzzler case – an iconic, yet unadopted panel report that clarified the scope of national treatment under the GATT, and especially the role of the controversial 'aim-and-effect' test that provided greater latitude for regulatory distinctions. Subsequently, as a chair of several WTO panel proceedings, Cottier had the opportunity to imprint his name while adjudicating certain watershed trade disputes. Cottier was appointed the chairman of the panel in *EC – Hormones*,[4] a sanitary and phytosanitary (SPS) controversy, which turned out to be a legendary WTO dispute. A couple of decades later, Cottier was selected for the task of chairing the panel for *Canada – Feed in Tariff Measures*,[5] a case that presented novel claims and ushered in a series of disputes that challenged the interface between industrial policy and climate change response.[6] Cottier had also adjudicated several other major cases at the WTO, but these remain as two of the standout disputes in the three-decade history of the WTO's dispute settlement system.

In this short piece, I explore Cottier's contribution to our understanding of subsidy disciplines. Obviously, it is challenging to speak about Cottier's direct contribution to WTO disputes, as WTO panel rulings do not reveal much about an adjudicator's intellectual contributions or court craft. There are no individual opinions in WTO disputes, and even dissenting opinions are anonymous. However, Thomas Cottier has expressed his ideas through multiple platforms, and his academic writings suggest the need for fresh thinking in some of these areas.[7] In 2023, Cottier was open and candid while participating in a discussion relating to the challenges in developing subsidy disciplines at the Society of International Economic Law (SIEL) biennial conference held in Bogota, Colombia. Cottier noted that the neoliberal movement of the 1990s was visibly absent in contemporary economic relations or trade policy.[8] In the early 1990s, neoliberal dogmas were adopted to bring disciplines to curb state power. The core idea of neoliberalism – often described as market fundamentalism without (or with minimal) state intervention – has lost its zeal. Abundant subsidies and state support are today readily visible in different sectors of national economies. Geopolitics, national security, supply chain resilience and climate change concerns have

[3] GATT Panel Report, *United States – Taxes on Automobiles*, DS31/R, 11 October 1994, unadopted.

[4] *European Communities – Measures Concerning Meat and Meat Products (Hormones)* WT/DS26.

[5] WTO Panel Reports, *Canada – Certain Measures Affecting the Renewable Energy Generation Sector/Canada – Measures Relating to the Feed-in Tariff Program*, WT/DS412/R/WT/DS426/R and Add 1, adopted 24 May 2013, as modified by Appellate Body Reports WT/DS412/AB/R/WT/DS426/AB/R, para 7.318.

[6] *India – Certain measures relating to Solar Cells and Solar Modules*, WT/DS456/R.

[7] Thomas Cottier, Garba Malumfashi, Sofya Matteottie-Berkutova, Olga Nartova, Joelle de Sepibus and Sadeq Z Bigdeli, 'Energy in WTO Law and Policy. The Prospects of International Trade Regulation: From Fragmentation to Coherence' (2011) NCCR Trade Working Paper, www.wto.org/English/res_e/publications_e/wtr10_7may10_e.pdf.

[8] Thomas Cottier's intervention in Panel 27 titled 'Reimagining Subsidy Controls' at the Eighth Biennial Global Conference of the SIEL 2023, Bogota (Colombia) (notes on file with author).

overtaken the neoliberal consensus.[9] Notably, a major proportion of the subsidies are granted for bolstering the domestic capacity to address concerns such as national security and security of supply, as well as for building new critical technologies and strategic competitiveness. According to the New Industrial Policy Observatory run by the St Gallen Endowment for Prosperity Through Trade, the USA and the EU dominate the subsidy race, with ostensible security and climate policy justifications. Not only developed countries, but also large developing countries are providing subsidies tied to industrial policy. According to the World Bank, the subsidy-type measures implemented annually since the mid-2010s have nearly tripled.[10] In essence, no country would like to lose the race to establish a mark in the technologies of the future.

The role of industrial policy in combating climate change is contentious. There are some who believe that development of green technologies is a global public good and that only an industrial policy push can jolt breakthrough innovations in this field.[11] While green transition measures are essential, how countries achieve such objectives is the core concern. Several scholars point out that twentieth-century trade rules cannot govern the dynamic twenty-first-century trade, especially in supporting various sustainable development goals and accelerating the path to a world of net zero emissions.[12] The WTO's tight subsidy disciplines, according to some, can curtail the ability of a state to respond to the grave challenges posed by climate challenge.[13] At the same time, a review of green energy measures reveals that countries are increasingly using such subsidies to covertly favour domestic industries, especially in the production of inputs and intermediate components.[14] Governments are increasingly forsaking reliance on free markets and engaging in protectionist measures, including targeted support for industries such as semiconductors, electric vehicles, solar panels, integrated circuits or even steel and aluminium. Although such subsidies may not fall within the category of prohibited measures, they may nonetheless produce adverse effects on the trade of other WTO members and are actionable. According to Gary Hufbauer, subsidies on

[9] John Narayan, '(After) Neoliberalism? Rethinking the Return of the State' (*Developing Economics*, 10 January 2022) https://developingeconomics.org/2022/01/10/after-neoliberalism-rethinking-the-return-of-the-state/.

[10] Alessandro Barattieri, Aaditya Mattoo and Dara Taglioni, 'Trade Effects of Industrial Policies: Are Preferential Trade Agreements a Shield' (2024) World Bank Policy Research Working Paper, https://documents.worldbank.org/en/publication/documentsreports/documentdetail/099310406172411550/idu154197ea11b0ca145c81a7371f9425c7549d7.

[11] Philippe Aghion, Celine Antonin and Simon Bunel, *The Power of Creative Destruction: Economic Upheaval and the Wealth of Nations* (Belknap Press, 2021).

[12] Elena Cima and Daniel C Etsy, 'Making International Trade Work for Sustainable Development: Towards a New WTO Framework for Subsidies' (2024) 27 *Journal of International Economic Law* 1, 2.

[13] ibid. See also Todd N Tucker, 'Recent WTO Rulings May Complicate Green Industrial Policies' *Washington Post* (20 December 2022) www.washingtonpost.com/politics/2022/12/20/recent-wto-rulings-may-complicate-green-industrial-policies/.

[14] Maria Grazia Attinasi, Lukas Boeckelmann and Baptiste Meunier, 'Unfriendly Friends: Trade and Relocation Effects of the US Inflation Reduction Act' (Centre for Economic Policy Research, 3 July 2023) https://cepr.org/voxeu/columns/unfriendly-friends-trade-and-relocation-effects-us-inflation-reduction-act.

products such as semiconductors are susceptible to countervailing duty (CVD)[15] investigations.[16]

Tension is indeed brewing as countries resort to confrontation, and not engagement, in relation to addressing subsidies on green goods. The USA and, more recently, Canada have imposed duties on Chinese electric vehicles.[17] Trade remedies – anti-dumping and CVD measures – have suddenly received an impetus in targeting green industrial goods such as auto parts, solar panels, lithium-ion batteries, biofuels and other critical goods.[18] The question is who is winning the war on subsidies?[19] The deeper the purse, the greater the possibility of encouraging the industries of the future. There is a larger issue of whether the world trading system can support climate change measures by ensuring that the trade rules do not stand in the way of the WTO members using state policies to encourage green energy transitions but at the same time not allowing such flexibilities as a mask for protectionism. Adjudicators in complex subsidy disputes have the unenviable task of ensuring that the legal disciplines serve the purpose for which they have been designed.

Before reverting to cases that Thomas Cottier had an opportunity to shape and interpret, it is important to appreciate how the subsidy disciplines emerged under the GATT and its successor, the WTO. Subsidy disciplines did not gallop into trade agreements; they came in slowly and with great resistance. The initial objective of subsidy rules, as explained below, was to discipline a limited category of CVD measures. There was no concrete approach to treat subsidy measures comprehensively. In the field of agricultural domestic support, there were hardly any disciplines until the end of the Uruguay Round of multilateral trade negotiations, and the disciplines were hurriedly negotiated as part of the Blair House Accord, some of which are heavily contested even today.[20]

In services, despite the call for negotiations under the General Agreement on Trade in Services (GATS), nothing worthwhile has happened. In the context of fisheries subsidies, while an initial set of rules were agreed as part of the WTO's 12th Ministerial Conference, the quest for a more comprehensive set of

[15] CVD measures are a unilateral remedy to offset the injurious effects of a specific subsidy in the domestic market of the importing WTO member.

[16] Gary Clyde Hoffbauer, 'Semiconductor Subsides and WTO Rules' (Columbia Centre on Sustainable Investment, 2 September 2024) https://ccsi.columbia.edu/sites/default/files/content/docs/fdi%20perspectives/No%20391%20-%20Hufbauer%20-%20FINAL.pdf.

[17] Promit Mukherjee and Akash Sriram, 'Canada to Impose 100% Tariff on Chinese EVs, Including Teslas' (Reuters, 27 August 2024) www.reuters.com/business/autos-transportation/trudeau-says-canada-impose-100-tariff-chinese-evs-2024-08-26/.

[18] See Edwin Vermulst and Madison Meng, 'Dumping and Subsidy Issues in the Renewable Energy Sector' in Thomas Cottier and Ilaria Espa (eds), *International Trade in Sustainable Electricity: Regulatory Challenges in International Economic Law* (Cambridge University Press, 2017).

[19] Guy Chazan, Sam Fleming and Kana Inagaki, 'A Global Subsidy War? Keeping Up with the Americans' *Financial Times* (13 July 2023) www.ft.com/content/4bc03d4b-6984-4b24-935d-6181253ee1e0.

[20] Jennifer Clapp, 'WTO Agriculture Negotiations: Implications for Global South' (2006) 27(4) *Third World Quarterly* 564.

rules in relation to overcapacity and overfishing is proving time-consuming and challenging.[21] In this regard, it is important to understand how subsidy disciplines emerged in the GATT and the WTO over time and how the regime can address complex issues, including the debate on harnessing subsidies for fast-tracking green energy transition.

This chapter proceeds by providing a history of the initial provisions under the GATT. Subsequently, the chapter examines some of the novel features of certain subsidy disputes in which Cottier was involved.

I. Disciplines on Subsidies under the GATT/WTO

Subsidy disciplines have taken years to evolve at the GATT and the WTO. Article XVI of the GATT dealt with subsidies on primary products. Article XVI recognised the possibility of harmful effects of certain export subsidies on the contracting parties. Although there was no prohibition of export subsidies on primary products (grains, dairy, meat, vegetable oils, seed, eggs, etc), Article XVI required that such subsidies are not applied in a manner such that a contracting party acquires more than an 'equitable share of world export trade' in that product.[22] This was in consonance with Article 25 (Line 3) of the Havana Charter.[23] Importantly, in relation to subsidies that affect production, including income or price support measures, the agreed obligations were even weaker. The only requirement was that if such subsidies operated to directly or indirectly increase exports of any product or reduce imports of such products into its territory, the country granting the subsidies was required to notify the contracting parties.[24] In fact, in a Memorandum submitted by Denmark in 1957 on the Export of Subsidized Eggs and Cattle from the United Kingdom,[25] it was alleged that the UK subsidies had led to serious prejudice to Danish exports. The only redress that Denmark sought was to limit the effect of UK subsidisation, which was weak in nature and mostly unenforceable.[26] The initial disciplines were more focused on notification and consultation.

The major weakness, however, was the scope of some of the substantive elements, such as the definition of subsidy itself. The Panel on Subsidies noted that it was neither necessary nor feasible to arrive at an agreed interpretation of what constitutes a subsidy.[27] It was believed that subsidies can have effects on negotiated

[21] Tristan Irschlinger, 'Fisheries Subsidies: Will World Trade Organization Members Finish the Job at MC13?' (International Institute for Sustainable Development, 11 January 2024) www.iisd.org/article/policy-analysis/fisheries-subsidies-wto-mc13.

[22] GATT, Art XVI:3(3).

[23] GATT/CP.2/22/Rev.1, adopted on 1 and 2 September 1948, II/39, 44.

[24] GATT, Art XVI(1)(5).

[25] *Export of Subsidized Eggs and Cattle from the United Kingdom* GD/42 L/627 (24 April 1957).

[26] ibid.

[27] GATT Panel on Subsidies, Report on the Operation of the Provisions of Article XVI, L/1442, 19 April 1961, para 23.

tariffs. The GATT contracting parties had a reasonable expectation that the value of concessions would not be nullified or impaired by the subsequent introduction or increase of domestic subsidy measures.[28]

The loose framework ensured that the subsidy disciplines had no real bite. In the GATT Panel on Subsidies, a view was expressed that, as opposed to restrictive instruments such as quantitative restrictions, subsidies have an in-built limitation.[29] By their very nature, subsidies will entail a charge on national budgets, including revenue foregone, which would have a restraining effect on the grant of subsidies.[30] The fact that no government, however well endowed, has the unlimited capacity to splurge public money tempted the contracting parties to believe that tough disciplines were not necessary.

The Tokyo Subsidies Code[31] provided an initial yet useful template for a comprehensive set of disciplines on subsidies. Subsidies as a concept involved an element of financial contribution. The Tokyo Code elaborated on the ways in which financial contributions can take place. However, neither the Tokyo Code nor the subsequent WTO Agreement on Subsidies and Countervailing Measures (ASCM) differentiated subsidies on the basis of their policy objectives or social purposes. At the same time, both the Tokyo Code and the ASCM recognised that subsidies other than export subsidies can serve as instruments for the promotion of social and economic objectives. Both agreements contain several hortative statements. A shortcoming, however, was that they both failed to make a distinction between subsidies that address market failures from those producing economic harmful effects. Interestingly, both the Tokyo and Uruguay Round agreements created a category of prohibited subsidies that included export subsidies, with the exception that the prohibition did not extend to primary agricultural products nor to developing countries.

The ASCM importantly has a category of subsidies called 'non-actionable' subsidies which can be traced to Article 11 of the Tokyo Subsidies Code. The non-actionable subsidies included exceptions for certain categories of expenditure incurred for research and development, and for addressing industrial, social and economic disadvantages of specific regions, as well as subsidies granted for the purpose of helping firms to adapt to certain environmental requirements. However, the category of non-actionable subsidies expired at the end of 1999 and was never renewed. By virtue of the expiry, no category of subsidies, however desirable they may be, can claim any safe harbour under the provisions of the ASCM.

The Tokyo Code, on the other hand, made several improvements in regulating the CVD investigations. The Tokyo Code was, in many ways, negotiated to curb the use of CVD measures. However, the definition of subsidy measures remained

[28] ibid para 27.
[29] ibid para 5.
[30] ibid para 22.
[31] Agreement on Interpretation and Application of Articles VI, XVI and XXIII of the General Agreement on Tariffs and Trade.

broad and ambiguous. The type of financial contribution that can qualify as a subsidy was also not elaborated. In addition, the important element of 'specificity' was not introduced in the Tokyo Code.

The ASCM brought significant clarity in the definitional elements of a subsidy. In a clear improvement over the provisions of the Tokyo Code, the ASCM clearly spelled out the types of financial contributions that can qualify as a subsidy. The ASCM also stipulates that for a subsidy to exist, a 'benefit' has to be 'thereby conferred'.[32] However, certain cracks in the scope and definitional elements of the ASCM have already opened up. As this chapter will explain, while WTO panels and the Appellate Body have, to some extent, clarified the meaning of the term 'benefit', it still arguably lends itself to multiple interpretations. The ASCM does not directly address the question of the location of the recipient of a subsidy vis-à-vis the location of the granting authority. In addition, the ASCM does not directly stipulate that for a countervailing duty investigation, the concerned subsidy must be provided by the government of the exporting member. In the age of transnational corporations and extra-territorial provision of financial incentives, some of these jurisdictional concerns require improved treatment.

II. New Challenges

Developments since the Rio Declaration emphasised the need for trade rules to accommodate environmental concerns. The United Nations Framework Convention on Climate Change,[33] despite the absence of clearly defined goals and policies, provided an important impetus for the transition towards renewable energy production. More recently, the Paris Agreement represent the climate goal of keeping the temperature rise well below 2°C above the pred-industrial levels.[34] As Cottier himself acknowledges, the transition from fossil fuel-based electricity production to renewable energy is slow.[35] Certain levels of state intervention can be a panacea for attracting investment in some of the new age industries, where the initial investments could be heavy and potentially risky.

The WTO treaty text on subsidies is, by and large, agnostic to climate change or related concerns. Most commercially traded products, including electricity, are insufficiently addressed in WTO law. The basic question of whether electricity should be treated as a good or not was itself subject to treaty interpretation. In addition, the electricity markets have been predominantly domestic, and

[32] Agreement on Subsidies and Countervailing Measures, Art 1.

[33] United Nations Framework Convention on Climate Change, Rio de Janeiro, 9 May 1992, 771 UNTS 107, Art 2.

[34] Paris Agreement, 12 December 2015, Art 2(1)(a).

[35] Thomas Cottier, 'Renewable Energy and Production Process, The E15 Initiative, Strengthening the Global Trade and Investment system for sustainable development' (ICTSD, August 2015) www.greenpolicyplatform.org/sites/default/files/downloads/resource/Renewable Energy and Process and Production Methods.pdf.

cross-border trade in this sector is possible only among limited jurisdictions. While the production and trade in energy products form an essential component of public international law, there is a feeling that existing trade rules are not sufficiently clear to bring about an effective and efficient transition towards green energy sources.

At the same time, international law cannot remain static. It should be open to embracing changes. The evolutive interpretation in the *USA – Shrimp*[36] case paved the way for how treaty rules can change with passing times. The Canada – *Feed-in Tariff (*FIT*)* case further demonstrates how WTO law, when used correctly, can provide the macro-legal conditions for moving to a carbon-neutral future.

The next section examines a couple of cases where Thomas Cottier acted as the chair of a WTO panel, including the Canada – FIT case, where subsidy disciplines under the WTO were implicated.

III. Green Energy Transition and the *Canada – FIT* Case

Canada – Renewable Energy/Canada – FIT Program presented several challenging issues. This case was decided around 2012, at a time when the WTO dispute settlement system was arguably operating at its best, and was healthy and robust. A well-functioning two-tier system ensured that panel determinations were subject to appellate review and that the panel findings could be reversed, modified or confirmed. This case discussed, among others, how state support to operators in the emerging field of renewable energy – where market-based mechanisms to sufficiently price in the social costs of climate change remain insufficiently low – could be addressed in dispute settlement.

The case dealt with the operation of a FIT scheme wherein the Canadian province of Ontario sought to increase the generation of wind and photovoltaic electricity by entering into purchase contracts that guaranteed certain fixed prices for long periods, extending from 20 to 40 years. However, the guaranteed prices came with a rider: in order to qualify for the guaranteed prices, the producers had to use a certain percentage of wind turbines or solar panels produced in Ontario.[37] Japan and the EU, the complainants, had little difficulty in establishing that the Ontario FIT programme violated Article III of the GATT. It was a discrimination based on origin, and was clearly a violation of Article III:4 of the GATT and 2.1 of the Agreement on Trade-Related Investment Measures (TRIMs Agreement). The requirements also fell clearly within the scope of the illustrative list of measures prohibited by the TRIMs Agreement.[38]

[36] *USA – Import Prohibition of Certain Shrimp and Shrimp Products* WT DS/AB/R.

[37] Steve Charnovitz and Carolyn Fischer, 'Canada – Renewable Energy: Implications for WTO Law on Green and Not-so-Green Subsides' (2015) 14(2) *World Trade Review* 177, 180.

[38] ibid 192.

More challenging was establishing a violation of the provisions of the ASCM. Import substitution subsidies – subsidies that are conditional on the use of domestic over imported products – are clearly inconsistent with the disciplines of the ASCM. However, the hurdle for the complainants was to establish that there was a subsidy in the first place. Even within this enquiry, the challenge was not in establishing that there was a financial contribution; rather, the challenge was in conclusively establishing that a 'benefit' was thereby conferred.

The concept of 'benefit' was examined in several cases in the past. In Canada – Aircraft, Brazil argued that support to Bombardier encompassed certain advantages, which became the touchstone for 'benefit' analysis in subsequent subsidy disputes. The Appellate Body in Canada – Aircraft[39] affirmed a fairly well-known reasoning of the panel.

> [T]he ordinary meaning of 'benefit' clearly encompasses some form of advantage ... In order to determine whether a financial contribution (in the sense of Article 1.1(a)(i)) confers a 'benefit', *i.e.*, an advantage, it is necessary to determine whether the financial contribution places the recipient in a more advantageous position than would have been the case but for the financial contribution. In our view, the only logical basis for determining the position the recipient would have been in absent the financial contribution is the market. Accordingly, a financial contribution will only confer a 'benefit', *i.e.*, an advantage, if it is provided on terms that are more advantageous than those that would have been available to the recipient on the market.

The Appellate Body further observed:

> We also believe that the word 'benefit' as used in Article 1.1(b), implies some kind of comparison. This must be so, for there can be no 'benefit' to the recipient unless the 'financial contribution' makes the recipient 'better off' than it would otherwise have been, absent that contribution. In our view, the marketplace provides an appropriate basis for comparison in determining whether a 'benefit' has been 'conferred' because the trade-distorting potential of a 'financial contribution can be identified by determining whether the recipient has received a 'financial contribution' on terms more favorable than those available to the recipient in the market.[40]

It is important to understand the operation of the FIT scheme in order to understand how the comparison benchmarks can be chosen. Electricity as a product is physically fungible and similar, irrespective of the production sources or technologies used. Consumers often do not distinguish electricity based on the production technologies or the base sources used. With energy and other products, unless the production means or process leaves a trace of certain characteristics within

[39] Appellate Body Report, *Canada – Measures Affecting the Export of Civilian Aircraft (Canada – Aircraft)* WT/DS70/AB/R, adopted 20 August 1999, para 149 (quoting WTO Panel Report, *Canada – Measures Affecting the Export of Civilian Aircraft (Canada – Aircraft)* WT/DS70/R, adopted 20 August 1999, upheld by Appellate Body Report WT/DS70/AB/R, para 9.112).

[40] ibid para 5.188.

the product, distinguishing between such products is an arbitrary and whimsical process.[41] The WTO panel noted that 'consumers of electricity in Ontario, whose demand instantaneously determines the purchases made at the wholesale level, do not distinguish electricity on the basis of different generation technologies, either by way of price or usage'.[42] Based on this logic, the market concerned with determining the benefit was the single market for electricity generated from all forms of energy, conventional and non-conventional.

The WTO treaty text addressing the issue of benefit determination obviously does not refer to any market, least of all a 'relevant market'. However, based on past rulings, especially in the Canada – Aircraft and subsequent cases, the Canada – FIT case discussed the issue of identifying the relevant market. Based on demand-side factors, the complainants sought to argue that the relevant market was the 'competitive wholesale electricity market as a whole' in Ontario.[43]

If such a comparison market were used in order to determine the conferment of benefit, there would hardly have been any doubt that the FIT programme bestowed a benefit on the producers of wind and solar photovoltaic (PV) electricity who had long-term contracts. However, it was a conscious choice of the Government of Ontario to opt for a particular mixture of energy supplies. From a practical point of view, without the FIT programme and the guaranteed contracts, the market for wind and solar PV electricity would not have existed. Despite the demand-side substitutability, the supply-side factors indicated that without government intervention, the existence of the market for wind and solar PV electricity would have been unlikely. In other words, there were crucial and notable differences between the various forms of energy production in terms of cost structures and operating costs.[44] This was also affirmed by the Appellate Body.

> A distinction should be drawn between, on the one hand, government interventions that create markets that would otherwise not exist and, on the other hand, other types of government interventions in support of certain players in markets that already exist, or to correct market distortions therein. Where a government creates a market, it cannot be said that the government intervention distorts the market, as there would not be a market if the government had not created it. While the creation of markets by a government does not in and of itself give rise to subsidies within the meaning of the SCM Agreement, government interventions in existing markets may amount to subsidies when they take the form of a financial contribution, or income or price support, and confer a benefit to specific enterprises or industries.[45]

[41] Cottier (n 9) 2.
[42] Panel Report, *Canada – Renewable Energy/Canada – Feed-in Tariff Program*, para 7.318.
[43] Appellate Body Report, *Canada – Certain Measures Affecting the Renewable Energy Generation Sector/Measures Relating to the Feed-in Tariff Program* (*Canada – Renewable Energy/FIT Program* (2013)), WT/DS412/DS426/AB/R, para 5.178, 173–75.
[44] ibid.
[45] ibid para 5.188.

While the Appellate Body reversed certain parts of the panel's reasoning, an examination of the market and the economic conditions that were vital for the success of the renewable energy programme marked a shift in direction in the legal analysis.[46] Previously adopted dispute settlement body reports have supported the use of demand-side and supply-side substitutability as a relevant consideration in determining markets, although not in the context of a benefit determination. There is also a tendency to assume the existence of a benefit in situations where governmental financial outlays are involved. While the Appellate Body was unable to complete its analysis in the absence of comparison benchmarks, which the panel could have identified, there is no denying that choosing an undistorted comparison market within the jurisdiction of the granting authority is a burdensome and overly demanding task.[47] In the first place, such an undistorted market may not exist at all or the price discovery may not be feasible especially in relation to renewable energy products, where government intervention has been common and pervasive.

The panel and the Appellate Body approaches demonstrated how the WTO dispute settlement fora can advance discussions on sustainability issues in legitimate cases. Interestingly, pursuant to the Canada – FIT case, subsequent challenges to renewable energy subsidy programmes under WTO dispute settlement have not involved a claim under the ASCM, or importantly a claim under prohibited subsidies.[48] In other words, the ASCM is not considered to be a major constraint in providing subsidies for renewable energy programmes, unless such subsidies are tied to the use of local contents or are otherwise significantly distortive. However, there is always a danger that sustainability-couched measures may be pursued to promote inherently industrial policy measures, a possibility that should be adequately disciplined.

IV. India Sugar Disputes

Cottier was also the chair of the WTO panel in *India – Sugar and Sugarcane*,[49] a dispute that has not attained finality. The case is before the defunct Appellate

[46] I Espa and G Marín Durán, 'Renewable Energy Subsidies and WTO Law: Time to Rethink the Case for Reform Beyond Canada – Renewable Energy/FIT Program' (2018) 21 *Journal of International Economic Law* 621, 625–28.

[47] The WTO Appellate Body in the *Softwood Lumber* dispute stated (with respect to the local Canadian timber market) that when determining 'benefit', the investigating authority 'may use a benchmark other than private prices in the country of provision … if it is first established that private prices in that country are distorted because of the government's predominant role in providing those goods'. Appellate Body, USA, *Final Countervailing Duty Determination with Respect to Certain Softwood Lumber from Canada*, WT/DS257/AB/R, adopted 17 February 2004, para. 90.

[48] See *India – Solar*; *USA – Renewable Energy*, etc.

[49] *India – Measures Concerning Sugar and Sugarcane* WT/DS 579/R, WT/DS 580/R, WT/DS 581/R.

Body.[50] However, this dispute presented a very important question of whether the market price support under Annex 3 of the WTO Agreement on Agriculture entailed some form of government support or revenue foregone.[51] As explained in this chapter, the concept of a subsidy involves the notion of certain financial contributions or income or price supports from the government or a public body.[52] One of the key issues in this dispute is whether paragraph 2 of Annex 3 of the Agreement on Agriculture (AoA) limits the scope of subsidies to 'budgetary outlays' and 'revenue foregone'.[53] Paragraph 2 provides that 'Subsidies under paragraph 1 shall include both budgetary outlays and revenue foregone by governments or their agents'.[54]

Under its Sugar Price Control Order (implemented in terms of the Essential Commodities Act),[55] India fixed a fair remunerative price (FRP) regarding the sale and purchase of sugar cane. The FRP set the price at which sugar cane could be purchased by the sugar mills from producers, but did not entail any expenditure or budgetary outlays from the government. The matter for the panel's consideration was whether a measure could be characterised as a 'market price support' and calculated for aggregate measurement of support (AMS) purposes under paragraph 8 of Annex 3 if it did not meet the condition of paragraph 2 of the Annex.[56]

India, in its defence, argued that market price within the meaning of paragraph 1 of Annex 3 should be in the nature of a subsidy, and that the subsidies are limited to budgetary outlays and revenues foregone. In other words, India raised the previously unexplored question of whether domestic support measures were or could only be in the form of 'subsidies'.[57]

While the WTO panel took into account the long-term objectives of the AoA, including the need to address distortions in agricultural markets,[58] it comes as a surprise that the tools of the Vienna Convention on the Law of Treaties (VCLT), especially Articles 31 and 32, were not extensively engaged or that reference to the VCLT was explicitly omitted in an important discussion on domestic support measures. Although this appeared somewhat unusual, perhaps it may be part of

[50] *India – Measures Concerning Sugar and Sugarcane, WT/DS 579/R; WT/DS 580/R; WT/DS 581/R Notification of Appeal by India under Article 16.4 and Article 17.1 of the Understanding on Rules and Procedures Governing the Settlement of Disputes (DSU) and Under Rule 20(1) of the Working Procedures for Appellate Review.*

[51] Annex 3 of Agreement on Agriculture 1995.

[52] Agreement on Subsides and Countervailing Measures, Art 1.1(a)(1).

[53] Panel Report, *India – Measures Concerning Sugar and Sugarcane WT/DS 579/R; WT/DS 580/R; WT/DS 581/R*, para 2.1.

[54] Agreement on Agriculture 1995, Annex 3, para 2.

[55] The FRP is allegedly determined by the Central Government annually, based on the recommendations of the Commission for Agricultural Costs and Prices.

[56] Panel Report, *India – Measures Concerning Sugar and Sugarcane*, para 7.2.5.

[57] ibid para 7.1.1.

[58] ibid paras 7.3–7.7.

the effort to indicate that the dispute settlement process is not excessively legalistic or semantic in nature.

The dispute also raised certain interesting issues regarding the operation of the duty remission/drawback schemes, which have increasingly become the subject of WTO disputes since the panel decision in *EU – PET*,[59] which introduced the concept of 'excess remission'. India's Duty-Free Import Authorisation scheme, which was challenged in that dispute, allowed the remission of import duties on a post-export basis based on standard input–output norms. The panel ruling suggested that for a duty drawback or remission scheme to be compatible with footnote 1, irrespective of the internal verification mechanism, the exported product should be made from the same input or intermediate products subject to remission or drawback.[60] In other words, to be compliant with the scheme of footnote 1, according to the panel, the product subject to remission should have been physically incorporated in the product that is exported.[61] This was an unexplored area in the context of the ASCM and perhaps would require a more comprehensive analysis.

V. Conclusion

Subsidy regulations have historically functioned on the basis of a minimal set of rules from the early days of the GATT. Considering the hesitation of GATT and WTO members to have horizontally agreed rules for subsidies, there are fundamental concerns, including matters relating to definition and scope. Some of the disputes explained in this chapter demonstrate the complexities relating to such basic conceptual issues. However, the global commitment to meeting sustainable development goals and the recent focus on expediting the green transition point to the need for a substantial overhaul of subsidy disciplines. While this process could take some time, at least interpretative clarity through disputes would be a welcome change. While tighter disciplines will have their challenges in terms of meeting broad acceptance, the rules should ensure that environmental and social objectives will not set to naught negotiated market access commitments, which, after all, remain one of the central objectives of entering into trade agreements.

Achieving positive outcomes in trade negotiations needs a unique occurrence of circumstances – or, as Thomas Cottier puts it, a rare matching of 'endemic and endogenous factors'.[62] The Uruguay Round provided one of those rare occurrences.

[59] *European Union – Countervailing Measures on Certain Polyethylene Terephthalate from Pakistan* WT/DS 486.

[60] ibid para 5.77.

[61] Panel Report, *India – Sugar and Sugarcane*, paras 7.289–7.291.

[62] Cottier (n 1).

While Cottier had a chance to preside over some of these complex subsidy issues, he knew better than anyone that adjudicatory solutions to complex trade issues are not realistically possible within a fragile global economic order.[63] However, Thomas Cottier has presided over dispute settlement proceedings that have led to an avalanche of academic literature on the topic of reimaging subsidy disciplines in the realm of international trade law. The process of reforms could take time, but the cases that I have discussed in this chapter where Thomas Cottier had a major role to play could enrich the relevant discussions.

[63] For details of the academic literature on the subsidy disciplines under WTO, see Aaron Cosbey and Petros C Mavroidis, 'A Turquoise Mess: Green Subsidies, Blue Industrial Policy and Renewable Energy – the Case for Re-drafting the Subsidies Agreement of the WTO' (2014) 17(1) *Journal of International Economic Law* 11; Paolo Davide Farah and Elena Cima, 'The World Trade Organization, Renewable Energy Subsidies, and the Case of Feed-in Tariffs: Time for Reform Towards Sustainable Development' (2015) 27 *Georgetown International Environmental Law Review* 515; Steve Charnovitz, 'Green Subsidies Under the WTO' (Robert Schuman Centre for Advanced Studies, 2014) Research Paper No RSCAS 2014/93; Avidan Kent and Vyoma Jha, 'Keeping Up with the Changing Climate: The WTO's Evolutive Approach in Response to the Trade and Climate Conundrum' (2014) 15(1–2) *Journal of World Investment and Trade* 245.

6

Litigating National Security in the WTO Era

PETROS C MAVROIDIS[1]

I. It's a New Ball Game

From one dispute between 1948 and 1994, there have now been 14 requests for a panel establishment (based on the General Agreement on Tariffs and Trade (GATT), Article XXI – the exception for national security) during the World Trade Organization (WTO) era (1995–now). The majority of them ended up in the issuance of a panel report, all of which were issued after 5 April 2019. As the WTO Appellate Body has been dysfunctional as of November 2019, no appellate report has been issued. Appeals have been lodged, but as there is no Appellate Body to entertain them, they were lodged 'into the void', thus depriving the panel reports of any legal significance.[2]

The panel reports constitute only the tip of the iceberg. There are dozens of notifications, and a high number of specific trade concerns have been raised before WTO bodies. A likely explanatory variable is that, unlike the GATT (which was established by the winners of WWII, who, with minor exceptions, were like-minded players, initially at least),[3] the WTO has been a global institution *ab initio*.

[1] I would like to express my gratitude to Charles M Cantore, Henrik Horn, Rodd Izadnia, Merit E Janow, Clarissa Long, Gabrielle Marceau, Bradley McDonald, Damien J Neven, Håkan Nordstrøm and Mona Pinchis for helpful comments and discussions.

[2] I discuss 'appeals into the void' in Petros C Mavroidis, *The WTO Dispute Settlement System: How, Why and Where?* (Edward Elgar Publishing, 2022). Suffice to note here that the legal significance of the issued reports is not the same. The panel report in DS512 was formally adopted. This was not the case with the panel report in DS556 and a few others which were appealed into the void. DS544, 547, 548, 550, 551, 552, 554, 556 and 564 are all separate reports issued following challenges by various WTO members against the US safeguards on steel products. This is not the place to discuss the reasons that led to the demise of the Appellate Body. For an excellent account in this respect, see Thomas Cottier, 'Recalibrating the WTO Dispute Settlement System: Towards New Standards of Appellate Review' (2021) 24 *Journal of International Economic Law* 515.

[3] John H Jackson, *World Trade and the Law of GATT* (Bobbs-Merrill Company, 1969); Douglas A Irwin, Petros C Mavroidis and Alan O Sykes, *The Genesis of the GATT* (Cambridge University Press, 2008) www.cambridge.org/core/books/genesis-of-the-gatt/796EE0ABCE00A2F8DD46812AFD9DD0CC; Benn Steil, *The Battle of Bretton Woods: John Maynard Keynes, Harry Dexter White, and the Making of a New World Order* (Princeton University Press, 2013).

Swayed by the spirit of a unipolar world,[4] it gradually encompassed heterogeneous players. Frictions between them, like the Ukraine–Russia conflict, were translated into trade frictions as well. Geopolitics, as Hoekman et al have argued, have had a lot to do with the observed phenomenon.[5]

With this in mind, here is the full list of the panel reports issued so far and a brief commentary for each one of them.

II. National Security-Related Disputes before the WTO[6]

A. Russia – Traffic in Transit (DS512)

Ukraine challenged a number of Russia's practices that were denying it the right to transit embedded in Article V of the GATT.[7] The panel agreed that this had indeed been the case. To justify its measures, Russia raised the national security exception. The panel adopted an approach to address national security claims that has been followed in all subsequent cases.[8] The main points can be summarised as follows:

- GATT, Article XXI is justiciable (§§7.54ff, and especially §§7.102–03);
- The test for reviewing consistency with GATT, Article XXI is two-tiered:
  - Was Russia at war with Ukraine, or facing an emergency?
  - If Russia was indeed at war, and only if yes, had it adopted the necessary measures to the end, that is, to protect its national security?

The panel held that GATT, Article XXI could be lawfully invoked only within this particular set of circumstances, that is, if measures had been taken within a war or war-like (emergency) context (§7.82). It insisted that the legality depended on 'when' the challenged action was taken. Complying with the first condition was a necessary but not sufficient condition for complying with Article XXI. Nevertheless, the panel recognised that Russia enjoyed substantial latitude when determining its 'essential security interests' (§7.98). The phrase 'it considers necessary' appearing in Article XXI(b) granted Russia wiggle room to assess the necessity of its actions. The panel held that Russia's defence must meet a 'minimum

[4] Francis Fukuyama, *The End of History and the Last Man* (Free Press, 1992).

[5] Bernard M Hoekman, Petros C Mavroidis and Douglas R Nelson, 'Geopolitical Competition, Globalisation and WTO Reform' (2023) 46 *The World Economy* 1163.

[6] This section borrows from Petros C Mavroidis, *Industrial Policy, National Security, and the Perilous Plight of the WTO* (Oxford University Press, 2024).

[7] Trade transiting through Russia amounted to a sizeable amount of its overall trade, as Ukraine traded a lot with the Commonwealth of Independent States, a coalition of 10 former Soviet Union countries, including Russia, and especially with Belarus. A very substantial percentage of its trade with China, its biggest trading partner, transited through Russia as well. https://wits.worldbank.org/CountryProfile/en/Country/UKR/Year/LTST/Summarytext.

[8] Pramila Crivelli and Mona Pinchis-Paulsen, 'Separating the Political from the Economic: The Russia – Traffic in Transit Panel Report' (2021) 20 *World Trade Review* 582.

requirement of plausibility' in this respect (§7.138). It understood this standard as akin to the well-known 'appropriateness' test: could the employed means appropriately have served the intended purpose irrespective of their trade-restrictiveness and/or effectiveness? If yes, they would be judged 'necessary'.

Necessity in GATT, Article XXI and GATT, Article XX should not be understood in an identical manner (§7.82 and §§7.139ff).[9] Using similar language in §7.137, the panel held that the respondent had passed the test of consistency since 'Russia's articulation of its essential security interests is minimally satisfactory in these circumstances'.

The request for consultations was submitted in September 2016, 30 months after the hostilities in the Crimean peninsula had ended. The panel provided an indicative list of 'emergencies', namely, latent armed conflict, heightened tension and general instability (§§7.765ff). The UN's recognition of an emergency in the region tilted the balance in the panel's view and found in Russia's favour (§7.122). That was it. As long as the UN had acknowledged its existence, there was no need for further proof that the Russian measures had indeed been adopted during an emergency. The measures passed the (self-imposed) 'minimally satisfactory' test.[10]

Opinions about necessity will not be lightly disturbed as long as the facts support their pertinence. All subsequent panels have repeated this test. As long as the 'when' leg of the test has been satisfied, the 'what' or 'how' becomes an easy-to-meet test. §7.230 of the panel report in DS567 *Saudi Arabia – IPRs*, the only case so far where a measure did not pass the 'minimally satisfactory' test (as I explain later on), offers an appropriate illustration of the influence that the test developed in *Russia – Traffic in Transit* has had on subsequent case law.

Note that neither this nor any other panel report dealing with a national security claim was appealed, so the WTO Appellate Body (now in indefinite hibernation) has yet to endorse this analysis.

Why did the DS512 panel decide this way? In the realm of GATT, Article XX, WTO panels will have to limit their assessment to the means. They cannot put into question the right to pursue the end itself. The chapeau of Article XX includes language implying that a control of ends could be possible: 'Subject to the requirement that such measures are not applied in a manner which would constitute a means of arbitrary or unjustifiable discrimination between countries where the same conditions prevail, *or a disguised restriction* on international trade' (emphasis added).

The two concepts (arbitrary or unjustifiable discrimination; disguised restriction of trade) have been discussed in various cases, the leading cases being DS2 (*USA – Gasoline*) and DS332 (*Brazil – Retreaded Tyres*). In both instances, the

[9] In a prior case, DS394 *China – Raw Materials*, a case involving restrictions on exports imposed by China, the panel had alluded to a deferential standard of review that should be applicable in cases involving claims under GATT, Art XXI (§7.276).

[10] Justice Kagan, in her concurring opinion in *Reed v Town of Gilbert* 576 US 155 (2015), referred to the 'laugh test'. The panel demanded more than that: it demanded appropriateness. Its standard of review is reminiscent of a quote attributed to former US Senator Daniel Patrick Moynihan: 'everyone is entitled to his own opinion, but not to his own facts', *Washington Post* (18 January 1983).

Appellate Body understood them as closely related and saw an even-handedness requirement there to apply, say, an environmental law in the same manner to both domestic and imported goods. If panels refrain from questioning ends in the realm of GATT, Article XX, they should do so all the more in the realm of GATT, Article XXI. Panels are thus left with the question of whether the measures employed were necessary to achieve their objective. But how does one measure 'necessity' in the context of Article XXI? The 'lexicographic' ordering of preferences suggests that national security comes out on top: nations spare nothing to defend their national security. World history is full of examples of inefficient and/or heroic (even if ineffective) measures to promote national security. In fact, ineffective (heroic) action might be a good proxy to conclude that a WTO member is really concerned about its national security. This is probably what led the panel to adopt the 'minimally satisfactory' test, besides, of course, the wording of the provision.

With ends non-justiciable and deference towards means warranted, the panel thought the timing of the adoption of measures was the one thing it could seriously review. This is a very plausible construction. What is implausible is to infer that measures taken outside armed conflict (or emergency narrowly defined) are impermissible.

B. USA – Steel and Aluminum Products (DS544 etc)

Upon assuming power, President Trump resuscitated Section 232 of the Trade Expansion Act of 1962 (19 USC §1862), an almost forgotten legal instrument. He invoked it to restrict imports of steel products in the name of national security. Section 232 had been enacted in 1955 and forms an integral part of the Trade Agreements Extensions Act. This instrument had almost fallen into desuetude.[11] The Trump administration imposed tariffs against a host of nations, namely Canada, China, the EU, India, South Korea, Mexico, Norway, Russia, Switzerland and Turkey, all in the name of national security.[12] But why did the USA not impose plain vanilla safeguards?

Unlike US section 201 (implementing Article XIX of the GATT and the WTO Agreement on Safeguards), section 232 provides the President with very

[11] Tucker mentions that it had been used six times only in the past: once by Presidents Eisenhower and Kennedy jointly (they faced 23 petitions); once by President Nixon (four petitions); once by President Ford (one petition); once by President Reagan (six petitions); and twice by President Carter (three petitions). President Johnson never used it (four petitions), and the same is true for Presidents Bush Sr (four petitions), Clinton (three petitions) and Bush Jr (one petition). In total, only 6/49 petitions had been met with presidential approval until President Trump arrived in power. Todd N Tucker, 'Are National Security Tariffs Legal?' (Medium, 16 February 2018) https://toddntucker.medium.com/are-nationalsecurity-tariffs-legal-2e8b0188a170. See also David D Knoll, 'Section 232 of the Trade Expansion Act of 1962: Industrial Fasteners, Machine Tools and Beyond' (1986) 10 *Maryland Journal of International Law* 55, 68ff.

[12] South Korea was exempted because it agreed to limit its exports to 70% of the volume during a previous representative period: Anne O Krueger, *International Trade: What Everyone Needs to Know* (Oxford University Press, 2020) 65ff. To do that, President Trump had to renegotiate some aspects of the Korean–US Free Trade Agreement: ibid 116.

substantial wiggle room:[13] it is not the effect of imports on the marketplace that is the concern addressed through section 232. It is their potential unavailability in case of emergency. Knoll, citing archival records,[14] claimed that the absence of a definition of 'national security' and the fact that the existence of a threat suffices to trigger this section explain why discretion is wide. Peter Navarro, Assistant to the President and Director of the Office of Trade and Manufacturing Policy, had this to say:

> Under the banner of 'economic security is national security,' the Trump administration's corporate tax cuts now spur investment and catalyze innovation. A wave of deregulation is making American businesses more globally competitive. Steel and aluminium tariffs and strengthened 'Buy American' rules help bolster two key pillars of our defence industrial base. Renegotiated trade deals with South Korea and the long-needed NAFTA update – the United States, Mexico, Canada agreement – will soon help level the playing field for America's factory workers.[15]

The efficiency of the measures adopted by the Trump administration has been criticised widely. Hufbauer and Jung[16] estimated that the steel tariffs imposed by the Trump administration preserved 12,700 jobs at a cost of $900,000 per job saved. Gertz[17] showed that President Trump saved steel jobs but lost car jobs. The same goes for jobs in other downstream industries hit by retaliatory measures against the USA. Gregg[18] estimated that, eventually, the steel tariffs led to the loss of 75,000 jobs.[19]

It is no exaggeration to state that this event triggered a chain reaction, the ripple effects of which the WTO is still going through. The Trump administration claimed that these measures constituted a reaction to protectionist measures that others had previously adopted.[20]

[13] See the analysis in Brock R Williams, 'Trump Administration Tariff Actions: Frequently Asked Questions' (Congressional Research Service, 2020) Report R45529, https://sgp.fas.org/crs/row/R45529.pdf.

[14] Knoll (n 11) 56ff.

[15] Peter Navarro, 'Why Economic Security Is National Security' (9 December 2018) www.realclearpolitics.com/Articles/2018/12/09/why_economic_security_is_national_security_138875.html.

[16] Gary Clyde Hufbauer and Euijin Jung, 'Steel Profits Gain, but Steel Users Pay, under Trump's Protectionism' (Peterson Institute for International Economics, 20 December 2018) www.piie.com/blogs/trade-and-investment-policy-watch/steel-profits-gain-steel-users-pay-under-trumps.

[17] Geoffrey Gertz, 'Did Trump's Tariffs Benefit American Workers and National Security?' (*Brookings*, 10 September 2020) www.brookings.edu/Articles/did-trumps-tariffs-benefit-american-workers-and-national-security/.

[18] Samuel Gregg, *The Next American Economy: Nation, State, and Markets in an Uncertain World* (Encounter Books, 2022) 72ff.

[19] In May 2023, the United States International Trade Commission (ITC) published a report in which they made it clear that while s 232 tariffs had little impact on the price of US steel, they had a larger (and on occasion substantially larger) impact on US downstream industries. ITC, 'Economic Impact of Section 232 and 301 Tariffs on US Industries' (2023) Publication Number 5405, 124ff, www.usitc.gov/publications/332/pub5405.pdf.

[20] Many years back, Robinson had asked why should we 'dump rocks in our harbours because other nations have rocky costs': Joan Robinson, *Contributions to Modern Economics* (Academic Press, 1978) 192. This is yet another lesson that successive administrations have failed to grasp.

Voices inside the USA opposed it. Before the WTO litigation had been initiated, the US administration had lost a very similar case before the US Court of International Trade (CIT). In *American Institute for International Steel Inc et al v United States and Kevin K McAleenan*,[21] the US CIT judge (Honorable Claire R Kelly) faced a claim by the US industry to the effect that the invocation of national security was self-judging by the President and not subject to judicial scrutiny. She dismissed the claim and, with it, the lawfulness of President Trump's actions. The Trump administration decided to ignore the court judgment and went ahead to initiate section 232 proceedings.

One reason why commentators found the US actions scandalising as well is that Canada, a country exempted from the Committee on Foreign Investment in the USA review on national security grounds, suddenly was considered a threat to the US national security when it came to trading steel. So, Canada could easily invest in the US steel industry in Ohio or Michigan, but it could not trade steel from Alberta, Manitoba or Saskatchewan. Lighthizer mentions that Canada and Mexico, the USA's partners in the USMCA (the USA–Mexico–Canada Trade Agreement, the successor to NAFTA), had initially been exempted from the imposition,[22] but the *quid pro quo* for their exemption would have been for them to voluntarily limit exports to the USA. When they declined to do so, they were inserted into the list of targets. As Lighthizer put it:[23] 'The Trump administration was willing to ruffle diplomatic feathers to advance its trade agenda.'[24]

All targeted countries introduced complaints against the USA. I will base my discussion of the disputes on the key findings of the report issued in DS556, where Switzerland had acted as the complainant. The panel found that the US measures were inconsistent with Articles I, II and XI of the GATT. The question arose before the panel whether the US measure qualified as a safeguard. In a lengthy passage (§§7.85–7.119), the panel decided that this was not the case (based on US domestic law, unilateral US declarations and notifications). What mattered for the panel was the intended function, and not the nature of the measure. While this finding did not matter much for Switzerland in DS556, it did matter in DS558, a dispute that I will discuss later on. Having established a violation of Articles I, II and XI, the panel then asked whether the challenged measures could be justified through recourse to Article XXI as per the US argument. The DS556 panel ended up where the DS512 panel had landed.

[21] Case No 18-00152, 25 March 2019, https://law.justia.com/cases/federal/appellate-courts/cit/18-00152/18-00152–2019-03-25.html.

[22] Robert Lighthizer, *No Trade Is Free: Changing Course, Taking on China, and Helping America's Workers* (Broadside Books, 2023) 235ff.

[23] ibid 235.

[24] On 8–9 June 2018, the 44th G7 meeting was held in Charlevoix, Québec. Lighthizer reports that Canada, Mexico and the USA almost struck a 'cars and cows' deal: Canada would offer additional access to its dairy market, Mexico would make some concessions with respect to the automobiles exported from its territory and the USA would move both countries off its list of steel safeguards. Canada leaked to the press a document indicating that negotiations had reached the final stage, a ploy that did not go down well with the Washington, DC crowd, who called the deal off. ibid 236ff.

The USA argued that Article XXI was self-judging (§7.123). The panel dismissed this claim, stating that nothing in the GATT and/or the WTO Dispute Settlement Understanding (DSU) warranted such an approach, as the national security provision had not been exempted from judicial review by panels (§§7.141ff, culminating at §7.146).[25] Having lost its threshold argument, the US invoked GATT, Article XXI(b)(iii) to justify its measures, arguing that its measures were justified because (§§7.151ff):

- there was an emergency resulting from the excess capacity in the steel market, and that much had been acknowledged by the G20 Global Steel Reform Forum, the OECD, and also the EU Trade Commissioner; and
- the unexpected change brought about by the revolution in steel production with the advent of new products had contributed to the reigning climate of uncertainty.

The panel did not side with the USA, holding that:

- the existence of (war or) an international emergency is a threshold issue for the applicability of Article XXI (§7.155);
- the action taken and the occurrence of the emergency must coincide time-wise (§7.158); and
- the displacement of the domestic industry by imports, the adverse impact of imports on the profitability of the domestic industry and the excess capacity of steel and aluminium worldwide (§7.160) exhibited both a national and an international dimension (§7.163):
  - the term 'war' informs the term 'emergency in international relations'(§7.157);[26] and
  - the present case fell short of this standard as cooperative efforts were being undertaken to redress the excess steel capacity and production (§7.166).

This report did not go down well with the US authorities. Assistant United States Trade Representative (USTR) Adam Hodge had this to say:

> The United States strongly rejects the flawed interpretation and conclusions in the World Trade Organization (WTO) Panel reports released today … The United States

[25] Case law under Art XXI is probably the only area where panels have consistently looked at the negotiating history. The panel report on DS512 includes a short appendix on this issue, and DS597 also discusses negotiating history. The DS556 report includes a 70-page-long appendix on the negotiating history of Art XXI and non-treaty materials, examining one by one all of the documents submitted by the USA. What emerges from the negotiating history, according to the panel, can be roughly summarised as follows. First, there is no shared unanimous understanding to the effect that Art XXI is entirely self-judging. And second, negotiators understood that discretion would be somehow limited. This latter finding weighed heavily in the panel's finding that the provision was not self-judging (and in its ensuing decision to reject the US argument along these lines).

[26] The French and Spanish versions of Art XXI(b)(iii) mention 'grave tension' in international relations, an element that supports the panel's approach. The panel mentioned the different linguistic versions in §7.157.

> will not cede decision-making over its essential security to WTO panels. The Biden Administration is committed to preserving US national security by ensuring the long-term viability of our steel and aluminum industries, and we do not intend to remove the Section 232 duties as a result of these disputes.[27]

The USA appealed this report into the void, thus depriving it of any legal significance.[28] USTR Katherine Tai went one step further and, in language that could be perceived as a threat to the multilateral institution, stated that the WTO was skating on 'very, very thin ice'.[29] This tone did not make her any new friends in Geneva, but she won the approval of former USTR, Robert Lighthizer, a former steel lobbyist and notorious 'hawk' in the previous US administration.[30]

Following the change of guard in Washington DC, the Biden administration opened negotiations with a few affected players. Australia, Canada and Mexico were excluded from the tariffs, and tariff quotas were negotiated with Japan, South Korea and the UK. The EU and the USA notified a mutually agreed solution to put their dispute on hold and attempt to resolve it bilaterally. The more comprehensive solution would promote environmental protection as well.

Negotiations have proved thornier than anticipated. A promise for a 'green deal' (to agree to the removal of tariffs while promoting a switch to environment-friendly production) remains out of reach, at least for now.[31]

C. Saudi Arabia – IPRs (DS567)

This is the only case where a panel refuted a national security defence. Saudi Arabia and Qatar brought their political differences to the trade table as well.

[27] 'Statement from USTR Spokesperson Adam Hodge' (Office of the United States Trade Representative, 9 December 2022) https://ustr.gov/about-us/policy-offices/press-office/press-releases/2022/december/statement-ustr-spokesperson-adam-hodge.

[28] WTO Doc WT/DS556/221 of 30 January 2023. Pinchis-Paulsen notes that after the dispute had ended the USA had notified, on 26 January 2023, the dispute settlement body of its decision to appeal to the (non-existent) Appellate Body certain issues of law in the reports. The USA gave Norway and Switzerland (members that had not undertaken unilateral rebalancing of concessions) options, as it was willing to find a solution. The USA offered the possibility to engaging in good offices, conciliation or mediation pursuant to DSU, Art 5, and/or to consider a non-violation complaint pursuant to Art XXIII:1(b) of the GATT 1994 as described in DSU, Art 26.1. There was no follow-up to the offer. Mona Pinchis-Paulsen, 'Negotiating After a Loss – ADR and the US Steel Tariff Cases' (*International Economic Law and Policy Blog*, 10 May 2023) https://ielp.worldtradelaw.net/2023/05/negotiating-after-a-loss-adr-and-the-us-steel-tariff-cases-.html.

[29] 'WTO on "Thin Ice" with Metals-Tariff Ruling, US Trade Chief Says' (*Bloomberg.com*, 19 December 2022) www.bloomberg.com/news/Articles/2022-12-19/wto-on-thin-ice-with-metals-tariff-ruling-us-trade-chief-says.

[30] Lighthizer (n 22) 79 and 201.

[31] See WTO Doc WT/DS/436/23 of 18 July 2023. On the ongoing EU–US steel negotiations, see Barbara Moens, Steven Overly and Sarah Anne Aarup, 'We Can Work It Out, Say US and EU, but Trade Disputes Linger' (*POLITICO*, 26 June 2023) www.politico.eu/article/us-eu-trade-dispute-electric-car-tax-credit-steel-valdis-dombrovskis-katherine-tai/. On requests and exclusions, see https://232app.azurewebsites.net/. India and the USA notified their mutually agreed solution in DS547 without detailing its content, WTO Doc WT/DS547/R of 8 August 2023.

It all started when Saudi Arabia accused Qatar of violating the treaty it had signed with it in 2014. In its view, by engageing in diplomatic relations with Iran, Qatar was espousing terrorism and extremism, and thus constituted a threat. The dispute soon escalated. Al Jazeera, a Qatari broadcasting company, expressed criticism of Saudi Arabia and the political beliefs it represented and was propagating.

Saudi Arabia responded by breaking all links with Qatar. For Saudi Arabia to protect itself from the ensuing threats, a total break from Qatar was necessary (§7.280). Breaking all links included the adoption of measures violating the Agreement on Trade-Related Aspects of Intellectual Property Rights (TRIPS Agreement) as well. Qatar complained before the WTO. Saudi Arabia invoked Article 73 of the TRIPS Agreement (which echoes almost verbatim GATT, Article XXI) to justify its measures.

To evaluate the Saudi claim, the panel applied the standard of review employed in DS512 *Russia – Traffic in Transit*. It first asked whether Saudi Arabia was facing an emergency. It decided that this was indeed the case, based on two elements. The first was that Saudi Arabia had severed diplomatic and consular relations with Qatar, and consequently trade and economic relations as well (§§7.258ff). In its view, severance of diplomatic relations was the ultimate state expression of the existence of an emergency. Second, the panel paid particular attention to the fact that Qatar had repudiated regional agreements aimed at protecting the neighbouring states against terrorism and extremism. The resulting security threat was, thus, a legitimate cause of concern for Saudi Arabia (§§7.263ff). The panel then articulated its standard for evaluating the lawfulness of the Saudi defence in §7.281:

> [T]he standard applied to the invoking Member was whether its articulation of its essential security interests was 'minimally satisfactory' in the circumstances. The requirement that an invoking Member articulate its 'essential security interests' sufficiently to enable an assessment of whether the challenged measures are related to those interests is not a particularly onerous one, and is appropriately subject to limited review by a panel.

What exactly was the Saudi measure? It had prevented beIN, the Qatari broadcasting company, from taking the opportunity to hire a Saudi legal counsel in order to enforce its intellectual property rights before Saudi courts and tribunals. The question thus before the WTO panel was whether blocking beIN from taking such action was necessary to defend national security. But this was not all. Saudi Arabia had also established a platform called beoutQ.[32] beoutQ organised screenings in public with unauthorised broadcasts of World Cup 2018 football games, and eventually sold the hardware to private citizens to enjoy similar broadcasting from home. Saudi Arabia did not refute the facts, and only stated that it did not 'promote or authorize screenings of beoutQ broadcasts'.[33] Saudi Arabia did not

[32] The name was chosen deliberately to mock the name of a Qatari TV platform beIN: beoutQ stands for 'be out Qatar'.
[33] §7.160 of the panel report on *Saudi Arabia – IPRs*, DS567, issued on 16 June 2020.

penalise beoutQ, the actions of which were affecting other suppliers as well. Saudi Arabia had also adopted 'anti-sympathy measures'.[34] The panel found that it was not implausible that similar measures were promoting national security (§7.286), but could not find justification for the refusal to allow Qatar to hire a legal counsel (§7.289). The panel echoed the standard of review that the panel on *Russia – Traffic in Transit* had originally adopted: 'whether its articulation of its essential security interests was "minimally satisfactory" in the circumstances' (§7.281).

Saudi Arabia had not even articulated why the refusal to allow Qatar to hire a counsel (which did not require any interaction with Qataris) was necessary to protect Saudi security.

Unsurprisingly, then, the panel found that Saudi Arabia had not met its burden under Article 73 of the TRIPS Agreement (§§7.290ff). The Saudi measure was, in the panel's eyes, orthogonal to the objective pursued, since the objective was to break all links with Qatar. Saudi Arabia could, of course, have claimed that it simply did not want to enrich Qatar, the threat to its security, and all its measures were serving this objective. But it did not.

D. USA – Origin Marking (Hong Kong, China) (DS597)

The USA had adopted legislation that obliged all products originating in Hong Kong, China to carry a label indicating that they were 'Made in China' (and not 'made in Hong Kong, China', as used to be the case before). Hong Kong, China is, of course, part of China, but it is also a member of the WTO in its own right, as it constitutes a separate customs territory.[35] The rationale was that, in the USA's view, Hong Kong, China did not enjoy sufficient autonomy from China to justify a separate indication of origin. Hong Kong, China complained, arguing that the US measure was discriminatory as the USA had adopted no similar conduct towards other WTO members. The USA made its submission publicly available.[36] The centrepiece of its defence was the invocation of the national security exception. The USA was yet again raising the self-judging nature of Article XXI.

The panel saw the US measure as a marking requirement, and reviewed its consistency only with Article IX of the GATT. The panel found that, unlike what it had been practising with respect to imports from other WTO members, when importing from Hong Kong, China the USA was not endorsing a correspondence between the determination of origin by the exporter and the marking of origin

[34] This term covered measures aiming to tarnish Qatar's reputation in Saudi Arabia, and break all links and contacts with it.

[35] Art XII.1 of the Agreement Establishing the WTO pertinently reads to this effect: 'Any State or separate customs territory *possessing full autonomy in the conduct of its external commercial relations* and of the other matters provided for in this Agreement and the Multilateral Trade Agreements may accede to this Agreement, on terms to be agreed between it and the WTO' (emphasis added).

[36] *USA – Origin Marking Requirements* (DS597), First Written Submission of the United States of America, 2 July 2021, https://ustr.gov/sites/default/files/enforcement/DS/DS597/USSub1.fin.pdf.

for the same products by the importer (§7.234). As a result, Hong Kong, China had suffered damage since its exports could not benefit from the reputation of products originating in its territory (§§7.237–39).[37] Having established its inconsistency with this provision, the panel asked whether the measure could still be justified under Article XXI. The panel rejected the US claim that Article XXI was self-judging (§§7.177–85).[38] It then went on to decide whether the US measure could have been justified under Article XXI(b) of the GATT. It held that this was not the case, because:

- there was no emergency in international relations (§7.281), as the understanding of this term should be informed by the meaning of the term 'war' (§7.312); and
- the situation before the panel could not qualify as an emergency, because
  - the USA had taken measures against Hong Kong, China and not against China, which was supposedly the target of the measures; and even
  - trade between the USA and China showed no signs of breakdown, unlike the disputes DS512 and DS567 (§7.354).[39]

The ultimate conclusion was that the US measures were taken outside of war (emergency).

It is one thing, of course, to base findings on the existence of war/emergency, as the DS512 panel did; it is a different thing to base findings on the absence of war/emergency, as this panel did. Panels seem to equate the absence of emergency (defined in light of 'war') as the absence of justification for adopting national security measures. This is wrong, as countries might possess confidential information about threats.

Byman and Waxman note that legal scholars focus too much on what states do, rather than what they threaten to do.[40] Yet, so much more of international

[37] Both these findings are questionable to say the least. The exporter marks the origin, but the importer can review it for purposes of customs valuation upon entry. During the Uruguay Round of multilateral trade negotiations, negotiators could not agree on harmonised rules of origin. The resulting Agreement on Rules of Origin condones regulatory diversity: each WTO member unilaterally defines its rules of origin and applies them to all other WTO members in non-discriminatory terms. Consequently, Hong Kong, China and the USA could very well disagree in the methodology they use to confer origin. It is even more puzzling that the panel did not even compare the treatment afforded to products originating in Hong Kong, China by US authorities to the obviously comparable counterfactual: the treatment afforded to products originating in Macau, China. The finding that the USA had violated the most favoured nation (MFN) requirement embedded in Art IX of the GATT is grounded on a wrong understanding of the manner in which origin is being conferred. The panel further reached the conclusion that Hong Kong, China had suffered damage because of the MFN violation without any evidence at all that its products had indeed suffered damage.

[38] The panel also made *en passant* a reference to Art 2.2 of the TBT (Technical Barriers to Trade), when in §7.147 it underscored the justiciability of invocations of national security.

[39] The US appealed the panel report, WTO Doc WT/DS597/9 of 30 January 2023. As there is no functional Appellate Body anymore, the appeal is into the void, and hence the panel report will not have any legal effect.

[40] Daniel Byman and Matthew Waxman, *The Dynamics of Coercion: American Foreign Policy and the Limits of Military Might* (Cambridge University Press, 2002).

relations is about threats rather than actions. When actions are taken, they are often intended as signals of other actions yet to come. WTO members might be quite incentivised to withhold information regarding their national security, and/or even to bluff about it. Absence of an overt 'emergency', in other words, should not automatically lead panels to decide that no emergency exists.

E. China – Additional Duties USA (DS558)

Following the imposition by the USA of additional duties under section 232, China reacted. Claiming that it had not agreed with the USA on compensation as per Article 8 of the WTO Agreement on Safeguards, it went on to exercise its rights and imposed additional duties on US exports unilaterally (§7.65). The USA complained, and the panel had to consider whether China had lawfully exercised its rights under Article 8. It held that the ordinary meaning of the terms of Article 8.2 linked the right to suspend concessions or other obligations to the application of a safeguard measure by another member (§§7.74–7.82). The question thus was whether the USA had indeed imposed a safeguard.

Echoing the approach adopted in DS556, the panel refuted the claim by China. The key passage of the report concerned the understanding of the term 'pursuant to'. Article 11.1(c) of the WTO Agreement on Safeguards requests members taking emergency action to address the situation envisaged in Article XIX only 'pursuant to' the provisions embedded in the WTO Agreement on Safeguards. Adopting measures *pursuant to* the Agreement on Safeguards, in the panel's view, should not be equated with adopting measures that are *consistent with* the various provisions of this agreement (§§7.91–99). What mattered was the intent of the party adopting the measures. In §§7.102–13, based on US law and unilateral US notifications and declarations that the USA made before WTO bodies, the panel concluded that the measure was all about protecting US national security. In §7.111, the panel said it all in these words:

> In the Panel's view, the abovementioned features of the Section 232 measures demonstrate that they were *designed and expected to operate to address the threat to national security* that the United States had determined to arise from rising levels of aluminium and steel imports. (emphasis added)

Having established that the US measure was not a safeguard, the panel found that the Chinese measure was in violation of Articles I and II of the GATT.

The approach in this report is not right. Relying (almost exclusively) on US law is one of its errors. What should matter is not the US description of the measure, but the WTO description. After all, it is consistency with WTO law that is at stake. The panel also conflated the nature of the challenged measure (eg its constituent elements) with the intent behind it. Instead of asking the question of whether the measure should be viewed as a tariff (and/or a quantitative restriction) or a safeguard, the panel embarked on an enquiry about the alleged intent of the USA when enacting the measure. A tariff can be used to affect terms of trade or to promote national security. But under both scenarios, recourse has been made to a tariff. The purpose can vary, but the instrument does not change. In the present case, the instrument was an additional duty. The panel should have characterised it as a duty or a safeguard. A lot of case law especially draws a clear line between tariffs and safeguards.[41] It is hard to understand why the panel was not inspired by it.

The text of Article 11.1(c) comes from the previous 'Dunkel draft', §22(c) of the Agreement on Safeguards draft. The privileged expression 'pursuant to' was chosen to draw a wedge between safeguard actions under specific agreements (eg agriculture, textiles) and the general safeguard clause. This provision wanted to eliminate confusion between sector-specific safeguards and the subject matter of the Agreement on Safeguards.[42] As the panel asserted, it was not chosen to distinguish between intent and consistency. Finally, this report opened the road to circumvention. Anyone can claim an objective to mischaracterise adopted measures even if the challenged measure is a far cry from whatever the WTO framers had in mind.

The panel's finding is hard to defend for one more common-sense reason. Practically the same measure that had been judged inconsistent with GATT, Article XXI in DS554 was found to be 'pursuant to' GATT, Article XXI in DS558. In DS544, the panel had found that the USA had not successfully invoked the national security exception. And yet, a few months later, in DS558, the panel found that the US measures had been adopted 'pursuant to' Article XXI. When issuing its report, the panel was well aware that the US measures had fallen short of Article XXI.

III. Brief Conclusions

Elsewhere, I have taken the view that the panel process is ill-suited to address national security-related concerns.[43] The manner in which panels understand the term 'measure' is an issue. Take DS512 as an illustration. The report looks reasonable. The panel found it legitimate for Russia to invoke national security to justify the restriction it had imposed on Ukrainian transit trade because of the ongoing

[41] Echoing Switzerland's claims, the EU (§§19ff) argued that for a measure to be a safeguard, it must have two constituent features: it must suspend, in whole or in part, a GATT obligation (or withdraw or modify a GATT concession); and the suspension, withdrawal or modification in question must be designed to prevent or remedy serious injury to the member's domestic industry (caused or threatened by increased imports of the relevant products). The merit of this approach is that for a measure to be characterised a safeguard, it is WTO law that should serve as benchmark, not the domestic law of a WTO member.

[42] The negotiating record is reflected in Terence P Stewart and Myron Brilliant, 'Safeguards' in Terence P Stewart (ed), *The GATT Uruguay Round: A Negotiating History (1986–1992)* (Kluwer, 1993).

[43] Mavroidis, *Industrial Policy* (n 6).

crisis in their relations. A number of UN documents provided the evidence to this effect. Now take one step back. Russia infiltrated Crimea through its 'little green men' in February and March 2014. Following Ukraine's defence, Russia aimed to asphyxiate it economically by denying transit to its trade through its territory. On 5 April 2019, the panel issued its report justifying Russia's action. But who is the aggressor here and who is the aggressed party? The panel effectively allowed the aggressor to invoke national security to justify its aggression. On 24 February 2022, Russia completed the job by invading Ukraine.

Would a discussion in a political/diplomatic setting have reached the same result as the DS512 panel did? It is highly doubtful, to say the least. And the reason why the panel diverged from common sense has probably to do with the nature of judicial review and the manner in which panels understood 'measure' as artificial segments of a wider strategy.

Furthermore, how would panels react if the party invoking GATT, Article XXI consistently made use of the first paragraph, namely not to divulge any information contrary to its security interests?

Would they go ahead and draw adverse inferences? The cost of error extends beyond trade damage, of course. Who would trust an adjudicating body that cannot safeguard the quintessential function of states, the pole of power in Wolfers's (1951)[44] inimitable expression?

Ideally, we would like to see Tucker's idea (to condition participation in international fora upon acceptance of a pact of non-aggression) implemented in the WTO as well.[45] But this is not on the cards at this point in time. Consequently, for now, the most reasonable approach would be to remove national security-related disputes from the docket and submit them to a committee process.[46]

[44] Arnold Wolfers, 'The Pole of Power and the Pole of Indifference' (1951) 4 *World Politics* 39.

[45] Paul Tucker, *Global Discord: Values and Power in a Fractured World Order* (Princeton University Press, 2022) https://academic.oup.com/princeton-scholarship-online/book/46242.

[46] This idea was fleshed out in Hoekman et al (n 5).

7

The New Roles of the World Trade Organization in Trade and Climate Change

GABRIELLE MARCEAU AND MARIA GEORGE*

I. Introduction and Overview

The Marrakesh Agreement Establishing the World Trade Organization (WTO Agreement) was a monumental multilateral undertaking, aimed at achieving disciplined trade liberalisation through a robust rules-based framework. The preamble of the WTO Agreement explicitly notes that trade relations should be conducted 'in accordance with the objective of sustainable development'.[1] This reference introduces an element of balance inherent to the mandate of the WTO: that policies of trade liberalisation are guided by the three pillars of sustainability: economic development, environmental protection and social justice.[2] This has been a crucial guiding light in navigating the work undertaken by the WTO with respect to environmental matters, and underscores the emergence of 'new' roles of the WTO in addressing the trade–climate change nexus.

Although the issue of climate change is not explicitly found in the WTO Agreement, the reference to 'sustainable development' opened the door for

* All opinions expressed are those of the authors and do not bind WTO Members and WTO Secretariat. The authors would like to thank Daniel Ramos and Ludivine Tamiotti for their useful comments. All mistakes are those of the authors only.

[1] 'Report of the World Commission on Environment and Development: Our Common Future – A/42/427' (4 August 1987) ch II, www.un-documents.net/wced-ocf.htm. The 'Brundtland Commission Report' compellingly defined 'sustainable development' as follows: 'Sustainable development is development that meets the needs of the present without compromising the ability of future generations to meet their own needs. It contains within it two key concepts: the concept of 'needs', in particular the essential needs of the world's poor, to which overriding priority should be given; and the idea of limitations imposed by the state of technology and social organization on the environment's ability to meet present and future needs.'

[2] Karen Whitfield, 'Quick Guide to Sustainable Development: History and Concepts' (National Assembly for Wales – Research Service, 9 March 2015) https://policycommons.net/artifacts/3788760/quick-guide-to-sustainable-development/4594521/.

discussions on the interconnected nature of trade and climate change. On the one hand, climate change impacts trade. Climate change-induced effects can adversely impact trade by raising costs and disrupting supply chains. At the same time, measures taken by governments to combat climate change can also have an adverse impact on trade. On the other hand, trade impacts climate change. Trade, specifically emissions from the manufacture of goods and their transportation, contributes to climate change. However, this relationship is not a one-way street: trade and trade policy have also become important tools in the arsenal of states in adapting to, and mitigating, the effects of climate change. This multifaceted and interconnected relationship between trade and climate change highlights the important institutional function of the WTO in the global response to a changing climate. This institutional function has evolved since its inception, both in response to the geopolitical landscape and in addressing the changing priorities of WTO Members. We term this the 'new' role of the WTO.

This chapter explores four institutional functions of the WTO and how they have evolved in the context of the emerging climate crisis. This provides the substantive content of the 'new' role of the WTO beyond its traditional mandate, representing a concerted effort to bring the trade and climate change regimes closer and in congruence with each other. In understanding the origin and potential of this new role, the chapter subsequently examines the evolving priorities of WTO Members, starting from the outcome document from the Twelfth Ministerial Conference (MC12) and specific Member proposals dealing with climate change. Lastly, the chapter looks at three ways in which the potential of this new role can manifest itself in the future work undertaken by the WTO: in promoting coherence between trade-related climate measures and environmental principles; in addressing the gap in trade rules for challenges arising from climate change; and in addressing the climate finance gap.

II. The WTO's Evolving Institutional Role

In 2016, Cottier and Payosova had examined the potential of the WTO to sufficiently respond to the needs of combating climate change as a 'common concern'.[3] They observed that the WTO could provide avenues for addressing climate change through multilateral trade negotiations, and through disciplines governing unilateral trade measures.[4] We seek to build on this scholarship and understand the

[3] Thomas Cottier and Tetyana Payasova, 'Common Concern and the Legitimacy of the WTO in Dealing with Climate Change' in Panagiotis Delimatsis (ed), *Research Handbook on Climate Change and Trade Law* (Edward Elgar Publishing, 2016).

[4] ibid 22–29. See also Thomas Cottier, Philipp Aerni, Baris Karapinar, Sofya Matteotti, Joëlle de Sépibus and Anirudh Shingal, 'The Principle of Common Concern and Climate Change' (2014) 52 *Archiv des Völkerrechts* 293, discussing how the WTO can establish the limits and basis for climate change related unilateral action.

'new' role of the WTO with respect to climate change. We trace the evolution of *four institutional functions* that make the WTO a key player in the global response to climate change. We start by looking at the manner in which discussions on trade and climate change have evolved, from formal committees to other informal discussion groups. We then look at how the WTO has assumed a leadership role in the efforts taken by multiple intergovernmental organisations (IGOs) in response to climate change, culminating in its active participation at the 28th Conference of Parties of the United Nations Framework Convention on Climate Change in December 2023. Given the unique nature of climate change, we further explore how the WTO provides a ready-made deliberative platform for engagement with the private sector. Lastly, we look at the dedicated research and publication efforts undertaken by the WTO in establishing the key role of trade in combating climate change.

A. Forum for Discussion: From Formal Committees to Other Informal Discussion Groups

Given the interconnected nature of trade and climate change, the WTO has historically provided a forum for its Members to exchange information and engage in open discussions through its various committees. The Committee on Trade and Environment (CTE), established in 1995 pursuant to the Marrakesh Ministerial Decision on Trade and Environment,[5] is considered the primary forum for such discussions. The mandate of the CTE is to examine the relationship between trade and the environment through various means, including by providing a forum for the open exchange of information between WTO Members. In addition to the CTE, the Committee on Technical Barriers to Trade (TBT Committee) also provides an important forum specific to climate change-related matters. The TBT Agreement imposes obligations on Members to share information on technical regulations that have an impact on trade.[6] This is especially relevant because measures adopted by states to combat climate change can take the form of such technical regulations. This is notably the case of product standards on energy efficiency or labelling requirements on emissions control. The discussions in formal committees are primarily aimed at congruence between trade rules and climate change-related measures adopted by Members through information sharing.[7]

[5] Marrakesh Ministerial Decision on Trade and Environment, www.wto.org/english/docs_e/legal_e/56-dtenv.pdf.

[6] TBT Agreement, Art 2.9.2.

[7] As elaborated below, discussions now also include finding opportunities for enhanced trade cooperation to achieve climate-related goals, identifying best practices, etc.

The WTO Secretariat's Environmental Database (EDB)[8] plays an important role in promoting enhanced transparency with respect to discussions relating to climate change at the WTO. The EDB covers information on: (i) environment-related measures notified under WTO Agreements and notification obligations; and (ii) environment-related measures mentioned in Members' trade policy reviews. The most recent Note by the Secretariat prepared on the EDB identified 74 environment-related measures expressly linked to adaptation, mitigation and other climate-related objectives.[9] The EDB database also provides a platform to view the notification status of individual Members,[10] including those specifically aimed at climate change mitigation and adaptation.

The role of the WTO is no longer restricted to the formal committee work noted above. Two new deliberative initiatives related to trade and climate change have created a space for policy discussions at the WTO outside formal committees:[11] the Trade and Environment Sustainability Structured Discussions (TESSD) and the Fossil Fuel Subsidies Reform (FFSR) discussions.

1. *TESSD*: The discussions were launched in November 2020 through four informal Working Groups on (i) Environmental Goods and Services; (ii) Trade-related Climate Measures; (iii) Circular Economy – Circularity; and (iv) Subsidies. The TESSD initiative features 76 Members as co-sponsors and is open to the entire membership. Its four areas of work represent a move towards recognising the facilitative role of trade in combating the climate crisis. The Statement by the TESSD Co-Convenors at the Thirteenth Ministerial Conference (MC13) highlights the progress of the Working Groups.[12] Specifically, the Working Groups moved beyond information sharing and identified concrete policy steps for tackling trade-related climate measures.[13] Further, with respect to aiding the green transition, the Working Group on Environmental Goods and Services identified relevant goods and services, and narrowed the approaches for promoting and facilitating trade in those goods and services.[14] However, such a new form of deliberation is not distinct or separate from the regular work of the WTO Committees.

[8] The 1996 Report of the Committee on Trade and Environment (WT/CTE/1) directed the Secretariat to compile and update annually all environment-related notifications to the WTO. In October 2018, web-based EDB application was developed. For the web-based EDB, see www.wto.org/edb or https://edb.wto.org/.

[9] Environmental Database for 2022, Chart 1.5, 7, note by the Secretariat, 14 March 2024, WT/CTE/EDB/22.

[10] https://edb.wto.org/members.

[11] The Dialogue on Plastics Pollution and Environmentally Sustainable Plastics Trade is also an example of discussions outside formal committees, although not directly related to climate change. For further information, see www.wto.org/english/tratop_e/ppesp_e/ppesp_e.htm.

[12] For a detailed overview of the progress, see Ministerial Conference, Thirteenth Session, Abu Dhabi, 26–29 February 2024, Trade and Environmental Sustainability Structured Discussions (TESSD), Statement by the TESSD Co-convenors, 19 February 2024, WT/MIN(24)/11.

[13] ibid Addendum (WT/MIN(24)/11/Add.2).

[14] ibid Addendum (WT/MIN(24)/11/Add.3).

TESSD intend to complement multilateral work in the WTO (including that pursued through the CTE).[15]

2. *FFSR*: These discussions were officially launched in December 2021,[16] with 48 Members as co-sponsors, and are open to the entire membership. The Work Plan adopted at MC12 sets up a forum to take stock of international efforts on FFSR.[17] At MC13, the Ministerial Statement on Fossil Fuel Subsidies reaffirmed the objective of the initiative: to achieve rationalisation, and to phase out or eliminate harmful fossil fuel subsidies. The three pillars identified were: enhanced transparency; crisis support measures; and identifying and addressing harmful subsidies.[18] The work programme sets out specific options under each of these pillars that showcase the new roles envisioned for the WTO in facilitating the green transition. For example, one of the deliverables identified under crisis support measures is monitoring and encouraging the reduction and/or removal of temporary fossil fuel support measures adopted to address the recent energy crisis.[19] This is intended to be achieved through the periodic review of Members' temporary crisis support measures and efforts to reform, reduce and remove these.

TESSD and FFSR are two examples of a new type of discussion being explored at the WTO involving smaller groups of like-minded Members interested in achieving progress on specific issues facing the wider membership.[20] In the context of climate change, given the urgency of the crisis and the important facilitative role that trade can play, such discussion groups represent a new forum for discussion at the WTO. However, such groups do not take away from the multilateral nature of the organisation and complement the work undertaken through formal WTO Committees.

B. Collaboration with Other IGOs: From Participation to Leadership at CoP28

The WTO has always participated in IGO efforts to collaborate and coordinate the global response to multifaceted challenges.[21] The emergence of a new role can be seen in the leadership role assumed by the WTO in initiatives relating to climate change.

[15] For a detailed overview of the progress, see ibid para 9.

[16] Ministerial Statement on Fossil Fuel Subsidies, 14 December 2021, WT/MIN(21)/9/Rev.1.

[17] Ministerial Statement on Fossil Fuel Subsidies, June 2022, WT/MIN(22)/8.

[18] Ministerial Statement on Fossil Fuel Subsidies, 26 February 2024, WT/MIN(24)/19.

[19] ibid Annex 1, Entry B(iii).

[20] Other examples are seen through the Joint Statement initiatives on e-commerce, investment facilitation for development, domestic regulation of services, and MSMEs.

[21] WTO, 'IGOs in Which the WTO Regularly or Occasionally Participates as an Observer' www.wto.org/english/thewto_e/coher_e/wto_observership_e.htm.

In April 2023, the Action on Climate and Trade was launched by the World Economic Forum (WEF), the World Bank and the WTO. The initiative is a collaboration between IGOs to leverage their analytical and capacity-building programmes to help participating developing economies,[22] especially less developed countries, to use trade to meet their climate change mitigation and adaptation goals. Jointly produced analytics are intended to be adapted to each country's specific needs, highlighting how trade policy can support the achievement of Nationally Determined Contributions under the Paris Agreement. This lends support to the work of the WTO, equipping concerned Members to engage on a stronger footing in forums like the CTE and TESSD.

The leadership role of the WTO became clear at the United Nations Framework on Convention on Climate Change (UNFCCC) Conference of Parties (CoP28), held in December 2023. The WTO Secretariat co-led the CoP28 Presidency Committee on Trade, bringing together the United Nations Conference on Trade and Development (UNCTAD), the International Chamber of Commerce, the WEF and the Abu Dhabi Department of Economic Development, with one day specifically devoted for trade and climate change (so-called 'Trade Day').[23] As elaborated in section II.C and II.D below, CoP28 also saw the release of several papers by the WTO Secretariat in collaboration with other IGOs and relevant stakeholders.[24]

The WTO further mobilised the Joint Task Force on Climate Action, Carbon Pricing, and Policy Spillovers comprising the Organisation for Economic Co-operation and Development (OECD), the International Monetary Fund, the World Bank and United Nations Trade and Development (UNCTAD), tasked with discussing common methodological approaches to carbon pricing and carbon markets.[25] This initiative came in the wake of a technical workshop organised by the WTO Secretariat in March 2023, at which a new analytical framework for variable national carbon pricing was presented to Members. The participants also discussed the potential for reinvestment of part of the funds generated by any such Border Tax Adjustment or other mechanism to support Members adversely affected by climate change.

The above initiatives showcase how the specific expertise of the WTO with respect to trade and climate change is recognised by fellow IGOs. This represents evolution from mere participation in such initiatives to a 'new' leadership role in joint efforts for global trade governance.

[22] WTO, 'WTO, World Bank, WEF Launch Joint Effort to Provide Tailored Trade and Climate Analysis' www.wto.org/english/news_e/news23_e/envir_20apr23_e.htm.

[23] WTO, 'WTO Secretariat at Climate Change CoP28' www.wto.org/english/tratop_e/envir_e/wto_cop28_e.htm.

[24] See ss II.C and II.D below.

[25] 'WTO Launching Global Carbon Price Task Force – Okonjo-Iweala' (Reuters, 17 October 2023) www.reuters.com/sustainability/wto-launching-global-carbon-price-task-force-okonjo-iweala-2023-10-17/. The first report of the Joint Taskforce entitled 'Working Together for Better Climate Action: Carbon Pricing, Policy Spillovers, and Global Climate Goals' was released on 23 October 2024, https://www.wto.org/english/news_e/news24_e/igo_24oct24_e.htm.

C. Platform for Private Sector Communication: Moving Away from Purely State-centric Responses

Climate change is also a unique challenge facing the global community, given that greenhouse gas (GHG) emissions are most directly the result of private actors.[26] This implies that a large portion of critical data on emissions is under the control of non-state actors. The private sector also has a wealth of expertise on emerging technology that plays a crucial role in the green transition. Therefore, the response to climate change must necessarily take account of the perspectives and expertise provided by private actors. The momentum to deepen engagement with the private sector at the WTO picked up during the COVID-19 pandemic and has continued in the context of discussions on the trade–climate change nexus.

The WTO Trade Forum for Decarbonization Standards in the Steel Sector, held in March 2023, brought together some of the biggest steel companies from around the world (such as ArcelorMittal, POSCO, Gerdau), with government representatives, other IGOs (OECD, International Energy Agency) and industry associations (World Steel Association, Responsible Steel). The landmark forum saw the steel industry actively request the WTO's participation in the development of steel decarbonisation standards, as a facilitator of dialogue between different governments, and between industry and government. Four specific aspects were highlighted that hint towards the new role of the WTO with respect to climate change and private sector participation:

(i) promoting international cooperation and discussion in a landscape of heterogeneity;
(ii) encouraging the use of the principles of equivalence and mutual recognition of standards between countries, particularly through various WTO committees, including the CTE and TBT committees;
(iii) offering a deliberative forum with equal and inclusive participation of developing and least developed countries; and
(iv) facilitating transparency and information sharing on standards between industry, standard setting bodies, Member countries and other stakeholders.

This forum eventually led to the 'Steel Standards Principles' Report, launched at CoP28 by the WTO Secretariat in partnership with standard-setting bodies, IGOs and the private sector. As intended, the report establishes common principles for measuring GHG emissions in the iron and steel sector.[27]

Further, TESSD provides informal avenues for interaction with stakeholders from the business community, civil society, academic institutions and other

[26] Charlotte Streck, 'Filling in for Governments? The Role of the Private Actors in the International Climate Regime' (2020) 17 *Journal for European Environmental & Planning Law* 5, 5–28.
[27] WTO, 'Steel Standards Principles' (1 December 2023) www.wto.org/english/tratop_e/envir_e/steelstandprincippartner_e.htm.

international organisations.[28] More specifically, TESSD informal working groups allow relevant private actors to enrich the discussions with their technical expertise. This is yet another example of a new role undertaken by the WTO in moving away from a purely state-centric response to the climate crisis and providing a unique platform for global public–private dialogue as well.

D. Building Dedicated Research: Assessing How Trade Can Best Respond to Climate Change

Although not strictly a new role for the WTO, the growing number of analytical contributions the WTO has been making recently with respect to trade and climate change bears recalling. As early as 2009, the WTO and the United Nations Environment Programme released a report entitled 'Trade and Climate Change' that identified complex linkages between the two regimes. The most significant contribution to studying these linkages was seen through the World Trade Report 2022 on Climate Change and International Trade.[29] This was further operationalised at CoP28 when the WTO Secretariat launched its 'Trade Policy Tools for Climate Action'[30] paper. The paper proposes 10 trade policy options that may be employed by Members to respond to climate change (for example, tariffs, government procurement, agriculture policies, trade facilitation).[31] Such measures can be incorporated into the Nationally Determined Contributions of Members under the Paris Agreement.[32]

Various other reports were also launched at CoP28, showcasing the WTO's commitment to building a dedicated research base. The WTO and the International Renewable Energy Agency launched the International Trade and Green Hydrogen Report.[33] This report outlines actions for policymakers, inter alia, in addressing trade barriers along the green hydrogen supply chain, developing a sound quality infrastructure for green hydrogen trade and fostering international cooperation on green hydrogen. As highlighted above, the 'Steel Standard Principles' were also released at CoP28.

Therefore, although the WTO has always undertaken research on interlinkages between the trade and climate change regimes, the recent publications culminating at CoP28 helped to cast trade as an essential part of the solution to climate change. This contributes to, and is a facet of, the 'new' role of the WTO in climate change.

[28] Trade and Environmental Sustainability Structured Discussions, 'Brief on TESSD and Its Package for MC13' www.wto.org/english/tratop_e/tessd_e/tessd_brief_mc13_e.pdf.

[29] WTO, 'World Trade Report 2022: Climate Change and International Trade' (2022).

[30] WTO, 'Trade Policy Tools for Climate Action' (2023) (Toolkit).

[31] ibid.

[32] ibid.

[33] WTO and IRENA, 'International Trade and Green Hydrogen: Supporting the Global Transition to a Low-Carbon Economy', www.irena.org/Publications/2023/Dec/International-trade-and-green-hydrogen-Supporting-the-global-transition-to-a-low-carbon-economy.

The next section explores the origins of these new roles and examines the Member-specific proposals that highlight the potential trajectory of the WTO's interaction with the trade-related challenges flowing from a changing climate.

III. Member-Driven Evolution of the WTO's 'New Role' Regarding Climate Change

The 'new' role of the WTO in climate change-related matters cannot be understood in isolation from the evolving priorities of its membership. This is most evident in the Outcome Document adopted at the WTO's Twelfth Ministerial Conference in June 2022. The very first paragraph of the Outcome Document reaffirms the commitment of Members to sustainable development and cooperation in relation to the protection and preservation of the environment.[34] The concluding paragraph explicitly recognises emerging global environmental challenges like climate change and notes the role of the CTE as a standing forum dedicated to dialogue among Members on such issues.[35] Additionally, the Members also recognised the need for strengthened collaboration and cooperation with IGOs and other relevant stakeholders in effectively addressing current and future multidimensional challenges.[36] Therefore, the emergence of the 'new' roles was not *suo moto*, but rather a response to the changing priorities and needs of WTO Members.

To understand this evolution further and also explore the potential for 'new' roles, it is necessary to examine the specific climate change-related proposals advanced by WTO Members. We have categorised the proposals according to their substantive function, identifying three areas where Members have requested the WTO to provide guidance: (i) promoting coherence in trade-related environmental measures and environmental principles; (ii) strengthening WTO rules and devising new rules to respond to emerging challenges; and (iii) supporting the facilitative role of trade in addressing climate change: the transfer of Environmentally Sound Technologies (ESTs).

However, the proposals we have examined are not exhaustive. They have been identified keeping in mind the specific functions they address and the engagements with those functions by other Members.

A. Promoting Coherence in Trade-Related Environmental Measures and Environmental Principles

The greatest number of proposals we have examined look to the WTO to provide a platform to discuss and guide Members in employing trade-related

[34] MC12 Outcome Document, para 1.
[35] ibid para 14.
[36] ibid para 12.

environmental measures to combat climate change. WTO Members are increasingly taking urgent action to combat climate change through policy measures for mitigation and adaptation. The important role of trade policy in aiding the green transition, incentivising decarbonisation and spreading green technologies is well established. As the number of such measures is increasing, WTO Members have recognised the need to have conversations on the effectiveness and impact of those measures.

As early as March 2023, China introduced a proposal for dedicated multilateral discussions on certain environmental measures that have a significant impact on trade pursuant to the MC12 mandate.[37] The proposal sought to engage the CTE as a platform for such discussions, going further than the mere exchange of information and positions. China elaborated further on its proposal in June[38] and November 2023,[39] finally focusing on Carbon Border Adjustment Mechanisms (CBAMs) and taking the EU's CBAM as a starting point. They proposed five key elements that could guide the discussions: (i) basic operating mechanism, focusing on underlying methodologies; (ii) policy design and implementation; (iii) environmental effects, focusing on the contribution of the measure to the intended environmental objectives; (iv) trade impacts, especially on developing countries; and (v) inclusiveness, focusing on how measures can be implemented in a more open, non-discriminatory and non-arbitrary manner.

Colombia's proposal on principles and parameters that should guide and support policies and measures on trade and environment also looked to the CTE to engage in key initial discussions and, later on, to ground such principles/parameter-specific discussions on policies and measures of interest to the entire membership.[40] The principles suggested by Colombia included: (i) international cooperation; (ii) common but differentiated responsibility (CBDR); (iii) non-discrimination; and (iv) prevention in policy formulation, ensuring adequate use of scientific evidence. In this case, we see a very specific reference to a principle of environmental law, the CBDR principle, being raised in a WTO setting. While several Members expressed caution in addressing this principle before the WTO as it belongs to other forums, Colombia is not alone in its position of wanting to bring congruence between the two regimes.

The African, Caribbean and Pacific Group of States have similarly advanced a proposal aimed at reinvigorating discussions in the CTE on issues and areas at the nexus of trade and environmental measures, including a focus on the needs

[37] 'A Proposal for Dedicated Multilateral Discussion on the Trade Aspects and Implications of Certain Environmental Measures', Communication from China, 13 March 2023, WT/CTE/W/251.

[38] 'Further Elaboration on Dedicated Multilateral Discussions on the Trade Aspects and Implications of Certain Environmental Measures', Communication from China, 12 June 2023, JOB/TE/81, now de-restricted.

[39] 'Policy Issues for Dedicated Multilateral Discussions on Border Carbon Adjustment', Communication from China, 10 November 2023, WT/CTE/W/258.

[40] RD/CTE/221, referenced in Report (2023) of the Committee on Trade and Environment, 13 December 2023, WT/CTE/30 (CTE Annual Report) para 8.6.

and priorities of developing countries.[41] They reference the Nairobi Declaration on Climate Change and Call to Action,[42] which calls for the development of 'global metrics and market mechanisms' to accurately value and compensate for the protection of the climate system. In this regard, they suggest that the CTE could provide an avenue to discuss the possible harmonisation and mutual recognition of such standards. Such work is already underway at the WTO, most recently evidenced through a Staff Working Paper.[43] While this is an important first step, the broader aspect of equivalences beyond price-based frameworks has yet to be explored.

India's paper, 'Concerns on the Emerging Trend of Using Environmental Measures as Protectionist Non-Tariff Measures',[44] underlines the importance of following foundational UNFCCC principles of equity and CBDR. The paper claimed that there was increasing use of unilateral measures impacting trade, which were justified as environmental measures, with potential inconsistencies with WTO rules and undermining multilateral environmental agreements. However, other Members noted the right to take WTO-consistent unilateral measures to address climate change, provided they do not unjustifiably and arbitrarily discriminate amongst Members or constitute disguised restrictions to trade.[45]

Similarly, the African Group Proposal on 'Principles Guiding the Development and Implementation of Trade-related Environmental Measures' brings a 'development approach to trade and environment'.[46] The proposal suggests that trade and environment discussions should be in line with the CTE mandate, focusing on the reference to 'sustainable development' in the preamble to the Marrakesh Agreement. They suggest 12 guiding principles to serve as the basis for engagement in the WTO on trade-related environmental measures: (i) compliance and interplay with existing WTO rules; (ii) common but differentiated responsibilities and respective capabilities; (iii) special and differential treatment; (iv) historic responsibility; (v) polluter pays; (vi) transparency; (vii) non-discrimination; (viii) access to and transfer of technology; (ix) technical assistance and capacity building; (x) environmental integrity and effectiveness; (xi) environmental impact assessment; and (xii) responsible business conduct. The proposal derives such principles from other relevant instruments, such as the 1992 Rio Declaration

[41] 'Proposal for Dedicated Multilateral Discussions on the Trade Aspects and Implications of Certain Environmental Measures, Communication from Samoa on behalf of the African', Caribbean and Pacific Group of States, 9 February 2024, WT/CTE/W/259.

[42] African Union, 'The African Leaders Nairobi Declaration on Climate Change and Call to Action' https://media.africaclimatesummit.org/Final+declaration+1709-English.pdf?request-content-type=%22application/force download.

[43] WTO, 'A Global Framework for Climate Mitigation Policies: A Technical Contribution to the Discussion on Carbon Pricing and Equivalent Policies in Open Economies' (6 March 2024) Staff Working Paper: Research ERSD-2024-03.

[44] JOB/TE/78, referenced in CTE Annual Report (n 40) para 1.4.

[45] CTE Annual Report (n 40) para 1.4.

[46] 'Principles Guiding the Development and Implementation of Trade-Related Environmental Measures', Communication from the African Group, 13 July 2023, WT/CTE/W/255.

on Environment and Development, the UN Convention on the Law of the Sea and the UNFCCC.

Another important proposal concerned a Ministerial Declaration on the Contribution of the Multilateral Trade System to Tackle Environmental Challenges,[47] made by Paraguay on behalf of a group of developing country members.[48] The proposal called upon Members to, inter alia, intensify work in the CTE to analyse the key principles of international environmental law that are relevant to the design and implementation of trade-related environmental measures, with the aim of enhancing coherence and mutual supportiveness between international environmental regimes and trade regimes in the design and implementation of trade-related environmental measures. Further, they also sought to strengthen discussions in the CTE and other relevant bodies of the WTO on how the multilateral trading system can best contribute to global responses to the climate crisis, taking into account the relevant principles of international environmental law.

Most recently, the USA has also made a proposal on 'Understanding the Opportunities and Challenges of the Green Transition: Coherence and Interoperability of Trade-related Climate Measures [TrCMs]'.[49] The proposal notes that greater coherence and interoperability between different TrCMs improves their effectiveness in addressing climate change, while reducing trade costs and tensions. The proposal seeks to provide a range of options for deepening the understanding of WTO Members in two areas: (i) policy design and implementation; and (ii) data and methodology. The specific options highlight various aspects that suggest 'new' roles to be taken up by the WTO, specifically in developing Good Regulatory Practices to improve the coherence of trade-related climate measures, and multi-stakeholder events that move away from a state-centric response to climate change.

Additionally, the US proposal also appreciates the work already underway through forums like TESSD, providing an informal incubation space to engage and explore emerging environmental issues in an open and inclusive format. They note that specific topics of TESSD discussions should eventually be broadened and developed, where possible, into concrete and practical policy options and tools. This would help to bring such topics back into the regular work of the relevant WTO Committees.

Through the Member(s) proposals discussed above, Members themselves have acknowledged the new roles of the WTO and requested guidance in order to fill

[47] Ministerial Declaration on the Contribution of the Multilateral Trade System to Tackle Environmental Challenges, 29 February 2024, WT/MIN(24)/28.

[48] The proposal was made by Argentina, Bangladesh, Barbados, Plurinational State of Bolivia, Brazil, Cabo Verde, Colombia, Ecuador, Egypt, Honduras, Indonesia, Kazakhstan, Panama, Paraguay, Peru, South Africa, Uruguay, Bolivarian Republic of Venezuela and the African Group.

[49] 'Understanding the Opportunities and Challenges of the Green Transition: Coherence and Interoperability of Trade-related Climate Measures', Communication from the USA, 4 April 2024, WT/CTE/W/260; G/C/W/843.

the gaps in the existing system. The discussions around the above proposals also reveal that there is growing support for the CTE to play an expansive role as a standing forum for discussions on the relationship between trade and environmental measures. This further builds on the reference to the CTE in the MC12 Outcome Document. Additionally, there is increasing acceptance of the utility of discussions taking place under informal forums like TESSD. The proposals also demonstrate the intention of some Members to arrive at guiding principles to bring coherence between trade-related climate measures, taking into account the relevance of environmental principles and data.

B. Strengthening WTO Rules and Devising New Rules: Responding to Emerging Challenges

Formally, there is a distinction between interpretations of[50] and amendments to the WTO Agreements.[51] Decisions are taken in accordance with the customary practice of decision-making by consensus.[52] However, amendments that alter the rights and obligations of Members shall take effect for a Member only after acceptance by them. The same rule applies to new agreements, such as the Agreement on Fisheries Subsidies adopted at MC12 and open for acceptance by Members.[53] While section III.A above focused on Member proposals relating to interpretations of existing rules, in this section, we examine Member proposals on the amendment of existing rules or the introduction of new rules.

The EU proposed two specific recommendations that hint at a 'new' role of the WTO. First, similar to the earlier proposals, the EU also proposes to reinforce deliberation on trade and global environmental challenges in the CTE. The aim is to make it a forum for transparency, coordination and policy dialogue on trade-related environmental measures. Secondly, relating to state intervention in support of industrial sectors, the EU recognises that well-designed subsidies can make an important contribution to achieving the climate transition while certain other subsidies can have a detrimental impact. However, they note that WTO rules are not presently equipped to deal with such situations, and a lack of transparency in such state interventions can increase trade conflicts and hinder the climate

[50] As per Art IX(2) of the WTO Agreement, the Ministerial Conference and the General Council have the exclusive authority to adopt interpretations of the WTO covered agreements.

[51] The procedure for amendment is laid down in Art X of the WTO Agreement.

[52] With respect to waivers and accessions, refer to 'Decision-Making Procedures Under Article IX and XII of the WTO Agreement', Statement by the Chairman as agreed by the General Council, 24 November 1995, WT/L/93. See also para 20 of Procedures for Appointment of Directors-General: Adopted by the General Council on 10 December 2002, 20 January 2003, WT/L/509.

[53] At MC12, the Amendment Protocol to insert the Agreement on Fisheries Subsidies into Annex 1A of the WTO Agreement was adopted. The Protocol was opened for acceptance by Members. As per the Protocol, it shall enter into force upon acceptance by two-thirds of the Members, in accordance with Art X:3 of the WTO Agreement.

transition. In addressing this gap, the EU suggests that the deliberative function of the WTO can be a place for initiating such discussions focused on transparency. Further, the aim would be to establish international consensus on the design of such measures, keeping in mind the developmental aspects of state intervention in industrial sectors.

The developmental aspects were further explored by the African Group in its proposal on 'Policy Space for Industrial Development – a Case for Rebalancing Trade Rules to Promote Industrialization and to Address Emerging Concerns such as Climate Change, Concentration of Production, and Digital Industrialization'.[54] They call for focused discussions by WTO Members to address the constraints inherent in certain WTO agreements that limit the policy space to drive industrialisation, economic diversification and structural transformation programmes, including the ability to respond to emerging challenges such as climate change. This submission is also a call to focus on multilateralism as a means through which new trade rules can be adopted to address the climate crisis.

Members recognise the potential of WTO rules to adapt to present challenges while envisaging the potential for new rules to address emerging challenges. These two facets are rooted in strengthening the deliberative function of the WTO to promote discussions and information exchange, and to build consensus on the shared needs of Members.

C. Supporting the Facilitative Role of Trade in Addressing Climate Change: Transfer of ESTs

The last function we explore relates to proposals by Members on strengthening the facilitative role of trade in aiding the green transition. Proposals relating to ESTs are an important example. They have been defined as technologies that have the potential to significantly improve environmental performance relative to other technologies, including know-how, procedures, goods and services, equipment, as well as organisation and managerial procedures for promoting sustainability.[55] ESTs are an important intersection between trade, intellectual property rights and climate change. It is well established that solutions should be explored to ensure IPRs are enablers, and not bottlenecks, in addressing climate change.[56]

[54] 'Policy Space for Industrial Development – a Case for Rebalancing Trade Rules to Promote Industrialization and to Address Emerging Concerns such as Climate Change, Concentration of Production, and Digital Industrialisation', Communication from the African Group, WT/GC/W/868, G/C/W/825 WT/COMTD/W/270, IP/C/W/695 WT/WGTTT/W/33, 1 March 2023.

[55] UNEP, 'Environmentally Sound Technologies' www.unep.org/regions/asia-and-pacific/regional-initiatives/supporting-resource-efficiency/environmentally-sound.

[56] UNCTAD's Trade and Development Report 2021.

The proposal by India and South Africa, entitled 'Concerns on Emerging Trend of Using Environmental Measures as Protectionist Non-Tariff Measures',[57] emphasised the collective nature of climate change, and the need to promote concrete solutions on climate finance and technology transfers. They propose that the CTE facilitate such solutions, including through the creation of a Trade and Environment Fund. Building on this proposal, India pursued this aspect in its proposal on 'Reinvigorating Discussions on the Relationship Between Trade and the Transfer of Environmentally Sound Technologies to Developing Countries to Address Climate Change'.[58] They specify that WTO Members need to operationalise the IPR system to ensure the free flow of ESTs. Pointing to the 2001 Doha Declaration on TRIPS and Public Health and the TRIPS waiver decision on COVID-19 vaccines at MC12, they argue that similar innovative solutions are required to provide access to patent-protected green technology, which is critical in combating the climate crisis. The paper contains a roadmap for future work that can be undertaken in this regard at the WTO. Such a roadmap features the following elements:

- *Creation of a financial mechanism* to promote the transfer of ESTs at reasonable prices, grants to developing countries, and financing appropriate environmental technical assistance and capacity-building programmes.
- *Creation of a database for ESTs* to promote transparency and exchanges of information. The proposal also highlights the need for synergies between other existing platforms, such as IO-run platforms like the UNFCCC, the Climate Technology Centre and Network, and WIPO Green. Such a platform is intended to connect providers and seekers of ESTs.
- *Streamlining licensing practices* to promote open and adaptable technology licensing for results from publicly funded projects on climate change and ESTs.
- *Enabling developing countries to use TRIPS flexibilities*, for example, through compulsory licensing, reduction of patent terms, waivers on patents on climate-friendly products and ESTs, and granting of royalty-free voluntary licences to address climate crises.

Two recent submissions of the African Group, entitled 'Role of Transfer of Technology in Resilience Building: Climate Change Mitigation and Adaptation'[59] and 'Principles Guiding the Development and Implementation of Trade-Related

[57] Concerns on Emerging Trend of Using Environmental Measures as Protectionist Non-Tariff Measures, Communication from India and South Africa, JOB/TE/78/Rev.1, referenced in Report of the Meeting Held on 13–14 and 16 November 2023, note by the Secretariat, Committee on Trade and Environment, WT/CTE/M/79, de-restricted on 2 February 2024.

[58] 'Reinvigorating Discussions on the Relationship Between Trade and the Transfer of Environmentally Sound Technologies to Developing Countries to Address Climate Change', JOB/TE/82 and JOB/TE/82/Corr.1, referenced in Report of the Meeting (n 56).

[59] WT/GC/W/883.

Environmental Measures',[60] emphasise the importance and necessity of providing developing countries with greater access to ESTs and facilitating the transfer of these technologies on favourable terms.

The above submissions indicate the deference of Members to the WTO to facilitate ways in which trade can aid the green transition and address the bottlenecks that exist. In so doing, the role of the WTO moves beyond a forum of exchange of ideas, with critical outputs being discussed in terms of financial mechanisms and the creation of e-platforms for coordination with other IGOs.

IV. Conclusion: Potential for Action

From the above discussions, we see that, presently, the 'new' roles of the WTO are being embraced through formal committees, as well as through informal forums of discussion. These discussions are moving beyond the traditional exchange of information, and Members are increasingly looking to the WTO to provide a forum where solutions can be devised. Building on this, the first potential for further action lies in the context of trade-related climate measures, where discussions before the WTO can bring coherence between the differing measures undertaken by Members and identifying the appropriate place for environmental law principles in such measures. Such coherence can lead to effective responses to climate change and aid the green transition. The informal forums of discussion like the TESSD working groups provide incubators where ideas and proposals in this regard can be tested, and thereafter brought into the regular work of the WTO in committees like the TBT Committee.

The next aspect is related to addressing gaps in existing WTO rules with respect to issues like state intervention for industrial promotion, for example, through subsidies. The work of the Fossil Fuel Subsidies Reform initiative and the TESSD Working Group on Subsidies holds significant potential for addressing such concerns. The tested solutions can thereafter be brought before the CTE to consider new rules in this regard. The conclusion of the Fisheries Subsidies Agreement offers a promising example of new rules that move beyond trade-only considerations and embrace sustainable development. Similarly, the urgency of the climate crisis can prompt deliberations on new disciplines or addressing gaps in existing rules.

Finally, the potential of the WTO to address concerns on climate finance and technology transfer through the establishment of a Trade and Environment Fund is emerging through some proposals put forth by Members. Such a fund could provide the means to transfer necessary ESTs to developing countries at reasonable prices, and finance technical assistance or capacity-building programmes.

[60] WT/GC/W/894.

The leadership role of the WTO in partnership with other IGOs will be crucial in the establishment and effective implementation of such a fund, for example, through cooperation with the UNFCCC Secretariat. Further, given that green technologies themselves are in the hands of private entities, the WTO already has a communication channel with such entities to facilitate technology transfer mechanisms.

These three aspects are merely indicative of how the WTO can leverage its 'new' roles to respond to Member demands with respect to the climate crisis and the potential ways in which future work can contribute to the global fight against climate change.

The trade and climate change regimes are no longer considered distinct, and there is today international consensus on their interlinked and interdependent relationship. The new roles of the WTO are means through which the relationship can be one where trade is a useful and necessary tool in combating climate change. Deputy Director General Paugam recently described this as a global 'win–win' approach for trade and environment.[61] He also highlighted the need to embrace new forms of trade cooperation, like plurilateral commitments, flexibilities in the adoption of trade commitments and even commitments that move beyond traditional hard law instruments. We believe the 'new' roles of the WTO are critical in successfully concluding innovative forms of global cooperation to combat climate change.

[61] 'DDG Paugam – WTO at a "Crossroads" in Addressing Trade and Climate Nexus' (*WTO News*, 4 July 2024) www.wto.org/english/news_e/news24_e/ddgjp_04jul24_e.htm.

8

Forever Searching: How Far Can We Go?

CHRISTIAN HÄBERLI

I. From Reciprocity to Multilateralism – And Back to Regionalism?

The Bretton Woods Institutions and the General Agreement on Tariffs and Trade (GATT) 1947 – and the United Nations framework established at the same time – came as a powerful tool for peace after two world wars. On the trade side, replacing reciprocity with multilateral rules provided both a base for unprecedented trade expansion and a sobering assessment of its shortcomings in terms of 'development' and 'fairness'.

The climax of multilateralism was reached on 15 April 1994, when 124 governments and the European Communities convened in Marrakesh to sign 30,000 pages of World Trade Organization (WTO) Agreements and Schedules of Concessions. This 'single undertaking' contained new commitments for trade in goods, services and intellectual property, and only a few holes to be filled by 'review clauses' and 'reform process' undertakings. A brand new dispute settlement mechanism without 'foreign judges' making new rules would provide proper rules reading and interpretation.

Multilateralism remains the *voie royale* of trade and investment liberalisation. However, with the wisdom of hindsight, one might surmise that a more progressive view of comprehensive liberalisation, in particular in North–South agreements, would have avoided today's visceral disputes on the adequacy of 'trade only' agreements ….

As for Thomas Cottier and his co-thinkers, it is probably fair to say that views on multilateralism and regionalism did not stop at recording the numbers, and discussing the (WTO) compatibility, of regional trade agreements (RTAs), including 'mega-regionals'. Early on, they also discussed whether the defensive but imprecise formulation of GATT, Article XXIV allowed a harmonious coexistence of multilateral and regional values and treaties – especially with developing countries.

II. Rethinking Multilateralism versus Regional Trade Liberalisation

Cottier and his World Trade Institute team wondered whether the rapidly increasing number of North–South trade agreements warranted a review of the WTO rules on development aspects of regional trade agreements. They pointed out that 'current RTA disciplines, particularly Article XXIV GATT, serve neither development nor trade needs'. For instance, there is a 'tariff bias' when only liberalisation in goods is taken into account in determining compatibility with the original meaning of GATT, Article XXIV. Moreover, this key provision for the relationship between multilateral and reciprocal trade disciplines 'creates a system of perverse incentives that benefit neither the parties to the agreement, nor, when seen from a proper perspective, third party WTO Members'. Hence, some reform of this provision might be required to bring it up to date. They outlined a series of legal options and a new view of measuring RTA liberalisation in which account is also taken of a broader set of economic interests – including services, aid-for-trade and trade facilitation.[1]

Those were also the years when the gigantic Common Market project of the European Communities made its best progress, pragmatically called 'two steps ahead, one step back'. Geographic expansion confirmed the success of an integrated Europe based on ever-deepening rules securing free trade, investment and movement of persons. For Thomas Cottier, this was also the perfect template for a closer relationship with Switzerland and other stand-alone countries. A customs union being out of reach, these other Europeans united in the European Free Trade Association, set up in 1960 by its then seven Member States for the promotion of free trade and economic integration between its members.

Many RTAs remain cloistered in tariff-only provisions, with a few steps addressing some non-tariff measures, but without subsidy limitations or mutual recognition agreements, let alone common market features. When the EU added a chapter on 'Trade and Sustainable Development' to its Economic Partnership Agreements with African, Caribbean and Pacific partner countries, it purposely excluded dispute settlement from those provisions and avoided a revision of measuring the development impact of these treaties. A vast field of action for future modernisation was left behind – with a silent GATT, Article XXIV.

[1] Lorand Bartels, Sacha Silva, Hadil Hijazi, Hannes Schloemann and Thomas Cottier, 'Re-Thinking Reciprocity: A New Framework for WTO Disciplines on North–South Regional Trade Agreements' (1 May 2013) NCCR Trade Regulation Working Paper No 2013/20/University of Cambridge Faculty of Law Research Paper No 14/2013.

III. The Pragmatic Spirit of the GATT

Ratifications were fast and expectations were high, especially for the trade impact of the new rules. Scholarship had its heyday, and the skies were blue for all traders. World trade expanded. Never mind funny terms like non-trade concerns, development and rural development needs and intellectual property technology transfer. Unfinished business remained, of course. Preambular language and legal loopholes allowed voluntary export restraints and food export restrictions. But all of these would be addressed in new ('development') negotiation rounds. Adjudicators (instead of the General Council) could also clarify unclear rules. Most dispute settlement rulings were duly implemented, albeit at times at the expense of third parties.

IV. Judicial Review: Reading National Law

Article 11 of the WTO's Dispute Settlement Understanding enjoins panels to 'make an objective assessment of the facts'. Cottier repeatedly contributed to the long-debated question on the standards of review, insisting that there is no room for deference to interpretations given by Member States in accordance with their domestic policies and interests. There is a fundamental difference between domestic and international review: adjudication on the level of international law has, in principle, no jurisdiction to construe and interpret domestic rules. Unlike domestic law, it is not a matter of interpreting both constitutional rules and statutory law (and possibly treaty rules in case of direct effect and consistent interpretation). Here, domestic rules are conceptually dealt with as questions of fact and not of law. Whether or not domestic law is in compliance with international obligations is based on a comparison of national law as reasonably stated by the respective member and as interpreted by its authorities and of WTO rules construed and applied by the WTO bodies. Panels and the Appellate Body cannot exclusively rely upon the reading of national law as submitted by the defending party (naturally in an alleged WTO-compatible way), and at least apparent misperceptions and interpretations short of a sound rational basis cannot be accepted. The assessment, therefore, does entail legal analysis, but it has to be dealt with as a matter of evidence, ie as to whether a defending party is in a position to demonstrate the alleged meaning and scope of its own and domestic law challenged by the complainant.[2]

[2] Thomas Cottier, 'Recalibrating the WTO Dispute Settlement System: Towards New Standards of Appellate Review' (2021) 24(3) *Journal of International Economic Law* 515–33; Thomas Cottier and Krista Nadakavukaren Schefer, 'The Relationship Between World Trade Organization Law, National and Regional Law' (1998) 1(1) *Journal of International Economic Law* 83; Krista Nadakavukaren Schefer and Serge Pannatier, 'The Banana Dispute and Implementation of WTO Legal Rulings' (1999) 11(2) *European Legal Developments Bulletin* 16; Thomas Cotter and Krista Nadakavukaren Schefer, 'Non-Violation Complaints in GATT/WTO Dispute Settlement: Past, Present, and Future' in

V. The Battle of Seattle: Just a Glitch?

The first clouds came soon enough, and without multilateralist pundits noticing.

One of the first anti-globalisation movements got together for the Third WTO Ministerial in Seattle, in November 1999. Protests by trade unionists, farmers and anti-genetically modified organism demonstrators clad in Monarch butterflies and peace and human rights activists ended in tear gas clouds instead of a dialogue. A group of trade ministers selected by US Trade Representative Charlene Barshefsky spent four days talking about agriculture in the Green Room before the talks collapsed at 4 am on day 5, with African and other ministers complaining about being treated like lost luggage and without the planned adoption of a negotiating mandate for a new negotiation round.

No such problems occurred when ministers reconvened to adopt the 'Doha Development Agenda' in November 2001 – with post-9/11 bombs falling on Afghanistan only 1000 km away. New and ambitious 'Singapore Issues' (transparency in government procurement, trade facilitation/customs issues, trade and investment, and trade and competition) provided a palatable menu package. The People's Republic of China and Chinese Taipei triumphantly joined as new WTO members.

Other issues were ignored or postponed. Many development, environmental and social concerns went unheeded. More snags came later, after intensive but fruitless negotiations and more ministerial reunions. The (misnomer) 'Doha Development Agenda' was amputated in 2003. The revised Doha Round 'modalities' proposals dated 6 December 2008 failed to obtain a go-ahead to reach a package solution.

No room for development and more coherence? Thomas Cottier never thought so.

VI. More Labour Protection under Trade Law?

In most of his publications, Cottier looks out for more equity and fairness. Adequately addressing labour standards in international trade regulation – a big topic for more than 200 years, and one with many ramifications – requires deference to the notion of public morality and a balance of interests in applying standards of necessity and fair competition. This is a highly sensitive issue in every country, and the tripartite process of the International Labour Organization (ILO) still appears to be the best formalisation of international standards. Looking at *EC – Seals*, Cottier argues that assessing the policy space of members of the WTO allows closer linkages between trade and ILO core labour standards.[3]

Ernst-Ulrich Petersmann (ed), *International Trade Law and the GATT-WTO Dispute Settlement System* (Kluwer Law Publishers, 1997) 145–83.

[3] Thomas Cottier, 'The Implications of EC – Seal Products for the Protection of Core Labour Standards in WTO Law' in Henner Gött (ed), *Labour Standards in International Economic Law* (Springer, 2018) 69–92.

The first and only multilateral trade agreement concluded since the WTO was established, the Trade Facilitation Agreement, entered into force in 2017.

VII. Sectoral Policies Benefiting from WTO Law?

Proposals for bringing trade-relevant sectoral policies into the WTO always faced opposition. For instance, the invitation to the Director General of the International Labour Organization to attend the first WTO Ministerial Meeting in Singapore (1996) had to be cancelled, replaced by a permanent inter-Secretariat dialogue without tangible results. Nevertheless, labour issues popped up in WTO disputes, albeit with very limited success. Labour, to be sure, was always a special topic for Thomas Cottier.

Other labour issues potentially affecting trade appeared in one WTO dispute (USA versus EU and Japan about public procurement of forced labour products in Myanmar) and two bilateral trade disputes (USA versus Guatemala about freedom of association, and EU versus Korea about ILO Convention's compliance in their free trade agreement (FTA)). Vietnam's commitments in this respect towards the USA (a side letter in the Draft Trans-Pacific Partnership Agreement) and the EU (a chapter on trade and sustainable development in the EU–Vietnam Trade Agreement) have not been challenged so far. Several articles report the views taken by Thomas Cottier et al. He repeatedly probed into the trade law impact of forced labour provisions existing under public international law.

VIII. Forced Labour Prohibition with International Economic Law?

Trade lawyers have tried in different ways to bring peremptory labour standards into the fold of multilateral trade disciplines. In her *Habilitationsschrift* completed under the supervision of Thomas Cottier and published in 2007, Christine Kaufmann places the debate under a human rights and international economic law (IEL) perspective starting in 1967, when the UN Economic and Social Council passed Resolution 1235, drawing the line at gross and systematic violations of human rights. This bottom-up approach further developed to define some human rights as being so basic or essential that they must be considered universal (*erga omnes*) obligations or even *ius cogens* proper. Such core labour rights would hence apply to any human activity in the workplace. They would be binding at least for all ratifying ILO members, and, in view of the large number of ILO Member States, come close to being universal, private international law-based obligations for all states.

Cottier and Oesch claim that the 'essence of non-discrimination in international economic law' is the 'creation of equal conditions of competition among domestic and foreign products and competitors, with respect to trade in goods, services, investment and labour'.[4]

IX. Can Switzerland Integrate with the EU Common Market? How?

The Swiss–EU relationship remains at the centre of Cottier's personal, political and legal agenda. He had always wanted more: his *ceterum censeo* was EU accession, but he looked further than full accession in his search for Swiss cosmopolitan policies. Cottier apparently regretted, for example, the lack of a dispute settlement mechanism in the unequal alliance based on the 1972 FTA with the EU (still the main pillar of the Swiss–EU trade treaties). The Swiss vote against joining the European Economic Area Agreement in 1992 also came as a bitter experience in Cottier's moving forward agenda. He had to wait until 1999 and the achievement of the so-called 'Bilaterals II' package to see a big step forward towards a common market.

More coherence remained central in Cottier's thinking, as much as for other reflections on sovereignty and market integration.

A. The Five-Storey House for Cosmopolitans

Many trade-related issues must be addressed in a wider public international law context. The doctrine of the 'five-storey house', taking into account cosmopolitan political theory, is informed by the idea that all layers of governance are of equal importance and reflect human interaction. It no longer makes a fundamental difference between domestic and international law in terms of allocating powers to regulate and enforce. It is similar to the perception of 'sovereignty-modern' developed by the late John H Jackson. It essentially argues that all levels of governance, from local to global, entail human conduct and behaviour, and share basic traits in terms of legal foundations and sources, albeit in very different constellations and compositions. In particular, it assists in distinguishing global, regional, national and local concerns and corresponding public goods. It also helps allocate powers in terms of power-sharing among different layers beyond federalism.[5]

[4] T Cottier, and M Oesch, 'Direct and Indirect Discrimination in WTO Law and EU Law. NCCR Trade Regulation' (Swiss National Centre of Competence in Research, 2011); C Kaufmann, *Globalization and Labour Rights: The Conflict between Core Labour Rights and International Economic Law* (Hart Publishing, 2007) 75.

[5] T Cottier and Z Ahmad (eds), *The Prospects of Common Concern of Humankind in International Law* (Cambridge University Press, 2021) 49.

After the failure of a seven-year 'pre-negotiation' process for a Framework Agreement covering several hundred Swiss–EU agreements, the 2024 decision by the EU Commission and the Federal Council to actually start new negotiations, called 'Bilaterals III', has brought Cottier *emeritus nec invictus* a sigh of relief – including a new approach for dispute settlement without 'foreign judges'.

B. Bilaterals III – A Fair Deal for Switzerland and the EU!

Securing market access to the common market and supplying security for Switzerland are paramount conditions for the most integrated European country after Luxembourg. This coming negotiation includes education and research, electricity, food safety, health and a better integration into the European labour market. It promises participation in decision-making and dispute settlement based on bilateral treaty law – without those foreign judges that a legendary William Tell had thrown into a stormy Lake Lucerne back in 1291.[6]

X. Restoring Trust Badly Needed

With the slowly but persistently darkening clouds over the multilateral trading system, where could academia take the lead? In 2018, Cottier contributed to Peter Van den Bossche's Festschrift on 'restoring trust in trade' with his ideas on equitable trade.

A. Equity as a Precondition

The global financial crisis eroded trust in the international trade regime, which was also suffering from the mood of Brexit and the Trump administration's unilateral trade policies. Restoring trust in the international trading system is essential to prevent the rise of economic nationalism and beggar-thy-neighbour policies, which history has shown to be a threat to global welfare and peace.

We can get back to a 'trustworthy' rules-based multilateral trading system, which has left a lasting legacy, by focusing on: (i) a robust institutional framework that promotes the rule of law over power politics; (ii) safeguarding the integrity and effectiveness of trade dispute settlement; and (iii) ensuring that

[6] Thomas Cottier, 'Die Bilateralen III sind ein faires Bündnis' (*Vereinigung La Suisse en Europe*, 5 February 2024) https://suisse-en-europe.ch/die-bilateralen-iii-sind-ein-faires-buendnis-von-thomas-cottier/. For earlier discussions about 'foreign judges', *cf* Thomas Cottier and Krista Nadakavukaren Schefer, 'Switzerland: The Challenge of Direct Democracy' in John H Jackson and Alan Sykes (eds), *Implementing the Uruguay Round* (Oxford University Press, 1997) 334–63.

substantive international trade rules appropriately balance trade and non-trade interests.[7]

New concerns and new issues cropped up continuously. Here is just a quick look at environmental concerns and the climate agreement.

B. Environment and Climate: Justifying 'Good' Protectionism?

Environmental concerns and global warming brought new tools under the name of 'noble' or 'good' protectionism. The EU Green Deal, announced in 2019, is a 'train' of over 50 policy proposals providing a framework for the EU to reach its carbon neutrality targets without losing competitiveness and avoiding carbon leakage. It includes the 'Fit-for-55' climate package published in July 2021. The EU Emission Trading System (ETS) will be revised and extended to new sectors, including the transportation sector. In this context, the Carbon Border Adjustment Mechanism was proposed as a new mechanism to complement the EU ETS and gradually replace the ETS-free allowances to prevent the risk of carbon leakage.

Cottier produced multiple texts, lecturing students and coaching PhD candidates for these concerns. He recognised the basic obligations of states and technology holders, comprising not only that of international cooperation and duties to negotiate, but also unilateral duties to act to enhance the potential of public international law to produce appropriate public goods.[8]

Perhaps the most important WTO agreement for Switzerland in economic terms is the Agreement on Trade-Related Aspects of Intellectual Property Rights (TRIPS Agreement).

C. Intellectual Property Reforms for More Development?

One of the chief architects of the TRIPS Agreement, Cottier never let go of the need to develop this treaty with a special interest for Switzerland. He often claimed that a good regulatory framework for intellectual property would help home states, foreign and local businesses to reinforce systemic, substantive and enforcement-related issues arising from plurilateralism (versus multilateralism for developing countries). At the same time, Cottier is always aware of the TRIPS

[7] Thomas Cottier, 'The Prospects of Equity in International Economic Law' in Denise Prévost, Iveta Alexovicova and Jens Hillebrand Pohl (eds), *Restoring Trust in Trade: Liber Amicorum in Honour of Peter Van den Bossche* (Hart Publishing, 2018) 119–38.

[8] Thomas Cottier, 'Preparing for Structural Reform in the WTO' (2007) 10(3) *Journal of International Economic Law* 497; Thomas Cottier and Sofya Matteotti-Berkutova, 'International Environmental Law and the Evolving Concept of "Common Concern of Mankind"' in Thomas Cottier, Olga Nartova and Sadeq Z Bigdeli (eds), *International Trade Regulation and the Mitigation of Climate Change* (Cambridge University Press, 2009) 21–47.

objective ('to the mutual advantage of producers and users of technological knowledge and in a manner conducive to social and economic welfare' – Article 7) of the public health challenge (Article 31*bis*/compulsory licences), and of the never fulfilled obligation of developed countries to 'provide incentives to enterprises and institutions in their territories for the purpose of promoting and encouraging technology transfer to LDC Members' (Article 66/2). This development dimension kept him permanently on the lookout for fair solutions – including through better protection of new inventions.[9]

But this was also the time of RTAs and 'mega-regionals' claiming compatibility with GATT, Article XXIV (except the Transatlantic Trade and Investment Partnership), bilateral investment treaty expansion and unfettered new trade arrangements, sometimes at the limits of most favoured nation (MFN) treatment and national treatment (NT).

D. Migration: Mission Impossible?

International regulation of the three key international production factors – trade, investment and migration – remains highly fragmented, even contradictory and self-defeating. Cottier and Sieber-Gasser show how migration regulation on the international level is lagging behind that of trade and investment. Stronger coordination, consideration of migration in trade and investment policy and stronger international cooperation in migration will provide the foundations for a coherent international architecture in the field.[10]

Still, the community of traders, governments and scholars remained optimistic. Dispute case initiations and settlements reached an all-time high, with over 200 cases in each of the years 1998–2000. Besides recording and commenting on the development of this peaceful conflict settlement tool, Thomas Cottier was also one of the most prolific WTO panellists of all time.

XI. Trade Wars and Solutions

The first across-the-board break-in into the holy MFN provision of GATT, Article I came when US President Donald Trump thought he could double the

[9] Thomas Cottier and Marion Panizzon, 'Legal Perspectives on Traditional Knowledge: The Case for Intellectual Property Protection' (2004) 7(2) *Journal of International Economic Law* 371; Thomas Cottier, 'The Doha Waiver and Its Effects on the Nature of the TRIPS System and on Competition Law: The Impact of Human Rights' (2007) NCCR Trade Regulation Working Paper No2006/21; Pedro Roffe et al, 'Current Alliances in International Intellectual Property Lawmaking: The Emergence and Impact of Mega-Regionals' (CEIPI & ICTSD, 15 September 2017) Global Perspectives and Challenges for the Intellectual Property System No 4.

[10] Thomas Cottier and Charlotte Sieber-Gasser, Labour Migration, 'Trade and Investment: From Fragmentation to Coherence' in *The Palgrave Handbook of International Labour Migration* (Palgrave Macmillan, 2015).

USA's bound tariffs for imports from China (and other countries). The punitive tariffs under sections 232 and 301 (which he called an 'easy win') hit the fan in the dispute settlement body (DSB) with a reinvented national security interpretation of Article XXI. China quickly retaliated in kind and added a DSB complaint over a slew of US state-level renewable energy programmes.

XII. National Security: Fake Only?

For decades, GATT, Article XXI and General Agreement on Trade in Services (GATS), Article XIV*bis* were invoked only to (unsuccessfully) justify balance-of-payment measures protecting sectoral interests or the domestic production of military boots. This almost benign neglect of a potentially powerful trade blocker ended when governments used trade restrictions and prohibitions to fight real (and alleged) wars. Their claims that security issues were involved which could not be addressed otherwise never succeeded. But when big countries like Russia and the USA fail to solve their problems with either wars or diplomatic means, a dispute settlement ruling may be the most efficient (and least expensive) way of solving a problem, assuming, of course, compliance.[11]

Cottier thought that due weight should be given to the adjective 'essential' before 'security interests', but that states should be given broad rights to define 'security interests'. Iryna Bogdanova explores in her PhD thesis, completed under the supervision of Thomas Cottier and published in 2022, the legality of unilateral economic sanctions, ie those imposed by individual states without authorisation of the UN Security Council, under international law. She considers that GATT, Article XXI and GATS, Article XIV*bis* prescribe the security exception quite clearly. The 'self-judging' nature of the national security determination of such scope inevitably includes a discussion of the self-judging nature of the clause. The panel report in *Russia – Traffic in Transit* distinguished between objective and subjective elements of the national security clause, as well as identifying the scope of the reviewability of the subjective elements.[12]

The negative impact of unilateral coercive measures on the enjoyment of human rights came as collateral damage way beyond the multilateral trading system. The costs of the trade war to the USA increased rapidly, however, especially to US agriculture. In 2018, the US Department of Agriculture authorised

[11] Panagiotis Delimatsis and Thomas Cottier, 'Article XIV bis GATS: Security Exceptions' (2008) 6 *Max Planck Commentaries on World Trade Law, WTO – Trade in Services* 329.

[12] Iryna Bogdanova, *World Trade Institute Advanced Studies Vol 9. Unilateral Sanctions in International Law and the Enforcement of Human Rights. The Impact of the Principle of Common Concern of Humankind* (Brill Nijhoff, 2022) https://boris.unibe.ch/173691/. See also Iryna Bogdanova, *Human Rights and Unilateral Economic Sanctions: A New Perspective on a Twisted Relationship*, European Yearbook on Human Rights (Intersentia, 2023) 171–203. For earlier discussions about 'national security' *cf* Michael J Hahn, 'Vital Interests and the Law of GATT: An Analysis of GATT''s Security Exception' (1991) 12 *Michigan Journal of International Law* 558, https://repository.law.umich.edu/mjil/vol12/iss3/3.

$12 billion for three programmes aimed at shielding US farmers and ranchers from retaliatory tariffs imposed on US goods. Together with other farm (and electoral) support programmes, the USA thus probably exceeded WTO bindings starting in 2019.[13]

XIII. Beyond the Boxes for *Ius Cogens*

On his way forward to the highest circle of scholars *emeritus*, Cottier launched a multi-year and multi-author research programme probing *de lege ferenda* borders of IEL, with help from international law, showing the emergence of new principles of law.

A. Common Concern of Humankind in International Law

Traditional treaties are rooted in the pursuit of national interests based upon reciprocity and do not generally accept a 'responsibility to protect' (R2P) by governments and corporations. According to Cottier, and his team of young researchers, climate change, protection of biodiversity, marine pollution, genetic resources and cultural diversity require essentially one-sided efforts. Benefits are not directly mutual, and the essential element of reciprocity in terms of interests and benefits is lacking. This incentivises unilateral policies of free riding and attitudes of wait and see, and leaves adjustments to others. The sustainable production of such global public goods requires new forms of cooperation and commitments, and a multilevel governance agreement. It implies some kind of enhanced commitment and obligations to international cooperation, starting with cogent law (*ius cogens*) and reinforcing the shift of classical international law from coexistence to cooperation, recourse to equity, public trust doctrine, community interests, preserving peace and security, and ultimately to integration and legal harmonisation in specific regulatory areas addressing shared problems and transboundary preoccupations.

The landmark Cambridge publication edited by Cottier and Ahmad contains seven areas of application in international law showing the emerging new Principle of Law:[14]

- Trade-Related Measures to Spread Low-Carbon Technologies: A Common Concern–Based Approach (by Zaker Ahmad)
- Marine Plastic Pollution as a Common Concern of Humankind (by Judith Schäli)

[13] In 2019, Joseph Glauber described the US Market Facilitation Program and found that, despite massive increases in domestic support, US agricultural exports to China fell from almost $22 billion in fiscal year (FY) 2017 to $7.3 billion projected for FY 2019: Joseph W Glauber', Agricultural Trade Aid' (American Enterprise Institute, November 2019).

[14] Cottier and Ahmad (n 5).

- Exploring the Recognition of New Common Concerns of Humankind: The Example of the Distribution of Income and Wealth within States (by Alexander Beyleveld)
- Reshaping the Law of Economic Sanctions for Human Rights Enforcement: The Potential of Common Concern of Humankind (by Iryna Bogdanova)
- Migration as a Common Concern of Humankind (by Thomas Cottier and Rosa Maria Losada)
- International Monetary Stability as a Common Concern of Humankind (by Lucia Satragno)
- Financial Stability as a Common Concern of Humankind (by Federico Lupo-Pasini)

A rich harvest for future interaction and reality checks between academia and policy-making at both national and international levels![15]

XIV. Conclusion: How Far do We Have to Go?

This 'vertical' glance through some of Cottier's works is not a summary in a nutshell. It only tries to show where academia can play its fact-finding and advisory role for rule-makers and other opinion leaders. After six fruitless trade and climate ministerial conferences, the time has come for academia to call a spade a spade, letting governments reassemble at the level of commitments required by present circumstances and challenges to humankind. Today's trade scholars need to address fragmentation and pluralism, not speculating whether the glass of WTO rules is half full or half empty. Work starts at home. Academia must help trade and investment regulators find their place in a changing world where a little-qualified prohibition of discrimination cannot be the only yardstick. Thomas Cottier's preferred way is for mending IEL and dispute settlement with the help of Public International Law, whereas for me, governments must acknowledge that the present rules are a part of the problem. International governance is the first victim of the refusal to initiate negotiations on fundamental problems. Today, most governments neglect even the most burning issues, such as standard harmonisation or mutual recognition agreements for 'like' products and processing methods. We thus need to find new ways to avoid 'green subsidy' rows, whereby every state subsidising and promoting the decarbonisation agenda is accused of distorting trade. This underscores the need for the whole scholarship to provide facts, data assessments and legal opinions on the options available inside and outside the box.

[15] Thomas Cottier and Krista Nadakavukaren Schefer, 'Responsibility to Protect (R2P) and the Emerging Principle of Common Concern' in Peter Hilpold (ed), *Die Schutzverantwortung (R2P): Ein Paradigmenwechsel in der Entwicklung des Internationalen Rechts?* (Martinus Nijhoff, 2013) 123–42.

PART II

Regional Trade Relations between Unequals: Switzerland, the EU and Beyond

9

From Rue de Martignac to Hallerstrasse – A Vision for Europe

CHRISTINE KAUFMANN

> Il faut une action profonde, réelle, immédiate et dramatique qui change les choses et fasse entrer dans la réalité les espoirs auxquels les peuples sont sur le point de ne plus croire.
>
> (Jean Monnet, 3 May 1950)

I. Quai D'orsay, 9 May 1950

On 9 May 1950, the French Ministry of Foreign Affairs announced a press conference at very short notice to take place later in the day. At six o'clock in the evening, Robert Schuman, the French Minister of Foreign Affairs,[1] took the floor in the Salon de l'Horloge at Quai d'Orsay, the ministry's headquarters, to open the briefing:

> Il n'est plus question de vaines paroles, mais d'un acte hardi, d'un acte constructif. La France a agi et les conséquences de son action peuvent être immenses. Nous espérons qu'elles le seront. Elle a agi essentiellement pour la paix. Pour que la paix puisse vraiment courir sa chance, il faut, d'abord, qu'il y ait une Europe.[2]

He then moved on to explain a proposal that the French government had just agreed upon a few hours before that was to be made at the upcoming meeting of the Western allied powers the next day.

[1] For a summary of Robert Schuman's life and career, see Rafael Domingo, 'Robert Schuman' in Olivier Descamps and Rafael Domingo (eds), *Great Christian Jurists in French History* (Cambridge University Press, 2019) 402.

[2] 'It is no longer a question of idle words, but of bold action, constructive action. France has acted, and the consequences of its action could be immense. We hope that they will be. France has acted essentially for peace. If peace is really to have a chance, there must first be a Europe.' François Fontaine, '30 jours qui ébranlèrent l'Europe' (1975) *30 jours d'Europe* no 202, 3 (available also in English at http://www.cvce.eu).

While all these preparations had taken place in secrecy and took most journalists as well as ministers by surprise, two days before, Robert Schuman had sent a letter to the German Chancellor, Konrad Adenauer. In the letter, he had informed the Chancellor of his intention to submit a Declaration on the relationship between France and Germany for approval to the French government and to make the decision public on 9 May 1950. He explained the spirit of the Declaration:

> La paix Mondiale ne saurait être sauvegardée sans des efforts créateurs à la mesure des dangers qui la menacent.
>
> La contribution qu'une Europe organisée et vivante peut apporter à la civilisation est indispensable au maintien des relations pacifiques … L'Europe ne se fera pas d'un coup ni dans une construction d'ensemble. Elle se fera si des réalisation concrètes créent d'abord une solidarité de fait.[3]

In order to overcome the historical opposition between Germany and France, which Schuman identified as a key obstacle to a lasting peace in Europe, the Declaration (which became known as the Schuman Plan) proposed to place the Franco-German production of steel and coal as a whole under a common High Authority, to be established in the framework of a new organisation. This organisation would also be open to other European countries.[4] It would be of a supranational nature and vest the new common High Authority with decision-making powers.[5] The idea was to build on 'solidarity in production' in order to reach the higher goal of positioning Europe as actively contributing to raising standards of living and promoting peace worldwide. Moreover, pooling the production of coal and steel under a new supranational body should pave the way towards the foundation of a European federation as a key prerequisite for maintaining peace.[6] With regard to the relationship between France and Germany, it was hoped that the coal and steel pool would make war between the two countries not only unthinkable but de facto impossible.[7]

Eventually, the Schuman Plan led to the establishment of the European Community for Coal and Steel in 1951,[8] the first building block for what later became the European Community and the EU. Five years after the end of WWII, it thus marked the birth of European integration and was a key 'constitutional moment' for Europe.[9] Schuman himself, while far from promoting his own role,

[3] Robert Schuman, Letter to Konrad Adenauer, 7 May 1950, reprinted in Fondation Jean Monnet pour l'Europe, Centre de recherches européennes (ed), *L'Europe une longue marche* (1985) 60–61.

[4] European Commission: Directorate-General for Communication, *La Déclaration Schuman du 9 mai 1950* [*The Schuman Declaration of 9 May 1950*] (Publications Office, 2015) https://data.europa.eu/doi/10.2775/065.

[5] Robert Schuman, *Pour l'Europe* (Nagel, 1963) 136–37.

[6] Déclaration Schuman (n 4).

[7] Raymond Aron, 'Le Pool industriel franco-allemand, II. L'Autorité Internationale' *Le Figaro* (7 June 1950).

[8] Treaty instituting the European Coal and Steel Community (original in French, German and Dutch), signed at Paris on 18 April 1951 by Belgium, France, Germany, Italy, Luxemburg and the Netherlands, in force from 23 July 1952 to 23 July 2002, 261 UNTS 140.

[9] Joseph HH Weiler, 'The Transformation of Europe' (1991) 100 *Yale Law Journal* 2403, 2478.

considered the Plan as revolutionary in terms of its design and range but peaceful in the way it was undertaken.[10] 'Realist' observers, however, particularly in the USA, considered the Plan to be 'unreal and presumptively unworkable'.[11] In their view, the idea that countries in Europe would surrender powers over their coal and steel industries and, thereby, parts of their sovereignty to a supranational body could not be regarded as a serious proposal. Similar arguments can be heard in the current discussion on Switzerland's relationship with the EU.[12] How was it possible, then, that in 1950, the 'peaceful' revolution would eventually prevail?

To answer this question, we need to travel a few blocks from the prestigious salon de l'horloge at Quai d'Orsay to offices on the rue de Martignac.

II. The 'Coup' of Rue de Martignac[13]

A meeting of the three Western allied powers in Washington, DC in the autumn of 1949 resulted in an agreement that France should be tasked with defining a common policy approach towards Germany, but it did not give any indication of how this could be achieved. For Robert Schuman, who received the mandate on behalf of France, overcoming the political deadlock in the relationship between France and Germany had long been a matter close to his heart, a sense which he shared with German Chancellor Adenauer. While he was convinced that bringing the coal resources of the Saar to the European level would be the key, there was no clear plan as to how this could be organised. Public opinion was split, but the general sense was that even if moving in this direction were to be considered, now would certainly not be the time.[14] Nevertheless, on 18 April 1950, the political directorate at Quai d'Orsay made it clear that acting defensively was not an option but that courageous initiatives ('initiatives audacieuses') should be developed instead.[15] Not surprisingly, at this stage, Schuman's team was not in a position to provide an adequate response. This was the moment when Jean Monnet, the head of the Planning Commission in charge of a national modernisation and development plan for France after the war, became active. Eventually, he and his team would bring Schuman's vision to life.[16]

[10] Schuman (n 5) 27–28; see also Domingo (n 1) 411.

[11] Raymond Vernon, 'The Schuman Plan – Sovereign Powers of the European Coals and Steel Community' (1953) 45 *American Journal of International Law* 183.

[12] For an in-depth (and demystifying) discussion, see Thomas Cottier and André Holenstein, *Die Souveränität der Schweiz in Europa: Mythen, Realitäten und Wandel* (Stämpfli, 2021); Matthias Oesch, *Die Schweiz und die Europäische Union* (EIZ Publishing, 2020).

[13] Fontaine (n 2) 3.

[14] ibid 4–5.

[15] Archives du ministère de l'Europe et des Affaires étrangères, France, 235 QO/57 Secrétariat général, vol 57, cited in Jean-Marie Palayret, 'Un saut dans l'inconnu? Pierre Uri, le Plan Schuman et les négociations du traité de Paris' in Alessandro Giacone (ed), *Pierre Uri* (Institut de la gestion publique et du développement économique, 2023) 71, para 7, https://doi.org/10.4000/books.igpde.17231.

[16] Boris Hazoumé, 'Jean Monnet, "l'inspirateur"' (2016) 33(3) *Inflexions* 31; François Fontaine, 'May 9, 1950, A Behind-the-Scene Account of What Happened' (1970) 134 *European Community* 4.

In 1946, the Planning Commission had moved into a small private house on the left bank of the river Seine at 18 rue de Martignac. Jean Monnet described the new office site as an 'island of peace' in the midst of ministry buildings. In his view, the baroque setting, with its labyrinthine corridors and stairs, contrasted with the intellectual order and rationality that the Commission was supposed to represent.[17] However, since it was, in the words of a staff member, as unbureaucratic a setting as could be, it seemed to fit well with the Commission's intention not to be a bureaucracy.[18]

Indeed, while walking in the Alps in April 1950, Monnet reflected on how this sense of being overwhelmed by challenges and obstacles given the current state of Europe could be overcome and what a response to the call from Quai d'Orsay could look like. What initiative could France take?

> D'une pareille situation, il n'est qu'un moyen de sortir: une action concrète et résolue, portant sur un point limité mais décisif, qui entraîne sur ce point un changement fondamental et, de proche en proche, modifie les termes mêmes de l'ensemble des problèmes … Il faut changer le cours des événements; pour cela, il faut changer l'esprit des hommes. Seule une action immédiate portant sur un point essential peut changer l'état statique actuel. Il faut une action profonde, réelle, immédiate et dramatique qui change les choses et fasse entrer dans la réalité les espoirs auxquels les peuples sont sur le point de ne plus croire … Il faut en changer les données en les transformant.[19]

Back at the office, Monnet started to work on a draft, together with Étienne Hirsch, Pierre Uri and Paul Reuter.[20] The team brought together a unique interdisciplinary expertise: Étienne Hirsch had an industrial background, with experience in the coal and steel sector; Pierre Uri brought in his economic expertise; and Paul Reuter was a highly renowned professor of international law.[21] The timing was critical, as a meeting of the Atlantic Council was scheduled for 10 May, during which the economic situation of Germany would have to be discussed. Any initiative to be launched then would therefore have to be accepted by the French government prior to the meeting, ie by 9 May.

The team discussed the general lines of action that Monnet had developed during his stay in the Alps and then moved on to elaborate on them. Discussions

[17] Jean Monnet, *Mémoires* (Fayard, 1976) 349.

[18] Jean-François Gravier, quoted in ibid 349.

[19] Jean Monnet, 'Note de réflexion, 3 mai 1950' (Fondation Jean Monnet pour l'Europe, Archives de Jean Monnet, AMG 1/1/5) 1–5. There is only one way out of such a situation: concrete, resolute action on a limited but decisive point. An action which brings about a fundamental change on that point and, step by step, alters the very nature of the problems … We need to change the course of events; to do that, we need to change people's minds … You have to change things by transforming them. Only immediate action on a vital point can change the current static state of affairs. What is needed is profound, real, immediate and dramatic action that will bring about real change and turn into reality the hopes that people are on the verge of losing … The facts must be changed by transforming them' (translation by the author based on translation DeepL).

[20] For an overview of the drafting process Palayret (n 15) para 2.

[21] Raymond Poidevin and Dirk Spierenburg, *Histoire de la Haute Autorité de la Ceca* (Bruylant, 1993) 10.

were far from easy. Based on the expertise of the team, each element was questioned and evaluated in depth, before eventually finding its way into the draft text:[22] Hirsch would ensure that the Declaration adequately reflected the current state and needs of the industry; Reuter focused on institutional aspects and thereby paved the way to the establishment of the High Authority. Last but not least, fully in line with Monnet's ambition to be as concrete as possible, Uri added structure and clarity to the text, for instance regarding the High Authority's jurisdiction.[23] In addition, he ensured coherence with regard to economic aspects, which would later allow for a seamless development of further elements, such as the notion of the common market. A further important element for the realisation of the Plan was Uri's idea to include transitional provisions.[24]

After nine drafts, the final version was ready for approval. Every word in it builds on the opening paragraph, which states that world peace cannot be safeguarded without the making of creative efforts proportionate to the dangers that threaten it. One of the key characteristics of the Declaration is that it does not stop at declaring the vision but translates it into practical political steps. Every word was weighed by the authors to facilitate acceptance by the countries and, at the same time, prevent loopholes and opportunities for turning back. Jean Monnet had originally intended to include a sentence for describing the relationship between sovereignty and European unity in abstract terms, by stating the intention 'to breach the rampart of national sovereignty, then lead the European states through the gap towards unity and federation'. However, along the drafting process, the authors decided that such a statement would raise unnecessary fears and concerns rather than serve the purpose. Instead, therefore, they opted to follow up on this theme with concrete proposals such as the design of the High Authority.[25]

In addition, as the drafting proceeded, the text moved away from addressing Germany only. Clearly, stabilising relations between Germany and France and eliminating the risk of another war between them was one of the key drivers for the Plan. This goal was ensured with three key elements. First, the Plan emphasised that France and Germany (as the biggest European countries) would need to work together and be at the heart of any European unity. Second, the creation of a single market for coal and steel would tie Germany's economy to the West. Third, the establishment of a common Higher Authority would provide a peaceful institutional setting for the industry.[26]

From the second draft on, though, participation by other European countries was included to complement the gradual extension to other areas of the economy, which had been included from the beginning. While coal and steel were

[22] Palayret (n 15) para 9.
[23] Éric Roussel, *Jean Monnet* (Fayard, 1995) 529.
[24] Monnet, *Mémoires* (n 17) 437.
[25] Fontaine (n 2) 6.
[26] William Diebold Jr, 'Imponderables of the Schuman Plan' (1959) 29 *Foreign Affairs* 114, 117.

the imminent issues to be addressed, they also served as an instrument to work towards a more ambitious plan.

Schuman and Monnet were fully aware that, as convincing and coherent as the Plan seemed to them, it was far from clear whether it would be accepted by the French Council of ministers, let alone how other countries would react. In what again turned out to be a pragmatic move, Schuman presented – and downplayed – the Plan to his colleagues as a necessary move by France, a goodwill gesture towards the other Western countries. Clearly, the style of the document was unusual, and there had not been enough time for an in-depth consultation with the ministries. In fact, civil servants in the French administration received the proposal at the same time as the other countries did – adding another 'revolutionary' element to the process.[27]

Today, we know that the Schuman Plan was a success in paving the way towards European integration. It is, therefore, worthwhile to ask what lessons can be drawn from the process. What were the ingredients for its success? It seems that three key elements can be identified: first, a clear vision indicating the overall goal; second, a focus on the practical and political implementation, combined with the stamina to discuss and test different options with a view to political acceptance; and third, the interdisciplinarity in the drafting process which ensured that the proposal was politically, economically and legally sound. These ingredients require people willing to bring in their expertise, question their assumptions in the light of other disciplines and views, and collaborate in the interest of the result.

Much of what has been said so far seems to resonate with Thomas Cottier's manifold activities throughout his career. So let us now move from Paris to Berne, from 18 rue de Martignac to Hallerstrasse 6.

III. The Spirit Travels: From Rue de Martignac to Hallerstrasse

After the conclusion of the Uruguay Round of multilateral trade negotiations, convened under the auspices of the General Agreement on Tariffs and Trade (GATT), it was clear to Thomas Cottier that the newly defined international trade law regime would not have traction on the ground without lawyers and economists being trained to understand and apply the new rules. Bringing the vision of free trade to life, therefore, required a practical initiative. In a very unusual move for the Swiss academic landscape, Thomas Cottier initiated the founding of the World Trade Institute (WTI) in Berne in 1995. Given the complexities of the Swiss academic landscape, the institute was initially integrated not as a formal institute in a university, but as a self-standing institution that partnered with the Universities of Bern, Fribourg and Neuchâtel. From the beginning, Thomas

[27] For a detailed account, see Fontaine (n 2) 3.

Cottier was convinced that a purely legal approach would not suffice to address the challenges of the new area of the international trade regime, but that economists and political scientists needed to be part of the conversation and, thus, of the new institute.

Dialogue and exchange need space, not only intellectually, but also physically. Similar to Jean Monnet, Thomas Cottier was, therefore, looking for a location. Close to the University of Berne, in the heart of the capital, would be ideal, but some safe distance would be appreciated. It was fortunate that the new WTI could move into the building of a former factory that was within walking distance to the University, as well as to the headquarters of the government and the Parliament. With its lofty open working space and offices with glass walls, the WTI has since then provided an ideal environment for breaking disciplinary silos.

Similar to 18 rue de Martignac, Hallerstrasse 6 quickly developed into an ecosystem of its own, while at the same time ensuring that it would not act in isolation from other actors and communities relevant to the topic. A key instrument to bring the world to the WTI has been an educational programme. The Master of International Law and Economics (MILE) programme was launched in 1999. Bringing to life the vision of the new international trade regime with the newly founded World Trade Organization (WTO) in 1995 required an interdisciplinary approach. However, this was not the way traditional academic education worked at the time. With the MILE, the WTI covered new ground by bringing academic communities together right from the start, requiring the participants as well as the teachers to find a common language and engage with diverse approaches across disciplines to current challenges in international trade. The programme quickly became the flagship programme of the institute and beyond. It was the first international interdisciplinary academic degree on international trade.

However, the WTI would not stop at serving as an institution for education, but also engaged in research and advising policy-makers. A milestone for bringing interdisciplinary training to the next level was again an initiative launched by Thomas Cottier: the National Centre of Competence for Research (NCCR) project, 'International Trade Regulation: From Fragmentation to Coherence'. Funded by the Swiss National Research Foundation, it brought together researchers from all parts of the world who, over 12 years, from 2005 to 2017, looked into solutions for overcoming the challenges of a highly fragmented international trade regime from a legal, economic and political science perspective. International trade and trade liberalisation were analysed with a view to their role of serving as a means to an end by increasing welfare, raising standards of living worldwide and eventually contributing to peace.[28] Apart from the more than 1000 publications, the most important impact of the project was the training of a new generation of academics to tackle key societal issues, including the increasing politicisation of trade and investment, and the rise of populism and nationalism from an interdisciplinary perspective.

[28] Thomas Cottier and Alexandra Dengg, 'Der Beitrag des freien Handels zum Weltfrieden' (2007) 81 *Basler Schriften zur europäischen Integration* 41.

Today, many of the participants of the MILE programme and members of the NCCR project work in governments and trade administrations, or are advising governments on international trade issues. In this role, they are facing similar challenges as did the team working at 18 rue de Martignac at the time. Thanks to Thomas Cottier's vision and his efforts to implement it in practice, they are well equipped to successfully navigate this complex environment.

In addition, and linked with the developments at the WTO, Europe has played an important role in the work conducted at Hallerstrasse 6. Even before the completion of the Uruguay Round, Thomas Cottier had emphasised the role of the GATT for European integration.[29] The founding of the World Trade Institute coincided with Switzerland redefining its relationship with the EU after the country's accession to the European Economic Area (EEA) was rejected in a popular vote on 6 December 1992.

Fully aware of the complexities that such an endeavour would entail, Thomas Cottier had strongly supported Switzerland's accession to the EEA. Unlike many observers at the time, he saw it not as an isolated move, but as a 'quantum leap' to position the country in an increasingly dynamic and globalised trade environment.[30] Looking back, this thinking very much resonates with Schuman's and Monnet's approach to shaping the European Coal and Steel Community as a starting, if not stepping, point towards a general common market.

During the following decades of bilateralism between Switzerland and the EU, Thomas Cottier would not lose sight of his broader vision: the bilateral sectoral agreements between Switzerland and the EU were not goals in themselves, but an instrument and important transitory step towards more integration.[31]

At the time of writing, as the multilateral system and a rule-based international order are under threat, Switzerland is again at a critical juncture in its relationship with the EU and in defining its position as a neutral country. It could, therefore, hardly be more timely to recall the opening paragraphs of the Schuman Plan calling for creative efforts and active state measures.

In the light of the spirit travelling from rue de Martignac to Hallerstrasse, two initiatives launched and supported by Thomas Cottier warrant mentioning.

First is the *Initiative for Europe – for a strong Switzerland in Europe*. Thomas Cottier substantially contributed to this popular initiative, which was launched in April 2024 and builds on the long history of Swiss–European relations.[32] It aims at

[29] Thomas Cottier, 'Die Bedeutung des GATT im Prozess der Europäischen Integration' in Olivier Jacot-Guillarmod, Dietrich Schindler and Thomas Cottier (eds), *EG-Recht und schweizerische Rechtsordnung: Föderalismus, Demokratie, Neutralität, GATT und europäische Integration*, Beihefte zur Zeitschrift für Schweizerisches Recht vol 10 (Helbing und Lichtenhahn Verlag, 1990) 139.

[30] Thomas Cottier, 'Recht und Macht im Europäischen Wirtschaftsraum' (1992) *Aktuelle Juristische Praxis* 1204, 1205.

[31] Thomas Cottier, 'Das Ende der bilateralen Ära: Rechtliche Auswirkungen der WTO auf die Integrationspolitik der Schweiz' in Thomas Cottier and Alwin R Kopše (eds), *Der Beitritt der Schweiz zur Europäischen Union/L'adhésion de la Suisse à l'Union européenne* (Schulthess, 1998) 87.

[32] Thomas Cottier and Rachel Liechti-McKee Abbott, 'Die Beziehungen der Schweiz zur Europäischen Union: Eine kurze Geschichte differenzieller und schrittweiser Integration' (2007) 81 *Basler Schriften zur europäischen Integration* 5.

breaking the current deadlock in the political discussion about the future relationship between Switzerland and the EU by defining in the Swiss Constitution first the federal government's active role regarding European integration and second the concrete means on how this role is to be implemented – with treaties between Switzerland and the EU. As shown below, a third paragraph addresses concerns about key societal values. Finally, a transition provision contains a concrete roadmap for achieving these ambitious goals. Should the initiative have reached the necessary verified 100,000 signatures by 2 October 2025, it will be submitted to Parliament for discussion. Following this discussion, if not withdrawn, it will eventually be subject to a popular vote. With the approval of the majority of citizens and the cantons (federal states), the Constitution would then be amended accordingly.

> *Initiative for Europe – for a strong Switzerland in Europe*[33]
>
> Article 54a Constitution
>
> [1] The Confederation shall actively participate in European integration.
>
> [2] To this end, it shall conclude international treaties with the European Union that enable secure and viable participation in the freedoms of the European internal market and in other areas of European cooperation, in particular culture, education, research and climate protection.
>
> [3] Within the framework of the applicable treaties, the Confederation and the cantons shall ensure the protection of fundamental democratic and federal values, natural resources and social balance in the community and on the labour market.
>
> Transitional provisions to Article 54a
>
> [1] The Federal Council shall conclude the necessary treaties with the European Union without delay at the latest after the adoption of Article 54a by the People and the Cantons. It shall submit the treaties to the Federal Assembly for approval within 12 months of the conclusion of the negotiations. At the same time, the Federal Council shall propose the measures required to implement Article 54a paragraph 3. In particular, these shall ensure that the European principle of equal working conditions for equal work in the same place is effectively and permanently implemented in Switzerland.

The initiative aims to position Switzerland in an active role in Europe and emphasises the importance of European cooperation not only for the welfare of Switzerland, but worldwide. Although this is not explicitly stated in the text of the initiative, it becomes clear from the context: the proposed Article 54a will – if accepted – complement Article 54, para 2, which reads as follows:[34]

> [2] The Confederation shall ensure that the independence of Switzerland and its welfare is safeguarded; it shall in particular assist in the alleviation of need and poverty in the world and promote respect for human rights and democracy, the peaceful co-existence of peoples as well as the conservation of natural resources.

[33] Translation by the author. Official text published in Bundesblatt 2024 733.
[34] This translation is provided by the federal government for information purposes only and has no legal force.

The similarities with the approach taken in the development of the Schuman Plan are striking. Similar to the Schuman Plan, the proposal looks at the potential of of European integration as a contribution to world peace, whilst being firmly grounded in the form of bilateral agreements under international law and the assignment of respective responsibilities.

There are, of course, other views on what the position of Switzerland in a globalised world should be. Another already submitted popular initiative, *Preservation of Swiss Neutrality (neutrality initiative)*,[35] also aims at introducing a new Article 54a into the Swiss Constitution. The proposed provision defines Swiss neutrality – which is currently not defined in the Constitution but rather a living concept – once and forever in very strict terms:[36]

> Article 54a Swiss neutrality
>
> [1] Switzerland is neutral. Its neutrality is perpetual and armed.
>
> [2] Switzerland shall not join any military or defence alliance. This shall not preclude cooperation with such alliances in the event of direct military aggression against Switzerland or in the event of acts in preparation for such an aggression.
>
> [3] Switzerland does not take part in military conflicts between third countries and does not take any non-military coercive measures against belligerent states. This is subject to obligations to the United Nations (UN) and measures to prevent the circumvention of non-military coercive measures by other states.
>
> [4] Switzerland uses its permanent neutrality to prevent and resolve conflicts and is available to mediate.

This approach is obviously very different from the Europe Initiative as it leaves no room for dynamic developments or adaptations. In addition, it applies a rather inward perspective and, apart from traditional mediation roles, does not address the active contribution of Switzerland to a peaceful world. Neutralising and petrifying Switzerland's role in such a manner and preventing it from playing an active role is in sharp contrast to the spirit of Hallerstrasse 6. To express this spirit and inspire the ongoing discussion, as a second initiative, a manifesto, *Neutrality for the 21st Century*, was presented by a group of scientists, diplomats and politicians at the WTI at Hallerstrasse 6 on 29 May 2024. It defines 10 key points to guide Swiss neutrality in the twenty-first century. In fact, with its neutrality policy in response to the war of aggression against Ukraine, Switzerland has manoeuvred itself into a situation that is hardly understood by other countries, including its partners and allies.

Indeed, applying the concept of neutrality in what Thomas Cottier, in an interview, called a very dogmatic manner has made Switzerland look powerless, with the risk of substantially weakening its position on the international stage. This situation somewhat resembles the state of French diplomacy in the run-up to the

[35] Submitted on 2 May 2024 with the necessary and verified number of signatures, Bundesblatt 2024 1206.

[36] Translation by the author.

Schuman Plan. To overcome this 'anemic' state,[37] a new and fresh initiative – the coup of rue de Martignac – was necessary to bring France back to play an active role among the great powers at the time. The authors and signatories of the manifesto on neutrality seem to act in the same spirit: preventing Switzerland from being paralysed by overly strict concepts, enabling it to play an active role, defending the shared values of democratic countries and contributing to a rule-based international order.

IV. What is Next?

Many of Thomas Cottier's ideas were first conceived, as he would put it, 'en face de l'Eiger'. He has often found inspiration in Grindelwald. First ideas were then discussed and further developed, revised or sometimes abandoned during lively discussions at Hallerstrasse 6. Whoever has had the privilege of working with Thomas Cottier will agree that the quest for contributing to a peaceful Europe and a peaceful world is deeply anchored in his DNA. Equally strong is his desire to bring vision and policies to life so that they have an impact on real people in their real lives. This takes creativity, innovation and stamina. He has inspired generations of young scholars who will continue on this path.

The current geopolitical environment with the accumulation of crises – the triple planetary crisis, looming financial instability, the impacts of severely disrupted supply chains – and the highest number of armed conflicts since WWII come with unprecedented challenges. Action is needed, and it is needed now. Recalling and reviving the spirit of rue de Martignac at Hallerstrasse gives a strong signal: the presented examples show that resignation in view of the challenges is not an option.

Travelling from 18 rue de Martignac to Hallerstrasse 6 is quite some distance. Perhaps a much shorter journey could get us even further sooner: just around the corner, at 28 rue de Martignac, is the home of the Swiss delegation to the OECD and, in the same block, the Swiss Embassy. Yes, you may say I am a dreamer, but I am not the only one – let this spirit travel; here is to Thomas Cottier!

[37] Fontaine (n 2) 4.

10

The EU–Switzerland Agreements and the Role of the Swiss Federal Supreme Court in the Five-Storey House of European Courts

MATTHIAS OESCH AND ELISA LUNARDON

I. Introduction

During his impressive academic career, Thomas Cottier has dealt with a notable variety of topics. However, one common aspect stands out and meanders like a red thread through all his writings: the endeavour to examine the various layers of government not individually, but instead holistically. Considering the different layers of government as an integrated whole allows the working out of similarities and differences between them, the definition of rules for the interaction of their authorities and for the allocation of competences, responsibilities and standards of review, and the developing of instruments to compensate for failures of one level with measures from another. Thomas Cottier has made a number of groundbreaking contributions: 'The Prospects of 21st Century Constitutionalism' of 2003, 'Multilayered Governance, Pluralism, and Moral Conflict' of 2009 and 'Towards a Five Storey House' of 2011.[1] These writings have been instrumental in the development of a better understanding of how the constitutional functions of our modern times can be secured across the different levels of governance, which – together – contribute to an overall constitutional system. Countless researchers around the globe have taken up Thomas Cottier's work and developed his conceptual thinking further, both theoretically and practically, also with a view to its application in specific policy areas.

[1] Thomas Cottier and Maya Hertig, 'The Prospects of 21st Century Constitutionalism' (2003) 7(1) *Max Planck Yearbook of United Nations Law* 261; Thomas Cottier, 'Multilayered Governance, Pluralism, and Moral Conflict' (2009) 16(2) *Indiana Journal of Legal Studies* 647; Thomas Cottier, 'Towards a Five Storey House' in Christian Joerges and Ernst-Ulrich Petersmann (eds), *Constitutionalism, Multilevel Governance and International Economic Law*, 2nd edn (Hart Publishing, 2011) 495.

This chapter takes up this thread and attempts to link the quest for multilayered governance with a second pillar of Thomas Cottier's *oeuvre*, namely Switzerland's integration into the EU legal area. The situation is complicated: Switzerland and the EU have developed a tight network of bilateral agreements, consisting of 20 main agreements, supplemented by over 100 secondary agreements, protocols and exchanges of letters.[2] Within this framework, various agreements, such as the Agreement on the Free Movement of Persons (AFMP), the Agreement on Air Transport (AAT) and the Schengen/Dublin Association Agreements (SAA, DAA), envisage the sectoral integration of Switzerland into the law of the EU and are based, for this purpose, on EU secondary law. Irrespective of this partially far-reaching integration, a two-pillar approach prevails at the institutional level. That means that each party (Switzerland and the EU) is individually responsible for the good functioning of the agreements. The same holds true with respect to legal protection. The Swiss Federal Supreme Court has no right to refer questions on the interpretation of the bilateral agreements to the European Court of Justice (ECJ) as, formally, it is not part of the EU's *Rechtsprechungsverbund*,[3] ie the EU's network of courts.

Currently, Switzerland and the EU are negotiating new institutional rules for those bilateral agreements which permit Switzerland's participation in the Union's internal market.[4] This includes a new dispute settlement model. The model envisages the setting up of a framework under which the EU and Switzerland can request the establishment of an arbitration tribunal if they disagree on the interpretation of any of the treaty provisions. However, such an arbitration tribunal must involve the ECJ when the interpretation of EU law is at issue. Moreover, the relevant authorities in the EU and Switzerland would interpret and apply the

[2] For general accounts on Swiss–EU relations, see Thomas Cottier and Rachel Liechti, 'Schweizer Spezifika: Direkte Demokratie, Konkordanz, Föderalismus und Neutralität als politische Gestaltungsfaktoren' in Fritz Breuss, Thomas Cottier and Peter-Christian Müller-Graff (eds), *Die Schweiz im europäischen Integrationsprozess* (Nomos, 2008) 39; Thomas Cottier, 'Swiss Model of European Integration' in Stefan Diezig and Astrid Epiney (eds), *Schweizerisches Jahrbuch für Europarecht, 2012/2013* (Schulthess, 2013) 377; Thomas Cottier et al, *Die Rechtsbeziehungen der Schweiz und der Europäischen Union* (Schulthess, 2014) passim; Thomas Cottier and Matthias Oesch, *International Trade Regulation: Law and Policy in the WTO, the European Union and Switzerland: Cases, Materials and Comments* (Staempfli Publishers, 2005) passim; Sandra Lavenex and René Schwok, 'The Swiss Way: The Nature of the Swiss Relationship with the EU' in Erik Oddvar Eriksen and John Erik Fossum (eds), *The European Union's Non-Members* (Routledge, 2016) 248; Matthias Oesch, *Switzerland and the European Union: General Framework, Bilateral Agreements, Autonomous Adaptation* (Dike Verlag Zurich, 2018). This contribution builds, in part, on the following publications: Matthias Oesch and Aliénor Nina Burghartz, 'The "Common Market" with Switzerland' in Robert Schütze and Takis Tridimas (eds), *The Oxford Principles of European Union Law*, vol II (Oxford University Press, forthcoming); Matthias Oesch, *Der EuGH und die Schweiz* (EIZ Publishing, 2023).

[3] For this term, see BVerfGE 140, 317 – Identitätskontrolle.

[4] See Federal Department of Foreign Affairs, Switzerland's European Policy, www.eda.admin.ch/europa/en/home.html; Thomas Cottier, 'Die Souveränität und das institutionelle Rahmenabkommen' (2019) 115(11) *Schweizerische Juristen-Zeitung* 345; Marc Maresceau and Christa Tobler (eds), *Switzerland and the EU: A Challenging Relationship* (Brill Nijhoff, 2023); Christa Tobler, 'The EU–Swiss Sectoral Approach Under Pressure: Not Least Because of Brexit' in Stefan Lorenzmeier et al (eds), *EU External Relations Law* (Springer, 2021) 107.

bilateral agreements in accordance with the case law of the ECJ – irrespective of whether the relevant judgment was issued before or after the signing of the agreement in question. These novelties will be remarkable as they will significantly affect the Federal Supreme Court's role in Swiss–EU relations.

In the following, we review the institutional features of the bilateral agreements, summarise the jurisprudence of the Federal Supreme Court on their interpretation and their supremacy in the event of a conflict with Swiss law, and critically assess the role of the Federal Supreme Court in accommodating the agreements in the Swiss legal system (section II). While the Swiss courts are not, formally, part of the EU's network of courts, the Swiss government regularly participates in preliminary ruling proceedings before the ECJ. *De lege ferenda*, it should be considered to grant the Federal Supreme Court the right to refer questions on the interpretation of the bilateral agreements to the ECJ (section III). An epilogue wraps up the findings (section IV).

II. Bilateral Agreements and the Courts

The institutional setting of the bilateral agreements is remarkably meagre: they follow traditional patterns of public international law based on a classic understanding of state sovereignty. A two-pillar approach, under which each party is individually responsible for the good functioning of the agreements, is predominant. This applies to legal protection as well. The Federal Supreme Court relies on the case law of the ECJ not only when interpreting the bilateral agreements involving Switzerland's participation in the internal market, but also when defining the intertwining of these agreements and Swiss law in the case of a conflict. Remarkably, for some agreements, it has established strict supremacy. In fact, the Federal Supreme Court's case law reveals its dual function: on the one hand, it acts as the final arbiter for the bilateral *acquis* in the 'Swiss pillar', similarly to the ECJ in the 'EU pillar'; and, on the other hand, it acts as the highest court of Switzerland, similarly to the national courts in the EU pillar.

A. Legal Protection

In the case of a dispute, the EU and Switzerland meet in joint committees to discuss pending issues and, ideally, to settle them. The agreements do not provide for common authorities to survey the correct interpretation and application of the agreements by the parties, to render authoritative interpretations or to grant legal protection. As there is no common surveillance authority (such as the European Commission or the European Free Trade Association (EFTA) Surveillance Authority) nor a common arbiter (such as the ECJ or the EFTA Court), the relevant authorities of the EU, its Member States and Switzerland, respectively, fulfil these tasks.

In the EU, the European Commission is responsible for supervising Member States to ensure that they are correctly interpreting and applying the agreements. It can do this by bringing any disputed measure before the ECJ (Article 258 of the Treaty on the Functioning of the European Union (TFEU)).[5] Legal protection for individuals is provided by administrative authorities and courts of the Member States. These are usually competent to implement and apply the bilateral agreements, thus ensuring the proper fulfilment of these tasks (Articles 216 and 291 TFEU). The ECJ is called upon to interpret the bilateral agreements by way of the preliminary ruling procedure; under this procedure, Member State courts can refer questions on the interpretation of EU law, including international treaties, to the ECJ (Article 267 TFEU). In practice, almost all ECJ judgments on the bilateral agreements to date have concerned preliminary rulings on the interpretation of the Agreement on the Free Movement of Persons. When the bilateral agreements are applied by the authorities of the EU, in particular by the European Commission and agencies, legal protection is provided by the General Court and the ECJ (Article 263 TFEU).

In Switzerland, there is no special body to supervise the correct interpretation and application of the bilateral agreements with the EU. Legal protection is provided by the administrative authorities and courts on the cantonal and federal levels. In any case, it is usually the Federal Supreme Court which acts as the court of last instance. There is no possibility for Swiss courts to request a preliminary ruling from the ECJ on the interpretation of the bilateral agreements. Nevertheless, Swiss courts have developed strategies to incorporate ECJ jurisprudence and thus to ensure that it is harmonised with the case law of the ECJ. They interpret the bilateral agreements, which are based on EU law and envisage Switzerland's sectoral integration into the EU legal order on the basis of specific methods of interpretation of EU law and in light of ECJ jurisprudence.[6] Furthermore, Swiss courts sometimes deliberately delay a decision on a legal question in the Swiss context and wait for a judgment of the ECJ on that question in the context of EU law.[7] This demonstrates the pragmatism with which Swiss courts often handle EU law issues.

Exceptionally, the Agreement on Air Transport (AAT) provides for a specific regime with respect to certain rights and obligations. The European Commission

[5] See, eg press release by the Commission, dated 30 September 2010, on the communication of a reasoned opinion to Greece with the request to respect the Savings Income Agreement of 2004; response of the Federal Council of 18 May 2011 to the motion 11.3157 'Beziehungen zwischen der Schweiz und Italien. Wogen glätten' regarding the Commission's request to Italy to respect its public procurement commitments towards Switzerland.

[6] See below.

[7] The Federal Administrative Court suspended an ongoing case for almost 10 months in 2008–09 in order to wait for an ECJ judgment on a legal question similar to the one at issue before the Swiss court; BVGer B-3064/2008 of 13 September 2010 (where, however, it was a matter of the Euro-compatible interpretation of a Swiss provision which had been aligned to EU law autonomously and not as a result of an obligation provided for in a agreement).

and the ECJ are responsible for surveillance and judicial review vis-à-vis Switzerland (Articles 11, 18 and 20 AAT).[8]

B. Interpretation

EU and Swiss authorities interpret the bilateral agreements based on the traditional methods of interpretation under public international law pursuant to Articles 31–33 of the Vienna Convention on the Law of Treaties (VCLT).[9] A special case concerns the interpretation of bilateral provisions based on EU law, the wording of which is identical with, or at least similar to, the relevant provision in EU law.

When called upon to interpret free trade and association agreements with third countries, the ECJ has consistently found that a parallel interpretation can only be considered if the purpose and the context of the provision in question are comparable to the purpose and the context of the parallel provision in EU law, especially when considering the degree of integration of the agreement.[10] According to the ECJ, these findings are also relevant for the interpretation of the agreements with Switzerland.[11] At the same time, the ECJ assumes – in particular in its more recent jurisprudence on the Agreement on the Free Movement of Persons – a presumption towards a parallel interpretation of a bilateral provision, which is based on EU law and envisages the sectoral integration of Switzerland into the EU legal order.[12] The ECJ does not hesitate to interpret the bilateral agreements in favour of a complaining party when such an interpretation is appropriate in light of its methods of interpretation; in doing so, the ECJ draws on its jurisprudence on EU law.[13]

[8] On this legal basis, the European Commission, the General Court and the ECJ decided the dispute on aeroplane noise pollution between Switzerland and Germany, Case C-547/10 P *Switzerland v Commission* EU:C:2013:139.

[9] BGE 149 II 129, con 6; BGE 133 V 329, con 8.4; BGE 132 V 53, con 6.3; Case C-70/09 *Hengartner and Gasser* EU:C:2010:430, para 36; Case C-581/17 *Wächtler* EU:C:2019:138, para 35; Thomas Cottier and Nicolas Diebold, 'Warenverkehr und Freizügigkeit in der Rechtsprechung des Bundesgerichts zu den Bilateralen Abkommen' *Jusletter* (2 February 2009) 237; Astrid Epiney, Beate Metz and Benedikt Pirker, *Zur Parallelität der Rechtsentwicklung in der EU und der Schweiz: Ein Beitrag zur rechtlichen Tragweite der Bilateralen Abkommen* (Schulthess, 2012); Benedict Vischer, *Einheitliche Auslegung im Bilateralen Recht* (EIZ Publishing, 2023) 8.

[10] Christa Tobler, 'Die EuGH-Entscheidung Grimme – Die Wiederkehr von Polydor und die Grenze des bilateralen Rechts' *Schweizerisches Jahrbuch für Europarecht* (SJER) 2009/2010, 369; see also Johannes Antonius Maria Klabbers, 'The Reception of International Law in the EU Legal Order' in Robert Schütze and Takis Tridimas (eds), *The European Union Legal Order*, Oxford Principles of European Law, vol I (Oxford University Press, 2018) 1208, 1216–20.

[11] Case C-351/08 *Grimme* EU:C:2009:697, para 29; Case C-70/09 *Hengartner and Gasser* EU:C:2010:430, paras 41–42; Case C-547/10 P *Switzerland v Commission* EU:C:2013:139, para 80; Case C-355/16 *Picart* EU:C:2018:184, para 29.

[12] Astrid Epiney, '"Brexit" und FZA' *Jusletter* (20 March 2017) Rz 5.

[13] For an overview on such cases, see Matthias Oesch and Gabriel Speck, 'Das geplante institutionelle Abkommen Schweiz-EU und der EuGH' SJER 2016/2017, 257, 267.

The same pattern has emerged in the jurisprudence of the Swiss Federal Supreme Court and the Federal Administrative Court. They interpret those bilateral agreements, which are based on EU law and aim at Switzerland's sectoral integration into the EU legal order, pursuant to the specific methods of interpretation of EU law and in view of the ECJ jurisprudence.[14] This is particularly relevant for the Agreement on the Free Movement of Persons and the Schengen/Dublin Association Agreements. Nonetheless, the Federal Supreme Court emphasises that certain agreements entail a less far-reaching level of integration than EU law does and, thus, must be interpreted autonomously. This holds true for the Free Trade Agreement of 1972: in a judgment of 2005, the Federal Supreme Court confirmed that this agreement was 'in principle to be interpreted and applied autonomously', but simultaneously pointed out that ECJ jurisprudence on parallel provisions in EU law is 'not irrelevant'.[15]

Occasionally, bilateral agreements explicitly oblige the authorities in Switzerland and the EU to consider the case law of the ECJ. This applies in particular to the Agreement on the Free Movement of Persons and the Agreement on Air Transport. Pursuant to Article 16(2) of the former, authorities shall take account of the relevant case law of the ECJ prior to the date of signature of the agreement, ie, prior to 21 June 1999, 'insofar as the application of this Agreement involves concepts of Community law'. The wording of Article 1(2) of the latter is similar. Both provisions impose an obligation to provide information with respect to ECJ judgments rendered after the date of signature of these agreements; if appropriate, the joint committee shall determine the implications of such case law. The Schengen/Dublin Association Agreements also deal with the interpretation of EU secondary law by Switzerland. However, they do not explicitly oblige Swiss authorities to take the case law of the ECJ into account (Articles 8 and 9 SAA, Articles 5 and 6 DAA). All of these provisions constitute *leges speciales* in relation to Articles 31–33 VCLT.

The Federal Supreme Court has repeatedly been called upon to interpret Article 16(2) AFMP.[16] In doing so, it has found that the case law of the ECJ on parallel provisions in EU law issued prior to 21 June 1999 is binding (*massgebend*) and, consequently, that Swiss authorities are obliged to follow it (*Befolgungspflicht*).[17] With respect to the case law of the ECJ issued after that date, there is an obligation to take it into consideration (*Beachtungsgebot*), but Swiss authorities may deviate from it in case there are cogent reasons to do so.[18] In practice, the distinction between ECJ judgments issued prior to 21 June 1999 and those issued after that

[14] See, eg BGE 142 II 35, con 5.2, where the Swiss Federal Supreme Court explicitly referred to the 'effet utile' as interpretative method.

[15] BGE 131 II 271, con 10.3 (own translation); see also BGE 118 Ib 367, con 6; BGer 2A.593/2005 of 6 September 2006.

[16] See, in particular, BGE 136 II 5, con 3.4; BGE 136 II 65, con 3/4; BGE 136 II 177, con 3.2; BGE 139 II 393, con 4; BGE 142 II 35, con 3.

[17] BGE 139 II 393, con 4.1.

[18] ibid.

date plays a subordinate role in the jurisprudence of the Federal Supreme Court. The court considers precedents of the ECJ on questions related to the bilateral relations analogously, disregarding the date of their issuance. As a result, a 'dynamic adaptation of the case law' arises.[19] As far as can be seen, the Federal Supreme Court has hitherto never explicitly deviated from an ECJ judgment based on an autonomous interpretation found to be more appropriate. However, according to the Federal Supreme Court, deviations are possible if a bilateral provision pursues a different purpose than the similarly worded provision of EU law does (that is, if the objective is not to extend EU law to the Swiss–EU relations). According to the Federal Supreme Court, this is the case of conditions that must be met for the expulsion of a criminal foreigner to be compatible with the Agreement on the Free Movement of Persons: the Federal Supreme Court does not interpret Article 5 of Annex I AFMP 'in the context of criminal law' analogously to the practice in EU law since this agreement 'is essentially an economic law agreement'.[20] According to the Federal Supreme Court, a deviation is also necessary if claims are not (primarily) based on traditional rights of free movement (in conjunction with the principle of non-discrimination), but rather on EU citizenship or its core elements.[21]

Seemingly, the Federal Supreme Court has not yet dealt with the scope of Article 1(2) AAT.[22] Presumably, considerations similar to those made regarding the interpretation of the Agreement on the Free Movement of Persons are also applicable here.

C. Supremacy

The principle of *pacta sunt servanda* (Article 26 VCLT) provides a starting point for determining the relationship between the bilateral agreements, on the one hand, and EU and Swiss law, on the other hand. A breach of an obligation under bilateral agreements by the EU or Switzerland gives rise to a responsibility under international law. However, the issue of international obligations differs from the question of the supremacy of the agreements within the EU and Swiss legal order. Such a question is to be answered through EU and Swiss constitutional law.

According to well-established ECJ case law, international treaties are situated between primary and secondary EU law in the hierarchy of EU law.[23]

[19] Andreas Zünd, 'Grundrechtsverwirklichung ohne Verfassungsgerichtsbarkeit' (2013) 22 *Aktuelle Juristische Praxis* 1349 (own translation).

[20] BGE 145 IV 364, con 3.4.4 (own translation); see also BGE 145 IV 55, con 4.2.

[21] BGE 139 II 393, con 4.1.2; BGE 136 II 5, con 3.6.3; BGE 136 II 65, con 4.

[22] For a case in which a communal court took a different route, see the judgment of the Court of Bülach of 2 February 2016, FV150044-C/U AB/ad, con 4.2. In interpreting the Air Passenger Rights Regulation (EC) No 261/2004, which is referred to in the AAT, the court deliberately deviated from the ECJ ruling in Case C-402/07 *Sturgeon* EU:C:2009:716.

[23] Joined Cases C-402/05 and C-415/05 *Kadi v Council and Commission* EU:C: 2008:461; Paul Craig and Grainne de Burça, *EU Law: Text, Cases and Materials*, 7th edn (Oxford University Press, 2020) 367, 406.

It can be assumed that this hierarchy applies to the relationship between EU law and the bilateral agreements as well. EU primary law, including the Charter of Fundamental Rights, thus takes precedence over bilateral law in the event of a conflict. By contrast, bilateral law is binding on the EU legislator and the Member States, and takes precedence over secondary EU law as well as over national law.

In Switzerland, the principle of primacy of international law generally applies (see Article 5(4) Swiss Constitution).[24] However, the Swiss Federal Supreme Court has consistently held that the authorities shall apply a federal act when the Federal Assembly has intentionally enacted that legislation contrary to a treaty obligation and is consciously prepared to face international responsibility. This exception to the principle that international law supersedes federal acts in the case of a conflict is known as the *Schubert* exception, established by the Federal Supreme Court in 1973.[25] Notwithstanding the *Schubert* exception, treaties that guarantee fundamental rights, such as the European Convention of Human Rights, must be respected in any circumstance (*PKK* counter-exception, pursuant to the plaintiff's name in the relevant case, the Partiya Karkerên Kurdistanê).[26] Moreover, the *Schubert* exception does not apply to the Agreement on the Free Movement of Persons, which must always be respected without any possibility of intentional deviation for the Federal Assembly (*AFMP* counter-exception).[27] Lastly, in 2022, the Federal Supreme Court extended the strict supremacy to the Dublin Association Agreement and held that Article 28 of the Dublin III Regulation, which is referred to in this agreement, as interpreted by the ECJ, took precedence over a conflicting provision of the Federal Act on Foreign Nationals and Integration.[28] It underscored that strict supremacy always takes place in cases where 'obligations on the part of Switzerland concerning human rights and the free movement of persons' are at stake.[29] While these rulings are far-reaching, they also have given way to various questions which remain, for the time being, unanswered.[30] In particular, it is unclear whether supremacy is indeed unconditional or whether the Federal Supreme Court reserves the right to deny supremacy in exceptional cases and to apply a Swiss rule instead.

[24] For these issues in general, see Walter Haller, *The Swiss Constitution in a Comparative Context*, 2nd edn (Dike Verlag, 2016); Patricia Egli, *Introduction to Swiss Constitution Law*, 3rd edn (Dike Verlag, 2024).

[25] BGE 99 Ib 39, con 3/4.

[26] BGE 125 II 417, con 4d.

[27] BGE 142 II 35, con 3.2.

[28] BGE 148 II 169, con 5.2, referring to Case C-60/16 *Khir Amayry* EU:C:2017:675.

[29] ibid E 5.2.

[30] *cf* Giovanni Biaggini, 'Die "Immerhin liesse sich erwägen"-Erwägung im Urteil 2C_716/2014: Über ein problematisches höchstrichterliches obiter dictum' (2016) 117(4) *Schweizerisches Zentralblatt für Staats- und Verwaltungsrecht* 169; Astrid Epiney, 'Ist die "Schubert-Rechtsprechung" noch aktuell? Zur Frage des Verhältnisses zwischen Völker- und Landesrecht' [2023] *Aktuelle Juristische Praxis* 699, 708–09; Matthias Oesch, *Der EuGH und die Schweiz* (n 2) 103–06.

D. The Federal Supreme Court's Dual Function …

The Federal Supreme Court's case law on the interpretation and supremacy of the bilateral agreements reveals its dual role in the process of European integration.

On the one hand, it acts as the final arbiter for the bilateral *acquis* in the Swiss pillar. Here, its function is similar to that of the ECJ as the supreme court for the internal market in the EU pillar. Hence, a supranational perspective dominates. Adhering to the case law of the ECJ – the Federal Supreme Court has never referred to cogent reasons in order to deviate from an ECJ ruling – ensures the uniformity of the law. From such perspective, the justification for the markedly consistent Euro-compatible interpretation of the agreements and their supremacy is based on a comprehensible logic: Switzerland participates sectorally in the internal market, similarly to the Member States. From here, it is a small step to call for strict supremacy in analogy to EU law and thus to ensure the proper functioning of the agreements. Against this background, it is not surprising that the Federal Supreme Court – in addition to other considerations (democratic legitimation through the acceptance in a referendum, guarantee of legal protection) – also referred, in order to justify strict supremacy, to the ECJ rulings in *van Gend en Loos* and *Costa/Enel*, the two groundbreaking rulings that paved the way for the ECJ to triumphantly establish the basis for the primacy of EU law and its constitutionalisation.

On the other hand, the Federal Supreme Court, acting as the highest court of Switzerland, represents the hinge between the bilateral *acquis* and national law. This also involves a specifically Swiss perspective. To date, the Federal Supreme Court has not addressed this perspective in its supremacy jurisprudence – admittedly a delicate terrain. When acting in this competence, its role resembles that of the highest courts of the Member States, which respect the unconditional primacy of EU law and the ECJ's prerogative to have the last word on its validity and interpretation generously, albeit not without limits.[31] In one form or another, primacy is accepted in most Member States on the condition that EU law duly guarantees the protection of fundamental rights, that the EU institutions act on the basis of existing competences (*ie* they do not act ultra vires) and that EU law respects the identity of the national constitution (or at least its fundamental content). This means that the Member States retain the last word on the effect of EU law in the national context. Various national courts have not shied away from declaring a Union act or a judgment of the ECJ incompatible with constitutional requirements. Recent examples include the ruling by the German Federal Constitutional Court in 2020 on the ECJ's acceptance of the European Central Bank's public sector purchase programme and the ruling by the Polish Constitutional Court in 2021 on the

[31] Craig and de Burça (n 23) 314, 328–56; Koen Lenaerts, Piet van Nuffel and Tim Corthaut (eds), *EU Constitutional Law* (Oxford University Press, 2021) 23.025–23.030.

ECJ's lack of competence to interpret the EU treaties regarding the independence of national judges.[32]

E. … but without the Right to Refer Questions to the ECJ

In the EU, the preliminary ruling procedure provides a mechanism for national courts to refer questions on the interpretation of the EU Treaties and on the validity and interpretation of EU legal acts to the ECJ (Article 267 TFEU). As the ECJ has noted in 1973, this procedure 'is essential for the preservation of the Community character of the law established by the Treaty and has the object of ensuring that in all circumstances this law is the same in all States of the Community'.[33] It is 'the jewel in the crown of the EU legal system'[34] and the 'keystone'[35] for the good functioning of the EU as a 'union based on the rule of law'.[36] It formalises cooperation and, ideally, contributes to a fruitful dialogue between the ECJ and the national courts, both being jointly responsible for ensuring that EU law is observed when interpreting and applying the EU Treaties (*cf* Article 19 of the Lisbon Treaty on European Union). National courts are 'juges de "droit commun" de l'ordre juridique de l'Union'[37] or 'agents of the Community order … as de facto Community judges'.[38] With their integration into the European network of courts, they have increased their influence: 'This dialogue is probably the source of the ECJ's success in strengthening the power of national courts at the national level and making them allies against national governments.'[39]

The national courts are well advised to give the ECJ the opportunity to comment on a disputed legal act or judgment before an open confrontation, explaining to the ECJ the reasons why it should choose their proposed solution and formulating a preferred judgment.[40] Thereby, a question of interpretation can also be referred to the ECJ more than once. Vice versa, the ECJ is well advised to consider the sensitivities of the national courts and to take their objections to presumably unconstitutional EU legislation seriously, as well as to avoid ignoring

[32] For an overview on such cases, see Renata Uitz, 'The Rule of Law in the EU: Crisis, Differentiation, Conditionality' (2022) 7(2) *European Papers* 929, 933; Matthias Oesch, *Der EuGH und die Schweiz* (n 2) 68–72; Vischer (n 9) fn 104.

[33] Case 166/73 *Rheinmühlen Düsseldorf* EU:C:1974:3, para 2.

[34] Kai Purnhagen and Lawrence W Gormley, 'Court Cases' in *Oxford Encyclopedia of EU Law* (2022) para 6, https://opil.ouplaw.com/home/OEEUL.

[35] Case C-619/18 *Commission v Poland* EU:C:2019:531, para 45.

[36] Case C-583/11 P *Inuit* EU:C:2013:625, para 91.

[37] Case C-1/09 *Gutachten Patentgericht* EU:C:2011:123, para 80.

[38] Alec Stone Sweet, 'The Juridical Coup D'État and the Problem of Authority' (2007) 8 *German Law Journal* 915, 925.

[39] Samantha Besson, *Droit constitutionnel européen*, 2nd edn (Stämpfli Verlag, 2023) para 549 (own translation).

[40] Art 107(2) of the ECJ's Rules of Procedure expressly encourages a national court to state in urgent preliminary ruling procedures what answer it proposes to the questions referred for a preliminary ruling.

any complaint concerning overly integration-friendly judgments. Thus, the ECJ adjusted its case law after Italy's Corte Costituzionale had announced that it would not implement an ECJ ruling in a dispute concerning limitation periods for VAT offences, as the said ruling was considered to violate the Italian Constitution.[41] The ECJ and the national courts thus influence and control each other in a system of vertical separation of powers. The President of the ECJ, Koen Lenaerts, shares the view of Andreas Vosskuhle, then President of the German Federal Constitutional Court, according to which 'the relationship between the ECJ and national constitutional courts … is not about superiority or subordination, but about an appropriate division of responsibility and allocation in a complex system of multi-level governance'.[42]

A decisive feature of the Federal Supreme Court's role in interpreting and applying the bilateral agreements is that, formally, the highest Swiss court is not part of the Union's network of courts. It has neither a right nor an obligation to refer questions on the interpretation of the bilateral agreements to the ECJ, and, consequently, it is not involved in the process of joint judicial decision-shaping and decision-making between the ECJ and the national courts. This is a shortcoming of the institutional set-up. Currently, the informal dialogue between Luxemburg and Lausanne resembles a one-way street, with the ECJ hardly ever invoking the case law of the Federal Supreme Court.[43] Exceptionally, in a judgment of 2009, the ECJ referred to a judgment of the Federal Supreme Court of 2004 and declared that it would take due account of it in accordance with Article 1 of Protocol 2 to the Lugano Convention.[44] However, this explicit reference to a judgment of the Federal Supreme Court by the ECJ remains, as far as can be seen, an isolated case. In interpreting the Agreement on the Free Movement of Persons, the ECJ has never referred to the practice of the Federal Supreme Court (or other Swiss courts); a disappointing record.[45] In the case of bilateral agreements, which aim to integrate Switzerland sectorally into the internal market, the Federal Supreme Court is at least *factually* part of the Union's court system. Even though the ECJ's style

[41] Matteo Bonelli, 'The Taricco Saga and the Consolidation of Judicial Dialogue in the European Union: CJEU, C-105/14 Ivo Taricco and others, ECLI:EU:C:2015:555; and C-42/17 M.A.S, M.B., ECLI:EU:C:2017:936 Italian Constitutional Court, Order no. 24/2017' (2018) 25(3) *Maastricht Journal of European and Comparative Law* 357, passim.

[42] Koen Lenaerts, 'Kooperation und Spannung im Verhältnis von EuGH und nationalen Verfassungsgerichten' (2015) *EuR* 3, 25 (own translation).

[43] At least, judges of the Federal Supreme Court meet regularly with judges of the ECJ (as well as other courts such as the ECtHR and the constitutional courts of neighboring states) to discuss legal issues, *cf* Bundesgericht, Geschäftsbericht 2022, 14, www.bger.ch. In the draft institutional agreement between the EU and Switzerland of 2018, the Federal Supreme Court and the ECJ would have been committed to a dialogue in order to promote a uniform interpretation (Art 11). This concern should be taken up again in the new negotiations.

[44] Case C-394/07 *Gambazzi* EU:C:2009:219, paras 35–38.

[45] Raphael Dummermuth, 'Im Auslegen seid frisch und munter!' (2023) 3 *recht – Zeitschrift für juristische Weiterbildung und Praxis* 175, 179.

of judgment is geared towards brevity, and, with the exception of the European Court of Human Rights (ECtHR), it generally does not refer to judgments of foreign courts, the Federal Supreme Court's role as the final arbiter on the interpretation of the bilateral agreements in the Swiss pillar would be acknowledged more adequately if the ECJ were to take note of its case law. A side view at the European Economic Area (EEA) reveals that the ECJ is conscious of the EFTA Court's important role in the 'EEA EFTA pillar' and regularly cites its case law.

III. Participation of Switzerland in ECJ Procedures

While the Federal Supreme Court formally is not part of the EU's network of courts, the Swiss government is able to participate in preliminary ruling proceedings before the ECJ (A). *De lege ferenda*, it should be considered to grant the Federal Supreme Court the right to refer questions on the interpretation of the bilateral agreements to the ECJ (B).

A. Government

(i) Preliminary Ruling Procedure

Special provisions of certain agreements allow Switzerland to participate in preliminary ruling proceedings before the ECJ concerning the interpretation of EU law which is also relevant for Switzerland due to the Schengen/Dublin Association Agreements or the Lugano Convention. The Lugano Convention authorises Switzerland to submit statements or written observations if a court of an EU Member State refers a question to the ECJ for a preliminary ruling on the interpretation of the Convention or a legal act referenced therein (Article 2 of Protocol 2 to the Lugano Convention). Analogous provisions can be found in the Schengen/Dublin Association Agreements (Article 8 SAA; Article 5 DAA).

Switzerland makes extensive use of this opportunity. In fact, between the entry into force of the agreements in 2008 and the beginning of 2023, the ECJ Registry notified Switzerland of 191 relevant proceedings based on the Schengen/Dublin Association Agreements. As there is a risk that the agreements will be terminated if Switzerland does not respect an ECJ ruling relevant to the Schengen/Dublin Association Agreements (Articles 9 and 10 SAA; Articles 6 and 7 DAA), it is not entirely surprising that Switzerland has submitted a statement in 42 of these cases.[46] The Federal Office of Justice decides whether a submission will be made

[46] The Federal Office of Justice maintains a publicly accessible list of these proceedings, www.bj.admin.ch/bj/de/home/sicherheit/schengen-dublin/uebersichten.html. Switzerland has never taken part in oral proceedings.

in proceedings and, subsequently, coordinates its preparation, which will then be sent to Luxembourg via diplomatic channels. Swiss submissions are generally not accessible to the public.[47] In the ECJ's deliberations, EU institutions, EU Member States and associated third states submitting a statement or an observation are listed; however, their content is generally not reproduced.[48] The Swiss government has summarised its practice as follows:

> Switzerland consistently makes use of the opportunity to comment on requests for preliminary rulings in order to exert its influence on legal developments in the EU. However, it refrains from commenting if it can be assumed from a precise analysis of the facts that the answer to the questions of interpretation posed will not have any repercussions on Swiss legislation and practice.[49]

Switzerland's active participation is remarkable as it potentially influences the ECJ's decision-making to the same extent as the statements of EU institutions (whereby the Commission is involved in practically all proceedings) and EU Member States (whereby participation varies considerably) do.[50] Switzerland thereby assumes co-responsibility for the development of case law in an area of EU law in which it is effectively treated as a Member State by virtue of its association. Swiss statements to the ECJ resemble the practice of *decision* (or *proposal*) *shaping* (which Switzerland practises within the framework of the Schengen/Dublin association when new EU legal acts are drafted by the European Commission), which is now also transferred to the judiciary.[51] Ideally, when drafting its statements, Switzerland consults with other states sharing similar interests related to currently debated issues to increase the impact of their arguments.

De lege ferenda, it is worth considering extending Switzerland's right to issue statements and written observations to other agreements that aim to integrate Switzerland into the internal market and are based on EU law for this purpose. This should be considered in the ongoing negotiations concerning new institutional rules. The Statute of the ECJ expressly allows for participation by third countries on the condition that it is provided for in the agreements concerned (Article 23 of the ECJ's Statute).

[47] *Prima vista*, neither Art 3, para 1, lit a, nos 4 and 5 of the Federal Act on Freedom of Information in the Administration of 2004 (documents relating to international dispute settlement proceedings and to constitutional and administrative judicial proceedings) nor Art 7, para 1, lit d of this act (affecting Switzerland's interests in matters of foreign policy and international relations) seems relevant, which means that there is a right of access to such statements. The Federal Office of Justice grants access to individual submissions if an applicant is interested in receiving a submission.

[48] On the function and influence of such statements and observations in ECJ proceedings in general, see Christoph Krenn, *The Procedural and Organisational Law of the European Court of Justice: An Incomplete Transformation* (Cambridge University Press, 2022) 59–73.

[49] Eidgenössisches Justiz- und Polizeidepartement, Fünfter Bericht des EJPD vom 17. März 2014 zuhanden der GPK-EJPD Stand der Umsetzung von Schengen/Dublin 2013/2014, 33, www.bj.admin.ch/bj/de (own translation).

[50] For statistics, see Krenn (n 48) 59–63.

[51] For an example of such decision (or proposal) shaping, see below.

(ii) Other Procedures

Switzerland was prevented from participating in the proceedings before the ECJ related to Directive 91/477/EEC (Weapons Directive), despite being a particularly affected party. The Weapons Directive, which belongs to the Schengen *acquis* relevant to Switzerland, was amended in 2017 with Directive (EU) 2017/853. It was clear that Switzerland had to adopt this amendment (*cf* Recital 36). Switzerland had previously succeeded in shaping the content of the new directive in a remarkable manner. As part of the *decision* (or *proposal*) *shaping*, it persuaded the Commission, the Council and the Parliament to include a provision specifically tailored to the circumstances of Switzerland – albeit formulated in general terms – and thus to install a 'Swiss finish', as it were (Article 6). The Czech Republic filed an action for annulment against the new directive with the ECJ, arguing, inter alia, that the Swiss finish was discriminatory because it led to an unjustified advantage for Switzerland compared to the EU Member States. The ECJ rejected this plea.[52] Nevertheless, Switzerland was not invited to submit a statement in these proceedings. In accordance with the above-mentioned agreements, the right to submit a statement or a written observation only exists in preliminary ruling proceedings. *De lege ferenda*, it would be conceivable to grant Switzerland the right to submit statements and written observations in annulment and infringement proceedings before the ECJ as well.

Moreover, in preliminary ruling proceedings, Switzerland's participation is actually limited to questions regarding the interpretation of an EU legal act relevant to the Schengen/Dublin Association Agreements or the Lugano Convention. Questions of validity are excluded from this, even though, in such cases, it is not only the validity of a legal act that is at stake, but also questions of interpretation with de facto prejudicial effect for the associated Schengen/Dublin states, and the annulment of an EU legal act might entail that the legal situation must also be adjusted bilaterally.[53]

B. Federal Supreme Court

The implementation and application of the bilateral agreements in Switzerland generally works well. Many lawyers are remarkably adept at finding their way through the jungle of EU law and are capable of accomplishing the 'translation' of this law into the bilateral context. Authorities interpret those agreements, which aim to integrate Switzerland into the internal market, consistently with the ECJ's jurisprudence. According to Andreas Zünd, judge at the Federal Supreme Court

[52] Case C-482/17 *Czech Republic v Parliament and Council* EU:C:2019:1035.

[53] For instance, such an adjustment would have been inevitable if the ECJ had declared the Air Passenger Rights Regulation (EC) 261/2004 null and void in Case C-12/11 *McDonagh/Ryanair* EU:C:2013:43.

until 2021 and thereafter judge at the ECtHR, the EU 'can rely on the fact that the application of the EU legal acts adopted by Switzerland remains compatible with the interpretation within the EU'.[54] The overtly generous interpretation of the conditions for the expulsion of foreign criminals by the Federal Supreme Court and the ruling of the Bülach District Court on the Air Passenger Rights Regulation are exceptions that confirm the rule.[55] With regard to those legal questions not yet subjected to any ECJ practice, Swiss courts have a 'first mover advantage'.[56]

Decisively, however, the Federal Supreme Court has no right to refer questions of interpretation to the ECJ. In view of the dicta from Lausanne, according to which the Agreement on the Free Movement of Persons and the Dublin Association Agreement take precedence over federal laws, and in view of the obligation envisaged in the ongoing negotiations to strictly comply with ECJ rulings independent of the date of their issuance, the need to formally integrate the Federal Supreme Court into the EU's network of courts is evident. The highest Swiss court should be competent to refer questions on the interpretation of a bilateral agreement to the ECJ.[57] The Federal Supreme Court would then be in the position to propose an interpretation that is preferable from a Swiss perspective and to actively shape the development of the law. It could also ask the ECJ to reassess unconvincing practices. The newly envisaged dispute settlement mechanism, according to which an arbitration tribunal would have to refer questions on the interpretation of EU law to the ECJ, would not exclusively be responsible for clarifying controversial issues of interpretation based on the input rendered by the ECJ. With a right of referral, it would primarily be up to the Federal Supreme Court to formulate the relevant questions of interpretation within a specific legal dispute and to refer them to the ECJ, instead of an arbitration tribunal in interstate proceedings.[58]

Models for such a set-up are already visible when glancing at agreements between the EU and other third countries:[59]

- The EEA–EFTA states Iceland, Liechtenstein and Norway can allow a court to ask the ECJ to rule on the interpretation of EEA provisions that correspond

[54] Andreas Zünd, 'Gastkommentar: Das Bundesgericht verliert seine Bedeutung' *Luzerner Zeitung* (23 March 2019) passim (own translation).

[55] See BGE 145 IV 364, con 3.4.4 (own translation); BGE 145 IV 55, con 4.2.

[56] This term originates from Carl Baudenbacher, 'Gastkommentar: Der EFTA-Gerichtshof ist unabhängig' *Neue Zürcher Zeitung* (26 July 2018) passim, www.nzz.ch/meinung/wie-unabhaengig-ist-der-efta-gerichtshof-ld.1398959, in relation to the role of the EFTA Court in interpreting EEA law; for an area of law in which the Federal Supreme Court possesses such a first mover advantage, *cf* Benedikt Pirker, 'Verbleiberechte gemäss dem Freizügigkeitsabkommen Schweiz-EU' [2023] *Aktuelle Juristische Praxis* 860, passim.

[57] *cf* also Joëlle de Sépibus, 'Ein institutionelles Dach für die Beziehungen zwischen der Schweiz und der Europäischen Union – Wie weiter?' *Jusletter* (14 July 2014) para 56.

[58] *cf* also Zünd, 'Gastkommentar (n 54); for further suggestions to provide the Federal Supreme Court a role in the proposed dispute settlement model, see Benedict Vischer, 'Feilen am Streitbeilegungssystem in den bilateralen Beziehungen' *Jusletter* (22 January 2024) passim.

[59] For the participation of third country courts in preliminary ruling procedures before the ECJ in general, see Jörg Gundel, 'Die Öffnung des Vorabentscheidungsverfahrens zum EuGH für nichtmitgliedstaatliche Gerichte' [2019] *Europäische Zeitschrift für Wirtschaftsrecht* 934, passim.

to EU provisions (Article 107 and Protocol 34 of the EEA Agreement). This option has not been used so far, primarily because the courts of the EEA–EFTA states may raise questions on the interpretation of the EEA Agreement before the EFTA Court (Article 34 of the Surveillance and Court Agreement). These courts take advantage of this opportunity and periodically refer interpretative questions to the EFTA Court.

- The Treaty establishing the Transport Community between the EU and the six countries of the Western Balkans of 2017 and the Agreement on the Creation of a European Common Aviation Area between the EU and various European countries of 2006 contain provisions that allow courts of these countries to refer questions on the interpretation of treaty provisions or provisions of legal acts referred to therein that are substantially identical to corresponding rules of the EU Treaty and to acts adopted pursuant to the EU Treaty to the ECJ for a ruling if necessary for a judgment (Article 19 and Article 16, respectively). These countries are free to stipulate the modalities according to which their courts are to apply this provision. Domestic laws can provide for a general right of referral by national courts or for an obligation of those courts, against whose decisions there is no judicial remedy under national law (Annex IV). No question of interpretation has ever been referred to the ECJ on the basis of these provisions.

Similar to the courts in the EU Member States, the Federal Supreme Court would continue to have no access to infringement proceedings (Article 258 TFEU) or to annulment proceedings (Article 263 TFEU).

IV. Epilogue

The envisaged conclusion of new institutional rules for those agreements which aim to integrate Switzerland into the EU internal market and are based on EU law provides a welcome opportunity to assess whether the Swiss model of European integration can still truly be regarded as the Swiss *Königsweg* (the Swiss king's way), as the bilateral way has been labelled by many.[60] This critical endeavour affords the chance to consider whether there may be a more effective method of safeguarding Switzerland's interests in Europe; moving from the policy of simply reproducing developments in EU law towards a more constructive approach and the assumption of (co-)responsibility for policy-making on a pan-European level. A new institutional framework is arguably inevitable in the short term, so that such a bilateral relationship can be put on a more solid basis and new agreements

[60] See Dieter Freiburghaus, 'Königsweg oder Sackgasse?' in Dieter Freiburghaus (ed), *Königsweg oder Sackgasse?: Schweizerische Europapolitik von 1945 bis heute*, 2nd edn (Neue Zürcher Zeitung, 2015) passim.

can be concluded. However, it is questionable whether new rules – which would institutionalise the already apparent tendency of de facto delegating legislative and judicial competence to Brussels, Strasbourg and Luxemburg – would represent a sustainable long-term solution. Political common sense and foresight – *gouverner, c'est prévoir* – call for all policy options vis-à-vis the EU to be kept open and periodically assessed, including the prospect of opting for full EU membership.

Thomas Cottier has repeatedly pointed out that the current model of the Swiss policy towards the EU might only be a *provisoire qui dure*, functioning as a stepping stone towards deeper integration but not providing a stable long-term solution. In 2013, he stated:

> The countries in the fourth circle [such as Switzerland] will retain formal sovereignty, but largely lose self-determination except for the decision whether or not to join another level of European integration. They need to make up their own minds, taking into account not only their own history and constitutional precepts, but also the needs of present and future generations in Europe facing emerging powers.[61]

In 2014, he reiterated the quest for a re-evaluation of Swiss policy towards the EU:

> Switzerland's fate is inevitably linked to that of its neighbors and the continent, culturally and economically, socially and politically. The country would do better to play an active role in shaping the future of this continent than to try to defend old privileges in an anxious and politically isolated manner. All of this requires a new and changed understanding of sovereignty, which seeks self-determination in the long term through co-operation, participation and integration.[62]

It is to be hoped that these considerations fall on fertile grounds – in Switzerland and beyond. Thomas Cottier's constant and tireless commitment and his contribution to better understanding and further developing international cooperation and European integration, including the role that Switzerland plays in these processes, are most remarkable and commendable.

[61] Thomas Cottier, 'Swiss Model of European Integration' in Diezig and Epiney (n 2) 377, 393.
[62] Cottier et al (n 2) 604 (own translation).

11

The Role of the CJEU with Regard to Switzerland and Swiss Operators

MICHAEL HAHN AND ANA SIJAKOVIC KRESSNER

I. Introduction

Thomas Cottier's interest and expertise regarding the peaceful settlement of interstate disputes is second to none and has influenced many of his seminal works on dispute settlement in international economic law and the relationship between Switzerland and the EU. This rich *oeuvre* has shaped the following reflections.

The Court of Justice of the European Union (CJEU) appears to play a somewhat marginal role in the relationship between the Swiss Confederation and the EU.[1] While the readers of this chapter will certainly know that a number of provisions in the 120+ 'bilateral' agreements,[2] such as Article 16(2) of the Agreement on the Free Movement of Persons (AFMP),[3] Articles 8 and 9 of the Schengen Association Agreement (SAA)[4] and Articles 5 and 6 of the Dublin Association Agreement (DAA),[5] make explicit reference to the jurisprudence of the CJEU, this would be news for the general public. Even Article 20 of the Air Transport Agreement (ATA),[6] the unique provision that establishes a (very limited) jurisdiction of the CJEU for actions taken by Union institutions pursuant to Article 18(2)

[1] For an overview of the Switzerland–EU agreements, see www.eda.admin.ch/europa/en/home/bilateraler-weg/ueberblick.html. For an analysis, see Thomas Cottier et al, *Die Rechtsbeziehungen der Schweiz und der Europäischen Union* (Stämpfli Verlag, 2014).

[2] In the Swiss political and legal discussions, the treaties between Switzerland and the EU (and sometimes its Member States) are called the Bilaterals, or Bilateral Agreements, a choice of words not taken up on the EU side.

[3] Agreement between the Swiss Confederation, of the one part, and the European Community and its Member States, of the other, on the free movement of persons, SR 0.142.112.681; [2002] OJ L114/6.

[4] Agreement between the Swiss Confederation, the European Union and the European Community on the Swiss Confederation's association with the implementation, application and development of the Schengen acquis, SR 0.362.31; [2008] OJ L53/52.

[5] Agreement between the Swiss Confederation and the European Community concerning the criteria and mechanisms for establishing the State responsible for examining a request for asylum lodged in a Member State or in Switzerland, SR 0.142.392.68; [2008] OJ L53/5.

[6] Agreement between the Swiss Confederation and the European Community on Air Transport, SR 0.748.127.192.68; [2002] OJ L114/73.

ATA in Switzerland, has never been controversial. In fact, none of these provisions has triggered any interest in the Swiss political discourse so far.

The failed draft of the Institutional Agreement (IA)[7] was to change that. It provided for an arbitration mechanism that had arbitrators refer questions concerning Union law to the CJEU, mirroring somewhat the procedure laid down in Article 267 of the Treaty on the Functioning of the European Union (TFEU) for EU Member States' courts. At the end of 2023, Switzerland and the EU agreed upon a 'Common Understanding' (CU), containing the results of exploratory talks[8] intended to establish 'a solid and balanced basis'[9] for new negotiations, which started in spring 2024.[10] Building on the provisions of the IA, the CU defines 'landing zones' for a new comprehensive revitalisation of the limping bilateral treaties, ensuring Switzerland's continued access to many parts of the EU single market. The CU allocates to a bilateral arbitral tribunal the competence to decide upon disputes regarding the bilateral relationship *tel quel*, whereas the CJEU would remain the ultimate interpreter of all provisions that constitute, in substance, EU single market law. Thus, the CJEU's (now obvious!) influence on Swiss–EU relations and, more generally, on the Swiss legal order has become a topic of intense scrutiny in Swiss public discourse.

In the following sections, we will initially acquaint the reader with the most important institutional arrangements prescribed by the CU, with a particular emphasis on the role of the CJEU. Secondly, we will juxtapose the purported innovations in these institutional elements with the CJEU's current role in shaping Swiss–EU relations. Lastly, we will contemplate the potential repercussions of continued deterioration in Swiss–EU relations should new agreements fail to materialise.

II. The Role of the CJEU under the CU Model

The CU establishes the principle that each of the five existing 'market access agreements'[11] (as well as future agreements ensuring Swiss participation to sectors of the EU internal market) incorporates identical institutional arrangements.

[7] For information and documents on the Institutional Agreement, see www.eda.admin.ch/europa/en/home/bilateraler-weg/ueberblick/institutionelles-abkommen/informationen-dokumente.html.

[8] Common Understanding, 27 October 2023, commission.europa.eu/document/download/a6c33aa4-6da2-4843-9423-ba653ff9a437_en?filename=common_understanding_concluding_the_exploratory_talks_on_the_bilateral_eu-switzerland_relationship_ENpdf.

[9] Der Bundesrat, Bericht über die Ergebnisse der Konsultation zum Entwurf eines Verhandlungsmandats zwischen der Schweiz und der Europäischen Union über die Stabilisierung und Weiterentwicklung ihrer Beziehungen, 8 March 2024, 4, www.newsd.admin.ch/newsd/message/attachments/86563.pdf.

[10] The negotiations started officially on 18 March 2024, www.eda.admin.ch/eda/en/fdfa/fdfa/aktuell/news.html/content/eda/en/meta/news/2024/3/18/100438.html.

[11] These are: Agreement on Air Transport, Agreement on the Carriage of Goods and Passengers by Rail and Road, Agreement on the Free Movement of Persons, Agreement on Mutual Recognition in Relation to Conformity Assessment, and Agreement on Trade in Agricultural Products, all signed on 21 June 1999.

Building on the current status quo, the parties are expected to resort to consultations and negotiations in the respective treaty-specific joint or mixed committee to resolve disputes. The committee consultations offer a platform to clarify facts, reconcile differing stances and potentially settle disputes in a cost-effective manner.[12]

However, existing agreements fail to provide a remedy for situations in which amicable solutions cannot be reached.[13] The fact that the absence of a rules-based dispute settlement mechanism[14] may have unfavourable repercussions became apparent to the Swiss public in May 2021. When Switzerland terminated the negotiations on the IA, the EU reacted not only by refusing to participate in updating the equivalence listings of Swiss and EU technical regulations regarding medical devices[15] pursuant to the Swiss–EU's Mutual Recognition Agreement (MRA),[16] but also by terminating the recognition of already issued certificates without any grace period.[17] With regard to the discontinuation of already issued certificates of conformity, the EU measures raised legal issues[18] without a judicial forum available, despite the significant impact on the Swiss MedTech industry.[19]

The CU lays the ground for a more orderly method of dealing with disputes. If negotiations in the respective joint committee prove unsuccessful, parties will have recourse to an ad hoc arbitral tribunal that may render legally binding rulings. This evolution in Swiss–EU relations aligns with the trends observed in contemporary free trade agreements (FTAs), especially those aiming for extensive economic integration: independent third-party arbitration or even judicial or quasi-judicial dispute settlement mechanisms have become the norm rather than the exception.[20] The introduction of a dispute settlement mechanism which establishes an exclusive and effective avenue for redress and enforcement strengthens the credibility of the rights and obligations entered into. Furthermore, irrespective

[12] Yuriy Rudyuk, 'How the Trade Disputes between EU and Ukraine will be Settled under the EU–Ukraine Association Agreement?' [2017] *Lex Portus* No 2, 4.

[13] Art 19 of the Agreement between the European Community and the Swiss Confederation on mutual recognition in relation to conformity assessment, SR 0.946.526.81 (also [2002] OJ L114/369), grants parties to the Agreement the right to suspend either entirely or partially its application in the event of non-compliance by the other party. However, Switzerland, which aims for the fool implementation of the Agreement, cannot find satisfaction in this choice.

[14] Cesare PR Romano et al, 'Mapping International Adjudicative Bodies, the Issues, and Players' in Cesare PR Romano et al (eds), *Handbook of International Adjudication* (Oxford University Press, 2014) 4.

[15] Regulation (EU) 2017/745 on medical devices [2017] OJ L117/1.

[16] Swiss–EU MRA (n 13).

[17] See European Commission, DG for Health and Food Safety, 'Notice to Stakeholders: Status of the EU–Switzerland Mutual Recognition Agreement for Medical Devices' (26 May 2021) health.ec.europa.eu/system/files/2021-05/mdcg_eu-switzerland_mra_en_0.pdf.

[18] Sidley, 'EU/EEA Market Access for "Swiss Legacy Devices" Post Abandonment of Swiss–EU MRA' (Memorandum, 2 July 2021) www.swiss-medtech.ch/sites/default/files/2021-07/20210702_Sidley-Medtech%20Europe_Placing%20on%20the%20market%20of%20Swiss%20medical%20devices%20270107418_markedDDpdf.

[19] Swiss MedTech, 'Stellungnahme zum Entwurf des Mandats für Verhandlungen mit der EU' (13 February 2024) www.swiss-medtech.ch/sites/default/files/2024-02/Stellungnahme%2013.2.2024.pdf.

[20] Romano et al (n 14) 9; see, eg United States–Mexico–Canada Agreement, ch 31; Part Six, Annexes 48 and 49 of the Trade and Cooperation Agreement between the EU and the EAEC, of the one part,

of Switzerland's tradition of avoiding binding international adjudication as much as possible, effective enforcement of the rule of law notably benefits partners who carry less political or economic weight.

Although many aspects of the arbitral tribunal's final functioning are yet to be defined by the parties (including rules of procedure, criteria for arbitrators' selection and their appointment, and, most importantly, whether the use of compensatory measures will depend on prior approval by the arbitral tribunal[21]), certain foundational principles regarding the future dispute settlement mechanism have been outlined in the CU.

When disputes arise involving questions about the interpretation or application of *Union law concepts*, the arbitral tribunal is obliged to refer these questions to the CJEU. The CJEU's decision will be binding on the arbitral tribunal. Conversely, if the dispute pertains to *exceptions* to EU law agreed upon or if the interpretation of EU law concepts is not pertinent to the dispute, a referral to the CJEU is not necessary. In such instances, the arbitral tribunal will exercise exclusive jurisdiction over the proceedings and will adjudicate the dispute based on the respective agreement, in accordance with the customary rules of interpretation of public international law (including those restated in the Vienna Convention on the Law of the Treaties (VCLT)).

The CU's approach is in line with the CJEU's case law. In the context of relations between the EU and third states, the CJEU diligently considers the object and purpose underlying the terms of agreements, adhering to the principles set forth in the VCLT.[22] As a result, it distinguishes between the distinct realms governed by EU law *proper* and those governed by an international agreement, refraining from automatically applying lock-stock-and-barrel EU law concepts to FTA arrangements 'unless there are express provisions to that effect laid down by' said agreements.[23] Since such concepts can acquire a different connotation based on the wording, meaning and purpose of bilateral agreements, they necessitate interpretation within the framework of such agreements. Thus, referral to the CJEU's interpretation would only be necessary if the bilateral agreement explicitly

and the UK, of the other part [2021] OJ L149/10; ch 12 of the Trade and Economic Partnership Agreement between the EFTA [European Free Trade Association] States and the Republic of India (not yet in force); ch VIII of the FTA between Canada and the EFTA States, SR 0.632.312.32; ch X of the FTA between the EFTA States and the Republic of Chile, SR 0.632.312.451; ch IX of the Agreement between the EFTA States and Singapore, SR 0.632.316.891.1. It should, however, be added that none of these bilateral mechanisms have had a use even remotely on a par with the WTO dispute settlement mechanism.

[21] See Der Bundesrat, Definitives Verhandlungsmandat (gemäss Bundesratsbeschluss vom 8 März 2024) [Federal Council, Definitive negotiating mandate], 6.7.

[22] Case C-270/80 *Polydor* ECLI:EU:C:1982:43, para 18; Case C-351/08 *Grimme* ECLI:EU:C:2009:697, para 26 ff; Case C-70/09 *Hengartner and Gasser* EU:C:2010:430, para 36 ff; Case C-355/16 *Picart* ECLI:EU:C:2018:184, para 29; C-547/10 P *Swiss Confederation v Commission* ECLI:EU:C:2013:139, para 80.

[23] *Grimme* (n 22) paras 27–29; Case C-541/08 *Fokus Invest AG* ECLI:EU:C:2010:74, para 28. See also Peter Van Elsuwege, 'Sectoral Bilateralism: Lessons from the Case Law of the Court of Justice of the European Union' in Marc Maresceau and Christa Tobler (eds), *Switzerland and the EU: A Challenging Relationship*, vol 20 (Brill 2023) 97–116; Thomas Cottier, 'Der Rechtsschutz im Rahmenabkommen

stipulates that a notion of EU law was to be interpreted as in the context of the EU internal market.

It comes as no surprise that the role of the EU's highest court within the bilateral dispute settlement mechanism sits uncomfortably with the idea that the two contracting parties are equal partners.[24] Addressing these concerns requires a closer look at the rationale of the institutional arrangements between the EU and its third-country neighbour, Switzerland.[25]

The CJEU's exclusive power to interpret EU law[26] follows from Article 344 TFEU and is a matter of course. Who else other than the highest judicial body of an entity could have the competence to authoritatively interpret this entity's laws and regulations? Thus, the Swiss Federal Tribunal indisputably holds the ultimate authority over the interpretation of Swiss law; the same principle applies to the CJEU regarding the EU internal market law. However, whereas only Liechtenstein has opted to integrate partially with the Swiss legal order, the EU internal market, with over 450 million people, has become interesting for many neighbouring states. Notable examples include the three other EFTA states,[27] Ukraine[28] and the microstates Andorra and San Marino.[29]

Schweiz EU: Kernstück des Abkommens und Instrument schrittweiser Rechtsentwicklung' in Astrid Epiney and Petru Emanuel Zlătescu (eds), *Schweizerisches Jahrbuch für Europarecht 2020/2021* (Schulthess Verlag, 2021) 362–63.

[24] See especially Carl Baudenbacher, Rechtsgutachten zur Streitentscheidungsregelung des InstA zu Handen der Kommission des Nationalrates für Wirtschaft und Abgaben WAK, 6.

[25] Several international agreements concluded by the EU incorporate provisions for the potential involvement of the CJEU in a trade dispute between the EU and a third party (or third parties). See Art 25(2) of the EU–Turkey Association Agreement [1977] OJ L361/29; Arts 16 and 20 and Annex IV of the Multilateral Agreement between the European Community and its Member States, the Republic of Albania, Bosnia and Herzegovina, the Republic of Bulgaria, the Republic of Croatia, the former Yugoslav Republic of Macedonia, the Republic of Iceland, the Republic of Montenegro, the Kingdom of Norway, Romania, the Republic of Serbia and the United Nations Interim Administration Mission in Kosovo on the establishment of a European Common Aviation Area [2006] OJ L285/3; Art 10 of the Monetary Agreement EU–Vatican City State [2010] OJ C28/13; Art 10 of the Monetary Agreement EU–Principality of Andorra [2011] OJ C369/1; Art 10 of the Monetary Agreement EU–Republic of San Marino [2012] OJ C121/5; Art 12 of the Monetary Agreement EU–Principality of Monaco [2012] OJ C310/1; Art 267 Association Agreement EU–Georgia [2014] OJ L261/4; Art 403(2) of the Association Agreement EU–Moldova [2014] OJ L260/4; Art 322(2) of the Association Agreement EU–Ukraine [2014] OJ L161/3; and Arts 19(2) and 37(3) and Annex IV of the Treaty establishing the Transport Community [2017] OJ L278/3. While the dispute settlement mechanism under the EU–Ukraine Association Agreement was tested once (the case of *Ukraine wood export ban*, Panel Ruling from 11 December 2020), there has been no dispute thus far that has led to a reference to the CJEU or that was decided by the CJEU based on the aforementioned agreements. Under different modalities, the CJEU can play a role also in the EEA context, see Art 111(3) EEA, as well as Art 107 of and Protocol 34 to the EEA Agreement [1994] OJ L1/3.

[26] Case C-248/16 *Achmea* ECLI:EU:C:2018:158; Joined Cases T-624/15, T-694/15 and T-704/15 *Micula* ECLI:EU:T:2019:423; Case C-741/19 *Komstroy* ECLI:EU:C:2021:655; Case C-109/20 *PL Holding decision* ECLI:EU:C:2021:875.

[27] Agreement on the European Economic Area [1994] OJ L1/3.

[28] Association Agreement between the EU and its Member States, of the one part, and Ukraine, of the other part [2014] OJ L161/3.

[29] Commission proposes Association Agreement with Andorra and San Marino to the Council, Brussels, 26 April 2024, www.ec.europa.eu/commission/presscorner/detail/en/IP_24_2286.

It is in this context that the principle of autonomy of EU legal order[30] was expanded to include the insulation from 'concurring' or even dissenting interpretations by amicable fellow adjudicators,[31] since such a cacophony of interpretations was seen as a threat to the coherence and autonomy of the EU legal order. Protecting the 'public good' of a uniform and consistent application of EU law from external influences is certainly a valid rationale.[32] However, two things can be true simultaneously: agreeing with this concept in principle does not exclude the fact that the CJEU has, at times, come dangerously close 'to get[ting] high on its own supply'[33] and has 'selfishly' pushed the prerogatives of the Court,[34] sometimes in clear violation of the mandate accorded by the founding treaties.[35]

The role of the CJEU in the potential adjudicative proceedings between Switzerland and the EU would be a direct consequence of Switzerland's chosen path in its relations with the EU. Unlike the UK or Canada, which opted for agreements with the EU that only eliminate all (or nearly all) tariffs on mutual trade in goods,[36]

[30] Initially used as a demarcation line vis-à-vis the Member States, see eg Case 26/62 *Van Gend en Loos* ECLI:EU:C:1963:1. *cf* Francisco Miguel de Abreu Duarte, '"But the Last Word Is Ours": the Monopoly of Jurisdiction of the Court of Justice of the European Union in Light of the Investment Court System' (2019) 30(4) *European Journal of International Law* 1187, 1204.

[31] Opinion 1/91 *EEA Agreement* ECLI:EU:C:1991:490; Opinion 1/00, ECLI:EU:C:2002:23; Case C-459/03 *Commission v Ireland* ECLI:EU:C:2006:345; Joined Cases C-402/05 P and C- 415/05 *Kadi and Al Barakaat International Foundation v Council and Commission* ECLI:EU:C:2008:461; Opinion 1/09 ECLI:EU:C:2011:12; Opinion 2/13 *ECHR* ECLI:EU:C:2014:2454; Opinion 1/17 *CETA* ECLI:EU:C:2019:341; see also Jed Odermatt, 'When a Fence Becomes a Cage: The Principle of Autonomy in EU External Relations Law' (EUI, 2016) Working Paper MWP 2016/07. For a critical analysis of the CJEU's case law that 'places considerable constraints on the external action of both the EU and its Member States', see de Abreu Duarte (n 30). See also a recent decision of the Swiss Federal Court (4A_244/2023, 3 April 2024) regarding a challenge to an arbitral award rendered by a Swiss-seated tribunal in a dispute between a French investor and Spain under the Energy Charter Treaty (ECT). The Federal Court, as a non-EU court, held that it was not bound by CJEU case law on intra-EU international arbitration, particularly by the CJEU's decision in *Komstroy* (n 26). In *Komstroy*, the CJEU ruled that, to preserve the autonomy and particular nature of EU law, Art 26 ECT, which grants unconditional consent to investors to submit disputes to arbitration, must be interpreted as not being applicable to disputes between a Member State of the EU and an investor of another EU Member State concerning an investment made by the latter in the first Member State. The TF observed that EU institutions had been pursuing a 'crusade' againt intra-EU investment arbitations without regard for international law or principles of treaty interpretation (para 7.6.5). Unconvinced and unbound by CJEU case law, the TF conducted an analysis of the relationship between Art 26 ECT and EU law in the light of the principles of the VCLT, finding no grounds to render Art 26 ECT inapplicable to intra-EU disputes.

[32] Odermatt (n 31).

[33] Michael Hahn, 'Never Get High on Your Own Supply – "Autonomy of the EU Legal Order" and Effective Treaty-Based Dispute Settlement Mechanisms' in Michael Hahn and Guillaume Van der Loo (eds), *Law and Practice of the Common Commercial Policy* (Brill, Nijhoff 2020).

[34] Bruno De Witte, 'A Selfish Court? The Court of Justice and the Design of International Dispute Settlement Beyond the European Union' in Marise Cremona and Anne Thies (eds), *The European Court of Justice and External Relations Law* (Hart Publishing, 2014) 33–46.

[35] *cf* Opinion 2/13 (n 31); Art 6(2) of the Treaty on European Union.

[36] Trade and Cooperation Agreement between the EU and the European Atomic Energy Community, of the one part, and the United Kingdom of Great Britain and the Northern Ireland, of the other part [2021] OJ L149/10; Comprehensive Economic and Trade Agreement (CETA) between Canada, of the one part, and the European Union and its Member States, of the other part [2017] OJ L11/23.

Switzerland pursues a more ambitious strategy.[37] Already under the current status quo, Switzerland is linked with the EU in a manner surpassing 'ordinary' FTAs: not only are tariffs largely removed, but so are TBT and SPS barriers.[38] Without seeking EU membership, Switzerland has acquired an enhanced access to the EU internal market through a network of bilateral agreements, ensuring 'non-discriminatory market access' (the famous *gleichlange Spiesse*, ie a level playing field) for its formidable private sector industries. The EU's position that this barrier-free participation necessitates the application of identical or equivalent rules for goods and individuals in Switzerland and the EU has been accepted by the Swiss negotiators in principle. Switzerland, thus, would bear regulatory burdens similar to those imposed on EU Member States under the EU internal market *acquis*,[39] albeit with important exceptions and safeguard clauses. By agreeing to EU internal market law as the foundation of its contractual relationship with the EU, Switzerland has made it all but inevitable that the CJEU, as the EU's ultimate interpreter of internal market rules,[40] will have to be involved when questions of EU law are relevant in a dispute between Switzerland and the EU. Any solution that would endanger the CJEU's prerogative to authoritatively interpret EU law for *all* (ie original and 'associated'[41]) internal market participants would not withstand ex ante (pursuant to Article 218(11) TFEU) or ex post (pursuant to Article 263 TFEU) judicial scrutiny.[42]

Should the CU become an operational reality, CJEU rulings may indeed entail significant implications for Switzerland. However, the furthest-reaching consequences feared by some anti-CU proponents would seem to be based on a misunderstanding of the CJEU's role. Although it is an institution of 'the other contracting party' and its judges *are* foreign (*fremde Richter*), they would not sit in judgment over a Swiss–EU dispute. Rather, the CJEU would determine how an EU provision has to be understood. This decision would dictate the interpretation and application of the relevant provision in all subsequent cases, regardless of Swiss

[37] Der Bundesrat, Lagebeurteilung Beziehungen Schweiz–EU, 9 June 2023, 51, www.newsd.admin.ch/newsd/message/attachments/79359.pdf.

[38] For the difference between these concepts, see eg Catherine Barnard and Emilija Leinarte, 'Movement of Goods under the TCA' (2022) 13(Suppl 2) *Global Policy* 106.

[39] See, eg the preamble of the AFMP: '"the Contracting Parties" … Resolved to bring about the free movement of persons between them *on the basis of the rules applying in the European Community*, Have decided to conclude this Agreement'; the preamble of the ATA: '"the Contracting Parties" … AGREEING that is appropriate to *base* [rules for civil aviation within the area covered by the Community and Switzerland] *on the legislation which is in force within the Community*'; and Art 7 of the Road Transport Agreement Switzerland–EU: 'Switzerland shall adopt … arrangement that are *equivalent to Community legislation* on the technical conditions governing road transport' (all emphases added).

[40] Matthias Oesch, *Der EuGH und die Schweiz* (EIZ Publishing, 2023) 157.

[41] *cf* Art 217 TFEU.

[42] On the competence of the CJEU regarding the conclusion, interpretation and application of international agreements to which the EU is a party, see EPRS, 'European Court of Justice and International Agreements' (July 2021) www.europarl.europa.eu/RegData/etudes/BRIE/2021/696171/EPRS_BRI(2021)696171_ENpdf.

involvement. It would be overly self-confident to assume that the CJEU would interpret a provision with the intent of 'getting a win' over Switzerland, rather than being acutely aware that, in the process, it establishes a precedent that would shape internal market law for the foreseeable future.[43]

Moreover, the CJEU's function is to interpret EU law, ie the *foreign* legal framework to which Switzerland, via bilateral agreements, has committed and potentially will commit to adhere to sectorally. Thus, the impact of the CJEU's jurisprudence arises from the (partial) extension of the EU's internal market to Switzerland, thereby projecting both its advantages and burdens (freedoms and prohibitions) beyond the EU's borders. This is contingent upon a rather high level of integration into the EU internal market.[44] These 'rules of the game' apply to any and all states associated with the EU's internal market (Article 26 TFEU), irrespective of whether the EU partner state is a developed and advanced post-industrial Western economy with a well-established democratic tradition, advanced rule of law and robust human rights protection, such as Switzerland, or merely an emerging economy.[45] But would the involvement of the CJEU pursuant to the CU's master plan entail a notable shift for practical purposes? As the next section will show, the answer might lean towards the negative.

III. The Role of the CJEU within the Status Quo

The existing agreements between Switzerland and the EU do not contain provisions for resolving potential state-to-state disputes through adjudication; the only exception can be found in the Insurance Agreement.[46] Treaty provisions addressing the CJEU's jurisprudence are limited. In practice, however, the CJEU already exerts an important influence on Swiss jurisprudence, to the extent that CJEU case law has become an integral facet of legal practice in Switzerland.[47]

Several clauses in bilateral agreements require Swiss authorities to refer to the case law of the CJEU.[48] Swiss courts routinely consult CJEU case law before rendering decisions, somewhat following the Swiss legislator's practice pursuant to

[43] Overrulings of the CJEU are exceedingly rare indeed: see, eg Joined Cases C-267/91 and C-268/91 *Keck* ECLI:EU:C:1993:905; Case C-127/08 *Metock* ECLI:EU:C:2008:449.

[44] Michael Hahn, 'Legal Issues, Concepts and Typology of Integration' in Julien Chaisse and Christoph Hermann (eds), *The International Law of Economic Integration* (Oxford University Press, forthcoming).

[45] But see Baudenbacher (n 24) 6.

[46] Agreement between the European Economic Community and the Swiss Confederation on direct insurance other than life assurance [1991] OJ L205/3. Art 38 allows parties to refer a dispute to an arbitration tribunal. This option has never been utilised thus far.

[47] Oesch (n 40) 4, 101.

[48] These are Art 16(2) AFMP, Arts 8 and 9 SAA, Arts 5 and 6 DAA and Art 1(2) ATA. The Lugano Convention, which is a multilateral treaty and not a bilateral agreement, in its Protocol No 2, Art 1, obliges courts applying and interpreting the Convention to pay due account to decisions rendered by the courts of other states bound by the Convention and by the CJEU.

Article 141(2)(a) of the Parliament Act.[49] Despite the lack of obligation to maintain the parallelism between Swiss and CJEU jurisprudence, Swiss courts aim to ensure Switzerland's seamless integration into the Union's internal market and legal order by doing just that.[50]

A case in point is the AFMP. It mandates Swiss authorities to consider relevant CJEU case law predating the Agreement when applying Union law concepts. The Swiss Federal Tribunal (Tribunal Fédéral, TF) has opted to extend its consideration of CJEU judgments beyond that cut-off date, while always emphasising that it was under no obligation to do so.[51] The TF's decision is based on the Agreement's objective to establish freedom of movement pursuant to the pertinent EU provisions[52] and the parties' expressed intent to ensure rights and obligations equivalent to those found in EU legal acts referenced in Article 16(1) AFMP. In light of these stipulations, the TF incorporates post-cut-off CJEU case law into its considerations whenever the Agreement draws on concepts of EU law to facilitate the parallelism between the legal orders of the contracting parties. Through this approach, the Swiss legal system is already undergoing a form of dynamic alignment.[53]

The TF retains the authority to diverge from CJEU's jurisprudence, provided compelling reasons (*triftige Gründe*) warrant such action.[54] While the TF has almost never expressly departed from CJEU jurisprudence based on such compelling reasons,[55] it has, from time to time, interpreted the Agreement's provisions more restrictively or expansively, in particular when the CJEU's

[49] SR 171.10.

[50] Oesch (n 40); Francesco Maiani, 'CJEU Citations in the Case Law of the Swiss Federal Supreme Court' in Arie Reich and Hans-W Micklitz (eds), *The Impact of the European Court of Justice on Neighbouring Countries* (Oxford University Press, 2020) 81–114.

[51] BGE 136 II 5 E 3.4; BGE 142 II 35 E 3.1; BGE 147 II 1 E 2.3; BGer 2C_168/2021 E 4.2.

[52] *cf* the AFMP's preamble.

[53] Oesch (n 40) 109, citing A Zünd, 'Grundrechtsverwirklichung ohne Verfassungsgerichtsbarkeit' (2013) 22(9) *Aktuelle Juristische Praxis* 1349, 1357, refers to this process as the dynamic alignment of jurisprudence. Maiani (n 50) 100 characterises this as a 'dynamic rule of conform interpretation', opposed to a 'static rule'. An example of this scenario is the legal framework for family reunification. Art 42(2) of the Swiss Federal Act on Foreign Nationals and Integration (AIG, SR 142.20) allows foreign family members of Swiss nationals to reunite and obtain a residence permit if they have previously resided lawfully in a country with which Switzerland has a free movement agreement. This provision aligns with the 2003 CJEU judgment in Case C-109/01 *Akrich* ECLI:EU:C:2003:491. However, the 2008 CJEU judgment in Case C-127/08 *Metock* ECLI:EU:C:2008:449 rejected the prior lawful residence requirement for family members. Following this, the Swiss Federal Court ruled that this requirement no longer applies for relatives of EU citizens (BGE 136 II 5) or Swiss citizens who exercised their free movement rights under the Swiss–EU Agreement (BGE 136 II 120). Consequently, Swiss citizens relying solely on Swiss domestic law face reverse discrimination, as they do not receive the same rights as those governed by the Agreement, an issue yet to be addressed by the legislature.

[54] BGE 136 II 5 E 3.4; BGE 142 II 35 E 3.1; BGE 147 II 1 E 2.3; BGer 2C_168/2021 E 4.2.

[55] To the best of the authors' knowledge, the only instance so far where the TF expressly determined that compelling reasons necessitated a departure from the jurisprudence of the CJEU is in the case BGer 2C_484/2022 E 3.4.2. *cf* Oesch (n 40) 114; Christoph Bürki, 'Rezeption der EuGH-Rechtsprechung durch schweizerische Gerichte am Beispiel der Personenfreizügigkeit und des öffentlichen Beschaffungswesens' (Master's thesis, University of Bern, 2019).

interpretations leaned heavily on the concept of EU citizenship, rather than on the free-movement rights rationale that characterises the relationship between Switzerland and the EU.[56]

Even the much-discussed jurisprudence of the TF's Criminal Law Division concerning the expulsion of foreign criminal offenders from Switzerland (mandated by Swiss criminal law provisions in certain situations[57]) has ultimately followed that line. Initially marked by untenable assertions that Switzerland 'did not agree to freedom of movement for criminal foreigners', that it was 'not bound by the Agreement in legislating criminal law within its territory' and that expulsion for criminal offences had 'neither an economic nor a migration law component',[58] the TF's Criminal Law Division ultimately acknowledged that the rights afforded to individuals under the AFMP may preclude certain decisions on the expulsion. This approach aimed to avoid contradictions between Switzerland's international law obligations and the provisions of its criminal code. However, the TF initially departed from the CJEU's narrow interpretation of restrictions on the free movement of persons[59] and adopted its own interpretation of the public-order clause in Article 5 of Annex I of the Agreement.[60] Although the CJEU recognised the rights of Switzerland and the EU to determine the requirements of public policy and public order in line with national needs and emphasised that such determinations should be 'contemplated and interpreted in the context of the Agreement and in conformity with the objectives pursued by that Agreement',[61] it also emphasised the strict interpretation of derogations from fundamental rules. Whether the initial practice of the FT's Criminal Law Division adhered to this strict interpretation is debatable. In more recent jurisprudence, however, the Federal Court explicitly stated that expulsion decisions, while compliant with Swiss criminal law, must also undergo scrutiny in light of the Agreement.[62] It now conducts comprehensive assessments, evaluating the individual behaviour of the offender to prognosticate the future conduct and assessing the nature and extent of the potential legal interest at stake: the greater the threat, the lower the threshold for the acceptable risk of recidivism. This modus operandi appears to align with the principles formulated in pertinent CJEU case law.[63]

Considering the objectives articulated in the Schengen and Dublin Agreements, emphasising 'the most uniform possible application and interpretation' of the Schengen and Dublin *acquis*, to which Switzerland has committed, coupled with Switzerland's (soft!)[64] dynamic alignment obligation as enshrined

[56] BGE 139 II 393 E 4.1.2; see also BGE 136 II 65 E 4.2.
[57] Art 66a of the Swiss Criminal Code (StGB, SR 311.0).
[58] BGE 145 IV 55 E 3.3; BGE 145 IV 364 E 3.4.1.
[59] See, eg Case C-348/96 *Donatella Calfa* ECLI:EU:C:1999:6, para 23.
[60] For more recent case law, see 6B_149/2021 E 2.7; 6B_1264/2021 E 1.3.5.
[61] Case C-506/10 *Graf and Engel* ECLI:EU:C:2011:643, paras 32 and 33.
[62] 6B_205/2023 E 1.2.2. ff and 6B_149/2023 E 1.3.4 ff.
[63] See, eg *Donatella Calfa* (n 59); Case C-441/02 *Commission v Germany* ECLI:EU:C:2006:253.
[64] Switzerland is not legally obligated to apply and implement changes to the Schengen and Dublin *acquis* listed in the SAA and the DAA. According to Arts 2(3) and 7(2)(a) SAA and Arts 1(3) and 4(2)

in Article 2(3) SAA and Article 1(3) DAA, it is unsurprising that the Federal Court and the Federal Administrative Court adhere to the CJEU jurisprudence in these domains.[65]

Unlike the more modern Swiss–EU 'bilateral' agreements, which in certain areas enable Switzerland to participate in the EU internal market, the Swiss–EU FTA[66] is 'a pure trade agreement' that neither obliges Switzerland to harmonise its regulations covered by the Agreement with those of the EU nor gives pertinent incentives to do so.[67] Both parties retain the right of autonomous implementation, and no common institution is authorised to interpret the Agreement's provisions authoritatively for both parties. Nevertheless, the Federal Court has occasionally considered CJEU jurisprudence.[68]

In the tax dispute between the EU and Switzerland, spanning from 2005 to 2014, it was the Commission's reliance on current CJEU jurisprudence on state aid law that brought the two partners to loggerheads. The EU Commission identified certain Swiss corporate tax regulations as state aid incompatible with Article 23 FTA.[69] Article 23 FTA declares state aid that distorts or threatens to distort competition incompatible with the proper functioning of the Agreement if it may affect trade between Switzerland and the EU. This provision also allows for (appropriate) compensatory measures for the affected party under the procedure laid down in Article 27 FTA. Upon the conclusion of the Agreement in 1972, the EU (at that time, the European Economic Community, or EEC) communicated to its partner[70] that 'in the context of the autonomous implementation of Article 23(1) […], it would assess any practice contrary to that Article *on the basis of criteria arising from the application* of' (emphasis added) what are today Articles 101, 102, 107 and 108 TFEU. While such commitment to use CJEU jurisprudence issued after the signing of the FTA is limited to the EU's own 'autonomous implementation' and may not directly bind Switzerland, it has had considerable impact. The tax dispute only ended when Switzerland agreed to significantly reform its tax regime for holding corporations.[71]

DAA, Switzerland has the discretion to decide whether or not to accept and implement these changes. However, if Switzerland decides not to implement them, the consequences are specified in Arts 7(2)(b) and 7(4) SAA and Arts 4(4), 4(6) and 4(7) DAA.

[65] See, eg BGE 143 IV 264 E 2.1; BGE 146 II 201 E 4.2.3; BGE 147 IV 340 E 4.5.5; BGE 148 II 169 E 4.

[66] SR 0.632.401; [1972] OJ L300/189.

[67] BGE 131 II 271 E 10.3.

[68] See, eg BGE 131 II 271 E 10.3.

[69] EC Comm, 13 February 2007, Doc C(2007) 411 final, Decision on the incompatibility of certain Swiss company tax regimes with the Agreement between the EEC and the Swiss Confederation of 22 July 1972. For more details and for Swiss response to EU Commission's claims, see Botschaft zum Unternehmenssteuerreformgesetz III, 5 June 2015, BBl 2015, 5081 and 5189, www.admin.ch/gov/de/start/dokumentation/medienmitteilungen.msg-id-10796.html.

[70] Declaration by the European Economic Community concerning Article 23(1) of the Agreement [2003] OJ L300/189.

[71] Botschaft zum Unternehmenssteuerreformgesetz III, BBl 2015, 5082.

Swiss courts regularly refer to CJEU jurisprudence in areas of law where Switzerland autonomously aligns with the EU legal order, such as competition law,[72] even though no pertinent international obligation exists.[73] The Federal Tribunal's rationale is that Swiss courts will not sabotage the legislator's intention to align Swiss rules with EU law.[74]

The obligation or inclination to align with the practice of the CJEU extends beyond the judiciary. An example is the Swiss Regulation Governing the Placing of Plant Protection Products on the Market.[75] In substance, it relies heavily on EU legal norms, and encourages, and in certain instances mandates, the Swiss administrative authorities to base their decisions on evaluations and practices of the relevant EU institutions and bodies, including the CJEU.[76]

IV. What are the Shortcomings of the Status Quo for Switzerland and Swiss Operators?

If the ongoing negotiations between Switzerland and the EU end without reaching agreements, particularly on institutional matters, their relationship will continue to be governed by existing agreements. However, without amendments, these agreements will gradually erode, as the EU has clearly communicated that it will not update any existing market access regime without a new institutional fundament. The MRA, for example, has stopped being useful for the producers of medical devices due to the absence of a declaration that Swiss regulations are equivalent to the new EU legislation, and the same fate awaits the machinery industry. This scenario leads to significant challenges for economic operators who rely on these agreements for seamless access to the internal market. Like producers from other third countries, they would be (depending on the product category) required to demonstrate compliance with EU technical requirements and SPS measures when exporting to the EU. In certain cases, they may also need to undergo conformity testing in the EU by an EU-accredited body. This entails a significant administrative burden and imposes additional costs.

In the context of the gradual erosion of agreements, uncertainties and disputes regarding their application are likely to increase. When such issues remain unresolved by the contracting parties, Swiss individuals may be compelled to seek protection of their interests before the institutions of the EU Member States or the EU itself, and particularly the CJEU. This necessity arises because Swiss courts lack

[72] BGE 139 I 72 E 8.2.3.
[73] BGE 129 III 335 E 6.
[74] ibid.
[75] Verordnung über das Inverkehrbringen von Pflanzenschutzmitteln (SR 916.161).
[76] See, eg Arts 2(2), 4(3)(a), 8(1), 10(1), 10b(2), 12, 17(1bis)(4), 18(4), 24, 29a and 33 of Verordnung über das Inverkehrbringen von Pflanzenschutzmitteln.

jurisdiction to assess the actions of these foreign entities and are in no position to involve the CJEU directly.

However, the path to the CJEU is particularly burdensome. While Swiss operators may benefit from substantive rights and obligations derived from the primary and secondary EU law, including the EU's international agreements, their legal standing before the CJEU is constrained. Articles 263(4) and 265 TFEU afford natural and legal persons the right to challenge the acts of institutions, bodies, offices and agencies of the EU, or their failure to act, only if the challenged acts were 'intended to produce legal effects vis-à-vis third parties', were addressed to these persons or, alternatively, are of 'direct and individual concern' to them. The CJEU has construed these conditions narrowly, establishing a high threshold that is difficult to overcome in practice for non-privileged applicants. This approach ensures that the national courts of EU Member States remain the primary forum for individual complaints regarding the legality of EU acts, with (only) indirect recourse to the CJEU via Article 267 TFEU.[77] The recent experiences of Swiss applicants underscore the observation that the direct route to the CJEU is not an easy road to travel. Both processes, one initiated by Swissgrid AG[78] and the other by Atesos medical[79] before the General Court, ended with orders dismissing the actions as inadmissible.

Swissgrid AG, the sole transmission system operator (TSO) of electricity in Switzerland, supported by the other EU TSOs and the EU Agency for the Cooperation of Energy Regulators, sought, pursuant to Article 1(7) of Commission Regulation (EU) 2017/2195,[80] to participate on European platforms for the exchange of balancing energy, including the Trans European Replacement Reserves Exchange platform (TERRE). However, in a letter, the Commission first noted that Swissgrid's participation on these platforms was not compliant with EU law, in the absence of its prior authorisation. Secondly, it pointed out that the conditions for such participation had not been met, and finally, the TSOs were requested to exclude Swissgrid AG from the TERRE platform. Deeming this letter a decision refusing to authorise Switzerland's participation under Article 1(7) Regulation (EU) 2017/2195, Swissgrid AG petitioned the General Court to annul it. However, the Court found that the Commission's letter did not constitute a decision capable of producing legal effects vis-à-vis the applicant within the meaning of Article 263(1) TFEU.[81] Rather, it accepted the view that, while Article 1(7) of

[77] Astrid Kjeldgaard-Pedersen, *The International Legal Personality of the Individual* (Oxford University Press, 2018) 221.

[78] Case T-127/21 *Swissgrid AG* ECLI:EU:T:2022:868, appealed, case before the Court of Justice, C-121/23 P.

[79] Case T-764/21 *Atesos medical AG* ECLI:EU:T:2022:91, appealed, case before the Court of Justice, C-491/23 P.

[80] [2017] OJ L312/6.

[81] *cf* eg Case T-43/16 *Telecom v Commission* ECLI:EU:T:2018:660, para 46; Case C-141/02 P *Commission v T-Mobile Austria* ECLI:EU:C:2005:98, para 70; Case T-884/16 *Multiconnect v Commission* ECLI:EU:T:2018:665, para 41.

Commission Regulation (EU) 2017/2195 established a procedure for authorisation, it did not grant Swissgrid AG the right to request and obtain it, leaving the Commission's decision-making power discretionary. Hence, according to the CJEU, the letter did not change Swissgrid AG's legal position or infringe upon any individual rights.

Several Swiss manufacturers of medical devices (Atesos medical AG and others) encountered similar legal obstacles when pursuing annulment proceedings before the CJEU. These manufacturers, whose products had obtained certification from SQS (a designated Swiss conformity assessment body), faced challenges upon the enactment of EU Regulation (EU) 2017/745 on medical devices. Following the entrance into force of the Regulation, the EU Commission published a notice signalling the cessation of mutual recognition of medical devices between the EU and Switzerland. The cessation occurred because there were no amendments to the Swiss–EU MRA that would incorporate the new EU Regulation and the corresponding Swiss rules on medical devices. Consequently, the Commission announced that the certificates for medical devices issued by Swiss conformity assessment bodies would no longer be recognised, and the NANDO (New Approach Notified and Designated Organisation) database entry for SQS was updated to reflect the expiration of its designation under Directive 93/42.

The General Court dismissed the manufacturers' legal action against the Commission's decision on the NANDO entry as manifestly inadmissible and upon appeal the CJEU affirmed the General Court's decision. The Court ruled that the Commission's decision was not reviewable, as it did not produce legal effects capable of changing the applicants' legal position within the meaning of Article 263(1) TFEU and established case law.[82] Central to the Court's reasoning was the assertion that alteration to entries in the NANDO database did not impact the validity of SQS's designation or certificates. Instead, their expiration and invalidity resulted from the enactment of Regulation 2017/745, which repealed Directive 93/42, alongside the failure to amend the MRA. In essence, the contested decision lacked distinct legal effects beyond those triggered by the enactment of the new Regulation, thereby failing to meet the criteria delineated by case law.

While the distinction between acts 'intended to produce legal effects vis-à-vis third parties' and those that are not is not always straightforward and can pose challenges, nothing suggests that the CJEU applied the law differently to Swiss applicants compared to how it would treat EU applicants. These cases simply illustrate the restricted access private actors have to the CJEU under Article 263 TFEU, reflecting the systemic preference for private operators to initiate proceedings before a domestic court of an EU Member State, which would refer a question of EU law to the CJEU pursuant to Article 267 TFEU. This option is, however, never easily (and sometimes not at all) available to Swiss operators, or even Switzerland itself. Consequently, it appears that there are, and will likely continue

[82] See, eg Case C-31/13 P *Hungary v Commission* ECLI:EU:C:2014:70, paras 56–65.

to be, scenarios in which Swiss economic operators lack a legal remedy when they believe that their rights under the bilateral agreements or EU law proper have been affected.

The situation concerning another Swiss company, Stahlwerke Gerlafingen, claiming to be experiencing economic hardship due to another decision by the EU Commission, differs somewhat, albeit with no brighter prospects. Commission Implementing Regulation (EU) 2019/159[83] imposes a tariff-rate quota coupled with an additional duty of 25 per cent on steel products, including those from Switzerland, where Stahlwerke Gerlafingen operates. Given that the Swiss–EU FTA prohibits the introduction of new customs duties and charges equivalent to customs duties, it is arguable that the EU Regulation potentially violates the FTA. This is notwithstanding the FTA's provision for the adoption of appropriate measures in cases of significant disturbances in economic sectors (Article 26), subject to the procedural requirements outlined in Article 27 of the FTA. Despite Switzerland's repeated expressions of concern regarding the legality of the EU measure within the FTA Joint Committee, the EU has maintained its stance. As per the FTA, Switzerland's options are limited to initiating a procedure for potential WTO law violation before the WTO Dispute Settlement Body. Consequently, the affected company, Stahlwerke Gerlafingen, must contend with the repercussions of this measure on its own.

In this context, the sole available legal recourse for Stahlwerke Gerlafingen is to contest decisions issued by EU Member States' authorities imposing customs duties, asserting their illegality under Article 216 TFEU and the Swiss–EU FTA. However, pursuing this avenue, albeit available, would entail a protracted process involving decisions by various authorities and courts of an EU Member State, ultimately leading to a judgment of the CJEU under Article 267 TFEU. Such proceedings are inherently time-consuming and could span several years. Even in the event of a favourable outcome, it is likely to arrive too late for a company already grappling with the severe economic ramifications of the EU measure.

An examination of recent and potential Swiss experiences before the CJEU would be incomplete without highlighting the singular case so far in which Switzerland participated as a party to the proceedings.[84] This occurred following the decision by German authorities to establish procedures for instrument-guided landings and take-offs at Zurich airport, which set out several limitations on airport approaches.[85] Upon the Commission's approval of the German decision

[83] Commission Implementing Regulation (EU) 2019/159 of 31 January 2019 imposing definitive safeguard measures against imports of certain steel products [2019] OJ L31/27.

[84] It should be noted that Switzerland sporadically participates in preliminary ruling procedures by submitting written observations before the CJEU, as outlined in Art 8(2) SAA and Art 5(2) DAA. For a comprehensive list of cases in which Switzerland has submitted written observations, see www.bj.admin.ch/bj/de/home/sicherheit/schengen-dublin/uebersichten.html.

[85] The German measures prohibited low-altitude overflights of German territory near the Swiss border between 21.00 and 07.00 on weekdays and between 20.00 and 09.00 on weekends and public holidays to reduce noise exposure for residents. Consequently, the two northern landing approaches,

(2004/12/EC), Switzerland brought the action for annulment of the Commission's decision.

Known as the *(Zurich) Airport Noise Case*,[86] this dispute vividly illustrates the complexity inherent to the Swiss model of EU integration. The CJEU emphasised Switzerland's decisions to reject the EEA Agreement and abstain from joining 'the internal market of the European Union, the aim of which is the removal of all obstacles to create an area of total freedom of movement', forming the contextual framework for the CJEU's interpretation of specific provisions governing the relationship between Switzerland and the EU.[87] In the case at issue, they led to two major consequences: procedural and material rights disparities between Switzerland and EU Member States. Firstly, despite accepting CJEU jurisdiction pursuant to Article 20 ATA, Switzerland did not enjoy the same procedural privileges before the CJEU as Member States under Article 263(2) TFEU. Instead, it was 'downgraded' (without further elaboration) to the status of 'any legal person' (Article 263(4) TFEU), necessitating recourse to the General Court before pleading before the Court of Justice.

Regarding material rights, the CJEU reaffirmed the *Polydor*[88] principle, limiting the automatic extension of EU internal market interpretations to the Swiss–EU ATA, unless expressly provided for in the Agreement itself. In the event, the relevant EU law was EU Regulation No 2408/92, certain provisions of which, but not all, were included in the ATA. Switzerland's reliance on the *Malpensa* judgment[89] was dismissed since the ATA lacked provisions enabling air carriers to benefit from EU law provisions on the freedom to provide services. Reading Regulation No 2408/92 in the Swiss–EU context necessitates adherence 'only' to the principle of equal treatment of nationals and non-nationals (Article 3 ATA) when imposing conditions on traffic rights by air carriers (Article 15 ATA). The General Court concluded that the Commission's decision was justified and proportionate, and thus did not infringe upon the rights of Swiss carriers.

V. Conclusion

Swiss opponents of a CU-based treaty package view the envisaged involvement of the CJEU in all questions related to EU law as the clearest indication of an unequal

previously used as primary routes for flights landing at Zurich airport, were rendered unavailable during these specific time frames.

[86] *Swiss Confederation* (n 22) and case before the General Court T-319/05 ECLI:EU:T:2010:367.

[87] *Swiss Confederation* (n 22) paras 78 and 79; see also *Grimme* (n 22) paras 26 and 27; *Fokus Invest* (n 23) para 27.

[88] *Polydor* (n 22).

[89] Case C-361/98 *Malpensa* ECLI:EU:C:2001:29, in which the CJEU confirmed that Regulation No 2408/92 had introduced the freedom to provide services in the air transport sector prohibiting not only all discrimination on grounds of nationality against providers of air transport services, but also any restrictions.

treaty relationship. The rhetoric used includes references to colonial and quasi-colonial relationships.

This chapter has demonstrated that the CJEU's current impact on the Swiss legal order is far from negligible; the same is true for EU law in general. Switzerland's choice to remain outside the Union, while desiring to participate in the EU's internal market, has created a situation where, although nominally unburdened by the obligations of a Member State, it implements most of the internal market law, not unlike an EU or EEA Member State. At the same time, its interests are not being projected into the Union's decision-making process. Thus, whatever the CJEU pronounces on EU law unavoidably serves as a contextual reference for Swiss decision-makers applying (EU-based) Swiss law, even if the CJEU's decisions are not technically binding.

The CU's landing zone for the Swiss–EU dispute settlement mechanism would nonetheless be dogmatically a seismic shift. A rules-based arbitral tribunal would be in charge of settling disputes between the two partners regarding their market access agreements. With regard to the CJEU, the CU model would recognise its last word concerning the interpretation of EU law, a feature so far absent from the Swiss–EU agreements. In essence, though, not much would change with regard to the last point. At the time of writing, it is already the CJEU who authoritatively determines EU law. Moreover, the Swiss TF already accepts and follows CJEU rulings as if it were obliged to do so, despite asserting that it is legally free to dissent.

The CJEU's new role is part of a comprehensive arrangement that, on the whole, would greatly enhance legal certainty and predictability. Following the unilateral termination of treaty negotiations in 2021, the EU responses have included measures that have significantly affected Swiss private and state-owned entities, leaving Switzerland without an effective judicial remedy. Under the CU's architecture, Switzerland could request an arbitral tribunal to enjoin unlawful EU actions, thereby allowing Swiss private actors to avoid litigating in foreign courts under foreign laws and ensuring support from the Swiss Confederation for its private sector.

Regardless of the outcome of the current negotiations between the EU and Switzerland, the laws of economic gravity mandate that the foreign court, the CJEU, will remain extraordinarily important for one of the world's most successful exporting nations. Despite being second to none when it comes to sovereignty consciousness, Switzerland's deep economic ties with the surrounding market of 450+ million consumers ensure the relevance of the Court, which serves as the guardian of the Union's internal market regime.

12

Free Movement of Services between the EU and Switzerland – The Contours, Limits and Prospects of a Complex Relationship

PANAGIOTIS DELIMATSIS

I. Introduction

The relationship between Switzerland and the EU is, in all respects, extraordinary. Switzerland is not a member of the EU; the Swiss population rejected membership to the European Economic Area (EEA); and the country demurred in 2021 when faced with the chance to sign the institutional framework agreement that the two partners had agreed to work towards as early as in 2014 (and for which negotiations had essentially already stopped in late-2018).[1] At the same time, just a quick glance at a map would suggest that the fate of the two partners is inextricably intertwined, characterised by a high degree of interdependence due to their geographical proximity.

Indeed, the EU–Swiss bilateral relationship has been long-standing and dynamic, displaying a gradual but unmistakenly discernible deepening of economic integration. Although Switzerland chose to remain a non-member of the EU,[2] the EU is by far Switzerland's most important trading partner: in the area of goods, about 70 per cent of Swiss imports come from the EU, while the EU is the recipient of half of Swiss exports. With a value of goods trade exceeding €330 billion, Switzerland is the EU's fourth most important trading partner, after

[1] For a Swiss perspective on how these negotiations have evolved, including the reasons that led to the collapse of the bilateral negotiations, see Federal Council, 'Bericht betreffend die Verhandlungen über ein institutionelles Abkommen zwischen der Schweiz und der EU' (26 May 2021) www.newsd.admin.ch/newsd/message/attachments/66830.pdf.

[2] See, generally, Christa Tobler and Jacques Beglinger, *Grundzüge des bilateralen (Wirtschafts-) Rechts Schweiz–EU* (Dike Verlag, 2013); Matthias Oesch, *Schweiz-Europäische Union – Grundlagen, Bilaterale Abkommen, Autonomer Nachvollzug* (EIZ Publishing, 2020).

the USA, China and the UK. When it comes to trade in services, the economic relationship is no less significant. Switzerland is EU's third most important trading partner, accounting for 9 per cent of EU's total trade in services (some €230 billion). Being in the heart of Europe, Switzerland is an obvious trading partner for the EU; for Switzerland, the fact that it shares immediate geographical borders with the three most important EU consumer markets means that physical barriers to market access are substantially lower than those faced by certain EU Member States who are at the periphery of the EU territory.

This high degree of economic interdependence is translated into – and nurtured by – a wide matrix of preferential agreements between Switzerland and the EU (and an extensive number of decisions by joint committees), the most important of which is the 1972 Free Trade Agreement (FTA).[3] The FTA aimed at the elimination of bilateral tariffs, discriminatory taxation and quantitative restrictions to industrial goods but, being a traditional agreement of this type, did not foresee any harmonisation of laws – or a locked-in procedure that would gradually lead to such a result.[4] However, the FTA includes a provision that offers a certain dynamism to the potential extension of the Agreement to matters that the parties decided not to cover at the time, thereby allowing the parties to seek the coverage of new areas by submitting a reasoned request to the EU–Switzerland Joint Committee seeking the opening of negotiations.[5]

In the years that followed, the Agreement has been amended by a series of decisions by the Joint Committee,[6] but also by a large number of additional protocols and other supplementary documents. As the question of a potential membership in the EEA, aiming to extend the single market to the European Free Trade Association (EFTA) countries, was rejected in a referendum by the Swiss people in 1992, the EU and Switzerland agreed in 1999 on a package of seven bilateral agreements (Bilaterals I), supplemented by nine additional sectoral agreements in 2004 (Bilaterals II) and a series of additional agreements that covered various areas, notably in the field of taxation and police cooperation.[7]

These agreements can be regarded as proxies for EU membership in the light of Switzerland's long-standing reluctance to apply for full EU membership and to participate in the single market that the EEA agreement created between the EU and Norway, Iceland and Liechtenstein. The bilateral agreements perfectly enunciate the Swiss approach to differentiated integration with the EU: selective autonomous adaptation to the EU legal order based on national interests.[8]

[3] See Agreement between the European Economic Community and Switzerland [1972] OJ L300/189.

[4] See BGE 104 IV 175.

[5] See Art 32 of the Swiss–EU FTA.

[6] For a list of these decisions, see https://eur-lex.europa.eu/legal-content/EN/TXT/?qid=1474544988881&uri=CELEX:01972A0722%2803%29-20160201.

[7] For a complete list, see www.eda.admin.ch/content/dam/europa/de/documents/publikationen_dea/accords-liste_de.pdf.

[8] See also Matthias Oesch, 'The Swiss Model of European Integration' in Andrea Biondi, Patrick Birkinshaw and Maria Kendrick (eds), *Brexit: The Legal Implications* (Wolters Kluwer, 2019) 35, 42.

Such adaptation has varied from a wave of adopting EU compatible legislation in the aftermath of rejecting the EEA to the implementation of the Schengen *acquis* and the autonomous recognition of the *Cassis de Dijon* doctrine in 2010.[9]

Thus, in many respects, Switzerland participates in the EU internal market, often based on an approach driven by an autonomously implemented, market-oriented alignment to EU law, which, for some, amounts to a form of passive, or de facto, EU membership.[10] In recent years, however, this approach has been contested internally and by the EU: at the national level, a dynamic was developed for more Swiss differentiation, notably regarding free movement of persons; at the EU level, the opposite trend was observed, that is, offering less room for differentiation to Switzerland associated with an attempt to recalibrate the degree of potential divergence.[11]

Absent an institutional framework, updates of the Swiss–EU sectoral agreements only take place when they are in the interests of the EU. For example, the air transport agreement continues to be regularly updated. In contrast, important areas of the Mutual Recognition Agreement (covering, for instance, medical devices or machinery), the Land Transport Agreement or the Agreement on Agriculture have not been updated since 2018. This leads to a creeping erosion of Switzerland's level of integration, which makes it more difficult for Swiss companies to access the EU market. Thus, the bilateral framework is no longer capable of securing frictionless market access for the contracting parties.

As the current agreements concluded between the EU and Switzerland do not cover all commercial aspects of the EU–Swiss relationship, much EU–Switzerland trade is governed by international law, most notably the law of the World Trade Organization (WTO). This is the case in particular with regard to trade in services, although certain aspects of bilateral trade in services are covered through a dispersed set of agreements on insurance (currently the only agreement between the parties covering financial services), the free movement of persons, air transport, the carriage of goods by rail or road, and government procurement. Similarly, the current bilateral relationship does not incorporate a level of protection equivalent to the free movement of capital, which means that Switzerland is treated as a third country in this respect.[12]

In view of the comprehensive partnership that the two trading partners have cultivated for years, but also due to the importance of the service sector for the two economies (services account for over 70 per cent of both the Swiss and the EU economy), this constitutes an anomaly and an area where great economic potential remains untapped. While a fundamental pillar of the EU internal market – that

[9] Based on this principle, EEA products would be considered as meeting the Swiss technical requirements and standards when sold in Switzerland.

[10] See Thomas Cottier et al, *Die Rechtsbeziehungen der Schweiz und der Europäischen Union* (Stämpfli, 2014).

[11] See G Malet and S Walter, 'Have Your Cake and Eat It, Too? Switzerland and the Feasibility of Differentiated Integration after Brexit' (2023) 47(5) *West European Politics* 1150.

[12] See, eg Case C-541/08 *Fokus Invest* ECLI:EU:C:2010:74, paras 38ff.

is, the free movement of persons – is extended in the EU relationship through the Agreement on the Free Movement of Persons (AFMP) with Switzerland, at the current state of bilateral legal obligations, the freedom to provide and receive services is not guaranteed. However, both sides seemingly recognise that services should be part of a potential amendment of the legal framework binding the two trading partners,[13] although Swiss economic actors are worried that, by agreeing to a new institutional framework, Switzerland will lose sovereign control over flows of service suppliers and workers.[14]

If there is one European academic who has forcefully, daringly and convincingly argued for a nuanced approach to sovereignty and federalism that takes common values, interests and even common sense into account, it is Professor Thomas Cottier. Thomas has been an unwaveringly ardent advocate and an inspirational figure of the pro-EU movement in Switzerland, a voice of reason amidst heated debates notably on the Swiss side. In addition, and equally importantly, Thomas has trained various Swiss and European academics, creating a diverse group of academic scholars who are convinced and adamant about the benefits of further integration of Switzerland in the EU, and has joined all those voices calling for new approaches to how we view sovereignty in a world of accrued interdependence.[15] Thomas has insisted on viewing sovereignty in the EU–Swiss context as the possibility to have a say (*Mitsprache*) and to co-determine policies (*Mitbestimmung*).[16]

With respect to trade in services in particular, Thomas has underscored on multiple occasions the irony of Switzerland being a services economy with an oversized financial sector and yet not seeking in any active manner the conclusion of an agreement on services with the EU.[17] To honour his commitment to and impact on the cause of ever-higher levels of economic integration between the EU and Switzerland especially in the area of services throughout his entire career, my contribution will focus on a critical reflection of the existing framework covering trade in services between the EU and Switzerland. As the most important instrument facilitating trade in services in the current bilateral context, the AFMP is

[13] See, eg Council's conclusions on EU relations with the Swiss Confederation, 28 February 2017, para 6; Council's conclusions on EU relations with the Swiss Confederation, 19 February 2019, para 12. See also European Parliament resolution on EU–Switzerland relations, 2023/2042(INI), 4 October 2023, para 22. On the Swiss side, see, eg the comments by the Swiss employers association in Bundesrat, 'Bericht über die Ergebnisse der Konsultation zum Entwurf eines Verhandlungsmandats zwischen der Schweiz und der Europäischen Union über die Stabilisierung und Weiterentwicklung ihrer Beziehungen' (8 March 2024).

[14] Bundesrat (n 13).

[15] A famous academic who affected Thomas's thinking on sovereignty, new governance structures and the challenges of multi-level governance has been the late John Jackson: see J Jackson, 'Sovereignty-Modern: A New Approach to an Outdated Concept' (2003) 97(4) *American Journal of International Law* 782.

[16] See Thomas Cottier, 'Die Bilateralen III sind ein faires Bündnis, kein "Kolonialvertrag"' *Neue Zürcher Zeitung* (15 February 2024) www.nzz.ch/meinung/die-bilateralen-iii-sind-ein-faires-buendnis-kein-kolonialvertrag-ld.1777461.

[17] See, eg his interview at *Neue Zürcher Zeitung* (30 July 2018) www.nzz.ch/schweiz/wir-werden-uns-zwangslaeufig-staerker-an-die-eu-anlehnen-muessen-ld.1407586.

discussed extensively. Section II analyses the contours of the AFMP and issues of interpretation, while section III focuses on the freedom to provide and receive services under the AFMP, including certain systemic issues with respect to service supply in the bilateral context, touching upon the issue of recognition of professional qualifications of service providers as governed by the AFMP. Section IV concludes.

II. The Agreement on the Free Movement of Persons and Regulatory Convergence in the EU–Swiss Bilateral Relationship

A. Certain Contextual Observations

The relationship between the EU and Switzerland is *sui generis*, enunciated through a dense network of bilateral agreements. In the broadest terms, Switzerland's relationship with the EU continues to be governed by the 1972 Agreement relating to free trade and competition rules. However, this agreement does not offer a comprehensive or coherent framework to govern the bilateral relationship or regulatory approximation – and definitely not by today's standards, whereby FTAs have become very complex and sophisticated.

Following the rejection of accession to the EEA by the Swiss population in 1992, Switzerland has opted for a sector-based approach, potentially leading to a long-term rapprochement with the EU and a parallel process of regulatory approximation.[18] This approach led to the adoption of a series of agreements, starting with the Insurance Agreement in 1989. This relationship goes beyond trade and economic matters to also cover justice and internal matters. Since December 2008, Switzerland has been part of the Schengen area and has adopted the Schengen *acquis*, which entails above all the suppression of internal border controls and foresees dynamic regulatory alignment with EU law.

In a historic watershed moment in the bilateral context that aimed essentially to offer an alternative to the EEA framework, Switzerland concluded seven bilateral agreements with the EU (Bilaterals I) in 1999, thus complementing the 1972 FTA. Absent EEA membership for Switzerland, these agreements aimed at offering to Switzerland a similar level of access to the EU single market. This set of agreements is to be viewed within both parties' attempts to find substitutes for the Swiss rejection of legal instruments that the other EFTA members were keen to adhere to. In return, Switzerland agreed to a substantial financial contribution

[18] Hufbauer and Baldwin describe the EU–Swiss relationship as an example of 'hub-and-spoke' bilateralism. G Hufbauer and R Baldwin, 'The Shape of a Free Trade Agreement between Switzerland and the United States – A Report by the Institute for International Economics' (2005).

of over CHF 1 billion that was dedicated to addressing disparities and achieving cohesion in the newly acceding countries during the 2004 EU enlargement, but also later Romania, Bulgaria and, more recently, Croatia.[19]

The most important agreement within the two packages of Swiss–EU bilateral agreements is the AFMP. This was signed as part of a package of seven agreements by both the then-European Community and its Member States on the basis of Article 310 of the Treaty establishing the European Community (ECT) (now Article 217 of the Treaty on the Functioning of the European Union (TFEU)),[20] on the one hand, and Switzerland, on the other. The AFMP does not fall within the exclusive competence of the Community, but is considered a mixed agreement, where the competences as regards the regulation of free movement of (natural) persons are shared by the Community and its Member States.

Such mandatory delimitation of competences was confirmed in the Opinion of the Court relating to the signature of the WTO Agreement.[21] At stake was whether, in accordance with the Common Commercial Policy (CCP) provisions of the EC Treaty, the then-European Community had the exclusive competence to conclude the WTO Agreement. With regard to the General Agreement on Trade in Services (GATS), the Court of Justice of the European Union (CJEU) had to demarcate among the four modes of supplying services that the GATS recognises. As for Mode 1 (cross-border supply), whereas neither the supplier nor the recipient of the service moves, but only the service, the Court found that the Community has exclusive competence, as this Mode did not differ from 'traditional' trade in goods. As to the temporary movement of persons (Mode 4 in GATS vernacular), however, the Court ruled that the EC Treaty clearly aims to distinguish between the CCP and measures concerning the entry and movement of third-country nationals. According to the Court, 'the existence in the Treaty of specific chapters on the free movement of natural and legal persons shows that those matters do not fall within the [CCP]'.[22]

[19] This financial contribution is for all practical purposes similar to – in fact, proportionately higher than – the contribution paid by the other EFTA/EEA countries (Norway, Iceland and Liechtenstein). In 2022, the EU and Switzerland agreed on a second, slightly higher financial contribution of over CHF 1.3 billion, to be disbursed over a 10-year planning and implementation phase (until 2029) and based on bilateral agreements signed between Switzerland and each EU Member State concerned to support cohesion but also to address migration. See the Memorandum of Understanding signed by the EU and Switzerland, www.eda.admin.ch/content/dam/europa/en/documents/abkommen/MoU-CH-EU-zweiter-schweizer-beitrag-unterzeichnet_ENpdf. The current negotiations are aimed at, inter alia, the establishment by the beginning of EU's 7th multiannual financial framework (ie as of 2028 onwards) of a permanent, legally binding mechanism for Switzerland's regular financial contribution to EU's cohesion: see the Council's Decision 2024/995 authorizing the opening of negotiations with the Swiss Confederation [2024] OJ L 2024/995.

[20] Art 217 TFEU reads: 'The Union may conclude with one or more third countries or international organisations agreements establishing an association involving reciprocal rights and obligations, common action and special procedure.'

[21] See Opinion 1/94 *WTO Agreement* ECLI:EU:C:1994:384.

[22] ibid para 46. See also Markus Krajewski, 'Of Modes and Sectors – External Relations, Internal Debates, and the Special Case of (Trade in) Services' in Marise Cremona (ed), *Developments in EU External Relations Law* (Oxford University Press, 2008) 172, 189.

The Court reached a similar conclusion in Opinion 1/08, relating to the modification of the EU schedule under the GATS after the EU's Eastern enlargement.[23] With the entry into force of the Lisbon Treaty, though, the EU Member States clarified the question of exclusive competence regarding the conclusion of tariff and trade agreements covering trade in goods and services. In its famous Opinion 2/15 (*EU–Singapore FTA*),[24] the Court confirmed the broad substantive scope of application of the new Article 207 TFEU that establishes an exclusive competence in commercial matters for the EU, covering all aspects of trade in services, including transport services.[25]

B. The Contours of the AFMP

The AFMP constitutes the most decisive step towards further integration among the two economies, as it introduces in the bilateral relationship the arguably most important fundamental freedom in the EU internal market edifice, the free movement of persons. Regarding its scope of application, the AFMP applies to all EU Member States, in the aftermath of consecutive successful referenda on this score in Switzerland and despite the recent upheaval about whether the extension of free movement rights to Croatia is compatible with the Swiss popular vote in 2014 to limit immigration.[26] As demonstrated below, the AFMP is the expression of the current bilateral, fragmented, 'learning-by-doing' approach at its best: in one and the same agreement, certain provisions imply the full application of EU legal acts, considering Switzerland as an EU Member State (this is notably the case regarding the social security scheme), while other provisions of the same agreement call for a more restrictive application – and thus, integration – of Union law (this is notably evident in relation to the freedom of establishment and services).[27]

The AFMP consists of a framework agreement including 25 Articles, three Annexes and several Protocols. It ensures its forward-looking character by including

[23] See Opinion 1/08, ECLI:EU:C:2009:739.

[24] See Opinion 2/15, ECLI:EU:C:2017:376.

[25] See also Panagiotis Delimatsis, 'The Evolution of the EU External Trade Policy in Services – CETA, TTIP, and TiSA after Brexit' (2017) 20(3) *Journal of International Economic Law* 583.

[26] See Swissinfo, 'Switzerland Grants Full Free Movement Rights to Croatians' (22 October 2021).

[27] After the withdrawal of the UK from the EU, Switzerland and the UK agreed on a set of agreements that aim at ensuring continuity and a level of access similar to the AFMP post-Brexit. With respect to services in particular, the UK–Switzerland bilateral relationship is governed by a temporary services mobility agreement (SMA), which combines elements from the AFMP and the GATS and is valid until the end of December 2025 (https://assets.publishing.service.gov.uk/media/5fe2297be90e074525bf7bfb/uk-swiss-agreement-services-mobility.pdf), and a Citizen Rights Agreement, which guarantees the rights that service providers have established before the end of the implementation period (ie before the end of January 2020) www.sem.admin.ch/dam/sem/en/data/eu/fza/brexit/abkommen-ch-uk-brexit-e.pdf.download.pdf/abkommen-ch-uk-brexit-e.pdf. A look at the mobility agreement reveals that the protection offered to service providers is not exactly the same. For instance, recognition of professional qualification is left for the future through deliberations of a Working Group, whereas there is no provision covering service recipients.

a standstill clause, prohibiting new restrictive measures in the areas covered by the Agreement.[28] Crucially, the standstill obligation is not a grandfathering provision exempting measures taken prior to the date of signature of the Agreement from its scope. In *Finanzamt Köln-Süd*, the CJEU clarified that any exception to the fundamental principle of equal treatment should have been expressly included in the AFMP in order to be shielded from the scope of agreement.[29] Thus, it would be against the objectives of the Agreement relating to gradual liberalisation of free movement of persons if the parties to the Agreement could maintain restrictions which are otherwise prohibited just because they existed when the Agreement was concluded. Thus, the liberalising effect of the Agreement consists not only of preventing the introduction of future restrictions, but also of requiring that previous restrictions be eliminated.

The Agreement aims at strengthening the economic ties between the EU and Switzerland,[30] yet it does much more than that: in certain areas specifically prescribed by the established legal framework that binds the two parties, the two parties agreed to extend to Switzerland certain rights and obligations typically ascribed to EU Member States. However, the Agreement incorporates various provisions that aim at limiting or spelling out its material and temporal scope alike. Additionally, the Agreement contains an exceptions provision, which is part of Annex I but appears to apply to the entire AFMP. Similarly to the TFEU, Article 5:1 of Annex I allows restrictions to the rights under the AFMP only in case of overriding interests relating to public order, public security or public health.[31] In accordance with Union law, though, such justifications are to be interpreted strictly.[32] Importantly, the AFMP gives the right to persons covered by it to lodge an appeal against decisions by competent authorities regarding the application of the AFMP. Such decisions should be amenable to judicial review, according to Article 11, and the same would apply in case competent authorities do not take a decision within a reasonable period of time. Clearly, the Agreement then incorporates unequivocal rights for EU and Swiss citizens that derive directly from the AFMP.

The AFMP extends EU citizens' free movement rights to Switzerland in their quality as workers or self-employed persons. However, economically inactive persons also enjoy these rights provided that they can prove their financial independence and health insurance coverage. The Agreement is unequivocally focused on the movement of *natural* persons. Thus, legal persons cannot claim the rights that derive from the freedom of establishment and are offered to self-employed

[28] See Case C-506/10 *Graf and Engel* ECLI:EU:C:2011:643, para 35.

[29] Case C-627/22 *Finanzamt Köln-Süd* ECLI:EU:C:2024:431, paras 115–16.

[30] ibid para 33.

[31] See also BGE 145 IV 55, 63; and BGE 145 IV 364, 371. The Swiss Federal Court also noted in this latter case that any deviation from previous CJEU case law cannot be undertaken lightly.

[32] See *Graf and Engel* (n 28) para 33. See also BGE 139 II 121.

persons (including frontier self-employed persons) under the Agreement.[33] However, when it comes to the freedom to provide services, natural and legal persons can supply services for a brief duration, that is, a period of 90 days per year.[34] Even so, the AFMP clearly aims to cover all categories of natural persons covered in Union law by the free movement of persons and freedom of establishment – albeit with certain twists, depending on the right at stake.[35]

This reveals the AFMP parties' original intention to, first, and with the exception of the provision of services, cover any economic activity of a natural person, and, second, apply the totality of the *acquis communautaire* in this specific area. All concepts of Union law used in the AFMP, such as 'worker', 'employed person', 'self-employed person' or 'equal treatment', are to be interpreted in accordance with the case law of the CJEU.[36] This would include exceptions to free movement rights, including the non-exhaustive list of overriding reasons in the general interest that the Court has essentially created and expanded over the years and the principle of proportionality that the Court has meticulously crafted.[37]

Importantly, the CJEU clarified that nationals of both parties can claim rights under the AFMP not only against the state to which they exercise their right to freedom of movement, but also against their state of origin. For instance, in *Wächtler*, the Court found that the principle of equal treatment can be relied on against the state of origin of a self-employed person who meets the requirements laid down by the Agreement.[38] Indeed, the AFMP has been invoked in a relatively high number of cases, notably of fiscal nature, due to alleged restrictions that EU Member States imposed on EU nationals who moved their residence and/or economic activity to Switzerland but continued to be taxed (in part at least) in their state of origin.[39] In that regard, and with a minimal involvement by the Swiss state, the Court has confirmed the extension of its case law relating to free movement also to Switzerland.

However, in *Picart*, the Court underscored that the rights deriving from AFMP are *analogous* to those under Article 49 TFEU, although not exactly the *same*.[40]

[33] See also Case C-13/08 *Stamm and Hauser* ECLI:EU:C:2008:774, para 44; Case C-351/08, *Grimme*, ECLI:EU:C:2009:697, para 34. Companies can benefit from the freedom of establishment to a certain extent under the agreements on insurance or air transport.

[34] See Art 5 AFMP.

[35] See also AG Wathelet's Opinion in Case C-581/17 *Wächtler* ECLI:EU:C:2018:779, para 48. See also Case C-355/16 *Picart* ECLI:EU:C:2018:184.

[36] See, eg Case C-478/15, *Radgen* ECLI:EU:C:2016:705, para 47; *Finanzamt Köln-Süd* (n 29) para 83. For an application, see BGE 140 II 460. See also Minh Son Nguyen, 'Le travailleur, l'indépendant, le prestataire de services et le travailleur détaché en droit suisse des migrations économiques' in Minh Son Nguyen and Cesla Amarelle (eds), *Migrations et économie – L'accès des étrangers à la vie économique: les normes et leur appication* (Stämpfli, 2010) 67.

[37] See also Case C-581/17 *Wächtler* ECLI:EU:C:2019:138, para 63; *Radgen* (n 36) para 46; BGE 140 II 112, 125.

[38] *Wächtler* (n 37) para 53.

[39] See, more recently, *Finanzamt Köln-Süd* (n 29). See also Erik Ros, 'Free Movement of Persons Between the EU and Switzerland: 5 Quo Vadis?' [2022] *EC Tax Review* 238.

[40] See *Picart* (n 35) paras 17ff.

In that case, the Court found that the AFMP, contrary to Article 49 TFEU, does not cover the right for natural persons to set up and manage undertakings.[41] It merely covers access to economic activities and the right to pursue such activities as a self-employed person. Additionally, and contrary to Article 43, which prohibits any restrictions on the freedom of establishment, the AFMP only prohibits de jure and de facto forms of discrimination on grounds of nationality.[42]

By virtue of Article 15 of the Agreement, the Annexes and Protocols to the AFMP are to be considered as integral parts of the Agreement. Annex I elaborates on the rights and obligations enshrined in the Agreement as regards the free movement of persons. Annex II aims to regulate the coordination of social security schemes among the contracting parties by incorporating various EU Directives and Regulations. With respect to the coordination of social security schemes as enshrined in the AFMP in particular, the CJEU went so far as to find that, based on Article 8 and Annex II of the AFMP, Switzerland is to be equated with a Member State of the EU.[43] In this manner, the Court confirmed that the AFMP is an integration-oriented agreement, suggesting that the most adequate interpretation is one that considers principles and concepts of EU law as if the third state – in this case, Switzerland – was part of the EU. Thus, the relevant EU legislation shall be applied by analogy, and the third state is treated as a virtual EU Member State.[44] Finally, Annex III relates to the mutual recognition of professional qualifications and equally refers to a series of EU Directives, both horizontal and sector-specific.

The AFMP is clearly asymmetrical in that it is aimed to bring Switzerland closer to the EU rather than vice versa. First, this is evident in the Preamble, which provides that the two contracting parties are determined 'to bring about the free movement of persons between them *on the basis of the rules applying in the European Community*[*sic*]' (emphasis added). Furthermore, according to Article 16 of the Agreement, parties are required to take all measures necessary to ensure that rights and obligations equivalent to those contained in the EU's vast body of legislation to which reference is made are applied in their relations.[45]

These references to EU secondary law are static; in other words, the Annexes do not foresee a dynamic regulatory approximation or alignment. Rather, such adaptation can only be done through a decision by the Joint Committee, which in

[41] See Case C-470/04 *N* ECLI:EU:C:2006:525, para 27; Case C-251/98 *Baars* ECLI:EU:C:2000:205, para 22.

[42] See also *Graf and Engel* (n 28) para 26; BGE 131 V 209. Even so, such clauses calling for non-discriminatory treatment on the basis of nationality may have far-reaching implications: see Case C-265/03 *Simutenkov*, ECLI:EU:C:2005:2013.

[43] See Case C-247/09 *Xhymshiti*, ECLI:EU:C:2010:698, para 31.

[44] See Nicolas Rennuy and Peter van Elsuwege, 'Integration Without Membership and the Dynamic Development of EU Law: United Kingdom v Council (EEA)' (2014) 51 *CML Rev* 935, 945.

[45] The Swiss Federal Court has derived a requirement of parallelism from Art 16 AFMP: see BGE 140 II 112, 125; BGE 136 II 5.

the case of the AFMP has decision-making powers.[46] Still, these references imply for Switzerland a vast set of rights and obligations analogous, to a certain degree, to those set out in the TFEU. This static referencing has implications not only at the institutional level (in that it increases the transaction costs of maintaining the bilateral relationship), but also at the judicial level, as it leads to a shrinking (if not elimination) of any scope for a dynamic or teleological interpretation of the AFMP by the Courts.[47]

The incorporation of these references to the AFMP confirms two important observations: first, that the economic integration of the two parties takes place on the basis of EU law only, that is, the law of only one of the contracting parties; and second, that the rights and obligations enshrined in these legal documents are extended to Switzerland, which, for all practical purposes, is to be treated as an EU Member State in the fields covered by the bilateral agreements (which is essentially applicable only in the case of coordination of social security).[48] Indeed, the AFMP *amends* these EU secondary law instruments, which as a legal construct is quite interesting and unique, as an international treaty is used to amend EU internal legislation through the decision of a Joint Committee that follows the adoption of that legislation.

However, the CJEU has also confirmed that there are consequences deriving from the fact that Switzerland decided not to subscribe to the project of an economically integrated entity with a single market, based on common rules between its members. As Switzerland has not joined the EU internal market, it cannot claim the totality of rights that the EU Member States enjoy from the removal of all obstacles to create an area of total freedom of movement akin to a national market. Indeed, the Court noted as much in *Grimme*, and underscored that the interpretation given to the provisions of EU internal market law cannot be automatically applied by analogy to the interpretation of the Agreement, 'unless there are express provisions to that effect laid down by the Agreement [on the free movement of persons] itself'.[49]

[46] See, eg the admittedly complex negotiation, which, on the basis of Arts 17 and 18 AFMP, followed the adoption within the EU of Directive 2005/36 on professional qualifications, which replaced 15 Directives that Annex III of the AFMP referred to. See Botschaft zur Genehmigung des Beschlusses No 2/2011 des Gemischten Ausschusses EU–Schweiz zum Freizügigkeitsabkommen (Änderung von Anhang III des Abkommens, gegenseitige Anerkennung von Berufsqualifikationen) und zur Umsetzung des Beschlusses, BBI 2012 4401. This change led to the adoption of a new Annex III in 2011. In 2012, Annex II was also replaced to incorporate the new EU Regulation 883/2004. The current version of the AFMP that incorporates the decisions of the Joint Committee is at www.fedlex.admin.ch/eli/cc/2002/243/de. The EU side equally maintains a consolidated version whereby all decisions of the Joint Committee and Protocols can be viewed: https://eur-lex.europa.eu/legal-content/EN/TXT/?uri=CELEX%3A02002A0430%2801%29-20210101. The Professional Qualifications Directive was amended by Directive 2013/55/EU, but no agreement for an amendment has yet been reached at the level of the Joint Committee.

[47] See also AG Jääskinen's Opinion in Case C-70/09 *Hengartner and Gasser* ECLI:EU:C:2010:289, para 45.

[48] See also C-656/11 *United Kingdom v Council* ECLI:EU:C:2014:97, paras 58–59 and 65.

[49] *Grimme* (n 33) paras 27 and 29; see also *Picart* (n 35) para 29. In the case of the Air Transport Agreement, see Case C-547/10 P, *Swiss Confederation v European Commission*, ECLI:EU:C:2013:139,

Furthermore, in *Hengartner and Gasser*,[50] a case relating to the imposition of a discriminatory annual tax applied on Swiss nationals for the exercise of the right to hunt in an Austrian province, the CJEU rejected an interpretation by analogy of the principle of non-discrimination for service recipients that would essentially extend to Switzerland the application of the EU fundamental freedom to receive services because the EU–Switzerland Agreement and its Annexes lack an equalising provision in that field. The case is very interesting because at issue was whether a teleological interpretation of the relevant AFMP provision relating to equal treatment could in fact prohibit fiscal discrimination on grounds of nationality. This could be a reasonable outcome if the treaty at issue were of a dynamic or evolving character, like the EEA Agreement. However, in the Court's view, the static character of the economic integration model at issue agreed upon by the parties, the wording chosen and the nature of the objectives of the Agreement do not favour such an interpretation.

Additional elements in the AFMP would appear to support such a textual interpretation of the rights and obligations laid down by the Agreement. For instance, according to the Agreement, only CJEU case law delivered prior to the date of signature of the Agreement (1999) should be taken into account when interpreting the Agreement. Later on, however, the CJEU clarified (somewhat contrary to the wording of Article 16 AFMP) that subsequent CJEU case law should also be taken into account provided that it merely clarifies or confirms the principles established in the case law that existed prior to 1999 regarding EU law concepts that inform the AFMP.[51]

In addition, the Final Act includes a joint declaration from both parties to 'take the necessary measures to apply the *acquis communautaire* to nationals of the other Contracting Party in accordance with the Agreement concluded between them'.[52] Thus, the *acquis communautaire* takes centre stage as far as the EU–Swiss bilateral relations are concerned. This is the result of a process that started several decades ago.[53] However, while covering many areas of EU law, the coverage of the Agreement remains limited due to the specific nature of the provisions chosen by the parties (clearly, as a result of intensive negotiations).

Crucially, then, rather than having an open-ended, integrationist character, the Agreement contains provisions that are unequivocally designed to limit or to clarify its material or temporal scope (see, for instance, the limited character of

para 80. Note the contrast to the EEA agreement, which is premised on the principle of homogeneity regarding the interpretation of common rules. See, eg Case C-471/04 *Keller Holding GmbH* ECLI:EU:C:2006:143, para 48.

[50] See Case C-70/09 *Hengartner and Gasser* ECLI:EU:C:2010:430.

[51] See *Wächtler* (n 37) para 39.

[52] See Joint Declaration attached to the Final Act relating to the Agreement between the European Community and its Member States, of the one part, and the Swiss Confederation, of the other part, on the free movement of persons [2002] OJ L114/70.

[53] See also Adam Lazowski, 'Enhanced Multilateralism and Enhanced Bilateralism: Integration Without Membership in the European Union' (2008) 45 *CML Rev* 1433, 1436; Bericht über die Stellung der Schweiz im europäischen Integrationsprozess vom 24 August 1988, BBI 1988 III 249, 380.

Article 17 of Annex I, when compared to Article 56 TFEU) and which arguably are foreign to EU law.[54]

C. Interpreting the AFMP

While being an international treaty, the AFMP clearly aims to bring about the free movement of persons between the two parties *on the basis of the rules applying in the EU*.[55] However, absent a more comprehensive long-term vision of the Agreement, notably when compared to the so-called 'Europe Agreements' (preparing states for accession to the EU) or the EEA (extending the internal market rules to the EEA countries and incorporating the homogeneity principle), the Agreement can only be regarded as an ordinary international treaty that the EU concluded with a third country.[56] Thus, any textual parallelism alone would be insufficient to justify an interpretation that fully follows CJEU case law in internal cases touching upon free movement law.[57] Rather, homogeneous interpretation similar to the EEA Agreement can only occur in cases that the AFMP explicitly foresees such as in the case of social security coordination.[58]

As with the interpretation of every international treaty, the rules of interpretation of the Vienna Convention on the Law of Treaties (VCLT) are relevant. Article 31 VCLT provides that a treaty shall be interpreted in good faith in accordance with the ordinary meaning to be given to its terms in their context and in the light of its object and purpose.[59] The CJEU has thus recognised the importance of the terms in which a given international instrument is worded and its objectives.[60] For instance, when interpreting several association agreements that the EU concluded, the Court accepted the direct effect of provisions the wording of which resembled that of the free movement rules, thereby interpreting them in a way similar to the fundamental freedoms.[61]

[54] On this point, see AG Jääskinen's Opinion in *Hengartner and Gasser* (n 47) para 46.

[55] See also BGE 129 II 249, 259. However, and crucially so, it is not aimed at the establishment on an internal market through the abolition of all obstacles to the movement of goods, persons, services and capital. Again, a Joint Declaration of the parties to the Agreement requires that the parties take 'the necessary measures to apply the acquis communautaire to nationals of the other Contracting Party in accordance with the Agreement concluded between them'. See n 48 above.

[56] Even in the case of this type of agreement, the same wording may lead to stricter interpretations by the Court that diverge from its free movement case law because the level of ambition is lower: see, eg Case C-63/99 *Gloszcuk* ECLI:EU:C:2001:488.

[57] See also Peter Van Elsuwege, 'Sectoral Bilateralism – Lessons from the Case Law of the Court of Justice of the European Union' in Marc Maresceau and Crista Tobler (eds), *Switzerland and the EU: A Challenging Relationship* (Brill, 2023).

[58] See also C-551/16, *Klein Schiphorst*, ECLI:EU:C:2018:200, para 28.

[59] See also BGE 145 IV 55, 60.

[60] See *Wächtler* (n 37) para 35.

[61] See, inter alia, Case C-416/96 *El-Yassini* ECLI:EU:C:1999:107 (EU–Morocco Cooperation Agreement); Case C-438/00 *Kolpak* ECLI:EU:C:2003:255 (EU–Slovakia Association – or 'Europe' – Agreement); *Simutenkov* (n 42) (EU–Russia Partnership Agreement); Case C-97/05 *Gattoussi* ECLI:EU:C:2006:780 (EU–Tunisia Association Agreement); Case C-235/99 *Kondova* ECLI:EU:C:2001:489 (EU–Bulgaria Association – 'Europe' – Agreement).

The Court has further warned in *Polydor* that a simple similarity in a provision enshrined in the EU Treaties and of an international treaty that the EU concluded with a non-Member State cannot *ipso facto* be taken as interpreting that treaty in the same way as the EU legal texts.[62] The task of the Court will be to reach such a conclusion only after taking into account the aim pursued by each provision in its own particular context. More recently, the Court held that a term can be taken to have a special meaning only if it can be demonstrated that this was the intention of the parties.[63]

Contrary to other agreements that the EU has concluded, which aim at the creation of stronger ties with the EU through a multifaceted programme of integration or even accession to the EU, the EU–Switzerland Agreement is clearly focused mainly on the liberalisation of movement of *natural* persons.[64] In addition, and as noted earlier, this liberalisation appears to be undertaken in a rather static manner.[65] Thus, the only possible anchors for a type of teleological interpretation of a given provision are the second recital of the Preamble of the Agreement (calling for the establishment of free movement of persons 'on the basis of the rules applying in the [EU]') and Article 16:2 of the Agreement, which provides: 'Insofar as the application of this Agreement involves concepts of Community law, account shall be taken of the relevant case law of the [Court of Justice] prior to the date of its signature.' However, neither of these two elements has ever been invoked to justify a teleological interpretation of the AFMP – and rightly so, as the systemic repercussions of equating Switzerland to an EU Member State would be significant. Rather, the Court followed a textual and fairly formalistic approach in interpreting the AFMP.[66]

Regarding the static interpretation and the temporal limitation on the relevance of the CJEU case law, as noted earlier, subsequent case law of the CJEU can be considered as relevant if it clarifies or confirms concepts of EU law established prior to 1999. However, no mechanical or automatic extrapolation of CJEU case law to a situation involving the EU and Switzerland is permissible.[67] The Swiss Federal Court explicitly drew a similar conclusion when it found that CJEU case law subsequent to the signature of the Agreement can still be taken into account for interpretive reasons if it does nothing more than specify previous case law.[68]

[62] Case 270/80 *Polydor* ECLI:EU:C:1982:43, paras 14–21; see also *Kondova* (n 61) para 51.

[63] See *Finanzamt Köln-Süd* (n 29) para 47.

[64] In *Fokus Invest*, the CJEU found that the objectives of the Agreement pursuant to Art 1 are established for the benefit of nationals of the signatories, and thus for the benefit of natural persons, and that all the categories of persons covered by the Agreement, with the exception of persons providing services and recipients of services, are by their nature categories of natural persons: Case C-541/08 *Fokus Invest* judgment of 11 February 2010, para 29. See also *Grimme* (n 33) paras 33–34.

[65] See the Opinion by Advocate General Jääskinen in *Hengartner and Gasser* (n 47) paras 45–46.

[66] *cf* Stephan Breitenmoser, 'Sectoral Agreements Between the EC and Switzerland: Contents and Context' (2003) 40 *CML Rev* 1137, 1152.

[67] See AG Sanchez-Bordona's Opinion in *Finanzamt Köln-Süd* (n 29) para 43.

[68] See BGE 133 V 624, 631, con 4.3.2; see also Thomas Cottier and Erik Evtimov, 'Probleme des Rechtsschutzes bei der Anwendung der sektoriellen Abkommen mit der EG' in T Cottier and M. Oesch (eds), *Die sektoriellen Abkommen Schweiz-EG* (Stämpfli, 2002) 200.

However, developments in EU law are not to be taken automatically into account and will most likely require an amendment of the Agreement. This was at issue in *Xhymshiti*,[69] where the Court suggested that the scheme established in the Agreement (in this case, Annex II on social security) is not intended to also make applicable EU legislation subsequent to the signature of the Agreement. This would mean that legislation that was adopted after the signature of the AFMP and so is not explicitly mentioned in the text of the Agreement cannot be invoked by the parties as applicable to their relations, even if that legislation is an amendment or updated version of the EU Regulations mentioned in the Agreement.

Any interpretation other than a textual one would have suggested that such legislation may be applicable, especially if it concretises legislative acts explicitly mentioned in the Agreement. This view is also corroborated by Article 1:1 of Annex II to the Agreement, which provides that the contracting parties agree to apply EU Acts to which reference is made as in force in June 1999, *or rules equivalent to such Acts*. However, as noted above, the CJEU dismissed extensive claims of this type, drawing a clear line between the benefits of the EU free movement law and the more limited version of that which the AFMP constitutes.

Finally, with respect to direct effect, that is, the possibility of individuals to invoke rights enshrined in the AFMP directly before national courts, the CJEU has not discussed this point at length in its case law. Instead, it directly applied the AFMP provisions in all cases that were presented before it.[70] On the Swiss side, the Swiss Federal Court accepted that at least the provisions of the Agreement relating to the rights of the citizens of the contracting parties (notably those contained in Annex I) were sufficiently clear and precise, and thus should in principle be regarded as producing direct effect ('self-executing').[71]

III. Freedom to Provide and Receive Services under the AFMP

A. Freedom to Provide Services under the AFMP

(i) A Tale of Subsequent Failed Negotiations

The liberalisation of trade in services between Switzerland and the EU constitutes unfinished business. The AFMP sets the tone by underlining the parties' intention to facilitate the supply of services in their respective territories and to liberalise the

[69] *cf* Case C-247/09 *Xhymshiti* judgment of 18 November 2010, para 36.

[70] See, however, AG Colomer's analysis in an early case, where he confirms that several key provisions of the AFMP provisions are sufficiently precise and clear, and thus are directly applicable, based on the *Demirel* doctrine: AG Colomer's Opinion in Case C-339/05 *Zentralbetriebsrat der Landeskrankenhäuser Tirols* ECLI:EU:C:2006:307, paras 32ff.

[71] BGE 129 II 249, 257.

provision of services of brief duration (that is, up to 90 days per year). However, an intention for a more comprehensive liberalisation of services is equally enshrined in the Agreement, as it also incorporates a Joint Declaration whereby the EU and Switzerland committed themselves towards general liberalisation of service provision on the basis of the *acquis communautaire*.[72]

Such negotiations started in the framework of the Bilaterals II process in June 2002 but, after four rounds of discussions, the issue was decoupled from the remaining agenda items. Negotiations were postponed in 2003, and have never resumed.[73] Exploratory talks were initiated on financial services, but these were suspended in April 2015 in the aftermath of the Swiss February 2014 referendum on mass immigration. Thus, it remains a paradox that two so integrated economies and champions of services liberalisation have failed to advance negotiations on a comprehensive agreement on services. This is quite puzzling, all the more because in the last 20 years both parties have been active participants in the negotiations on services at the WTO level, notably the discussions on disciplines on domestic regulation.

(ii) Ratione Personae

While not being a fully fledged services agreement,[74] the AFMP includes certain provisions which aim to facilitate the provision of services among the signatories not only by natural persons, but also by companies.[75] The main provision of the AFMP relating to the provision of services is Article 5:1, which provides that service providers originating in the contracting parties shall have the right to provide a service in the territory of the other party for a period not exceeding a total of 90 days of actual work in a calendar year.

For a Swiss or EU service supplier, this would mean that it can supply services in all Member States, as long as the *aggregate* number of days does not exceed the three-month period in a calendar year.[76] Notably, in cases of cross-frontier services supply not exceeding 90 days of actual work per year, the Agreement establishes in Article 17 of Annex I an outright prohibition against any restriction on the supply

[72] The legal mandate took the form of a joint declaration in the final act of the Agreement on the free movement of persons: [2002] OJ L114/70.

[73] See also C Nufer, 'Bilaterale Verhandlungen wie weiter? Liberalisierung der Dienstleistungen zwischen der Schweiz und der EU: Gewinner und Verlierer aus Schweizer Sicht' (2006) Basler Schriften zur europäischen Integration No 798.

[74] See, among others, Walter Kälin, 'Die Bedeutung des Freizügigkeitsabkommens für das Ausländerrecht' in Cottier and Oesch (n 68) 28.

[75] See also Daniel Maritz, 'Der Dienstleistungsverkehr im Abkommen über die Freizügigkeit der Personen' in Daniel Felder and Christine Kaddous (eds), *Bilaterale Abkommen Schweiz-EU* (*Accords bilatéraux Suisse-Union européenne*) (Schulthess Verlag, 2001) 335.

[76] Art 21:1 of Annex I. See also Bundesamt für Berufsbildung und Technologie (BBT) Neue europäische Richtlinie über die Anerkennung von Berufsqualifikationen (RL 2005/36/EG) – Erläuternder Bericht (Anhörung) 2006, 15.

of the service or on the right of entry and residence, regardless of whether the service is supplied by a legal or a natural person.

Article 17:2 also extends the right of entry and residence to any employee of a person providing services regardless of the employee's nationality, as long as they are integrated in the labour market of the home state (typically a 12-month period is required). Interestingly, the Agreement does not refer here to prohibition of discrimination on the basis of nationality but rather on *restriction*, suggesting that the comprehensive case law of Article 56 TFEU (freedom to provide services) would most likely be applicable. Article 19 of Annex I to the Agreement incorporates a category-specific non-discrimination provision which states that during the 90-day period, the host Member States cannot impose on those service suppliers (legal or natural persons) who are nationals of one contracting party less favourable conditions vis-à-vis its own nationals.

The Agreement mainly aims to facilitate the movement of *natural* persons as service providers. The AFMP unequivocally focuses on the regulation of the stay of a service provider or recipient rather than full liberalisation of service supply pursuant to Article 56 TFEU.[77] As noted above, depending on the category of persons, the rights that they can claim when compared to an internal EU situation will vary. The treatment of legal persons, on the other hand, is less generous. Notably, under the AFMP, no right to establishment for legal persons is granted.[78] The latter right is given only to natural persons who are to be granted a five-year renewable residence permit if they wish to exercise a self-employed activity.[79] However, companies are granted the right to provide services under Article 5:1 of the AFMP and Article 18 of Annex I. These services cannot be provided for a period exceeding 90 days of actual work in a calendar year.[80]

For companies which send their workers to provide services in the territory of the contracting parties, what matters is the number of days on which the services are provided and not the total number of workers supplying those services. This greatly expands the leeway given to sizeable service providers, but also explains the recurring fear on the Swiss side about potential abuse in the case of posting of workers.[81] The Swiss authorities have also introduced an eight-day advance notice requirement in case a service provider or posted worker offers services in Switzerland for more than eight days per calendar year.[82] This flanking measure has been one of the most controversial points in the recent negotiations for

[77] See BGE 133 V 624, 635.

[78] *Grimme* (n 33) para 38.

[79] *Stamm and Hauser* (n 33) para 44.

[80] Art 21 of Annex I to the Agreement.

[81] For an account on this issue, see Kurt Pärli, 'The Swiss Posted Workers Act and Free Movement of Services' in Maresceau and Tobler (n 57) 117.

[82] For certain categories of service providers (such as gardening, cleaning, construction and security services), there is an obligation of notification from the first day of the service supply. Over 200,000 short-term service suppliers from the EU use the right to provide services every year: see Bundesrat, 'Lagebeurteilung Beziehungen Schweiz–EU' (9 December 2022) 23.

an institutional framework agreement between the EU and Switzerland. While Switzerland argues that Articles 22:2 and/or 22:4 of Annex I allow this type of additional administrative burden, the EU considers this to be a wrongful application of the AFMP, discriminating against EU service providers and violating the standstill obligation.

A valid identity card or passport clearly indicating the nationality of its holder – but no residence permit – is required for the provision of services not exceeding the 90-day limit. However, service suppliers can still be subject to laws, regulations and administrative provisions when providing their services within the 90-day period if such rules serve an imperative requirement in the public interest.[83] These would include requirements such as road traffic rules, rules concerning the development or use of land, town and country planning, building standards or administrative penalties imposed for non-compliance with such rules.

Additionally, the EU and Switzerland retain the right to regulate the activities of temporary and interim employment agencies. The same derogation applies to financial services when their provision is subject to prior authorisation and the host country imposes certain prudential requirements on financial service suppliers. Both derogations, however, are applicable only if they existed at the time of entry into force of the AFMP.

Pursuant to Article 5:2(b) of the AFMP in conjunction with Articles 17(b) and 20:2 of Annex I to the AFMP, the 90-day limit can be exceeded if the service provider has received authorisation to provide a service from the competent domestic authorities. In that case, a residence permit giving access to the entire territory of Switzerland or the EU Member States concerned is to be issued for a period equal to that of the supply of services.[84] In instances where prior authorisation is granted for a period longer than 90 days, the Agreement establishes a prohibition on any restriction on the right of entry and residence to those service suppliers (and the members of their family, irrespective of their nationality) established in one contracting party and wishing to supply their services in the territory of another contracting party.

The AFMP makes clear in Article 22:1 of Annex I that the rights for service providers mentioned above do not apply to activities involving the exercise of public authority in any of the contracting parties, even if this activity is undertaken on an occasional basis. Corresponding CJEU case law under Articles 51 and 62 TFEU[85] suggests that this exception has to be narrowly construed and applies to

[83] See Art 22:4 of Annex I to AFMP. For instance, the requirement that certain documents are translated into the host-country language and maintained onsite to allow host-country civil servants to monitor the activities were found by the CJEU to serve the legitimate objective of social protection of workers and the monitoring of such protection. See Case C-490/04 *Commission v Germany* ECLI:EU:C:2007:430, para 70. See also C-113/89 *Rush Portuguesa* ECLI:EU:C:1990:142, para 18.

[84] Art 20:2, 3 of Annex I to the Agreement.

[85] Art 51 TFEU provides that fundamental free movement rules shall not apply to activities which in a given Member State 'are connected, even occasionally, with the exercise of official authority'.

activities which have a *direct* and *specific* connection with official authority.[86] More broadly, the Court will apply the TFEU provisions to functions that are merely auxiliary and preparatory, notably when carried out by a private body which is supervised by an entity which effectively exercises official authority by taking the final decision.[87] The Swiss Federal Court has followed the CJEU case law in this regard and significantly narrowed down the scope of application of this exception in the case of self-employed persons, but also workers under the relevant AFMP provisions.[88] Thus, there is no indication whatsoever that it would find otherwise under Article 22.

B. Transitional Arrangements for Newly Acceding EU Member States

Crucially, Article 5:4 AFMP clarifies that the quantitative limitations imposed under Article 10 AFMP cannot be enforced against suppliers (both natural and legal persons) and recipients of services. However, Article 5:4 AFMP appears to have been superseded in part by the amendment of Article 10 AFMP, made to take account of the EU's enlargement (in particular of the accession of Bulgaria, Romania and, more recently, Croatia).[89]

For instance, Article 10:2a gave the possibility to Switzerland to maintain until the end of May 2007 controls (giving priority to the labour force already integrated in the Swiss market and reviewing wage and working conditions) on and qualification requirements for service providers from the new EU members (except Cyprus and Malta) in the following sectors: horticultural services; construction-related services; security services; and industrial cleaning. Similar conditions in the same sectors were applied after the accession of Bulgaria and Romania towards service providers originating in these countries. Similar controls and requirements were imposed for the most recent accession, that of Croatia.

Thus, through subsequent decisions by the Joint Committee, Article 10 was used as a legal basis to introduce market entry and access restrictions for nationals of newly acceding members, thereby defying the letter of Article 5:4. Such measures (and additional flanking measures)[90] taken by the Swiss side as of June 2004 onwards aimed at lessening the allegedly negative spillovers of liberalisation on Swiss society and standards of living, including most notably wages and working conditions.[91] Article 10 in its current form incorporates the phasing-in of labour

[86] Case 2/74 *Reyners* ECLI:EU:C:1974:68, para 45.

[87] *cf* Case C-404/05 *Commission v Germany* ECLI:EU:C:2007:723, para 38.

[88] See BGE 140 II 112, 123.

[89] The consolidated version of the AFMP can be found at https://eur-lex.europa.eu/legal-content/EN/TXT/?uri=CELEX%3A02002A0430%2801%29-20210101.

[90] For an overview of these measures, see Pärli (n 81) 118.

[91] See also Swiss Federal Council, 'Message relatif à l'approbation des accords sectoriels entre la Suisse et la CE' (23 June 1999) FF 1999 5440.

market integration, with a clear focus on the gradual opening towards nationals from countries that became EU members after 2004. Currently, such measures remain applicable only in the case of Croatian nationals.

Based on Article 10 and the accompanying Protocol to the AFMP, Switzerland invoked the relevant safeguard clause after full freedom of movement led to a rapid surge of Croatian workers in 2022. It currently maintains quantitative limitations against the entry of Croatian nationals until the end of 2024.[92] While restrictions against Croatian nationals will be lifted in 2025, transitional arrangements for Croatian nationals run until the end of December 2026. However, the quantitative limitations imposed on Croatian nationals are not applicable against Croatian service providers and companies interested in posting workers, as long as the services are limited to 90 days or less per calendar year.

C. Freedom to Receive Services under the AFMP

According to the Agreement (Article 5:3 in conjunction with Article 23 of Annex I to the Agreement), EU and Swiss nationals wishing to receive services in the territory of any contracting party have the right of entry and residence. If the consumption of the service at issue lasts longer than three months, then the service recipient should hold a residence permit equal in duration to the service. Such permits, as with all other types referred to earlier, are valid throughout the territory of the issuing state. Unrestricted geographical mobility is thereby ensured. Social security schemes may not be applicable to the service recipient during its period of residence. Thus, contrary to the right to provide services, the right to receive services is not subject to any temporal limitation.

In *Hengartner and Gasser*, a case discussed earlier,[93] the CJEU found that the element that gives rise to the discriminatory tax applied by the Austrian authorities was the grant to Messrs Hengartner and Gasser, in return for payment and under certain conditions, of the exploitation of a right to hunt in an area of land for a limited time. This, in the Court's view, constitutes a service of a cross-border nature supplied to the Swiss nationals. Therefore, one had to evaluate the purview of the provisions of the Agreement relating to the consumption of services.

After reviewing the nature and objectives of the AFMP along the lines explained earlier, the Court referred to the non-comprehensive nature of the non-discrimination principle enshrined in Article 2 of the Agreement, alluding to the analysis of the Advocate-General. The Court also accepted that other than a right to entry and residence, the AFMP does not include any provision that prohibits discrimination regarding the commercial transaction that underpins the

[92] See Swiss Confederation, 'Federal Council Extends Safeguard Clause for Croatia' (22 November 2023) www.sem.admin.ch/sem/en/home/sem/medien/mm.msg-id-98790.html.

[93] See n 50 and the accompanying text.

consumption of the service at issue.[94] Absent a general and absolute prohibition on all discrimination against nationals of the contracting parties,[95] the Court, following the above-mentioned textual and overly formalistic interpretive method, found that no provision in the Agreement is specifically intended to allow recipients of services to benefit from the principle of non-discrimination as regards fiscal provisions relating to the commercial transactions whose subject is the provision of services.[96]

Thus, the CJEU confirmed in *Hengartner and Gasser* that the non-discrimination obligation applies differently in the case of service *recipients* as compared to service *providers*. The former can claim equal treatment in the case of entry and residence requirements while the latter, according to Article 19 of Annex I to the AFMP, may also claim equal treatment with regard to the terms relating to the access and supply of the service at issue (which would arguably also include fiscal issues).

The Swiss Federal Court has demonstrated similar levels of rigidity in a series of cases relating to the reimbursement of medical costs of treatments that Swiss nationals had in an EU country. The Court suggested that the AFMP is aimed at the liberalisation of services only in part. Regarding the consumption of services in particular, the Court ruled that the AFMP merely aims to grant a right of entry and residence, as opposed to the modalities of supply and the consumption of medical services.[97] Following the argumentation of the CJEU, the Swiss Federal Court acknowledged that the objective of the AFMP is not the establishment of an internal market, but merely the facilitation of service supply, notably of brief duration. Absent any ambition for creating an area without internal frontiers, the far-reaching CJEU case law relating to reimbursement of medical costs is inapplicable.

As things stand, one can infer from the AFMP-related case law that both the CJEU and the Swiss Federal Tribunal appear to be fully aware of their important role in serving homogeneity and coherence despite the fact that no mechanism exists in the bilateral agreements that allows a request for preliminary reference on the side of the Swiss courts. Of course, the autonomous adaptation to EU law creates potential issues and leaves room for fragmented interpretation.

[94] *Hengartner and Gasser* (n 50) para 40. As the AG noted in this case, it would have been different if the discriminatory tax affected the right of entry and/or residence of the recipient of the service at hand.

[95] *cf* Art 21 of the Charter of Fundamental Rights of the European Union. See also Art 9 of Annex I to the Agreement, which seems to be much more absolute when it comes to employed persons residing in the territory of one contracting party. In fact, Art 2 of the AFMP, by its reference to the three Annexes to the Agreement, reflects varying levels of application of the non-discrimination principle among the different categories of persons coming under the scope of the Agreement.

[96] In that sense, TCNs residing within the EU may be treated more favourably than Swiss nationals wishing to receive services on an occasional basis through the cross-frontier consumption of a given service.

[97] Here the Court refers to the statements of the Federal Council and the fact that separate negotiations with a view to liberalising services were initiated according to the Agreement, but ultimately failed. See, eg BGE 133 V 624.

This is so even if the Swiss Federal Court has set the tone early on by referring to EU-conforming interpretation as a default rule when Swiss legislation seeks to align with EU law.[98] This alone obliges Swiss courts to follow both legislative and judicial developments within the EU.

D. Certain Systemic Issues Relating to the Freedom to Provide Services

(i) Definition of Services

The AFMP does not define services. In view of the AFMP's anchoring to Union law, including the extension of concepts that preceded the signature of the AFMP, it would appear that the parties converge around the EU definition – and ensuing classification – of services. This focuses on three constituent elements: cross-border nature; remuneration; and duration.[99] The first and third elements have been interpreted flexibly by the CJEU. Under the AFMP, duration is clearly delimited (90 days),[100] while the cross-border character appears to be substantively close to its meaning under Union law. On duration, it appears that the CJEU case law is equally applicable with respect to access to facilities and infrastructure necessary to provide the service. Thus, a service provider could, for instance, rent facilities for the entire year without this putting at risk her intention not to establish herself but to merely offer services.[101]

(ii) Turning against the Country of Origin

A systemic question in this regard is whether the CJEU and Swiss courts would consider as falling under the AFMP cases arising from the supply of a service by nationals to their home country while established in the other contracting party (for instance, a German living in Switzerland but supplying services of brief duration in Germany). Based on existing case law, this question would most likely be answered in the affirmative.[102]

Indeed, as the Court eloquently put it in *Wächtler*, 'The free movement of persons guaranteed by the AFMP would be impeded if a national of a contracting party were to be placed at a disadvantage in his State of origin solely for having exercised his right of free movement'.[103] Although this case was about a

[98] See BGE 129 III 335.
[99] See also Panagiotis Delimatsis, 'From *Sacchi* to *Uber*: 60 Year of Services Liberalization, Ten Years of the Services Directive in the EU' (2018) 37(1) *Yearbook of European Law* 188, 196.
[100] In *Grimme*, the CJEU clarified that no rights can be derived from the AFMP if the cross-frontier activity has a continuous character that exceeds the upper time limit of 90 days: *Grimme* (n 33) para 44.
[101] *cf* Case C-347/09 *Dickinger and Ömer* ECLI:EU:C:2011:582, para 38.
[102] *cf Wächtler* (n 37).
[103] ibid para 53.

self-employed person and related to the line of CJEU case law on the freedom of establishment, CJEU case law that existed before the signature of the AFMP equally allowed service providers to seek the elimination of restrictions on the freedom to provide services imposed by the Member State of origin.[104]

By the same token, the AFMP would cover restrictions imposed by the Member State of origin which impede or place at a disadvantage a domestic service supplier who wants to supply services in the territory of the other contracting party.[105] Thus, the inquiry about equal treatment would essentially amount to an analysis as to whether there is a situation of inequality brought about by the place of residence.

Although Article 19 of Annex I is not as elaborate as Article 9 of the same annex relating to employed persons, such an interpretation allowing a service provider to invoke the non-discrimination provision against its state of origin is logical. First, it would be in line with the AFMP objective to *liberalise* the provision of services of brief duration. Such an outcome would also be corroborated by the alleged intention of Article 17 of Annex I relating to service suppliers to eliminate any *restriction* on the cross-frontier supply of services.

This is contrary to other situations and categories of persons where the AFMP only focuses on non-discrimination on the grounds of nationality: in the case of service providers, the AFMP incorporates wording that resembles Article 56 TFEU. The use of the term 'restriction' would arguably suggest a broad scope of application,[106] prohibiting any obstacle (including non-discriminatory ones) that impedes service supply within the 90-day period.[107] Importantly, such restrictions can be imposed not only by public authorities, but also by private bodies, whose actions should also be regarded as covered by the AFMP if they constitute restrictions that discourage or otherwise impede the supply of a service.[108]

This would also be in line with the existing case law on the meaning of Article 16:2 AFMP. That suggests that EU law concepts that pre-existed the signature of the AFMP, such as equal treatment, should be taken up.[109] Finally, Article 19 of Annex I also supports this claim for a broad interpretation regarding the rights of service providers to free movement, as it obliges the host state not to impose on service providers terms less favourable than those imposed on its own nationals; the broad reference to 'terms' would again imply a broad scope of application, which is only to be curtailed by the temporal limitation of 90 days per calendar year. Overall, and taken together, it would appear reasonable to suggest

[104] See, eg Case C-384/93 *Alpine Investments* ECLI:EU:C:1995:126; Case C-60/00 *Carpenter* ECLI:EU:C:2002:434.

[105] ibid.

[106] To this effect, see also BGE 140 II 447, 4.5. For the conceptual scope of the term 'restriction', see Vassilis Hatzopoulos, *Regulating Services in the European Union* (Oxford University Press, 2012) 97.

[107] See also Delimatsis, 'From *Sacchi* to *Uber*' (n 99) 199.

[108] See Case 36/74 *Walrave and Koch* ECLI:EU:C:1974:140; Case 281/98 *Angonese* ECLI:EU:C:2000:296; also Delimatsis, 'From *Sacchi* to *Uber*' (n 99) 203.

[109] See also n 32.

that Articles 17–21 of Annex I of the AFMP aim at *unfettered* access to the parties' services markets – albeit only for up to 90 days.[110]

(iii) Remote Supply of Services under the AFMP

The supply of services through remote means (internet, post, etc) also falls under the scope of the Agreement, although this has been a controversial point. Against it would speak the very objective of the AFMP, ie an agreement allowing the free *movement* of natural and legal persons. Also, one could claim that if no actual movement of the service supplier was envisaged, then the contracting parties would have never contemplated a 90-day limit, simply because it is impossible to enforce.

In favour of the claim that remote supply of services is covered by the AFMP would speak various elements. First, the concept of services under EU law and how free movement has evolved conceptually in the area of services matches real-life technological advances and the increased servicification of the global economy.[111] Second, the AFMP speaks of a *right* of entry and residence, but no *obligation* to move. This would mean that not only the online supply, but also the online consumption of a service would be protected by the AFMP.

Moreover, the derogation of Article 22:3 of Annex I in fact brings additional confusion as to whether service supply without the relocation of the service supplier or consumer is covered by the AFMP: while the derogation under indent (i) relating to temporary and interim employment agencies would appear to suggest that the temporary movement of the service supplier was considered as warranted, the derogation under indent (ii) would appear to suggest the opposite. Although establishment of legal persons is not covered by the AFMP, services provision through remote means is allowed as long as an authorisation is granted by the prudential supervision authority of the host country.

This issue could have been solved as long ago as the early 2000s, when the *Fidium Finanz* case was before the CJEU.[112] At stake was whether a Swiss financial service supplier could lawfully provide financial services to German customers online without seeking prior authorisation from Germany's financial supervisor. The CJEU found that a third-country service supplier could not benefit from the freedom to provide services, nor could it rely on the AFMP because it had not

[110] Having said this, as noted earlier, the several flanking measures that Switzerland introduced over the years to curb such flows and level the playing field, ranging from the notification requirement to the differentiation among professions, has led to increasing discontent on the side of the EU, which claimed that Switzerland interprets the AFMP at will and has thus violated the agreement. See also René Schwok, 'Switzerland–EU Relations: The Bilateral Way in a Fragilized Position' (2020) 25(2) *European Foreign Affairs Review* 159, 165.

[111] Servicification aims to capture a dominant trend in the global economy whereby the manufacturing sector increasingly relies on services, whether as inputs, activities within firms or outputs sold bundled with goods.

[112] Case 452/04 *Fidium Finanz* ECLI:EU:C:2006:631.

entered into force in the material time. However, it would appear plausible that, after the entry into force of the AFMP, the Swiss provider could benefit from the limited liberalisation that the Agreement brought about subject to prior authorisation. Thus, while authorisation by the German authorities for cross-border activities in the financial sector would be needed in this case, no actual (temporary) relocation to provide the service would be warranted (as it would be for in-person supply of the service).[113]

In *L GmbH and M v Kantonsrat des Kantons Zürich*,[114] the Swiss Federal Court took a fairly broad and open-minded stance towards EU legal persons' right to provide services through remote means derived from the Agreement. At stake was whether a prohibition of litigation financing services was, inter alia, against the fundamental right of economic freedom enshrined in Article 27 of the Swiss Constitution and, if so, whether a foreign legal person could successfully raise such a claim. The latter had hitherto been allowed to foreign natural persons with a residence permit and to domestic legal persons only. The Swiss Federal Court was of the view that this right must also be granted to EU legal persons that wish to supply services in the Swiss market on the basis of the AFMP. Litigation financing is a legal service of a financial nature, and the Court found as much. Because the Agreement entitles EU suppliers of such services to undertake economic activity in Switzerland, the natural extension of this suggests that a right to raise a claim based on the right of economic freedom should be granted to those service suppliers.[115]

One problematic feature remains: this remote supply would have to be limited to 90 days to fall within the scope of application of the AFMP. The issue was eventually clarified in the recent *Viagogo* judgment.[116] The CJEU accepted the broad substantive scope of Article 5 of the Agreement, as well as Articles 17 and 18 of Annex I, allowing legal persons to provide services through remote means. Yet the Court underlined that the AFMP only covered online services of *limited* duration; thus, in that case, the Swiss company Viagogo could not rely on the application of the AFMP because, by its very nature, an activity via a website would imply a 'continuous, even permanent character'.[117] As there was no evidence of Viagogo limiting its online services to 90 days per calendar year, no rights could be derived from the AFMP for that company.

[113] In 2014, BaFin and FINMA signed a Memorandum of Understanding establishing a simplified exemption procedure that allows Swiss banks to offer their services to German clients without the need to set up a business in the German territory. See FINMA, 'Vereinfachtes Freistellungsverfahren für Schweizer Banken bei grenzüberschreitenden Tätigkeiten im Finanzbereich in Deutschland' (6 January 2014) www.finma.ch/de/~/media/finma/dokumente/dokumentencentre/4dokumentation/finma-mitteilungen/finma-mitteilung-54-2014.pdf?la=de; see also Deloitte, 'Simplified Exemption Procedure for Swiss Banks under the German Banking Act', www2.deloitte.com/ch/en/pages/financial-services/Articles/simplified-exemption-procedure-swiss-banks.html.

[114] BGE 131 I 223.

[115] ibid 226–27.

[116] See Case C-70/22 *Viagogo* ECLI:EU:C:2023:350.

[117] ibid para 37.

Incidentally, a careful reading of *Viagogo* would arguably suggest that, other than the 90-day temporal limitation, the Court seemed ready to extend to a Swiss service provider its case law under Article 56 TFEU.[118] This would be in line with my argument developed earlier regarding Articles 17 and 19 of Annex I of the AFMP. Importantly, and in deviation from EU law on Article 56 TFEU, this broad interpretation would only apply to the *supply* of services. For the *consumption* of services, the *Hengartner and Gasser* line of case law made it clear that Article 5:3 AFMP limits the scope of the Agreement to issues of entry and residence, but not access.

(iv) Third-Country Nationals as Service Providers

The AFMP applies to Swiss and EU nationals, and these are the main beneficiaries of the Agreement.[119] Third-country nationals (TCNs), however, can benefit from the right to entry and residence if they are employees of Swiss or EU nationals providing services and are posted for the provision of a service on behalf of their Swiss – or EU – employer.[120] For this purpose, TCNs have to be integrated into the labour market of a contracting party (typically for 12 months, with a residence and work permit). However, according to Article 22:2 of Annex I to the Agreement, referring to Directive 96/71 on the posting of workers, the contracting parties are free to apply laws, regulations and administrative provisions regarding the application of working and employment conditions to persons posted to provide a service.[121]

When combined with Article 16 of the Agreement, one could reasonably argue that the CJEU case law with regard to posting of workers will be taken into account to ensure that rights and obligations equivalent to those laid down in the Directive are applied to Swiss nationals (and, by implication, to TCNs).[122] This view is supported by the declaration included in the final act of the Agreement providing that the EU and Switzerland consider that the relevant EU legal provisions

[118] ibid para 34.

[119] *cf* also *Xhymshiti* (n 43).

[120] A Epiney and P Zbinden, 'Arbeitnehmerentsendung und FZA Schweiz – EG: Zur Tragweite und Auslegung der Dienstleistungsfreiheit im Freizügigkeitsabkommen Schweiz – EG' *Jusletter* (31 August 2009); see also Pärli (n 81).

[121] See also BGE 140 II 447. Like several EU legal acts mentioned in the EU–Switzerland bilateral agreements, Directive 96/71 was amended after the entry into force of the AFMP. Directives 2014/67 and 2018/957 have amended Directive 96/71 and introduced more protection for posted workers. More recently, Directive 2020/1057 introduced new rules for the posting of drivers in the road transport sector, although the Directive 96/71 remains applicable. See further Case C-815/18 *Federatie Nederlandse Vakbeweging* ECLI:EU:C:2020:976. None of these Directives form part of the legal framework applying to the EU–Swiss relationship.

[122] The relevant legal framework in Switzerland consists of the Entsendegesetz (EntsG, SR 823.20) and the Entsendeverordnung (EntsV, SR 823.201) www.fedlex.admin.ch/eli/cc/2003/231/de. For a discussion, see BGE 140 II 447, 453.

regulating posting of employees who are TCNs in the context of the cross-border supply of services should prevail.[123]

It is unclear whether TCNs can benefit from the Agreement as members of the family of the service provider who enters for 90 days, or more in exceptional cases. To start with, TNCs' rights in this respect are derived rights, that is, they follow because there is a close relationship with a Swiss or EU national. Members of the family, within the meaning of the AFMP, are:[124]

(i) a spouse and relatives in the descending line who are under 21 years old or are dependent;
(ii) relatives in the ascending line and those of a spouse who are dependent; or
(iii) in the case of a student, a spouse and dependent children.

In favour of a right for TCNs as family members to accompany the service provider, one could use the very structure of Annex I. The general provisions of this Annex, that is, Articles 1–4, are relevant not only for self-employed persons, but for all categories of persons mentioned in Annex I, including service providers and also service recipients. Article 3 of Annex I provides that EU and Swiss nationals who exercise their right to free movement and have the right of residence are entitled to be joined by their family members. This would appear to include service providers for the duration of their stay in the territory of the other contracting party.

An additional question is whether a posted person who is a TCN can also be accompanied by family members, regardless of their nationality. The argument mentioned above regarding the very structure of Annex I could be relevant in this case as well. However, the counter-argument in this case could be that Article 1 of Annex I refers to family members only for nationals of the contracting parties but does not seem to extend this to posted persons.

E. Professional Qualifications and Service Supply under the AFMP

The inclusion of disciplines on professional qualifications are not only important because they constitute an essential corollary of economic activity: they are equally crucial for an international treaty such as the AFMP because they set the foundations for a common education policy in which Switzerland expresses the desire to participate and be a part of. The AFMP initially determined that the previous EU regime relating to the recognition of professional qualifications

[123] See Declaration by the European Community and Its Member States on Articles 1 and 17 of Annex I [2002] OJ L114/72.

[124] See Art 3 of Annex I to the Agreement; see also BGE 129 II 249.

was relevant for the bilateral relationship. Thus, Directive 89/48, establishing a general system for the recognition of higher-education diplomas (three-year duration), and Directive 92/51, establishing a second general system covering regulated professions for which a diploma is not necessarily required, would be applied as a basis. This system was accompanied by a series of sectoral Directives which determined the conditions of recognition of professional qualifications and in part extended the system of automatic recognition discussed above within the context of the Swiss–EU relationship pursuant to Annex III to the Agreement.[125]

By a decision of the Joint Committee of September 2011, Annex III of the AFMP was replaced to reflect the changes in the EU professional qualifications regime introduced by the adoption of the Directive 2005/36[126] and the accession of Bulgaria and Romania to the EU.[127] Importantly, just like in the case of Annex II to the AFMP, Annex III provides that, for the purposes of recognition of professional qualifications and the EU acts mentioned in section A of the Annex, Switzerland is to be equated to an EU Member State.

The Professional Qualifications Directive (PQD) replaced three general and 12 sectoral Directives relating to recognition of qualifications. It applies to regulated professions[128] and covers both employed and self-employed activities. By recognising professional qualifications of individuals acquired in another Member State, the host Member State pledges to grant access to that same profession and allow the pursuit of that profession under the same conditions as host country nationals. A novelty of Directive 2005/36 and a crucial addition to the system of professional qualifications is the adoption of specific provisions on the conditions applicable to the cross-frontier provision of services. More specifically, one of the objectives of Directive 2005/36 is to ensure that less onerous conditions apply to the cross-border provision of services on a temporary basis than those applicable to the right of establishment. The Directive provides that access to the market of the host Member State cannot be made conditional on the recognition of qualifications by that Member State if the service supplier is legally established in a given Member State and pursues the same profession there. If the profession is not regulated in the home Member State, then the service supplier can legitimately be requested to provide evidence of two years of professional experience gained over the previous 10-year period.

The PQD creates a presumption that the qualifications of a professional entitled to pursue a regulated profession in one Member State are sufficient for the pursuit of that profession in other Member States. According to the PQD, the host Member State may require prior declaration on an annual basis. Additionally, it may require that the first declaration be accompanied by certain documents, such as: proof of the nationality of the service supplier; an attestation that she legally

[125] *cf* BGE 132 II 135, 141.

[126] Directive 2005/36/EC on the recognition of professional qualifications [2005] OJ L255/22.

[127] See Decision No 2/2011 of the EU–Swiss Joint Committee [2011] OJ L277/20.

[128] The definition of 'regulated professions' is a matter of EU law: Case C-298/14 *Brouillard* ECLI:EU:C:2015:652, para 36.

exercises professional activities in her home Member State; evidence of professional qualifications; and evidence of no criminal convictions if employed in the security sector. The service supplier may also be required to submit certain information to the service recipient related to: home-country professional qualifications; liability cover; membership of professional associations; or VAT identification number. However, authorities should strive to make the procedures the least burdensome possible and to avoid delays and additional costs.[129]

The Directive allows for the adoption of safeguards, for instance in cases of important safety or health concerns (and only for those regulated professions which do not come under the automatic recognition regime). In this case, local authorities can perform an a priori evaluation of the professional qualifications of the service provider at issue to avoid serious damage due to lack of professional qualifications. Such an evaluation can only take place prior to the first provision of the service at issue (thus, only once), and has to be proportionate to the objective pursued. However, as the entire system has been traditionally based on building mutual trust, it is for the competent authorities, as opposed to the service supplier, to act proactively.

In June 2008, the Swiss Federal Council agreed on the necessity of adopting Directive 2005/36, and this led to a new, revised Annex III.[130] The issue of the recognition of professional qualifications of EU nationals had already arisen previously. For instance, the Swiss Federal Court had to tackle the question of whether a German laboratory doctor could be regarded as having an equivalent education and vocational training level when compared to Swiss laboratory doctors.[131] The relevant Swiss authority (Schweizerischer Verband der Leiter medizinisch-analytischer Laboratorien – FAMH) answered the question in the negative. The Court took issue, and instead found that training, experience and the possibility to be heard should have been taken into account, in accordance with established case law and in full respect of the principle of non-discrimination enshrined in the AFMP.[132]

In Switzerland, service providers are required to submit a declaration under Swiss law[133] if they plan to offer services in regulated professions for a maximum of 90 days per calendar year.[134] This declaration should be submitted to the

[129] *cf* Case C-298/99 *Commission v Italy* ECLI:EU:C:2002:194.

[130] *cf* Bundesamt für Berufsbildung und Technologie (BBT), 'Übernahme der Richtlinie 2005/36/EG in der Anhang III des Abkommens über die Freizügigkeit vom 21. Juni 1999 – Bericht zu den Ergebnissen der Anhörung' (March 2008).

[131] BGE 133 V 33.

[132] Among many, Case C-340/89 *Vlassopoulou* ECLI:EU:C:1991:193.

[133] See *Bundesgesetz über die Meldepflicht und die Nachprüfung der Berufsqualifikationen von Dienstleistungserbringerinnen und -erbringern in reglementierten Berufen* of 14 December 2012; *Verordnung über die Meldepflicht und die Nachprüfung der Berufsqualifikationen von Dienstleistungserbringerinnen und -erbringern in reglementierten Berufen* of 26 June 2013.

[134] If establishment is rather the objective, then the professional is not required to follow the declaration procedure but has to request normal recognition of her professional qualification from the relevant competent recognition authorities in Switzerland. See www.sbfi.admin.ch/sbfi/en/home/education/recognition-of-foreign-qualifications/recognition-procedure-on-establishment/recognition-authorities.html.

State Secretariat for Education, Research and Innovation (SERI), and is required only if the profession or activity is included in the list that SERI maintains and regularly updates.[135] This requirement is separate from the notification procedure that applies to all service providers and posted workers, obliging them to notify to the State Secretariat of Migration of the period of services and place of work before the start of the service supply.[136] Declarations and notifications are dealt with at the cantonal level. Regarding the former, the declaration obligation for certain requirements may be applicable only to specific cantons. For instance, while an EU/EEA sworn translator will have to declare her services in Geneva, no such declaration is necessary in any other Swiss canton. In contrast, every canton requires dentists, medical doctors and midwives to declare their services.

The fast-track declaration procedure is predominantly aimed at self-employed service providers (EU/EFTA) and posted workers (regardless of nationality). For both categories, as noted earlier, no residence or commuter permit is necessary according to the AFMP if the 90-day limit is not exceeded. In the case of a self-employed service provider, proof that she is authorised to carry out the professional activity at issue in her home country is sufficient proof that the applicant comes within the definition of a service provider for the purposes of Directive 2005/36. According to Swiss law, it appears that service providers will have to submit the declaration anew every calendar year, which, depending on the situation, may not be fully aligned to the spirit of the PQD.

A final interesting point relates to the interpretation of the PQD.[137] This is of significance because, by definition, any case law produced by the CJEU under the PQD is *subsequent* to the date of signature of the AFMP. The objective of the AFMP of bringing about the free movement of persons on the basis of the rules applying in the EU, the reference of the new Annex III to clarity and rationality that led to the introduction of the new Directive, and the fact that the new Directive does not deviate from but rather spells out free movement rights enshrined in EU primary law would be sufficient reasons to argue that the CJEU case law on this legal act should be the guiding reference in cases arising before Swiss courts that relate to the recognition of professional qualifications either acquired or recognised in the EU/EEA.

IV. Conclusion

After the unilateral termination by Switzerland of bilateral negotiations on an institutional framework in May 2021, the EU and Switzerland agreed in October

[135] For the list of the professions that are subject to the declaration requirement, see www.sbfi.admin.ch/dam/sbfi/en/dokumente/2015/04/reglementierte_berufediedermeldepflichtunterstehen.pdf.download.pdf/professions_subjecttodeclarationrequirement.pdf.

[136] This notification should be submitted no later than one day before the first day of work for the service provider or posted worker.

[137] Note also that the PQD was amended by the Directive 2013/55, which most notably introduced the European Professional Card. This Directive is not incorporated as of yet in Annex III.

2023 on a Common Understanding about the content of the negotiations before adopting the respective mandates internally, an approach that would appear to be paying off.[138] The Council of the European Union authorised the opening of the negotiations in March 2024, abandoning the idea of an umbrella institutional framework and accepting the Swiss proposal for a package that encompasses institutional provisions in existing and future agreements with Switzerland. Homogeneity took centre stage in the EU negotiating mandate. The Council called for provisions that would allow: dynamic alignment with the Union *acquis*; uniform interpretation and application of those agreements and the Union *acquis*; and dispute resolution and state aid provisions to be included in existing and future agreements related to the internal market.[139]

The Swiss government prioritised a package deal that would also have tangible outcomes on electricity, food safety and health. In addition, the Swiss government sought the incorporation in the agreement of provisions which recognise the Swiss sensitivities regarding the posting of workers even if the current EU legal framework on the posting of workers is extended to Switzerland.[140] Finally, through the prospective framework, Switzerland aspired to establish a two-pillar approach, similar to the EEA, whereby each party has a certain autonomy on supervision and adjudication.

In December 2024, the EU and Switzerland announced the completion of negotiations, updating several agreements and adding six new agreements, including on food safety, electricity and health.[141]

Currently, the agreed text is not publicly available. However, certain elements emerged in public. For one, the parties agreed on the need for dynamic alignment in the fields covered by the bilateral agreements but with a certain leeway left to Switzerland regarding domestic transposition. In case of non-alignment, the EU can take compensatory measures in the same or another field relating to the internal market, which will have to respect the principle of proportionality. Additionally, new state aid rules will be introduced in the areas of electricity as well as air and land transport.

Furthermore, new provisions in the AFMP will limit the parties' right to impose free movement limitations. Switzerland apparently managed to ensure that sensitive issues related to expulsion, permanent residence or economically non-active persons and students will be accommodated. The new agreement foresees that alleged economic difficulties to justify limitations to free movement should be first discussed before the Joint Committee. Absent a solution, the issue should be brought before an arbitral tribunal. Thus, no unilateral determination will be possible. Disputes about any of the agreements should be handled by an

[138] See Common Understanding concluding the exploratory talks on the bilateral EU–Switzerland relationship (27 October 2023) https://commission.europa.eu/publications/common-understanding-concluding-exploratory-talks-bilateral-eu-switzerland-relationship_en.

[139] See Council Decision 2024/995 (n 19).

[140] See the Swiss negotiating mandate agreed on by the Federal Council on 8 March 2024, www.newsd.admin.ch/newsd/message/attachments/86562.pdf.

[141] See the European Commission's Press Release, https://ec.europa.eu/commission/presscorner/detail/en/ip_24_6562).

arbitral tribunal. Nevertheless, the new agreement requires that the arbitral tribunal submit questions to the CJEU on EU law questions and makes such decisions by the CJEU binding on the arbitral tribunal. Additionally, the new agreement clarifies that the EU case law is applicable to all agreements signed by the parties.

Finally, as expected, the new deal introduces a permanent mechanism for the Swiss contribution to EU cohesion. It foresees an annual contribution of 375 million Euros from its entry into force until 2036. Additionally, there will be an annual payment of some 140 million Euros as of end-2024.[142]

In the case of services, no details have been released to the public. As a reminder, the negotiating mandate sought to reset the regulatory dialogue on financial services to prevent friction between the two markets, which have recently been shaken by the non-extension of an equivalence decision by the European Commission regarding trading venues. For now, we only know that parties agreed to take proportionate compensatory measures in case of alleged non-compliance by the other party and, in principle, under the same agreement at stake. Otherwise, hopes were relatively low from the beginning of these negotiations: the Common Understanding did not refer to an extension of the current 90-day limit nor did it mention whether (and if so, how) the EU Services Directive could be relevant for the bilateral relationship.

This would seem to be a missed opportunity, as the timing would arguably be ideal due to the recent agreement at the WTO on a reference paper on domestic regulation in services and the participation of both the EU and Switzerland in improving transparency, predictability and efficiency.[143] Furthermore, as the new Commission prepares itself for a new mandate and the Letta Report as well as the Draghi Report gave an idea of the importance of services for reviving the EU economic capacity for further growth,[144] Switzerland would seem to be missing the opportunity to influence directions of regulatory policy in its immediate neighbourhood.

Overall, at the current stage of negotiations, there is a lack of vision and ambition on the Swiss political landscape regarding services, as the approach taken is rather defensive. On the EU side, on the other hand, it seems that negotiators are satisfied with bringing in the principle of homogeneity and dynamic alignment, which will settle the Swiss case for some time. They were also eager to crystallise the regularity of Switzerland's financial contribution before moving to substantive issues.

[142] See https://www.blv.admin.ch/blv/en/home/dokumentation/nsb-news-list.msg-id-103692.html#downloads.

[143] For the reference paper, see https://docs.wto.org/dol2fe/Pages/SS/directdoc.aspx?filename=q:/INF/SDR/2.pdf&Open=True.

[144] See Enrico Letta, 'Much More Than a Market – Speed, Security, Solidarity: Empowering the Single Market to Deliver a Sustainable Future and Prosperity for all EU Citizens' (April 2024) and Mario Draghi, 'The Future of European Competitiveness – Part A: A competitiveness strategy for Europe' (September 2024).

The economic integration of Switzerland into the EU is a work in progress, built on an inevitable path that geography and economic dependence prescribe. The current bilateral framework provides for à la carte integration, which, however, reflects a fragmented approach depending on the field. An optimist would see this as a reflection of the messy EU internal market. Much as the EU would like to see the internal market as indivisible, the internal market is a political construct marked by heterogeneity and at the mercy of political choices, both at the EU and the domestic level, that determine its shape and direction depending on the field.[145] Indeed, there are several internal markets, and the EU–Swiss bilateral framework, with its varying degrees of integration depending on the area and subject matter at stake, is no different.

The AFMP exemplifies that not only are the rules of the internal market *divisible* when exported outside the EU, they are also *divided*, to satisfy the demands of the contracting parties and allow them to reach a compromise not only on the legally binding text that will govern their relationship, but also on the financial contribution that unlocks access to the EU internal market. The AFMP sets out the conditions for gradual legal integration in a somewhat suboptimal manner that focuses on how to pragmatically allow for the gradual penetration of EU law into Swiss domestic law.[146] It is suboptimal not only because of the fragmented approach described in this chapter, but also because the general manner that the EU and Switzerland approach their relationship is inherently contradictory in that they demonstrate unexpected ease in settling certain issues (eg the recognition of professional qualifications or the recognition of social security systems) while showing reluctance and significant lack of flexibility in other areas (such as the posting of workers or the role of the CJEU in their relationship). Furthermore, the static character of the legal framework that binds the two sides is not conducive to giving an important role to the judicial actors active in this equation; this also justifies to a certain degree the level of unease that is often observed in rulings by the CJEU or the Swiss Courts.

Is, then, Switzerland a reluctant integrationist player in this equation? Not really. On the contrary, in its relations with the EU neighbours and partners, Switzerland has opted for a pragmatic, market-driven approach that puts economic matters above any political aspirations. It is the latter in particular that has sparked controversy in Switzerland and fuelled discussions about the outer limits and contemporary meaning of sovereignty. Surrounded by powerful European nations, such a careful approach may also to a certain extent be regarded as justified. However, from very early on, Switzerland has sought to strengthen and diversify its economic ties with European nations. Even before the FTA with the EU in 1972, Switzerland was a founding member of EFTA, together with Austria, Denmark, Norway, Portugal, Sweden and the UK. In addition, accession to the

[145] See Stephen Weatherill, 'Several Internal Markets' (2017) 36 *Yearbook of European Law* 125.
[146] *cf* Anne-Marie Burley and Walter Mattli, 'Europe Before the Court: A Politicial Theory of Legal Integration' (1993) 47(1) *International Organization* 41.

EEA was rejected by a very narrow majority of the Swiss population. And in many respects, one could reasonably argue that the current body of law that is applicable in the EU–Swiss economic relationship is not much narrower than the one applicable in the relationship between the EU and the EEA countries.

However, its differentiation has costs for both the EU and Switzerland. In the Swiss case, reputational cost is joined by an internal political cost, whereby political actors have to pretend that the hard core of Swiss sovereignty will never be affected. While presented in Switzerland as a pick-and-choose or cherry-picking exercise towards the EU, in effect the EU insists on (and is gradually moving towards) levelling the playing field in a way in which the rules are established by the EU alone. For the EU, extending the internal market comes at a cost. First, reaping the full benefits of the expansion of the internal market presupposes that such expansion is governed by a common set of rules, but also a plausible set of standards as requirements for those interested in participating in one of the most exciting economic projects ever undertaken by a group of countries in human history. Just the hint that cherry picking may be allowed raises eyebrows, and often leads to erroneous conclusions about the intentions of political leaders and cynical comments about the importance of financial contributions. Second, the emergence of various integration regimes (ie, the EEA; deep and comprehensive free trade areas with Ukraine, Moldova and Georgia; the bilateral agreements with Switzerland) weakens the coherence of the common legal space the EU wishes to create and maintain. Homogeneity or uniformity is not simply a hypothetical or theoretical objective;[147] whether it is achieved or not has real implications on businesses, people and communities.

[147] See Lazowski (n 53) 1445.

13

ASEAN Integration: A Case Study in Multilayered Governance

SUFIAN JUSOH AND INTAN MURNIRA RAMLI

I. Introduction

Multilayered governance refers to the distribution of authority and decision-making across multiple levels and jurisdictions, including national, regional and international entities. In the context of the Association of Southeast Asian Nations (ASEAN), multilayered governance is particularly relevant as it involves the interaction and coordination among various stakeholders, including member states, regional organisations and international institutions.

The purpose of this chapter is to analyse the role of multilayered governance in the integration process of ASEAN. The chapter explores the challenges and opportunities associated with the implementation of multilayered governance in ASEAN. Multilayered governance in ASEAN is driven by its constitutional document, the ASEAN Charter of 2007, which establishes ASEAN as an international organisation based in Jakarta, with a 10-country membership in Southeast Asia.

As an international organisation, ASEAN is not a supranational organisation, as is the case with the EU. Although the organisation is governed by the ASEAN Charter, it is not an international treaty, and much of the implementation of ASEAN initiatives and agreements are governed by the national governments of the member states.

A proper understanding of each layer of ASEAN's governance structure will assist the organisation to further its integration goals towards the ASEAN Vision 2045. This will assist ASEAN member states in implementing ASEAN agreements and initiatives, based on the rule of law, whilst enhancing the decision-making process. Multilayered governance is crucial for ASEAN integration, providing opportunities for more inclusive and participatory governance, as well as for the sharing of best practices and resources among member states. It emphasises the need for ASEAN to maintain a balance between the different layers of governance and ensure that the member states work together effectively to achieve the organisation's goals.

II. Thomas Cottier and the Theory of Multilayered Governance

The theory and concept of multilayered governance have been developed and refined by many leading scholars, chief among whom is Thomas Cottier. Multilayered governance generally deals with hierarchies, competencies and a rationale of common standards and principles, with a constitutionalist perspective of different layers of bodies, organisations and competence from the perspective of international law.[1] Such layers can span the municipal to the international level, where all relevant governance layers are embedded in an overall international system.[2] It starts with a basic assumption that 'a constitution (in a normative sense) is the sum of basic (materially most important) legal norms which comprehensively regulate the social and political life of a polity'.[3]

The model of 'multilayered constitutionalism' was influenced by Emer de Vattel, according to which a constitution mainly determines how public authority is to be conducted, without tying it to a certain political model.[4] In the first phase (2005–09) of an NCCR Trade Regulation project led by Thomas Cottier, the project linked the model of constitutionalism to basic 'constitutionalist' principles, values and instruments to improve the fairness and effectiveness of the international order and/or to compensate for the loss of constitutionalist order and people's rights protection on the national level.[5] Constitutional principles from the period of enlightenment, alongside key elements of contemporary constitutions, such as the rule of law, the balance of powers, human rights, participatory rights or democratic legitimacy,[6] are conceived as principles of good governance that should be reflected at the international level independently of a nation-state model where each system brings along its own specific purpose and core 'constitutional' principles to achieve its goal.

According to Thomas Cottier, multilayered governance means different layers of functions within an overall constitutional order. They share common elements of legitimacy outcome, the rule of law and representation (democracy). They share traits of the libertarian *demos* and deliberative schools of legitimacy. Yet, these

[1] Thomas Cottier and Maya Hertig, 'The Prospects of 21st Century Constitutionalism' (2003) 7 *Max Planck Yearbook of United Nations Law* 261, 264; Joost Pauwelyn, 'Bridging Fragmentation and Unity: International Law as a Universe of Inter-Connected Islands' (2004) 25 *Michigan Journal of International Law* 903.

[2] Sufian Jusoh, 'Harmonisation of Liability Rules in Transboundary Movement of Biotechnology Crops' (PhD Thesis, University of Bern, 2009).

[3] This is reflected in the NCCR Trade Regulation Phase 1 (2005–09), led by Thomas Cottier.

[4] Emer de Vattel, *Le Droit Des Gens Ou Principes de La Loi Naturelle Appliqués à La Conduite et Aux Affaires Des Nations et Des Souverains* (1758) bk I, ch III, §§27, 31, https://gallica.bnf.fr/ark:/12148/bpt6k865729. See also Anne Peters, 'Compensatory Constitutionalism: The Function and Potential of Fundamental International Norms and Structures' (2006) 19 *Leiden Journal of International Law* 579, 581.

[5] Cottier and Hertig (n 1) 264; Peters (n 4) 581.

[6] Cottier and Hertig (n 1) 264.

elements differ in mutual relations and composition on different levels of governance, ranging from local communities to institutions of global governance. While *demos* dominates locally and nationally, it is absent from international organisations, even in the EU at this point in time. Legitimacy based upon deliberation and interaction exists on all levels, yet in different forms and to a different degree. Libertarian traits protecting rights and the rule of law are shared equally by all levels, but assume a key role in international organisations and compensate for the impossibility of appropriately supplying other elements constituting legitimacy and, thus, faith and voluntary compliance.[7]

According to De Wet,

> multilayered governance relates to the constitutionalisation of the international order. References to the constitutionalization of the international legal order describe the process of (re)organization and (re)allocation of competencies among the subjects of the international legal order, which shapes the international community, and its value system and enforcement.[8]

Thus, the legal order may be applicable to different layers in the international community, which is assumed to be more integrated.

Eising presents three characteristics of multilayered governance that could assist our understanding of its effect on domestic groups.[9] For one, multilayered governance has a statist and institutional core, where public actors from at least two different levels of government share political authority in formal institutional arrangements. Public actors at the upper level are, to some extent, autonomous, but lower-level units 'are not subordinate' and participate in higher-level decision-making. While this does not separate multilevel governance from international organisations or federal policies, it helps to distinguish multilevel governance from any intra-organisational division of labour and from private governance arrangements. Second, functional tasks do not coincide with territorial competencies; rather, the former cut across the latter. The allocation of functional responsibilities to different levels of government can be decided for the short term or the long term. It can cover few or many policies and policy instruments, and can lead to the separation or to the sharing of responsibilities among governmental institutions. Third, multilevel governance combines various modes of interaction: competition, bargaining based on self-interests, negotiations to build consensus, majority decisions and hierarchical imposition.

[7] Thomas Cottier, 'Constitutionalism, Multilevel Trade Governance and Social Regulation (Studies in International Trade Law, Vol 9). Edited by Christian Joerges and Ernst-Ulrich Petersmann' (2007) 10 *Journal of International Economic Law* 424.

[8] Erika De Wet, 'The Emergence of International and Regional Value Systems as a Manifestation of the Emerging International Constitutional Order' (2006) 19 *Leiden Journal of International Law* 611, 611–32.

[9] Rainer Eising, 'Multilevel Governance and Business Interests in the European Union' (2004) 17 *Governance* 211, 216.

Cottier and Hertig suggest a model akin to a five-storey house in examining the role and application of multilayered governance in the ASEAN Economic Community, as illustrated in Figure 1.

Figure 1 The ASEAN Economic Community and multilayered governance

Source: Authors' depiction of Cottier–Hertig's five-layered Swiss house (2003).

These five levels are cantons or sub-federal entities and the federal structure. The fourth level amounts to the framework of regional integration, such as that of the EU. The fifth level is global. The global rule of law, which includes dispute settlement and the enforcement of rights, is likely to gradually develop constitutional and supranational structures binding upon states and organisations. Other international fora may re-emerge in response to global regulatory needs and call for adjustment at the regional, national and cantonal levels.[10]

The different levels include the states that are central to the process of international lawmaking and enforcement; international organisations with legal personality, which increasingly play a prominent role in international and regional issues; and individuals who also constitute members of the international community to the extent that they possess international legal personality.

Such a description fits De Wet's definition of the term 'constitution', which describes an embryonic constitutional order in which different national, regional and functional (sectoral) regimes form the building blocks of an international community that is underpinned by a core value system common to all communities and embedded in a variety of legal structures for its enforcement.[11] Thus, each of the parties to multilayered governance is to assume and exercise authority and power at a different layer of the governance.

[10] Cottier and Hertig (n 1) 300–01. See also Thomas Cottier, 'The Impact from Without: International Law and the Structure of Federal Government in Switzerland' in Peter Knoepfel and Wolf Linder (eds), *Verwaltung, Regierung und Verfassung im Wandel: Gedächtnisschrift für Raimund E Germann = Administration, gouvernement et constitution en transformation: hommage en mémoire de Raimund E Germann* (Helbing & Lichtenhahn, 2000).

[11] De Wet (n 8) 611–32.

According to Keohane and Nye, governance refers to the emergence and recognition of principles, norms, rules and procedures that both provide standards of acceptable public behaviour and are sufficiently followed to produce behavioural regularities.[12] Under multilayered global governance, the nation-state is supplemented by other actors – private and third sector consisting of pressure groups and non-governmental organisations – in a more complex geography. While the nation-state remains the most important player, it is not the only key actor in global politics. Hence, the concept of divided sovereignty is based on the concept of federalism. The notion of shared sovereignty refers to the division of powers between the federation and the sub-federal entities, and this could be extended to international and supranational governance structures.

In a system of multilayered governance, it is essential to define the role and relationship of each level of governance. The steady rise of international and supranational rules holds the potential of considerably shifting and upsetting the balance of traditional constitutional patterns.[13] From the viewpoint of the higher level of governance, this situation is unsatisfactory as some of those at this higher level of governance, such as the ASEAN Leaders Summit or the United Nations General Assembly, do not have the powers to implement and enforce obligations at the lower levels, yet have to assume international responsibility. From the perspective of the lower level, the situation is disturbing as the internal division of competence is being eroded by a higher level.[14]

Nevertheless, the role of the nation-state as the most important actor in multilayered governance should not be underestimated. To secure desirable outcomes in the international system, from peace to health to prosperity, international law must address the capacity and the will of domestic governments to respond to these issues at their sources. Where states are strong enough to combat these internal threats directly, international law can play a critical coordinating role to ensure that governments cooperate in addressing threats before they span borders. Where national governments are unable or unwilling to address the origins of these threats, such as through lack of capacity or knowledge, or because of inadequate law, international law may step in to help build their capacity or stiffen their will. Thus, multilayered governance is not so much as a label for the joint and interconnected governance of subnational, national, regional and global political actors.[15]

[12] Robert O Keohane and Joseph S Nye, 'Introduction' in Joseph S Nye and John D Donahue (eds), *Governance in a Globalizing World* (Brookings Institution Press, 2000).

[13] Cottier and Hertig (n 1) 300–01.

[14] ibid.

[15] Anne Peters and Klaus Armingeon, 'Introduction – Global Constitutionalism from an Interdisciplinary Perspective' (2009) 16 *Indiana Journal of Global Legal Studies* 385, 386.

III. ASEAN and its Constitutionalism

ASEAN is a regional intergovernmental organisation, founded in 1967 to promote political and economic cooperation among its members. ASEAN's primary objectives include promoting regional peace, stability and economic development. The organisation has 10 member states: Brunei, Cambodia, Indonesia, Laos, Malaysia, Myanmar, the Philippines, Singapore, Thailand and Vietnam. Timor-Leste has recently been granted observer status and will be accepted as the eleventh and potentially last member state when its accession process is completed.

From the perspective of constitutionalism and multilayered governance, ASEAN as an international grouping of nations has developed from a mere loose organisation under the Bangkok Declaration (generally known as the ASEAN Declaration) into a more structured organisation through various initiatives, including the Bali Accords I, II and III and the ASEAN Charter.

The organisation was initially formed by five member states – Indonesia, Malaysia, the Philippines, Singapore and Thailand – through the ASEAN Declaration, signed in Bangkok on 8 August 1967. Brunei joined the regional grouping in 1984, and the remaining members – Cambodia, Laos, Myanmar and Vietnam – joined in the 1990s and 2000s.[16]

The founding principles of ASEAN were to promote political and economic cooperation among its members, with the primary objective of maintaining regional peace and stability. ASEAN differs from other regional integration initiatives even though it serves the same purpose of ensuring the peaceful coexistence of its members. Compared with the EU, for example, ASEAN started as a political organisation, whereas the EU started as the European Economic Community under the Treaty of Rome 1957.

As stated in the ASEAN Declaration,[17] among the aims and objectives of ASEAN are to accelerate of economic growth, social progress and cultural development in the region in order to strengthen the foundation for a prosperous and peaceful community of Southeast Asian nations.[18] ASEAN's first step towards

[16] ASEAN, 'The Founding of ASEAN' https://asean.org/the-founding-of-asean/.

[17] The Bangkok Declaration or ASEAN Declaration is the main document that established ASEAN on 8 August 1967. It was signed by the Minister for Foreign Affairs of Indonesia, the Deputy Prime Minister of Malaysia, the Secretary of Foreign Affairs of the Philippines, the Minister for Foreign Affairs of Singapore and the Minister of Foreign Affairs of Thailand. Other aims include to promote collaboration and mutual assistance on matters of common interest, to provide assistance to each other in the form of training and research facilities, to collaborate for the better utilisation of agriculture and industry to raise the living standards of the people, to promote Southeast Asian studies and to maintain close, beneficial cooperation with existing international organisations with similar aims and purposes.

[18] To promote peace and stability in the region, ASEAN member states signed the Treaty of Amity and Cooperation (TAC), otherwise known as Bali Concord I, in 1976. Under Bali Concord I, ASEAN member states agreed that each will not use force but seek peaceful solutions in resolving conflicts. To date, 29 countries have signed the TAC, guided by important principles such as mutual respect for the independence, sovereignty, equality, territorial integrity and national identity of all nations; the right of every state to lead its national existence free from external interference, subversion or coercion; non-interference in the internal affairs of one another; settlement of differences or disputes by a peaceful manner; renunciation of the threat or use of force; and effective cooperation among themselves.

deeper regional integration started with the signing of Bali Concord II, which was endorsed at the Ninth ASEAN Summit in October 2003. Bali Concord II consists of three pillars, namely the ASEAN Security Community (now the ASEAN Political-Security Community), the ASEAN Economic Community and the ASEAN Socio-Cultural Community.

ASEAN adopted its constitution in the form of the ASEAN Charter in 2007. The ASEAN Charter came into force on 15 December 2008, when all member states ratified it. The ASEAN Charter provides ASEAN with a legal personality and makes it an international inter-governmental organisation. Unlike the EU, the ASEAN Charter turns ASEAN not into a supranational body, but rather a loose organisation of 10 member states.[19] The Charter enshrines core principles and delineates requirements for membership.

This characterises ASEAN as a rules-based and people-oriented international organisation. Under the ASEAN Charter, the main purposes of ASEAN are to maintain and enhance peace, security and stability, and further strengthen peace-oriented values in the region; to enhance regional resilience by promoting greater political, security, economic and socio-cultural cooperation; to preserve Southeast Asia as a Nuclear Weapon-Free Zone, free of all other weapons of mass destruction; and to ensure that the peoples and member states of ASEAN live in peace with the world at large in a just, democratic and harmonious environment.

On the economic front, the ASEAN Charter Blueprint 2015 and the ASEAN Blueprint 2025 Forging Ahead Together state that ASEAN aims to create a single market and production base which is stable, prosperous, highly competitive and economically integrated, with effective facilitation for trade and investment in which there is a free flow of goods, services and investment; facilitated movement of business persons, professionals, talents and labour; and the freer flow of capital.[20] Under the ASEAN Charter, ASEAN also aims to alleviate poverty and narrow development gaps within member states through mutual assistance and cooperation.

ASEAN Leaders celebrated the formal establishment of the ASEAN Community in 2015 and charted the ASEAN Community Vision 2025 by issuing the Kuala Lumpur Declaration on ASEAN 2025 *Forging Ahead Together* at the 27th ASEAN Summit in Kuala Lumpur. ASEAN Leaders adopted the ASEAN Community and further launched the ASEAN Community Vision 2025, the ASEAN Political-Security Community Blueprint 2025, the ASEAN Economic Community (AEC) Blueprint 2025 and the ASEAN Socio-Cultural Community Blueprint 2025. ASEAN Leaders agreed that ASEAN 2025 *Forging Ahead Together* succeeded the Roadmap for an ASEAN Community (2009–2015).[21]

[19] Hooman Peimani, 'Disintegration of the EU and the Implications for ASEAN' (2020) Asian Development Bank Institute (ADBI) Working Paper 1140, www.adb.org/publications/disintegration-eu-and-implications-asean.

[20] The ASEAN Charter, ch I.

[21] ASEAN, ASEAN 2025: Forging Ahead Together (November 2015).

Through the ASEAN 2025 *Forging Ahead Together* initiative, ASEAN Leaders aim to consolidate the ASEAN Community by building upon and deepening the integration process to realise a rules-based, people-centred ASEAN Community, with human rights and fundamental freedoms, higher quality of life and the benefits of community building, reinforcing a sense of togetherness and common identity, guided by the purposes and principles of the ASEAN Charter. ASEAN Leaders also envision a peaceful, stable and resilient ASEAN Community endowed with an enhanced capacity to respond effectively to challenges, and ASEAN as an outward-looking region within a global community of nations, while maintaining ASEAN centrality. ASEAN Leaders also underlined the importance and complementarity of the United Nations 2030 Agenda for Sustainable Development – generally known as the Sustainable Development Goals – with ASEAN community-building efforts to uplift the standards of living of ASEAN peoples.

Under the ASEAN Economic Community (AEC) 2025, *Forging Ahead Together*, ASEAN Leaders envisioned that by 2025, ASEAN should achieve a highly integrated and cohesive regional economy that supports sustained (high) economic growth by increasing trade, investment and job creation; improving regional capacity to respond to global challenges and megatrends; deeper integration in trade in services; and a more seamless movement of investment, skilled labour, business persons and capital.

The AEC 2025 also envisions a competitive, innovative and dynamic community which fosters robust productivity growth, including through the creation and practical application of knowledge, supportive policies towards innovation, science-based approaches to green technology and development, embracing evolving digital technologies, promoting good governance, transparency, responsive regulations and effective dispute resolution, as well as enhanced participation in global value chains.

ASEAN is now working on the ASEAN Vision 2045 to replace the ASEAN Vision 2025. ASEAN Vision 2045 will be supplemented by attendant documents, including five-year strategic plans. During the 43rd ASEAN Summit in Jakarta in September 2023, ASEAN Leaders adopted the core elements of the ASEAN Vision 2045. Moving towards 2045, ASEAN will continue to enhance itself as a rules-based Community of Nations that fosters mutual trust, respect and benefits, and adheres to the shared principles, purposes, values and norms enshrined in the United Nations Charter, the ASEAN Charter and other ASEAN instruments.[22]

[22] ASEAN, Chairman's Statement of the 43rd ASEAN Summit Jakarta, Indonesia, 5 September 2023, https://asean.org/wp-content/uploads/2023/09/CHAIRMAN-STATEMENT-OF-THE-43RD-ASEAN-SUMMIT-FINpdf.

IV. The ASEAN Economic Community and Multilayered Governance

ASEAN faces several challenges in achieving its regional integration aims. To address these challenges, multilayered governance can present opportunities. This approach involves a combination of regional, national and international cooperation to tackle issues that transcend individual country boundaries. Figure 2 attempts to explain the multilayered governance in ASEAN.

Figure 2 The multilayered governance of ASEAN

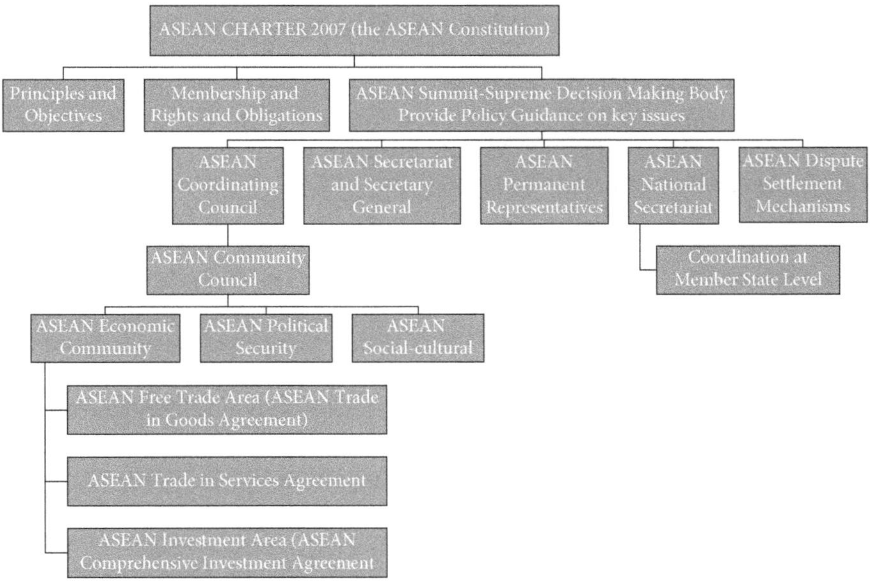

Source: Authors' own interpretation based on the ASEAN Charter and other ASEAN agreements.

The prospects of ASEAN integration, a case study in multilayered governance, are closely tied to the economic aspects of the association. ASEAN has been broadly successful in promoting political cooperation among its member states, but its efforts in economic integration have, on the whole, proven less successful.[23] The organisation has made much progress in areas such as trade liberalisation, but it has not yet achieved the level of economic integration seen in other regional blocs like the EU.[24]

[23] Donghyun Park, 'The Prospects for Further Economic Integration in ASEAN' (1999) 14 *Journal of Economic Integration* 382, 382–418.

[24] Hal Hill and Jayant Menon, 'ASEAN Economic Integration: Features, Fulfillments, Failures and the Future' (December 2010) ADB Working Paper Series on Regional Economic Integration 69, www.adb.org/sites/default/files/publication/28551/wp69-hill-menon-asean-economic-integration.pdf.

ASEAN, as provided for in the ASEAN Charter, respects the rule of law. The formation of the ASEAN Community is part of a regional effort to reinforce ASEAN centrality and its primacy as the driving force in regional stability.[25] ASEAN's focus on the rule of law requires ASEAN member states to respect democratic processes, good governance, human rights and negotiated dispute settlement.[26] ASEAN pursues the rule of law in managing conflicts through negotiated dispute settlement by promoting good governance, democratisation and human rights as the cornerstones of its current and future diplomatic stance. Its adaptation to the rule of law, defined here as the accountability of member states to the same laws, norms and regional practices, takes place in the context of several interrelated developments.[27]

At the global level, ASEAN has two ASEAN economic agreements and several preferential trade agreements (PTAs) governed by the rules of the World Trade Organization (WTO) on regionalism as provided for in Article 24 of the General Agreement on Tariff and Trade and Article V of the General Agreement on Trade in Services. The two ASEAN agreements are the ASEAN Trade in Goods Agreement 2010 (ATIGA) and the ASEAN Framework Agreement on Services 1995, which is being replaced by the ASEAN Trade in Services Agreement 2020 (ATISA). ASEAN PTAs include the ASEAN–Australia–New Zealand Free Trade Area, the ASEAN–China Free Trade Agreements, the ASEAN–India Free Trade Area; the ASEAN–Japan Free Trade Area, the ASEAN–Republic of Korea Free Trade Area, ASEAN–Hong-Kong Free Trade Area and the Regional Comprehensive Economic Partnership Agreement.

At the regional level, ASEAN and its member states are bound by the above preferential trade agreements. In addition, ASEAN and its member states are bound by the provisions of the ASEAN Charter, which acts as the de facto constitution of the organisation. Further, ASEAN also has a regional investment agreement, the ASEAN Comprehensive Investment Agreement (ACIA), which was signed in 2009 and came into force in 2012. The above-mentioned ASEAN agreements bind its member states and sub-national entities.

Ensuring compliance with the above arrangements and other ASEAN initiatives can be daunting. ASEAN has a complex institutional framework that involves various mechanisms and institutions to facilitate cooperation and

[25] The term 'ASEAN centrality' is based on the ASEAN Charter, Art 1.15, which states that ASEAN's main objective is to maintain ASEAN's centrality and proactive role as the main driving force for its relations and cooperation with external partners, in an open, transparent and inclusive regional architecture. As stated in the ASEAN Outlook on the Indo-Pacific, ASEAN centrality means ASEAN must become the dominant regional platform to overcome common challenges and engage with external power.

[26] Abdullah Mohd Kamarulnizam, 'Malaysia and ASEAN: The New Challenges of a Rule-Based Community' in Paul Evans and Sufian Jusoh (eds), *IKMAS Insights*, vol 1 (Institute of Malaysian and International Studies, Universiti Kebangsaan Malaysia, 2024) www.ukm.my/ikmas/wp-content/uploads/2024/01/IKMAS-Insights-Volume-1-2024-eISBNpdf.

[27] ibid.

integration among member states. Some of the key institutions and mechanisms include:

1. ASEAN Summit: The ASEAN Summit is the highest decision-making body in ASEAN, consisting of the heads of state or government of all member states. The summit provides a platform for leaders to discuss and make decisions on regional issues, including economic, political and security matters.[28]
2. ASEAN Secretariat: The ASEAN Secretariat is the executive arm of ASEAN and is responsible for implementing the organisation's policies and programmes. It is located in Jakarta, Indonesia, and is headed by a Secretary-General who is appointed by the ASEAN Summit.[29] In terms of implementation and compliance, ASEAN established the ASEAN Integration Monitoring Office within the ASEAN Secretariat to ensure the implementation of integration milestones.[30] These milestones and agreements have played a crucial role in shaping ASEAN's integration process and paving the way for deeper cooperation among member states. However, challenges remain, and continued efforts are needed to ensure the successful implementation of these initiatives and to address ongoing issues related to trade, financial integration and regional stability.
3. ASEAN Ministerial Meetings: These meetings involve the foreign ministers of ASEAN member states and are responsible for implementing the decisions made by the ASEAN Summit.[31]

The above institutions and mechanisms play a crucial role in facilitating ASEAN's integration efforts and ensuring the smooth functioning of the organisation. They provide a platform for dialogue, decision-making and cooperation on various issues, enabling ASEAN to address the challenges and opportunities of regional integration.

Furthermore, ASEAN undertakes several initiatives to ensure the compliance of the above-mentioned agreements and other ASEAN arrangements. For example, ASEAN initiates several harmonisation and mutual recognition arrangements, including in relation to standards in goods and mutual recognition agreements in professional services. However, the issue of harmonisation raises the issue of the sovereignty of nations in enacting their own domestic laws. As ASEAN member states are all sovereign nations, they remain free to develop and enact their own laws. Harmonisation processes may be hampered if some member states choose not to fully implement agreed outcomes or to enact their own set of laws that could be different from what is internationally agreed upon.

[28] Pattharapong Rattanasevee, 'Towards Institutionalised Regionalism: The Role of Institutions and Prospects for Institutionalisation in ASEAN' (2014) 3 *SpringerPlus* 556.

[29] ibid.

[30] Aladdin D Rillo, 'Asean Financial Integration: Opportunities, Risks,And Challenges' (2018) 14 *Public Policy Review* 901, 901–24.

[31] Rattanasevee (n 27).

Another initiative is the availability of dispute settlement mechanisms, state-to-state under the ATIGA, ATISA and ACIA and investor–state dispute settlement under the ACIA. ASEAN established the ASEAN Dispute Settlement Mechanism, which has not been tested in practice. Under the ASEAN Charter, disputes arising from ASEAN economic agreements such as the ATIGA, ATISA and ACIA may be resolved through the ASEAN Protocol on Enhanced Dispute Settlement Mechanism. Further, disputes relating to ASEAN instruments may be settled through the mechanisms provided for under such agreements.

Article 25 of the ASEAN Charter provides mechanisms to resolve disputes, including through arbitration. The implementation of Article 25 is provided for under the Protocol to the ASEAN Charter on Dispute Settlement Mechanism 2010 and the Instrument to Incorporate the Rules for Reference of Non-Compliance to the ASEAN Summit in 2012.[32] However, the dispute settlement mechanism is not the same as the European Court of Justice, which has judicial and enforcement power against offending EU Member States. The ASEAN dispute settlement mechanism has never been tested and therefore its effectiveness is unknown.

In addition, the ACIA provides investors with access to investor–state dispute settlement means. ASEAN investors, as defined in the ACIA, have access to the domestic courts of the host country or various forms of international arbitration and alternative dispute resolution mechanisms.[33] Under Article 32 ACIA, if an investment dispute has not been resolved within 180 days of receipt by a disputing member state of a request for consultations, the disputing investor may submit a claim under the ISDS mechanism, either to the domestic court or to international arbitration, but not both.[34]

V. Conclusion

Multilayered governance is particularly relevant to ASEAN as the regional grouping's evolution involves interaction and coordination among various stakeholders, including member states, regional organisations and international institutions.

Within ASEAN, there are three main layers of governance, at the global, regional and national levels. Globally, the WTO governs the AFTA, ATIGA and ATISA. These entities can influence ASEAN integration through their policies

[32] Hao Phan, 'Towards a Rules-Based ASEAN: The Protocol to the ASEAN Charter on Dispute Settlement Mechanisms' (2013) 5 *Arbitration Law Review* 254.

[33] See Julien Chaisse and Sufian Jusoh, *The ASEAN Comprehensive Investment Agreement: The Regionalisation of Laws and Policy on Foreign Investment* (Edward Elgar Publishing, 2016).

[34] In the event that ASEAN member states disagree about the interpretation of ACIA on matters other than disputes about the state's investment-related measure causing damage or loss to a foreign investor, ACIA incorporates the existing ASEAN state-to-state dispute settlement mechanism under the ASEAN Protocol on Enhanced Dispute Settlement Mechanism signed in Vientiane, Lao People's Democratic Republic on 29 November 2004.

and initiatives, as well as through their interactions with ASEAN institutions. The regional layer includes the ASEAN Secretariat, the ASEAN Summit and the ASEAN Regional Forum, which facilitate cooperation and decision-making among ASEAN members, shaping the regional integration process. At the national level, national governments are responsible for implementing policies and regulations within their own countries, which can influence the overall direction of ASEAN integration.

The interaction between these layers of governance is crucial for ASEAN integration. National governments must work together with regional and global institutions to ensure that policies and decisions are aligned and cohesive. This requires effective communication, coordination and cooperation among all stakeholders.

Although ASEAN's multilayered governance structure has at times led to a complex and fragmented decision-making process, it also provides opportunities for more inclusive and participatory governance, as well as for the sharing of best practices and resources among member states. As ASEAN continues to evolve and deepen its integration efforts, it will be essential to maintain a balance between the different layers of governance and ensure that they work together effectively to achieve the organisation's goals. Hence, it is important that ASEAN member states better understand the importance of working together and how doing so can contribute to making ASEAN's integration process more seamless.

PART III

Addressing Common Concerns and the Future Challenges to Trade Law

14

Sovereignty Strikes Back: Continued Relevance of Common Concern of Humankind in Times of Polycrisis

ZAKER AHMAD AND IRYNA BOGDANOVA

The doctrine of common concern of humankind (CCH), as shaped by Professor Thomas Cottier, envisages the identification of the most pressing shared global problems as common concerns and their effective redress through law, particularly by way of (i) cooperation, (ii) homework and (iii) unilateral responses. In doing so, the CCH doctrine advances a qualified reading of state sovereignty, creating room for deference to a rules-based global order. In practice, however, global affairs in recent years have taken a turn away from rules-based interactions between states. Aggression in the name of security and the race for subsidies in the name of climate action, among others, evidence an attempt to take control back from the global to the domestic level. Prompted by such developments, this chapter revisits the previously drawn conclusions on the utility of CCH doctrine in the areas of human rights enforcement via economic sanctions and low-carbon technology diffusion. It concludes that the doctrine remains more salient than ever, especially in moving towards a rule of law rather than a rule through power. With that in focus, the chapter updates the cooperation, homework and unilateral action agenda in the regimes mentioned above – opening an opportunity to compare and contrast the two and reinforcing the continued relevance of the doctrine in the current era of deglobalisation and crisis of the rules-based international order.

I. Introduction

From 2015, Professor Thomas Cottier led the project 'Towards a Principle of Common Concern in Global Law: Foundation and Case Studies' for four years, enlisting both of us as his PhD students. Although, looking back from 2024, the world in 2015 may look brighter, it was nothing but. Against the backdrop of the aftermath of the global financial crisis, unforeseen mass migration towards Europe, the occupation of Crimea by 'little green men', brewing tension over the nearing expiry of non-market economy controls in China's World Trade Organization (WTO) Accession Protocol and no long-term climate agreement yet in place, the prospects of international law resolving shared global challenges looked very poor. The project was framed as a response to those challenges. Its goal was, in many ways, emblematic of Professor Cottier's vision of international economic law – realistic yet forward-looking – as it sought to explore the possibility of the predominantly environmental principle of common concern of humankind to be recognised as part and parcel of international law and have a positive structural impact upon the regulation of common interests, going beyond existing principles like sustainable development, prevention of transboundary harm and the common heritage of mankind. This goal was to be fulfilled by attaching stronger normativity to the principle, in the form of specific obligations binding all stakeholders to cooperate and resolve shared problems.

By the end of 2021, in the midst of the COVID-19 pandemic, the project was completed. It produced a propositional framework – the doctrine of common concern of humankind[1] – and several PhD theses which tested its application to different pressing problems, such as monetary stability, global inequality, human rights-related sanctions, migration, marine plastic pollution and transfer of low-carbon technologies.[2] In all of those studied areas, propositions of the doctrine were found to be useful in addressing collective action problems. However, instead of making any progress along the proposed trajectories, actual world affairs have since displayed a continuous shift away from the values of global community and solidarity. The rise of authoritarian and populist regimes, me-first economic policies, unaccountable and illegal acts of aggression against other countries and a general decline in multilateral cooperation are but a few indicators of the crisis of our times.

This chapter revisits some of the key messages of the common concern project, which are also one of Professor Cottier's latest contributions to public international law. Our goal is to situate the propositions of the CCH doctrine with recent developments and look for a continued relevance of engaging with this evolving notion. To that end, we begin by briefly recalling the key findings and propositions of the CCH doctrine and its application in the fields of climate change and human rights. This is then followed by an account of subsequent developments. On the one hand, we note the positive reception of the notion in an emerging field of common interest, ie the protection of the atmosphere. On the other hand, we highlight the signs of parochialism's resurgence in international affairs. Against

[1] Thomas Cottier (ed), *The Prospects of Common Concern of Humankind in International Law* (Cambridge University Press, 2021).

[2] Zaker Ahmad, *WTO Law and Trade Policy Reform for Low-Carbon Technology Diffusion: Common Concern of Humankind, Carbon Pricing, and Export Credit Support* (Brill, 2021); Alexander D Beyleveld, *Taking a Common Concern Approach to Economic Inequality* (Brill, 2022); Iryna Bogdanova, *Unilateral Sanctions in International Law and the Enforcement of Human Rights* (Brill, 2022); Lucía Satragno, *Monetary Stability as a Common Concern in International Law* (Brill, 2022); Judith Schäli, *The Mitigation of Marine Plastic Pollution in International Law* (Brill, 2022).

this dialectical, contested backdrop, we conclude that not only does the doctrine remain more relevant than ever, but also that continued engagement with it in new fields through 'claims and responses' is an essential part of the progress of solidarity and common interest norms in international law. Suggestions outlining that path in the fields of human rights sanctions, climate change and international economic law are provided at the end.

II. The CCH Doctrine in Context

International cooperation in pursuit of long-term, shared interests is hardest when it requires a large group of heterogeneous stakeholders to sacrifice localised economic and political gains in the short term – such as in the case of anthropogenic climate change.[3] This premise gives an insight into the almost insurmountable difficulty surrounding the struggle for effective global arrangements, in the form of binding international treaties, to tackle existing and emerging transboundary problems. Progress, nonetheless, happens. In his celebrated 1994 lecture at the Hague Academy of International Law, Bruno Simma noted how the ideological acceptance of the international community as a 'higher unity' triggered a gradual evolution of the interstate and bilateral character of public international law towards becoming a value-based order.[4] In line with the idea of collective action problems, Simma accurately highlighted the paradox of building community interests on a bilateral state-centric foundation of international law, and suggested the development of concrete 'principles, institutions and rules' to overcome it.[5] Doctrinal expressions like *jus cogens*, he observed, serve an important compensatory function to progressively fulfil community interests through international institutions.[6] The emergence and growth of the legal principle 'common concern of humankind' should be seen as progress along that trajectory. In response to the need to highlight the global interest in addressing challenges that surpass state-territorial domains, 'common concern of humankind' emerged as a problem signifier in the early 1990s,[7] which was also the United Nations decade of

[3] Thomas Cottier, 'The Principle of Common Concern of Humankind' in Cottier, *The Prospects of Common Concern of Humankind in International Law* (n 1) 7–9; Mancur Olson, *The Logic of Collective Action: Public Goods and the Theory of Groups*, 17th printing (Harvard University Press, 1998); Paul G Harris, 'Collective Action on Climate Change: The Logic of Regime Failure' (2007) 47 *Natural Resources Journal* 195, 199–204; Elinor Ostrom, 'Analyzing Collective Action' (2010) 41 *Agricultural Economics* 155, 157–59; Inge Kaul, 'Global Public Goods: Explaining Their Underprovision' (2012) 15 *Journal of International Economic Law* 729, 736–43; Scott Barrett, 'Collective Action to Avoid Catastrophe: When Countries Succeed, When They Fail, and Why' (2016) 7 *Global Policy* 45.

[4] Bruno Simma, *From Bilateralism to Community Interest in International Law*, Recueil Des Cours: Collected Courses of the Hague Academy of International Law, vol 250 (Martinus Nijhoff Publishers, 1997) 234–35, 243–49.

[5] ibid 247–49.

[6] ibid 285–86.

[7] UNGA, 'Protection of Global Climate for Present and Future Generations of Mankind' (1988) A/RES/43/53; AA Cançado Trindade and David J Attard, 'I Meeting of the UNEP Group of Legal

international law.[8] Born alongside its more renowned sibling principle of sustainable development, the problems of climate change and biodiversity loss were its first fields of operation, although it is not, as we will later see, relegated exclusively to those regimes.

A. What is of 'Common Concern'?

To indicate the attributes that may earn a shared problem the label 'common concern', academics in the past have used expressions such as being truly fundamental, reflecting universal values or touching upon ethics of global significance.[9] While being emotionally evocative of the importance of underlying interests, these descriptions, either individually or all together, elude the formation of a concrete assessment metric – one that can serve the useful function of gatekeeping the boundary of common concern. Cottier et al were the first to propose a consistent normative content to be assigned to this principle.[10] Drawing analogies with the existing areas of recognised common concerns, it was argued that the essential starting point of framing a common concern is the 'existence of threat of a real transboundary problem, the resolution or prevention of which requires collective action and cooperation among two or more states'.[11] Extending it further, Cottier argued that the unique threshold for a common interest issue to become of common concern of humankind ought to lie in its likelihood of adversely affecting global peace, stability and welfare – the core functions of international law.[12] A consistent structural form and threshold then allows the assessment of existing and emerging shared problems, such as inequality, global monetary and financial instability, egregious violation of human rights, migration crisis and marine plastic pollution, through the lens of CCH.[13] It is noteworthy that the method of extending the application of CCH to a new, characteristically similar issue area through analogical reasoning has also been employed by the International Law Commission's (ILC) Special Rapporteur on the Protection of the Atmosphere, Shinya Murase. He

Experts to Examine the Implications of the "Common Concern of Mankind" Concept on Global Environmental Issues' (1991) 13 *Revista IIDH* 247. For a broad overview, see Cottier, 'The Principle of Common Concern of Humankind' (n 3) 11–16.

[8] UNGA, 'United Nations Decade of International Law' (1989) UNGA Resolution A/RES/44/23.

[9] Cottier, 'The Principle of Common Concern of Humankind' (n 3) 18–20; Friedrich Soltau, 'Common Concern of Humankind' in Cinnamon P Carlarne, Kevin R Gray and Richard G Tarasofsky (eds), *The Oxford Handbook of International Climate Change Law* (First edition, Oxford University Press, 2016) 207; Dinah Shelton, 'Common Concern of Humanity' (2009) 5 *Iustum Aequum Salutare* 33, 33–34.

[10] Cottier, 'The Principle of Common Concern of Humankind' (n 3) 25; Thomas Cottier et al, 'The Principle of Common Concern and Climate Change' (2014) 52 *Archiv des Völkerrechts* 293, 314–15.

[11] Cottier, 'The Principle of Common Concern of Humankind' (n 3) 37.

[12] ibid 39–41.

[13] Cottier, *The Prospects of Common Concern of Humankind in International Law* (n 1) chs 3–8.

used the approach to propose atmospheric degradation as a common concern of humankind. According to Murase, a deductive approach is justified to ensure the progressive development of international law in areas where 'the law has not yet been sufficiently developed in the practice of States', as long as it conforms to the emergent principles and rules of customary international law.[14]

We furnish two illustrations of how such an identification exercise may work out in distinct legal contexts. Firstly, within a formally recognised domain of CCH like climate change, its sub-issues also earn the same label to the extent they are connected to the main problem. This is the case, for example, of technology transfers.[15] Transfer of technology is a regulatory regime in its own right, some aspects of which function flawlessly. Other aspects, eg low-carbon technology transfer between developed and developing regions, face challenges. The recognition of climate change as a CCH would be applicable to those particular technology transfer challenges that problematise climate action.[16] Hence, the problem of inadequate transfer and diffusion of technologies necessary for adequate climate response deserves to be termed as a CCH. Secondly, key attributes of shared challenges formally recognised as a common concern, eg its gravity and urgency, and the indispensability of transboundary collaborative efforts, serve as comparative benchmarks to assess the potential of new problems to be inducted into the scope of CCH. Professor Cottier additionally proposed the notion of threat to global peace and security as a threshold indicator. These metrics identify the situations of grave and systematic breaches of human rights as producing negative externalities which potentially threaten international peace and security. One of the examples is massive refugee flows: they may range from violence-induced movements to crises caused by a dire economic situation that partly emanates from the persistent violation of economic and social rights, especially in cases of authoritarian regimes deriving their economic might from natural resource exploitation. Posing a threat to regional and international peace and security, such egregious human rights violations can be recognised as constituting a common concern calling for collective action.[17] Framing international human rights as common interests and community interests is hardly novel,[18] yet labelling them as a common concern calls for a new approach to the allocation of the states' rights and duties that is discussed in the next section.

[14] Shinya Murase, 'Second Report on the Protection of Atmosphere – 67th Session of the International Law Commission' (2015) A/CN4/681, para 34.

[15] Ahmad (n 2).

[16] ibid 76–89.

[17] Bogdanova (n 2) ch 5.

[18] Wolfgang Benedek, 'Humanization of International Law, Human Rights and the Common Interest' in Wolfgang Benedek (ed), *The Common Interest in International Law* (Intersentia, 2014); Samantha Besson, 'Community Interests in International Law: Whose Interests Are They and How Should We Best Identify Them?' in Eyal Benvenisti and Georg Nolte (ed), *Community Interests Across International Law* (Oxford University Press, 2018).

B. Normative Consequences Flowing from the CCH

Focusing on the inherent normative import of the term 'concern',[19] it was stated that the very normative dimension of designating a common concern translates into a call for a joint action,[20] which was proposed to be carried out by designating specific state obligations along three dimensions. These courses of action comprise international cooperation between states as well as inward and outward directed domestic actions undertaken within each involved state's jurisdictional boundary. While some of the suggested actions (eg cooperation) have limited independent existence in international law, the innovation of the doctrine lies in linking them as a normative consequence flowing from the CCH – something that is in its early stage of emergence in state practice.[21]

(i) Cooperation

Although international legal instruments are yet to formally endorse that a duty to cooperate emerges out of a recognised common concern, scholars broadly agree about such a normative linkage.[22] This is important because, at present, obligations to cooperate are not commonplace in international law.[23] They only exist in specific issue areas subject to prior state consent or as customary principles.[24] Combined with the principles of sovereign equality and independence, the status quo is that cooperation cannot be claimed as a right against other states to resolve all existing and emerging common concerns.[25] Due to the indispensability of cooperation in resolving common concerns of humankind, Cottier also holds that international recognition of a problem as a CCH is, *ipso facto*, an endorsement of the need for cooperation. The duty to cooperate can already be found in various legal regimes addressing common interests,[26] including the ones on

[19] Cottier, 'The Principle of Common Concern of Humankind' (n 3) 37–38.

[20] ibid.

[21] See section II.C below.

[22] See, among others, Mostafa K Tolba, 'The Implications of the "Common Concern of Mankind" Concept on Global Environmental Issues' (1991) 13 *Revista IIDH* 237, paras 16–17; Murase (n 14) para 37; Antônio Augusto and Cançado Trindade, *International Law for Humankind* (Brill Nijhoff, 2013) 347 https://brill.com/display/book/9789004255074/B9789004255074-s015.xml.

[23] Rüdiger Wolfrum, 'Cooperation, International Law Of' in *Max Planck Encyclopedia of Public International Law* (2010) para 39, https://opil-1ouplaw-1com-1p67dv9pt0089.han.sub.uni-goettingen.de/display/10.1093/law:epil/9780199231690/law-9780199231690-e1427?prd=MPIL; Jost Delbrück, 'Coexistence, Cooperation and Solidarity in International Law: The International Obligation to Cooperate – An Empty Shell or a Hard Law Principle of International Law? – A Critical Look at a Much Debated Paradigm of Modern International Law' in Holger P Hestermeyer et al (eds), *Coexistence, Cooperation and Solidarity: Liber Amicorum Rüdiger Wolfrum* (Brill Nijhoff, 2012) vol 1, 13–15.

[24] Cottier, 'The Principle of Common Concern of Humankind' (n 3) 59–60.

[25] ibid; Rüdiger Wolfrum, *Solidarity and Community Interests: Driving Forces for the Interpretation and Development of International Law*, Recueil Des Cours: Collected Courses of the Hague Academy of International Law, vol 416 (Brill Nijhoff, 2021) 182–85.

[26] ibid 188–208.

common concerns. However, what remains problematic is that this obligation is understood in a process-oriented fashion and not in a results-oriented manner. To resolve this, Cottier proposes that the obligation to cooperate should be carried out transparently, in good faith, through consultations for the establishment of appropriate institutional and support mechanisms for effective resolution of the common concern.[27] Such efforts should also influence the adjacent legal regimes (eg climate and trade, or human rights and trade). Cooperation should comprise not only rulemaking and determination of tasks, but should also extend to timely implementation of the same.[28]

With regard to addressing the common concern of low-carbon technology diffusion, it was proposed that cooperation should focus on strengthening existing mechanisms under the Paris Agreement with a view to creating enabling environments for technology transfers. Such efforts should also incorporate supporting activities in the adjacent regimes, such as WTO law, where the notion is not formally recognised at present.[29] Ultimately, international cooperation to facilitate the diffusion of low-carbon technologies should recognise the importance of the issue, put in place both demand and supply side incentives and requirements, and operationalise technology transfer mechanisms that are already in place.

In the human rights domain, the duty to cooperate entails rights and duties imposed on both the state where grave and systematic human rights violations occur and other states. To elucidate this point, it should be recalled that grave human rights violations are engendered either by a lack of resources necessary for effective human rights protection or by a state's intentional action to deprive its citizens of human rights guarantees.[30] In the former case, the state in need of assistance should act in a transparent and cooperative manner in providing accurate information and requesting assistance from other states, while other states acting in good faith should cooperate in resolving the crisis.[31] The historical record bears witness to instances of international cooperation of this sort: for example, in situations of natural disasters, states cooperate to provide humanitarian aid. The duty to cooperate, as a normative implication of the CCH, has the potential to reinforce existing practice by giving it the sense of a legal obligation. In case of a state's intentional action aimed at depriving its citizens of the human rights guaranteed under international law, the duty to cooperate elevated by the CCH to the level of an international obligation would require such a state to provide information and cooperate with other states willing to investigate the ongoing human rights crisis.

[27] Cottier, 'The Principle of Common Concern of Humankind' (n 3) 60–61.

[28] ibid 62.

[29] Thomas Cottier, 'The Principle of Common Concern of Humankind and the WTO' in *Elgar Encyclopedia of Environmental Law* (Edward Elgar Publishing, 2023) 146; Ahmad (n 2) 140–44.

[30] Emilie M Hafner-Burton, 'A Social Science of Human Rights' (2014) 51 *Journal of Peace Research* 273; Daniel Bodansky, 'What's in a Concept? Global Public Goods, International Law, and Legitimacy' (2012) 23 *European Journal of International Law* 651.

[31] Bogdanova (n 2) 300.

Non-compliance with this obligation to cooperate legitimises unilateral recourse to coercive measures.

(ii) Homework

The homework dimension of the proposed normative consequences of CCH connects the principle to making real-life impacts on people and communities affected by the shared problem. Expanding the current understanding of the scope of the CCH, Cottier advances homework as an obligation of a state to take adequate steps within its jurisdiction to address the common challenge, within the limits of available resources and capability, and in keeping with the principles of equity and distributional fairness.[32] In addition to implementing international obligations, homework measures are envisaged by Cottier to also cover autonomous measures, which may have an indirect extraterritorial effect beyond the border.[33] Given the utility of international trade policy measures to offer effective economic benefits or alternatively impose costs on partners ('carrot and stick' approach), trade policy measures feature as a prominent toolset of choice to further the shared objectives of common concern.[34] The practice of recourse to trade policy in pursuance of other objectives is not new. States in a position to do so have always used their economic might to leverage the achievement of unilateral policy objectives. The CCH doctrine is poised to further structure such recourses, approving those that advance common interests while rejecting protectionist ones.

Homework in the climate domain involves appropriate mitigation and adaptation policies in line with the long-term Paris Agreement goals. With particular regard to low-carbon technology diffusion, it is important for both developed and developing countries to adopt domestic measures that incentivise and encourage the transfer of technology in a complementary fashion.[35] Having effective forums for cooperation on low-carbon technology transfer facilitates that process. Furthermore, low-carbon technology transfer must be coupled with unilateral climate-motivated economic policy measures (eg border adjustment of carbon footprints) to alleviate any unreasonable costs on low and middle-income countries abroad.[36]

International human rights law is a non-reciprocal legal regime characterised by the absence of forces inducing compliance. According to Oona Hathaway, it is 'an area of international law in which countries have little incentive to police non-compliance with treaties or norms'.[37] This, combined with the weak enforcement

[32] Cottier, 'The Principle of Common Concern of Humankind' (n 3) 63.
[33] ibid 64–65.
[34] ibid 65–68.
[35] Ahmad (n 2) 129–31, 146–47.
[36] ibid 4.
[37] Oona A Hathaway, 'Do Human Rights Treaties Make a Difference?' (2002) 111 *Yale Law Journal* 1935.

mechanisms, is emblematic of the domain of human rights.[38] It is against this background that states often ratify human rights treaties without a strong desire or incentive to implement them domestically.[39] Building upon the cornerstone principle of international law – *pacta sunt servanda* – the CCH-derived homework responsibility can enhance the obligation on the part of states to prevent, avoid and remedy systemic violations of human rights as a matter of international law.

(iii) Securing Compliance Unilaterally

The final normative proposition of the doctrine involves the securing of compliance. Once again, stemming from the fact that inadequate compliance and free-riding tend to become the norm rather than the exception when it comes to other-regarding shared issues like climate change, it is proposed that recognition of a CCH logically would require all states to adopt appropriate countermeasures to preclude free-riding and non-compliance.[40] Cottier finds existing rights to act available to states under international law as insufficient, because states' willingness to exert such a right on common interest is dictated by politico-economic calculations, as well as by the ability to act.[41] Hence, it is foreseen that the principle of CCH should further facilitate the legal foundations of a responsibility to act, through the use of other-regarding extraterritorial measures, in pursuance of the concern.[42] Furthermore, it should also be noted that the obligation to act through countermeasures (including sanctions) is further structured by the doctrine. Recourse to such a measure would only be taken when necessary, and executed with prior information, proportionately and in a transparent manner.[43] Measures taken should also be subject to judicial review.[44]

The use of unilateral economic coercion to improve the performance of climate actions in general or low-carbon technology transfers in particular is problematic. Practically, sanctioning states unwilling to transfer low-carbon technologies to developing countries is difficult to implement, as large economies capable of imposing such sanctions are themselves the biggest source of low-carbon technologies. Alternatively, it is possible to think about sanctioning

[38] Bogdanova (n 2) ch 3.

[39] For motivations behind ratification of human rights treaties, see Oona A Hathaway, 'Why Do Countries Commit to Human Rights Treaties?' (2007) 51 *Journal of Conflict Resolution* 588; for empirical studies analysing the effect of human rights treaties on protection of human rights, see Bogdanova (n 2) 197–200.

[40] Cottier, 'The Principle of Common Concern of Humankind' (n 3) 69–70.

[41] ibid 72–73.

[42] ibid 75–76.

[43] ibid 76–77.

[44] ibid 77.

economies that are wilfully and unreasonably slow in adopting low-carbon technologies. Such an approach may even become feasible in regimes such as the WTO law, where states are allowed to adopt measures they consider necessary in the backdrop of an 'emergency in international relations'.[45] The challenge is that the existing law grants nearly unrestricted policy freedom in this regard, without any requirement for the sanctions to be proportional, or to respect the principle of common but differentiated responsibility.[46] The likely relevance of the doctrine of CCH in this regard will be to add further structure and limitations to the exercise of security-motivated trade sanctions in the climate context.[47]

The relatively widespread acknowledgement of the need to enhance human rights protection has not led to changes in the interpretation and application of the secondary rules of international law, such as rules on state responsibility. In other words, the dichotomy between an inspirational attitude towards human rights protection and the right to resort to third-party countermeasures persists.[48] Hence, individual states willing to respond to situations of grave human rights violations, for example by imposing unilateral economic sanctions, might find it difficult to justify these actions as permissible countermeasures.[49] To a significant extent, the same conclusion applies to the *lex specialis* regime established by WTO Agreements that explicitly carve out the applicability of the general rules on state responsibility and do not explicitly endorse the protection of human rights as an exception. The proposed CCH framework suggests that in situations of grave and systematic human rights violations that meet the threshold of being recognised as a common concern, individual states might act unilaterally if the state on whose territory these violations occur neither engages in international cooperation nor resolves the situation.[50] Seen this way, CCH puts forward a *de lege ferenda* proposition on how to distinguish between legal and illegal recourse to unilateral measures in response to human rights violations occurring abroad.

[45] See, among others, Art XXI(b)(iii) of the General Agreement on Tariffs and Trade 1994 (Marrakesh Agreement Establishing the World Trade Organization, Annex 1A, 1869 UNTS 299; 33 ILM 1197 (1994)); Ahmad (n 2) 265–67.

[46] Ahmad (n 2) 250–55.

[47] ibid 271–73.

[48] While the Draft Articles on Responsibility of States for Internationally Wrongful Acts do not explicitly endorse the right of non-injured states to rely upon countermeasures, the legality of third-party countermeasures (countermeasures in general interest) remains debatable. Martin Dawidowicz, *Third-Party Countermeasures in International Law* (Cambridge University Press, 2017); Martin Dawidowicz, 'Third-Party Countermeasures: A Progressive Development of International Law?' (2016) *Questions of International Law*; Martin Dawidowicz, 'Public Law Enforcement without Public Law Safeguards? An Analysis of State Practice on Third-Party Countermeasures and Their Relationship to the UN Security Council' (2007) 77 *British Yearbook of International Law* 333.

[49] Bogdanova (n 2) ch 4.

[50] ibid 302–05.

C. Subsequent Progress of the CCH

The CCH continues to thrive in the international arena as an emerging legal principle. Its evolution up till 2020 is well documented in the work of Professor Cottier.[51] It is somewhat counterintuitive that, since then, notwithstanding the crisis of the rules-based international order, states have continued to call upon the notion in established regimes like climate change. Decisions adopted by the Conference of the Parties serving as the meeting of the Parties to the Paris Agreement (CMA) have repeatedly referred to the CCH in the preamble of the Agreement and its connection to human rights guarantees. Work at the CMA has also transformed CCH into strict reporting obligations for state parties regarding, inter alia, market-based mitigation cooperation.[52] The notion has continued to be re-endorsed elsewhere too. In the legal regime on biodiversity conservation, the 2022 Kunming–Montreal Biodiversity Framework reiterated that 'reversing the loss of biological diversity, for the benefit of all living beings, is a common concern of humankind' and invited its implementation to be guided by the Rio Principles.[53]

The return of the CCH into the ILC guidelines for the protection of the global atmosphere,[54] where previous wide criticism led to the term 'pressing concern' being used,[55] is a strong testimony to the broad acceptance of CCH as a legal expression by the states and a shared interest in its continued use and growth. It

[51] Cottier, 'The Principle of Common Concern of Humankind' (n 3) 11–24.

[52] For example, the initial reporting obligation under Art 6, para 2 of the Paris Agreement requires a party to describe how each cooperative approach will reflect the 11th preambular paragraph of the Agreement, which recognises climate change as a common concern of humankind and requires parties to promote and consider human rights obligations. See para 18(h)(iii)(ii) of the Annex in UNFCCC, 'Guidance on Cooperative Approaches Referred to in Article 6, Paragraph 2, of the Paris Agreement: Annex' (UNFCCC 2021) FCCC/PA/CMA/2021/L.18 https://unfccc.int/sites/default/files/resource/cma2021_L18Epdf. Similar reporting obligation also exist under Art 6, para 4 of the Paris Agreement.

[53] UNEP, 'Decision 15/4: Kunming-Montreal Global Biodiversity Framework (GBF)', *Report of the Conference of the Parties to the Convention on Biological Diversity on the Second Part of Its Fifteenth Meeting, CBD/COP/15/17* (2023) Annex, para 7(k), www.cbd.int/doc/c/f98d/390c/d25842dd39bd8dc3d7d2ae14/cop-15-17-en.pdf.

[54] International Law Commission, 'Draft Guidelines on the Protection of the Atmosphere 2021', *Report of the International Law Commission: Seventy-Second Session, A/76/10* (United Nations 2021) paras 39ff, https://legal.un.org/ilc/reports/2021/english/a_76_10_advance.pdf. The preamble to the guidelines hold that 'atmospheric pollution and atmospheric degradation are a common concern of humankind'.

[55] Initially, Special Rapporteur Murase's proposal to incorporate common concern as a substantive guideline was criticised and rejected by the ILC members. See Cottier, 'The Principle of Common Concern of Humankind' (n 3) 21–23. As a result, the 'draft guideline 3 on the common concern of humankind [was] moved to the preambular section of the draft guidelines. The Drafting Committee recommended that the expression "common concern of humankind" should be changed to "pressing concern of the international community as a whole", and it was included in the preamble in that form.' Shinya Murase, 'Third Report on the Protection of Atmosphere – 68th Session of the International Law Commission' (2016) A/CN4/692, para 3. At the time, most ILC delegates (including China, Finland [on behalf of Nordic countries], France, Israel, Japan, Republic of Korea, Singapore, Spain, Sri Lanka) supported the change. Only a handful (Federated States of Micronesia, Germany, Portugal) preferred the original expression ibid 5, nn 8–9.

is also true that there are no comparable legal expressions available to the international community that can serve the purpose of highlighting the pressing need to work together on a specific challenge. Moreover, the use of different languages only deprives clarity in understanding states' roles regarding a common interest problem. Most importantly, after the return of CCH in the Paris Agreement, states' views on the relevance and utility of the notion changed overwhelmingly.[56] In the context of the Commission's mandate regarding the 'progressive codification of international law', the inclusion of CCH in a new area of shared interest not only cements its status as an emerging principle of global law, but also attaches great importance to the work of specifying its normative scope.[57] This is also where Professor Thomas Cottier's contribution lies.

During the negotiation phase of the recent Biodiversity Beyond National Jurisdiction (BBNJ)[58] Agreement, efforts were made, inter alia, by the International Union for Conservation of Nature (IUCN) to have CCH included as a general principle therein.[59] This evidences the growing interest among state and non-state stakeholders to adopt CCH as a legal principle. However, those efforts were not successful on this occasion. Given the close relationship between the BBNJ Agreement and the Law of the Sea Convention, as well as the recognition of the deep seabed area as a common heritage of mankind in the latter instrument,[60] the parties chose to side with the common heritage approach in the former.[61] Scholars have already pointed this out as a missed opportunity.[62]

Back in the climate change legal domain, CCH has also started to seep into formal legal claims and reasonings. In *Verein Klimaseniorinnen*,[63] the European Court of Human Rights has picked up on the repeated legal recognition of climate

[56] Germany, the Netherlands, Portugal, Finland, Japan and Antigua & Barbuda proposed the re-inclusion of the expression. UNGA, 'Protection of the Atmosphere: Comments and Observations Received from Governments and International Organizations' (International Law Commission, 72nd Session 2020) A/CN4/735.

[57] On behalf of the Nordic countries, Finland noted that 'Insofar as the omission of a reference to the protection of the atmosphere as "a common concern of humankind" was related to a lack of clarity as to the precise legal implications of the concept, the Nordic countries would consider the draft commentaries a worthy opportunity for the Commission to contribute to its clarification.' ibid 14–15.

[58] Agreement under the United Nations Convention on the Law of the Sea on the Conservation and Sustainable Use of Marine Biological Diversity of Areas Beyond National Jurisdiction (BBNJ Agreement) 2023.

[59] The IUCN argued that protection of biodiversity is already recognised as a common concern in IUCN, 'IUCN Briefing for BBNJ Negotiators: Principles and Approaches, Part I, Article V' www.iucn.org/sites/default/files/2022-07/iucn-briefing-principles-final.pdf IUCN.

[60] United Nations Convention on the Law of Sea 1982 (1833 UNTS 397) Art 136. It holds that 'The Area and its resources are the common heritage of mankind'.

[61] BBNJ Agreement, Art 7(b).

[62] Jingchang Li and Wangwang Xing, 'A Critical Appraisal of the BBNJ Agreement Not to Recognise the High Seas Decline as a Common Concern of Humankind' (2024) 163 *Marine Policy* 106131; Sarah Lothian, 'Forget Me Not: Revisiting the Common Concern of Humankind Concept in the BBNJ Context' (2021) 38 *Environment and Planning Law Journal* 189.

[63] *Verein Klimaseniorinnen Schweiz and Others v Switzerland* [2024] European Court of Human Rights Application No 53600/20.

change as a 'common concern of humankind' and its connection with intergenerational equity.[64] Drawing upon it, the court was able to strengthen the linkage between human rights and climate change,[65] and to enhance the legal standing of associations to strengthen the rights of future generations before the court.[66] The CCH is also expected to make an impact in the legal reasonings of the upcoming climate change advisory opinions from key international courts and tribunals. For example, in its written statement submitted to the International Court of Justice in relation to the advisory opinion on climate obligations of states, Switzerland relied on CCH to provide a wider meaning to the state's obligation to prevent harm, as well as to urge concerted action by all states.[67]

In the human rights field, CCH has not yet been explicitly endorsed. That said, recent developments point to the potential gap-filling function that the CCH doctrine can serve. In particular, the idea of utilising the CCH as an instrument legitimising the use of unilateral economic sanctions in situations of grave and persistent human rights violations has gained some interest and traction.[68] This should not come as a surprise: the recent scholarly debate increasingly discusses the interrelations between unilateral economic sanctions and the human rights obligations of states that impose such measures.[69] In this ongoing discussion, economic sanctions are instrumentalised either as an instrument to promote human rights and their enforcement, or as policies that violate human rights obligations of the states imposing them.[70] In a way, this discussion is part of a perennial overarching debate on the per se legality or illegality of unilateral economic sanctions. The latter, as well as the former, debates suffer from the same deficiency – there are hardly any deliberations on the rules or principles that might legitimise the use of unilateral economic sanctions. In this context, the CCH and its normative implications that apply as a logical sequence of steps provide a much-needed guidance on the permissible use of unilateral economic sanctions.

[64] ibid 104, 133ff.

[65] ibid 451.

[66] ibid 489 and 499.

[67] Swiss Confederation, 'Obligations of States in Respect of Climate Change: Written Statement by the Swiss Confederation' (18 March 2024) paras 20, 81. Copy held by the authors.

[68] Two reviews of the book *Unilateral Sanctions in International Law and the Enforcement of Human Rights: The Impact of the Principle of Common Concern of Humankind* by I Bogdanova paid particular attention to the part of the book wherein the role of CCH framework in legitimising unilateral economic sanctions is discussed. Alexandra Hofer, 'Iryna Bogdanova: Unilateral Sanctions in International Law and the Enforcement of Human Rights: The Impact of the Principle of Common Concern of Humankind' (2023) 83(3) *Zeitschrift für ausländisches öffentliches Recht und Völkerrecht* 545; Christina Seewald, 'Iryna Bogdanova (ed): Unilateral Sanctions in International Law and the Enforcement of Human Rights: The Impact of the Principle of Common Concern of Humankind' in P Czech et al (ed), *European Yearbook on Human Rights* (Intersentia, 2023) 685–88.

[69] Jean-Marc Thouvenin, 'International Economic Sanctions and Fundamental Rights: Friend or Foe?' in Norman Weiss and Jean-Marc Thouvenin (eds), *The Influence of Human Rights on International Law* (Springer, 2015); Iryna Bogdanova, 'Human Rights and Unilateral Economic Sanctions: A New Perspective on a Twisted Relationship' in Czech et al (n 68).

[70] Bogdanova, ibid.

III. Common Concern and Sovereignty: A Contested Relationship

A. A Nuanced Portrayal of Sovereignty in the CCH Doctrine

The doctrine of common concern of humankind is premised upon a nuanced understanding of national sovereignty. On the surface, its claim for strict state obligations flowing automatically in specific, objectively determinable circumstances and events (ie common concerns) may seem to go against the fundamental precepts of sovereignty, self-determination and liberty. However, Cottier dispels this misunderstanding with several arguments. First and foremost, he argues that the CCH does not do away with the importance of consent as it does not compel any state to subscribe to it.[71] Furthermore, tracing the emergence of sovereignty as a concept through history, Cottier shows that its roots lie in a state's legally assigned function of ensuring peace, security and welfare of those in its charge.[72] When citizens' welfare is inextricably linked to the availability of specific global public goods, sovereignty must be understood in such cooperative terms that make production of those goods feasible.[73] Modern notions of sovereignty call for a duty-oriented conceptualisation, endorsing states' responsibility to address common concerns as a part of discharging their role as a sovereign.[74] Hence, there are no conflicts between sovereignty, self-determination and addressing common concerns along the above-outlined avenues. This responsibility-oriented, cooperative understanding of sovereignty is also reflected in Cottier's work on another emerging principle, ie the 'responsibility to protect' (R2P).[75]

While sovereignty as a concept at the centre of present-day international law and relations is hardly ever questioned, its precise content and the limits imposed on it by international law remain a contentious issue. Framing sovereignty as a legally circumscribed notion containing core responsibilities, effective discharge of which is essential to the reflexive legitimation of sovereignty itself, is what Koskenniemi termed a 'legal approach'.[76] This approach is the foundation of many solidarist international legal arguments that suggest the use of equitable principles

[71] Cottier, 'The Principle of Common Concern of Humankind' (n 3) 55.

[72] ibid 56–57. Among others, Cottier draws upon the works of Jean Bodin, who proposes welfare as the defining responsibility of a sovereign. As we will see later, Koskenniemi also refers to Bodin as an example of legal approach to sovereignty. See Martti Koskenniemi, *From Apology to Utopia: The Structure of International Legal Argument: Reissue with a New Epilogue* (Cambridge University Press, 2005).

[73] ibid 58.

[74] ibid.

[75] Krista Nakavukaren Schefer and Thomas Cottier, 'Responsibility to Protect (R2P) and the Emerging Principle of Common Concern' in Peter Hilpold (ed), *The Responsibility to Protect (R2P)* (Brill Nijhoff, 2015) https://brill.com/view/book/edcoll/9789004230002/B9789004230002-s005.xml.

[76] Koskenniemi (n 72) 228–29. Among others, Koskenniemi gives examples of Bodin (sovereignty remains condition by the commands of the God and Nature), Kelsen, Hart and Verdross (state sovereignty and subjection to international law is one and the same thing), and equates the approach with the notion of 'international community'. ibid 229 and fns 15–17.

to balance conflicts of interests among competing sovereigns.[77] To prevent sovereignty from turning into a blank cheque of policy-making ('apologism', per Koskenniemi), the legal approach advocates for the assumption of a normative code, envisaged 'in terms of interdependence, common interests and shared progressive morality or legal logic'.[78] However, as Koskenniemi also points out, the challenge to a legal approach to sovereignty comes from the fact that states have little practical utility of a notion that cannot solely legitimise states' liberty to act and requires further normative validation itself. This leads to the opposing camp's view that law, including international law, must accommodate itself with (ie recognise the superiority of) the fact of sovereignty.[79] This approach fuels views such as the subjugation of international law to a state's will, the primacy of municipal law over international rules, the claim of domestic jurisdiction or that the functions of an international organisation are dependent on the mandate agreed by states.[80] Although Koskenniemi's account is from decades ago, it has a strong resonance with recent world affairs, to which we turn below.

B. Sovereignty Strikes Back

In many ways, recent developments in international affairs present themselves as the antithesis of the expectations placed on international relations by the doctrine of common concern of humankind. What can only be seen as a snowballing of parochialism fuelled by the self-serving actions of the powerful has magnified the distance between local and global interests over the past decade. This has played out along several routes – populism-triggered securitisation of economic rivalry, disregard of the rules-based global order and a concomitant weakening of multilateral institutions (eg the WTO, the UN Security Council). These developments are further exacerbated by what Tom Ginsburg terms as a turn towards an 'authoritarian international law'.[81] One of the distinctive features of this new approach to international law is that authoritarian regimes favour the absolutist notion of sovereignty and emphasise non-intervention/interference in internal affairs.[82]

[77] ibid 230–31.

[78] ibid 231 and fn 20. This aptly describes the founding basis of common concern and the supporting scholarly view. In a similar vein, Malcolm Shaw, in his recent contribution to the Hague Academy courses, underlined that 'the international community, essentially the community of States, has agreed to mitigate the absolute nature of territorial sovereignty to be able to confront and deal with challenges that transcend the boundaries of any one State': Malcolm Shaw, 'A House of Many Rooms: The Rise, Fall and Rise Again of Territorial Sovereignty?' (2021) Inaugural Lecture, Hague Academy of International Law.

[79] Koskenniemi (n 72) 231–32. 'To be a State is … a question of fact which the law can only recognize but cannot control' (232). Koskenniemi further draws upon Schmitt as example (226–27 and 231).

[80] ibid 232–33.

[81] Tom Ginsburg, 'Authoritarian International Law?' (2020) 114 *American Journal of International Law* 221.

[82] Ginsburg argues that authoritarian states are 'returning us to a world of Westphalian international law, primarily as a defensive measure': ibid 228.

What is more, authoritarian states are using existing norms and institutions – 'building on and repurposing some of the norms of the liberal era' – for purposes antithetical to these norms and institutions.[83] This is evident in the field of international human rights law, for the reason that authoritarian regimes are preoccupied with their survival, which could be achieved only through the oppression of any potential opposition domestically and through the lack of transparency.[84] Authoritarian regimes such as the People's Republic of China have been actively engaged in the work of international organisations responsible for monitoring and enforcing human rights globally. There is a growing body of literature on what instruments have been used to contest the perception of human rights as a matter of international concern, focusing on a narrowly defined approach to human rights as a matter of purely domestic concern that is shielded from international scrutiny by the notion of state sovereignty.[85] These changes also affect domestic human rights policies: according to Wayne Sandholtz, as the number of authoritarian regimes and their power grow, the effectiveness of international human rights law at the domestic level declines.[86] Put together, this can be seen as a resurgence of a fact-based outlook of sovereignty, as was described by Koskenniemi, asserting its precedence over the rules-based international order.

In the climate regime, the legal flexibility accorded to sovereigns under the Paris Agreement has led to a collective failure to live up to the Agreement's temperature reduction commitments.[87] Adverse consequences are already perceptible in the early onset of climate hazards and the imminent reaching of irreversible climate tipping points.[88] With regard to climate technology, economic and financial barriers continue to be the main hurdle in effective technology transfers to developing countries.[89] Such a deplorable pattern is reinforced by the trend of disproportionately low amounts of financial resources flowing into climate technology-related activities (eg renewable energy, electrification, green buildings, waste management)

[83] ibid.

[84] ibid.

[85] Yu-Jie Chen, '"Authoritarian International Law" in Action? Tribal Politics in the Human Rights Council' (2021) 54 *Vanderbilt Journal of Transnational Law* 1203.

[86] Wayne Sandholtz, 'Resurgent Authoritarianism, Rights, and Legal Change' in Nico Krisch and Ezgi Yildiz (eds), *The Many Paths of Change in International Law* (Oxford University Press, 2023).

[87] UNEP, *Emissions Gap Report 2023: Broken Record – Temperatures Hit New Highs, yet World Fails to Cut Emissions (Again)* (United Nations Environment Programme, 2023) 6–9, https://wedocs.unep.org/20.500.11822/43922. Just the USA and the EU were responsible for one-third of the global emissions between 1850 and 2021. The G20 countries together were responsible for 75% of emissions during the same period. In contrast, the least developed countries were responsible for only 4% of global emissions during that period (8).

[88] Intergovernmental Panel on Climate Change (IPCC) (ed), *Summary for Policymakers: Climate Change 2022 – Impacts, Adaptation and Vulnerability: Working Group II Contribution to the Sixth Assessment Report of the Intergovernmental Panel on Climate Change* (Cambridge University Press, 2023) 9–11, www.cambridge.org/core/books/climate-change-2022-impacts-adaptation-and-vulnerability/summary-for-policymakers/016527EADEE2178406C4A7CE7DEAEACA.

[89] UNFCCC, 'Fourth Synthesis Report on Technology Needs Identified by Parties Not Included in Annex I to the Convention' (2020) Note by the Secretariat, FCCC/SBI/2020/INF.1, 20–22.

in developing countries.[90] At the same time, domestic policies in the major economies are fuelled by industrial policy motivations, driving the agenda along the avenues of unilateral protectionism.[91] Economic rivalry in climate-related industries, perceived security threats and persistent non-cooperation have put economic multilateralism in an existential mode – so much so that improving existing institutional mechanisms or establishing new ones to enhance the contribution of global economic policy to climate adaptation and mitigation seem like a far cry from reality.

The above-outlined conflict between the expected nature of sovereignty and its actual exercise in practice allows us to draw conclusions along two dimensions. Factually, the benefit-to-cost ratio for engaging in multilateralism is declining for most of its prominent players. Apart from the traditional causes of collective action problems (eg heterogeneity, free riding) and the inability of the multilateral system to keep new powers from emerging and destabilising the balance, the rise of nationalist sentiments among the population that view common interest and cooperation as nothing but a burden explain this decline.[92] The broader, philosophical, conclusion is to see a Hegelian dialectical pattern in conflicting views on sovereignty. Like previous historical cycles, such as the 'end of history' era,[93] what we are presented with is essentially an interaction between a *thesis* (ie the CCH) and an *antithesis* (ie the pushback from sovereigns) in progress. What remains to be seen is whether the *synthesis* will bring us towards a shared global order. We turn to this question next.

[90] IPCC (ed), *Innovation, Technology Development and Transfer: Climate Change 2022 – Mitigation of Climate Change: Working Group III Contribution to the Sixth Assessment Report of the Intergovernmental Panel on Climate Change* (Cambridge University Press, 2023) 1684–85. In the urban context of the Asia-Pacific, see Peter Storey and Peter DuPont, *Climate Finance for Urban Technologies: Climate Technology Progress Report 2023: Speed and Scale of Urban Systems Transformation* (2023) 55–56.

[91] fDi Intelligence, 'Industrial Policies Are Mostly Motivated by Protectionism, Not Geopolitics' (17 January 2024) www.fdiintelligence.com/content/news/industrial-policies-are-mostly-motivated-by-protectionism-not-geopolitics-83358; Global Trade Alert, 'The Green Goods Trade War Is in Full Swing' (Globel Trade Alert; St Gallen Endowment, 2024) 9, www.globaltradealert.org/reports/131; Reda Cherif and Fuad Hasanov, 'The Pitfalls of Protectionism: Import Substitution v Export-Oriented Industrial Policy' (IMF, 2024) Working Paper 2024/086, www.imf.org/en/Publications/WP/Issues/2024/04/26/The-Pitfalls-of-Protectionism-Import-Substitution-v-546349; Kimberly Clausing and Catherine Wolfram, 'Putting Progress over Protectionism in Climate Policy' (PIIE, 19 December 2023) www.piie.com/blogs/realtime-economics/putting-progress-over-protectionism-climate-policy; Timothy Meyer, 'Copernican Revolution or Green Protectionism?' in Geraldo Vidigal and Kathleen Claussen (eds), *The Sustainability Revolution in International Trade Agreements* (Oxford University Press, 2024).

[92] Christine Schwöbel-Patel, 'Multilateralism' in Jean d'Aspremont and John Haskell (eds), *Tipping Points in International Law: Commitment and Critique* (Cambridge University Press, 2021).

[93] Francis Fukuyama, 'The End of History?' [1989] *The National Interest* 3; Roger Kimball, 'Francis Fukuyama and the End of History' [1992] *The New Criterion*, https://newcriterion.com/article/francis-fukuyama-and-the-end-of-history/.

IV. Contestation, International Order and Common Concern

Contestation remains an essential part of the evolution of a norm into a legal rule. For the purpose of this contribution, we apply the notion of a norm as an emerging pattern of state practice[94] whose scope as an applicable legal rule is not yet certain. Contestation tells the story of a legal rule's origin. However, once a norm is adorned with the legal form, its validity from a legal perspective depends on evidence consistency rather than contestability. This is why, compared to international relations studies, legal scholarship is less concerned with the understanding of contestations. Scholars of the former discipline are more accustomed to making structured analyses of the process of contestation in the context of norm life cycles.

Outlining a theory of contestation, Antje Wiener views the phenomenon as a 'meta-organising principle of global governance' and a necessary phenomenon for fundamental global norms to remain legitimate.[95] Contentions take place in four typical contexts: (i) regimes; (ii) international organisations; (iii) protest movements; and (iv) epistemic communities.[96] In each context, one of four modes – arbitration, deliberation, contention and justification – assumes a dominating role.[97] Wiener finds that norms operate in a tiered fashion. Sitting at the meta-level are fundamental type 1 norms (eg sustainability), which are of high moral importance but are less specific in content. Agreed at the highest level of governance, the type 1 norms require further flanking measures and support from adjacent norms to be implemented.[98] This is supplied by the organisational principles, or type 2 norms (such as common but differentiated responsibility), which are established through political practice at the interstate level (meso-level).[99] Lastly, type 3 norms are highly specific, with little or no room for negotiation. These are directives and regulatory measures that apply at the lowest (micro-)levels.[100] The degree of contestation increases as the norms go higher up the levels. Outlining a cyclical structure in the process of contestations validating norms, Wiener shows how such norms are not only validated formally, through negotiated settlements among high-level participants, but also socially recognised by groups and culturally validated by individuals.[101]

[94] Martha Finnemore and Kathryn Sikkink, 'International Norm Dynamics and Political Change' (1998) 52 *International Organization* 887, 891–93.

[95] Antje Wiener, 'A Theory of Contestation – A Concise Summary of Its Argument and Concepts' (2017) 49 *Polity* 109, 114.

[96] ibid 113.

[97] ibid.

[98] ibid 119.

[99] ibid.

[100] ibid.

[101] ibid 117, 121.

Using this framework, the doctrine of CCH can be seen as an evolving organising principle (type 2) that informs several overarching fundamental norms (type 1), ie peace and security, sovereignty, as well as sustainability, demanding specific balances and interrelations among the latter. Furthermore, normative consequences of common concern – obligations of cooperation, homework and engaging unilateral measures – call for further implementation through substantive regulation at the meso- and micro-levels (types 2 and 3). The framework is useful in elucidating the particularly challenging nature of the forward progress of the CCH doctrine, as it shows that CCH seeks to influence the issues where shared global interests falling under the aforementioned fundamental norms overlap. As it proposes to limit the application of sovereign freedom to the interests of global peace, security and sustainability, formal contentions arise through deliberative processes in international regimes, adjudicative processes and epistemic communities. The framework also reveals the existing disconnect between the CCH and social movements in daily life, addressing which can serve as important reinforcement, especially to prompt the nation-state sovereigns in the right direction. Lastly, the framework outlines the dialectical progress of CCH towards validation. While the withdrawal from multilateralism and the rise in unilateral redress are a portrayal of the reaction the doctrine currently faces in multilateral regimes such as the WTO, rising legal and judicial recognition of the principle,[102] as well as growing epistemic support, strengthened by the devoted and relentless works by experts such as Professor Cottier, counters those forces. The outcome of this process will potentially be determined by the manner in which such contestations find validation in social and cultural terms. This, in turn, indicates the importance of highlighting as well as strengthening the homework and unilateral dimensions of the doctrine.

Therefore, the overarching conclusion is that in the ongoing journey of the CCH to come full circle by gaining broader acceptance and legal normativity, contestation does not lead to its demise. In the same vein, Sandholtz rightly argues that a rejection of a legal norm does not per se lead to its death or dismissal.[103] In the ongoing attempts to deny the shared interest norms, Sandholtz does not see anything novel, holding that 'if current challenges to international norms represent in part a reassertion of sovereignty, they portend not the emergence of new values but a re-emphasis on values that have been central to international law all along'.[104] Seeing the process of contestation as a 'dynamic marketplace of rules', where actors make bids and counter-bids,[105] the view expressed by Sandholtz also corresponds with those of Wiener and Cottier. This is particularly aligned to the

[102] See section II.C above.

[103] Wayne Sandholtz, 'Is Winter Coming? Norm Challenges and Norm Resilience' in Heike Krieger and Andrea Liese (eds), *Tracing Value Change in the International Legal Order: Perspectives from Legal and Political Science* (Oxford University Press, 2023) 51–52.

[104] ibid 50.

[105] ibid 55.

system of claims and responses elaborated by Cottier, which draws attention to the process of inducting a new principle into the body of international rules. The marketplace metaphor aptly portrays the ebb and flow of a dynamic and ever-continuing process.

V. Outlook: The Continued Relevance of CCH

Looking forward, the doctrine of CCH remains particularly relevant in present times, as it spearheads the fight to curb the resurgence of an international order shaped by an agglomeration of authoritarian and populist sovereigns. It remains capable of filling the shortcomings of the existing body of rules addressing shared challenges and delivering meaningful solutions, the lack of which gave rise to some of the dissatisfaction with the current system to start with. In that process, the ongoing contestations provide learning opportunities to revise our expectations, set new targets and contribute further to the resilience of CCH as an emerging legal principle. In this connection, it is noteworthy that Sandholtz proposes institutionalisation as a strategy to improve norm resilience.[106] At the international level, institutionalisation is pursued by embedding a particular norm in a broader framework. At the domestic level, wider incorporation of the norm helps. Institutionalisation also opens the opportunity for the norm to be socially and culturally validated.

In the climate change regime, the process of further institutionalisation of CCH as a grounding principle is well underway. Looking forward, a few important tasks remain to be undertaken in this legal setting. First, CCH should continue to be incorporated in the domestic and international legal processes as a key hook connecting enhanced, adequate and timely climate response measures to state obligations. Second, as unilateral economic measures taken in the service of climate goals will continue to grow in the foreseeable future, it is important to ensure that CCH is not picked up as an excuse to engage in disguised protectionism. Emphasis on prior cooperation, the exercise of good faith and states' abidance by the principles of proportionality, equity and differentiated responsibilities, as suggested by the doctrine, will be key. Lastly, continued epistemic engagement with the doctrine, especially claiming for its integration into climate policy measures at the domestic level and climate-adjacent legal regimes at the international level (eg the WTO), will remain crucial to opening up the avenues for social and cultural validity of the norm.

The institutionalisation of the CCH in the field of international human rights has not gained the same traction as have developments in the climate change regime. This unfortunate outcome happens at a time when human rights and their

[106] ibid 58–60.

effective protection through enforcement of state obligations have fallen victim to other major developments in international law. Two examples mentioned before in this chapter illustrate this: first, attempts to narrow down the nature of human rights to the benefit of an absolutist notion of sovereignty; and second, attempts to de-legitimise the use of unilateral economic sanctions, including the ones imposed against repressive regimes, on grounds of their alleged incompatibility with human rights.

The CCH doctrine, by embedding an idea of common interest and community norms into formal legal frameworks with respective rights and duties, can be seen as a legal instrument aiming at the de-politicisation of human rights. Furthermore, the idea of entangling human rights protection and international economic law might be of relevance in light of recent developments. If the views of Professor Tom Ginsburg on the nature of international law dominated by authoritarian states hold true, we would observe a growing relevance of international economic law and a significant decline in human rights law and its enforcement.[107] If this assumption stands, then it is high time to entangle the protection of human rights with international economic law, including through the encouragement of international cooperation, domestic actions and unilateral responses as the measures of last resort, as is proposed by the CCH.

Instead of a final word, we leave the reader with this prescient quote from Professor Cottier:

> While recognised in environmental law, [CCH] has a long way to go in other areas … A fully fledged principle of CCH may eventually emerge in customary law as an amalgamation of all these efforts. Courts of law may shape it one way or the other. It may evolve as a legal principle of multilevel governance equally applying within regional integration and federal and subfederal levels in addressing shared pressing problems. The general principle, once recognised, will then apply by default. But even before that state is reached, the blueprint of CCH inspires and gives directions, showing the way forward. It expounds what at the end of the day should be achieved in order to redress fundamental deficiencies in addressing collective action problems and the lack of reciprocal interests of states in areas of vital importance to humanity and future generations.[108]

[107] Ginsburg (n 81).
[108] Cottier, 'The Principle of Common Concern of Humankind' (n 3) 83.

15

The Twenty-First Century 'Land Investment' or 'Land Grabs' in Africa as a Common Concern of Humankind

MALEBAKENG AGNES FORERE

I. Introduction

This chapter aims to show that land grabs, a term used to refer to large-scale transnational commercial dealings with the land[1] in Africa and other parts of the world, are a common concern of humankind (CCH), requiring international solutions. This is so because land grabs have the ultimate consequence of aggravating poverty, thereby defeating goals one and seven of the United Nations' Sustainable Development Goals (SDGs) and the antecedent forced migration out of Africa for survival.

The concept of CCH has been around for a few decades; however, its definition and constituent characteristics have been fluid despite it being enshrined in international treaties.[2] Such fluidity might be caused by the fact that the concept seems to be mentioned only in the preamble of the UN treaties where it is mentioned, leaving it as an underlying motivation and not a rule. Nevertheless, CCH has conceptually been used to address global problems, particularly those affecting shared resources such as the environment. Addressing issues that go beyond the jurisdictional borders of states requires concerted efforts from all states, hence the birth of the concept of CCH.[3] This concept is also used to address issues falling within national jurisdictions, such as biodiversity, but which other states have an

[1] Saturnino M Borras Jr et al, 'Towards a Better Understanding of Global Land Grabbing: An Editorial Introduction' (2011) 38 *Journal of Peasant Studies* 209, 209.

[2] Frank Biermann, '"Common Concern of Humankind": The Emergence of a New Concept of International Environmental Law' (1996) 34 *Archiv des Völkerrechts* 426; Edith Brown Weiss, 'The Coming Water Crisis: A Common Concern of Humankind' (2012) 1 *Transnational Environmental Law* 153, 164.

[3] Chelsea Bowling, Elizabeth Pierson and Stephanie Ratté, 'The Common Concern of Humankind: A Potential Framework for a New International Legally Binding Instrument on the Conservation and Sustainable Use of Marine Biological Diversity in the High Seas' (United Nations, date unknown) 3.

interest in or are experiencing similar problems with within their own borders.[4] The latter aspect is what distinguishes it from the common heritage of mankind.

The concept of CCH can be traced back to humanitarian and human rights treaties from as far back as 1946, although the exact term may not have been used.[5] The exact terminology was first used in 1988, when the UN General Assembly adopted Resolution 43/53 on the Protection of Global Climate for Present and Future Generations of Mankind, where it recognised climate change as a CCH.[6] In 1992, two multilateral treaties referred to the CCH as follows: the United Nations Framework Convention on Climate Change states that 'change in the Earth's climate and its adverse effects are a common concern of humankind',[7] and the Convention on Biological Diversity sees states affirm that 'the conservation of biological diversity is a common concern of humankind'.[8] Adopted in 2001, the International Treaty on Plant Genetic Resources for Food and Agriculture states that 'plant genetic resources for food and agriculture are a common concern of all countries, in that all countries depend very largely on plant genetic resources for food and agriculture that originated elsewhere'.[9] Similarly, the UNESCO Convention on Safeguarding Intangible Cultural Heritage states that 'safeguarding the intangible cultural heritage of humanity is a common concern'.[10] Most recently, the 2015 Paris Agreement further acknowledged in its preamble that climate change was a CCH.

Outside UN treaties, the concept has been used in Europe, where Article 99 of the European Community Treaty, adopted in the run-up to the creation of the EU and the adoption of the euro, refers to economic policies as a common concern. This is because the alignment of currencies as a prelude to the euro rested on the convergence in interest rates.[11] To this end, interest rate stability and the overall economic policy stances of individual European countries became common concerns for the European Community bloc to achieve its goal of becoming the EU with a single market. This construction shows that the concept of common concern can exist for a specific community or purpose. It need not necessarily be a concern at the global level.

[4] Laura Horn, 'The Implications of the Concept of Common Concern of a Human Kind on a Human Right to a Healthy Environment' (2004) 1 *Macquarie Journal of International and Comparative Environmental Law* 233, 233.

[5] Dinah Shelton, 'Common Concern of Humanity' (2009) 5 *Iustum Aequum Salutare* 33, 83.

[6] Protection of Global Climate for Present and Future Generations of Mankind, GA Res 43/53, UN Doc A/RES/43/53 (6 December 1988) www.un.org/documents/ga/res/43/a43r053.htm.

[7] United Nations Framework Convention on Climate Change, 9 May 1992, 31 ILM, 849, 851.

[8] Convention on Biological Diversity adopted 5 June 1992, 1970 UNTS 79, preamble, para 3.

[9] International Treaty on Plant Genetic Resources for Food and Agriculture, adopted 3 November 2001, 2400 UNTS 303, preamble, para 3.

[10] Convention for the Safeguarding of the Intangible Cultural Heritage, adopted 17 October 2003, 2368 UNTS 3, preamble, para 5.

[11] Zenon Kontolemis, 'Exchange Rates Are a Matter of Common Concern: Policies in the Run-up to the euro?' (September 2003) European Union Economic Paper No 191, 1–9, https://ec.europa.eu/economy_finance/publications/pages/publication852_en.pdf.

Aware of the importance of CCH in tackling global issues but lacking descriptive components, the international community within the United Nations Environmental Programme (UNEP) established a Group of Legal Experts to examine the concept of the 'common concern of mankind' in relation to global environmental issues. The report of the second meeting held in 1991 in Geneva is important for this work as the Group highlighted several principles in unpacking the concept of CCH.[12] The Group recognised that the concept could be applicable to issues outside of environmental ones. Without undermining state sovereignty, the expert group pointed to the need to balance state sovereignty with problems of common concern, further emphasising the need for equitable burden sharing. Scholars have also weighed in to unpack the principle of common concern, and there is general consensus over use of the word 'humankind'.

The word 'humankind' implies intergenerational rights, whereby the needs of the current generation must be met without compromising the needs of future generations, making current generations trustees or custodians of the needs of future generations.[13] Lastly, there is also consensus in scholarly circles that common concern depicts a linkage between human rights and problems of common concern.[14]

In recent years, Thomas Cottier has led other scholars in making compelling submissions on other defining aspects of CCH. This helps fill an important gap that was identified by the Group of Legal Experts regarding the fact that the concept did not create rights and obligations for states.[15] Such scholarly work submits that common concern creates rights and obligations to act and to do so beyond national territorial jurisdictions.[16]

It is these conceptions that will be used in this chapter to argue that land grabs in Africa are a CCH. I argue that this triggers a duty of cooperation among states to solve this problem and to create obligations and the right to act for all relevant actors within a multilevel governance framework in tackling the problem of land grabs.

In documenting how land grabs in Africa are a common concern by causing poverty and resulting in forced migration, this chapter is organised in five parts. Section two defines the phenomenon of land grabs in Africa and its consequences. Section three makes an argument that land grabs are a common concern, while section four provides a synopsis of how parties (local, national, regional and international) can act to prevent land grabs. Section five concludes the discussion.

[12] UNEP Secretariat, 'The Meeting of the Group of Legal Experts to Examine the Concept of the Common Concern of Mankind in Relation to Global Environmental Issues, Geneva, 20–22 March, 1991', https://digitallibrary.un.org/record/766634.

[13] Shelton (n 5); Horn (n 4); Biermann (n 2); Thomas Cottier et al, 'The Principle of Common Concern and Climate Change' (2014) 52 *Archiv des Völkerrechts* 293.

[14] Laura Horn, 'Globalisation, Sustainable Development and the Common Concern of Humankind' (2007) 7 *Macquarie Law Journal* 53, 58.

[15] UNEP Secretariat (n 12) para 4.

[16] Cottier et al (n 13).

II. Nature and Consequences of Land Grabs in Africa

The term 'land grab' refers to large-scale land deals, which include long-term use rights of land, enclosures, land concessions, global land rush and land concentrations.[17] Effectively, land grab has no concrete meaning, despite it being a subject of academic interest.[18] Forced removals and large-scale commercial land transactions fall in the same pot of land grabs. For scholars of foreign investment law, land grabbing presents conceptual challenges similar to non-compensable state conduct that constitutes indirect compensation and a state's legitimate regulatory conduct that does not require compensation.[19] These two have proved difficult to discern in theory and practice, as evidenced by contradictory decisions of arbitral tribunals. Despite the conceptual challenges of land grabs, any reference to land grabs in this chapter is limited to land deals affecting rural communities and land owned by government, also referred to as public land; thus, it does not refer to commercial land deals between enterprising entities, as doing so would render land a non-investible asset in Africa. The recommendations made in this work are therefore made against the backdrop of this limitation to deals that constitute land grabs.

The phenomenon of land grabs is not unique to Africa, but rather is a global problem, as depicted in a 2010 report by the World Bank.[20] Although it is dated, the report indicated that 45 million hectares of land were subject to commercial activity,[21] and the trend of large-scale land deals is continuing, as shown by studies that followed.[22] The issue that makes Africa stand out is that more than half of the land deals were in Africa,[23] a continent that only gained control of its natural resources in the mid-twentieth century, including land from colonialisation. Given that these land deals mainly involve Western countries, Asia and the Gulf,[24] this means that African land is once again under foreign control, achieved through the backdoor of foreign direct investment (FDI) for job creation and economic growth or through voluntary commercial contracts. There is also a rise in new actors (emerging economies) in Asia and South America that are aggressively acquiring land in Africa to guard against the rising risk and incidence of food

[17] Marc Edelman, Carlos Oya and Saturnino M Borras, 'Global Land Grabs: Historical Processes, Theoretical and Methodological Implications and Current Trajectories' (2013) 34 *Third World Quarterly* 1517; Christophe Golay and Irene Biglino, 'Human Rights Responses to Land Grabbing: A Right to Food Perspective' (2013) 34 *Third World Quarterly* 1630, 1631.

[18] Edelman et al (n 17).

[19] Ying Zhu, 'Do Clarified Indirect Expropriation Clauses in International Investment Treaties Preserve Environmental Regulatory Space' (2019) 60 *Harvard International Law Journal* 377, 378.

[20] World Bank Report, 'Rising Global Interest in Farmland: Can It Yield Sustainable and Equitable Benefits?' (2010).

[21] Ibid.

[22] GRAIN, 'The Global Farmland Grab in 2016: How Big, How Bad?', https://grain.org/e/5492.

[23] Sonja Vermeulen Lorenzo Cotula, 'Land Grab or Development Opportunity? Agricultural Investment and International Land Deals in Africa', www.iied.org/12561iied.

[24] Edelman et al (n 17).

insecurity.[25] This begs the question of how beneficial this form of FDI is to the African communities and economies. The section below provides a summary of land deals to help determine whether the world should be worried, ie is this a common concern or not?

A. The Nature of Land Grabs

The advent of colonialisation in Africa is still fresh in the minds of citizens throughout the continent as the majority of African countries obtained independence in the 1960s. The land and mineral resources underneath African land was controlled by the colonisers, leaving a bitter taste and desperation for Africans to regain control of their resources, including their land. The end of colonisation meant the end of foreign control of Africa, a continent rich in land. This land is used 'sustainably' in the sense that farming is mostly not for commercial gain but for subsistence, thereby using less chemicals that destroy the soil.

The term 'land grab' is suggestive of military takeover or colonisation of targeted territories, which used to be the main vehicle through which land was taken from its rightful owners. In this way, the phenomenon of land grab could be described in political terms to mean occupation and control of land.

Today, the term 'land grab' includes, as mentioned above, commercial transactions between a foreign (although some involve local people) buyer or lessee and a sovereign state or private seller/lessor, largely in response to a current or future food crisis or to meet the demands of growing economies such as BRICS member countries.[26] While wilfulness is emphasised in the new era of land grabbing, it must be underscored that there is a political and economic past that underpins land grabs, which is that of colonisation and of the poverty of those selling and leasing land today.[27] Accordingly, justifying land grabs with arguments that people have a right to dispose of their wealth or that states have a sovereign right to dispose of their wealth must be taken against the backdrop of poverty, power imbalance and the fact that capital is in the hands of those living in the Global North as well as in the emerging markets, which underpin the political economy of land grabs.[28]

It is important to highlight that colonialisation introduced two legal systems in the occupied countries – common or civil law and customary law – the latter governing relations among rural populations, including property rights such as land rights. With regard to rural communities, land was largely held by the sovereign in trust for their nation. With this land tenure system, land was allocated to the sovereign's subjects who required land, including for subsistence farming, and

[25] Eva Cudlínová et al, 'New Forms of Land Grabbing Due to the Bioeconomy: The Case of Brazil' (2020) 12 *Sustainability* 3395, 3396.

[26] ibid.

[27] ibid.

[28] Edelman et al (n 17) 1517.

normally there would be little or no proof of ownership in the form of title deeds. Land would then pass from generation to generation within a family or clan. As land is held by the sovereign in trust for the nation under their majesty's rulership, alienation and acquisition of land was subject to strict controls – in the main, no foreigners would be allocated land.

While this land tenure system, applied appropriately, fostered sustainability and generational equity by ensuring that a prodigal head of family could not alienate land to the detriment of future family generations, it nevertheless precluded rural communities from participating in the formal economy using their land as collateral for credit or selling it. Thus, alienation of rural land through the sale or pledging of the land to financial institutions in order to access capital for other projects was impossible in the absence of title deeds. This led to the era of formalisation and modernisation of rural land tenure systems. The movement was led by non-governmental organisations (NGOs) which decried the financial exclusion of rural communities and campaigned for the modernisation and formalisation of rural land tenure systems. The land tenure system in rural communities was often criticised for producing poor yields as it discouraged investments in the rural agriculture sector, resulting in the World Bank supporting governments that sought land reforms to obtain individual titles to land.[29] Today, the formalisation of land tenure systems for rural communities has facilitated large-scale land grabs by investors while leaving communities in dire straits.[30]

African communities are still largely rural, with an estimated 58 per cent of the continent's population living in rural areas in 2022, down from over 80 per cent in 1960.[31] Communities, chiefs and kings or queens control large tracks of land, most of which is used for subsistence farming due to lack of modern technologies and a lack of capital for large-scale farming, which requires heavy machinery, fertilisers, pesticides, herbicides and abundant water for irrigation. The small percentage of commercial farming in Africa is mainly done by European settlers or foreign investors.[32] For subsistence farming in the rural communities, there is little pressure to maximise production for every acre of land. Consequently, weeds are removed by hand hoe, cow dung manure is commonly used, and plants are watered by rain despite there being ample water from rivers and dams.

Land in Africa therefore presents itself as untapped gold. While arable land is more than ample in Africa, many African countries experience extreme levels of poverty, securing food donations (grain) from large-scale grain-producing countries such as the USA, Russia and Ukraine. Even African countries such as South

[29] Pauline Peters, 'Challenges in Land Tenure and Land Reform in Africa: Anthropological Contributions' (2009) 37 *World Development* 1317.

[30] Avispa Midia, 'World Bank Pursues Land Grabs for "Energy Transition"', https://farmlandgrab.org/post/32245-world-bank-pursues-land-grabs-for-energy-transition.

[31] 'Sub-Saharan Africa Rural Population 1960–2024', www.macrotrends.net/global-metrics/countries/SSF/sub-saharan-africa-/rural-population; World Bank, 'Rural Population (% of Total Population) – Sub Saharan Africa', https://data.worldbank.org/indicator/SP.RURTOTL.ZS?locations=ZG.

[32] Ivan I Potekhin, 'Land Relations in African Countries' (1963) 1 *Journal of Modern African Studies* 39, 39.

Africa and Zimbabwe that were historically grain exporters have become net food-importing nations. It is for this reason that, in 2014, African states, through the African Development Bank, adopted a turnaround strategy to transform the continent's agricultural sector by adopting mechanisms to move away from subsistence farming and towards commercial farming to maximise production.[33]

Against the backdrop of 'underutilised' land in Africa, countries around the world are waking up to the effects of global warming, which creates weather conditions that are increasingly becoming unfavourable to farming.[34] Simultaneously, African cities are ballooning due to overpopulation caused by (chiefly internal) migration in search of jobs. As cities expand, arable land diminishes because farmers sell land for non-agricultural developments.[35] Studies have shown that in future there is a real threat of food insecurity, and even those that have arable land find the cost of farming increasingly onerous due to both a degrading environment and the rising cost of capital that is needed for agricultural production. One example comes from Saudi Arabia, which, cognisant of the environmental footprint associated with growing wheat, banned its production domestically. Instead, the country decided to source land in Africa for wheat production.[36] The irony is that while Saudi Arabia aims to protect its skies from wheat pollution, environmental pollution knows no boundaries – pollution in Africa becomes a problem or concern to other nations thousands of miles away beyond the continent's shores.

Similar to the time when African countries were signing bilateral investment treaties in the hopes of attracting greater volumes of FDI,[37] which at times ended up haunting them, it seems that similar forces are at play on the continent today, albeit in a different form. Specifically, African countries are now concluding very long leases and/or selling land to foreigners as a means to attract FDI in the agricultural sector, hoping for job creation and accelerated economic growth.[38] There is now a new scramble for African land in which investors from all continents come to Africa in different sizes and forms, seeking the acquisition of land.[39]

[33] African Development Bank, 'Feed Africa: Strategy for Agricultural Transformation in Africa 2016–2025', www.afdb.org/fileadmin/uploads/afdb/Documents/Policy-Documents/Feed_Africa-Strategy-En.pdf.

[34] CE Richards, HL Gauch and JM Allwood, 'International Risk of Food Insecurity and Mass Mortality in a Runaway Global Warming Scenario' (2023) 150 *Futures* 103173; CE Richards, RC Lupton and JM Allwood, 'Re-framing the Threat of Global Warming: An Empirical Causal Loop Diagram of Climate Change, Food Insecurity and Societal Collapse' (2021) 164 *Climatic Change* 49.

[35] Sylvia Szabo, 'Urbanisation and Food Insecurity Risks: Assessing the Role of Human Development' (2016) 44 *Oxford Development Studies* 28.

[36] Lorenzo Cotula and Sonja Vermeulen, 'Deal or No Deal: The Outlook for Agricultural Land Investment in Africa' (2009) 85 *International Affairs* 1233, 1235.

[37] Andrew T Guzman, 'Why LDCs Sign Treaties That Hurt Them: Explaining the Popularity of Bilateral Investment Treaties' (1998) 38 *Virginia Journal of International Law* 639.

[38] Derek R Byerlee et al, 'Rising Global Interest in Farmland: Can It Yield Sustainable and Equitable Benefits?' (World Bank, 2011) 69.

[39] Sam Moyo, Praveen Jha and Paris Yeros, 'The Scramble for Land and Natural Resources in Africa' in Sam Moyo, Praveen Jha and Paris Yeros (eds), *Reclaiming Africa: Scramble and Resistance in the 21st Century* (Springer, 2019) https://doi.org/10.1007/978-981-10-5840-0_1; Margaret C Lee, 'The 21st Century Scramble for Africa' (2006) 24 *Journal of Contemporary African Studies* 303.

Some conclude private sale agreements or contract farming, while others enter into sale or lease agreements with governments. Both forms taken by the scramble for African land are explored below.

Starting with investor–state land agreements, investors often approach a given government in Africa, promising economic development and job creation in the agricultural sector. The proposals are immediately enticing to governments that are facing poverty and joblessness. Identified land is subsequently cleared (through the removal or relocation of communities occupying them) for a new development.[40] Madagascar is a case in point, where communities were removed from their land as a result of an agreement between the Government of Madagascar and Korea's Daewoo. This is a deal in which Daewoo had sought access to 1.3 million hectares of land, which is massive by any standard, for the purpose of growing maize for export back home. The local communities were never consulted about the agreement.[41] The move attracted public outcry, both inside and outside of Madagascar, leading to the overthrow of the government of President Marc Ravalomanana and the suspension of the land deal. Although the Daewoo deal failed, others have succeeded across the world, with an estimated 491 land deals spanning more than 30 million hectares spread over 78 countries recorded in 2016, of which 42 per cent of deals are in Africa.[42]

As the land grabs grew in number and started to attract international attention, investors shifted from patent forms of land grabs that transfer ownership of land to investors or foreign governments to subtler ones centred on production for export: 'To escape the social backlash, some investors are switching to more diffuse and subtle forms of land grabbing such as: contract farming, special economic zones, agropoles and infrastructure corridors. But any way you slice it, land concentration is increasing.'[43]

B. Consequences of Land Grabs in Africa

In this section, I consider the impacts of land grabs in Africa with a view to determining whether the world should be worried; that is, whether land grabs should be deemed a CCH. Whereas there can be possible other consequences of land grabs, here I identify poverty and forced migration pressures within and beyond Africa as real threats to both the continent and the world.

[40] Borras et al (n 1) 209.

[41] Renée Vellvé and Mamy Rakotondrainibe, 'The Daewoo–Madagascar Land Grab: Ten Years On' (Thomson Reuters, 16 November 2018) https://news.trust.org/item/20181116144408-pdi0a/.

[42] GRAIN (n 22); Caterina Conigliania, Nadia Cuffarob and Giovanna D'Agostino, 'Large-scale Land Investments and Forests in Africa' (2018) 75 *Land Policy* 652.

[43] Vellvé and Rakotondrainibe (n 41).

(i) Poverty

I have shown above that African communities, which are largely rural, chiefly use land for subsistence farming. Any agricultural surplus is usually sold to neighbours who, for one reason or another, do not have a large enough harvest to sustain them through the season, and the proceeds are used to buy household necessities.

Land grabs result in owners vacating their land or encourage them to sell their land, which they use for sustenance. The proceeds of such sales are enticing for poor households, who are not ordinarily used to such lump sums. However, it does not take long before the money runs out and the families are driven into destitution because the sale price is usually below market value, and the money gets depleted with usage in any event. As noted above, the traditional land tenure system in Africa is such that land is passed on from one generation to the next. Thus, selling land to investors creates generational poverty as the future generations of the family that sold the land will not have access to land for sustenance. Similarly, those who are evicted from their land to make way for investors are at considerable risk of heightened poverty.[44] From the human rights perspective, the end result of land grabbing is denial of the right to food for communities.[45]

For sales and long leases concluded with governments, the expectation on the part of governments typically concerns job creation and commercial exports of farm produce to earn foreign currency. The reality is that while some jobs are created, often seasonal ones, the produce is exported for food security reasons while potentially creating food insecurity in a country that has land and produces food. As a result, a government that was hoping to lease and/or sell land for food security and export would find itself grappling with the risk of greater poverty.

Long leases of land can also be a form of land grab that leads to poverty, especially if the use of land is unregulated, as is usually the case, and degrades the soil, thereby depriving the future generations of the use of such land, as noted by Cottier and Shingal: 'Importation of feedstuff and fertilizers should be limited to curbing intensive agriculture and stressing soil quality. Product and production standards need to contribute to preserving soil quality abroad and will be implemented with the cooperation of producers and importers.'[46]

[44] Lisa-Marie Rudi et al, 'Land Rights as an Engine of Growth? An Analysis of Cambodian Land Grabs in the Context of Development Theory' (2014) 38 *Land Use Policy* 564; Logan Cochrain, 'Food Security or Food Sovereignty: The Case of Land Grabs' [2011] *Journal of Humanitarian Assistance*.

[45] Golay and Biglino (n 17).

[46] Thomas Cottier and Anirudh Shingal, 'Migration, Trade and Investment: Towards a New Common Concern of Humankind' (2021) 55 *Journal of World Trade* 51, 64.

(ii) Forced Migration

The African proverb 'an empty stomach has no ears' holds true to those afflicted by poverty. Despite xenophobic attacks in countries such as South Africa[47] and boats capsizing in the Mediterranean Sea,[48] killing hundreds of people, those seeking to address their immediate basic needs are not seemingly dissuaded. Illegal immigrants and refugees continue to flock into South Africa and Europe despite host country destinations not being ready or willing to accommodate them.

While not discarding that commercial agricultural activity in Africa is significant in some countries, farming in rural Africa is often chiefly for sustenance, such that families that do not own land often experience the most extreme forms of poverty. With this in mind, when families alienate their land through sale, they can face poverty within a very short space of time after selling that land. This is exacerbated by the pricing of land in rural communities all too often being below the true market price.

Once poverty hits, people leave their homes in search of a livelihood.[49] Often, these people have poor educational qualifications, making them ineligible for any kind of work-related visa that requires skills. Accordingly, they are at risk of having to leave their countries to be refugees or illegal immigrants in other countries.

In Africa, South Africa is the top destination country for economic migrants from Sub-Saharan Africa and Asia. Specifically, after their economy tanked as a result of years of malgovernance, Zimbabweans flocked to South Africa in search of an improved livelihood. Tensions have ensued between Zimbabwean migrants in South Africa and the local population, as well as with the Government of South Africa, as the latter feels overburdened and wants to send the Zimbabweans home.[50] Similarly, there are thousands of economic migrants from other neighbouring countries, including Lesotho, Mozambique and Zambia, who take up menial jobs in South Africa just so they can meet basic needs. Meanwhile, South Africa deports between 15,000 and 20,000 illegal immigrants annually.[51]

Forced migration into Europe due to poverty has made global headlines, with Europe struggling to keep up with migration inflows from Africa and Asia.[52]

[47] 'GroundView: Aaron Motsoaledi's Shameful Outburst', www.groundup.org.za/article/groundview-aaron-motsoaledis-shameful-outburst/; Abigail Dawson, Sally Gandar and Sharon S Ekambaram, 'Xenophobia Fuelled by Minister Motsoaledi's Scapegoating' *Daily Maverick* (6 October 2019) www.dailymaverick.co.za/article/2019-10-06-xenophobia-fuelled-by-minister-motsoaledis-scapegoating/.

[48] James Hampshire, 'Europe's Migration Crisis' (2015) 6 *Political Insight* 8; Philippe Fargues and Sara Bonfanti, 'When the Best Option Is a Leaky Boat: Why Migrants Risk Their Lives Crossing the Mediterranean and What Europe Is Doing About It', https://cadmus.eui.eu/handle/1814/33271.

[49] Cottier and Shingal (n 46); Richards et al, 'Re-framing the Threat' (n 34).

[50] Pearl Khumalo, 'The End of the Zimbabwean Exemption Permit?' (ProBono.Org, 25 August 2023) https://probono.org.za/the-end-of-the-zimbabwean-exemption-permit/.

[51] Anthony Molyneauz, 'Government Plans to Get Tough with Spazas' *BusinessLIVE* (South Africa, 18 April 2024) www.timeslive.co.za/politics/2024-04-18-watch-spaza-shops-need-to-be-audited-and-pay-tax-motsoaledi-on-new-immigration-proposals/.

[52] Hampshire (n 48).

III. Land Grabs as a Common Concern of Humankind

I start this section on the generally accepted premise that the concept of CCH is not limited to environmental issues but extends to other areas, including freshwater access, plant genetic resources, common currencies,[53] internet access[54] and ecological warfare.[55] Some scholars describe the application of CCH as open-ended;[56] therefore, the argument that land grabs could be a CCH should not be frowned upon. To determine whether land grabs are a common concern, I apply the salient features of CCH to the phenomenon of land grabs.

A. Global Consensus on Land Grabs as a Common Concern of Humankind

Before an issue can be regarded as a common concern, there must be global consensus that such an issue is indeed a broadly shared concern, and usually such consensus is derived from treaties in the absence of customary international law to that effect.[57] Any common concern addressed by treaties and/or under customary international law would impose obligations upon states to address such an issue equitably. While there is not yet a treaty classifying land grabs as a CCH, the phenomenon has attracted global attention. To this end, land grabs are a concern for global groupings and organisations such as the Food and Agriculture Organization (FAO), G7, G20 and World Bank.[58] Specifically, the FAO adopted Voluntary Guidelines on the Responsible Governance of Tenure of Land, Fisheries and Forests in the Context of National Food Security in 2012 and revised them in 2022. This was as a response, in part, to the grabbing of land belonging to rural communities, which resulted in poverty and food insecurity on continents such as Africa, where tenure of land rights is not secure.[59] More compelling still is the

[53] Cottier and Shingal (n 46); Weiss (n 2); Nguyễn Hồng Thao and Marie Anne Cyra H Uy, 'Common Concern of Humankind in the Work of the International Law Commission on the Protection of the Atmosphere' (2023) 16 *Sustainability and Climate Change* 250. In fact, the flexibility of the concept of common concern is particularly seen in the EU, where exchange rates were viewed as of common concern, not of humankind but of the existence of the EU: 'Exchange rate stability is therefore seen as important both in terms of achieving, and facilitating, a single European market, but is also regarded as an important test for participation in the euro zone … The Treaty states explicitly [under Art 99 of the EC Treaty that "Member states shall regard their economic policies as a matter of common concern and shall coordinate them within the Council …"]' Zenon Kontolemis (n 11) 6.

[54] Antonio Segura-Serrano, 'Internet Regulation: A Hard-Law Proposal' (2006) Jean Monnet Working Papers 48, https://ideas.repec.org//p/erp/jeanmo/p0240.html.

[55] UNEP Secretariat (n 12) para 12.

[56] Jutta Brunnée, 'Common Areas, Common Heritage, and Common Concern' in Daniel Bodansky, Jutta Brunnée and Ellen Hey (eds), *The Oxford Handbook of International Environmental Law* (Oxford University Press, 2008) 564.

[57] ibid 565.

[58] Cudlínová et al (n 25) 3396.

[59] Food and Agricultural Organization, 'Voluntary Guidelines on the Responsible Governance of Tenure of Land, Fisheries and Forests in the Context of National Food Security' (2022) https://openknowledge.fao.org/server/api/core/bitstreams/4e08d38d-b1f5-4c74-8478-7cbd61a1e90a/content.

Policy Paper adopted by the International Criminal Court in 2016 outlining a plan to prosecute Rome Statute crimes committed by means of, among others, land grabbing,[60] which indicates that there is an emerging global consensus on land grabs being a common concern.

The consequences of land grabs – among them poverty and forced migration – have been found in other settings as issues of common concern, requiring global responses. To the extent that land grabbing has these debilitating effects, that is, causing poverty and forced migration, they must be regarded as of common concern. Poverty is a global crisis requiring a global response. Poverty threatens sustainability, hence poverty alleviation is at the top of the list of SDGs. States have undertaken to eradicate poverty, in all its forms, by the year 2030. This affects 670 million of the world's population, a large proportion of which are situated in Sub-Saharan Africa. Since key to sustainable development is 'meeting the demands of the world's poor',[61] there can be little doubt that land grabs, as a fertile source of poverty aggravation, are a common concern for humankind, and the adoption of SDG 1 is an indication that there is global consensus that poverty is a CCH. Cottier and Shingal have since outlined the need to preserve agricultural land because the degradation of land, which is extended to land grabs in this chapter, increases irregular migration as people face increased risks of poverty and struggle to make a living, especially in rural areas.[62] With regard to forced migration, this work aligns and builds on the work by Cottier and Shingal, who already pointed out that migration is a CCH.[63] Forced migration is a global crisis to the extent that migrants put pressure on systems such as health and housing in the receiving country, causing migrants to live in tents with inadequate sanitation, food, shelter and other basic needs. It then becomes a humanitarian crisis. Recalling that common concern was first used in relation to global problems such as environmental degradation and humanitarian crises, it must be accepted that land grabs, as potential breeding grounds for poverty that often trigger forced migration for the affected communities and result in a humanitarian crisis in the receiving country, are a common concern.

B. Land Grabs as Requiring a Global Response

The first question is whether land grabs in one part of the world affect the rest of the world. The Convention on Biological Diversity shows that a problem need not be occurring globally for it to be a common concern. Rather, it suffices that

[60] International Criminal Court, 'Policy Paper on Case Selection and Prioritisation' (2016) para 41, www.icc-cpi.int/sites/default/files/20160915_OTP-Policy_Case-Selection_Eng.pdf.

[61] World Commission on Environment and Development (WCED), 'Our Common Future' (1990) 87.

[62] Cottier and Shingal (n 46) 64.

[63] ibid.

other countries experience a similar problem.[64] Land grabs, which affect many countries in the world (over 78 as per data generated by GRAIN),[65] are indeed occurring on a very large scale, thereby warranting a search for global solutions. In fact, international organisations have raised global alarms regarding land grabs and their effect on the livelihoods of those whose land is grabbed. The argument made herein is that poverty undoubtedly increases migratory pressures, the latter having been argued elsewhere by Cottier et al that it is a common concern. The cause and the consequence need not happen simultaneously at the global scale. To this end, while the cause (land grab) happens in Africa, the consequence is felt in other parts of the world, such as in Europe. The use of CCH for the single currency in Europe shows that the concept can be used for specific policy challenges affecting specific jurisdictions. Therefore, land grabs as a specific issue can be a common concern for Africa as it is a driving force for poverty-stricken people to migrate to Europe as a destination continent. The pressure on basic services in Europe, and the denial of basic human rights in Europe in respect of migrants, could morph into a humanitarian crisis, calling all countries to assist Europe to address this crisis.

C. Temporal Element of Land Grabs

Second, the concept of CCH has a temporal element, similar to sustainable development, which requires that the rights and obligations of both present and future generations be safeguarded.[66] Land grabs become a common concern by not only affecting the needs of current generations [in Africa], but also those of future generations, thereby threatening human existence in areas facing poverty and forced migration due to land grabs. On this reasoning, land grabs must be seen as a CCH.

In the context of Africa, land runs through families – it is therefore a form of property that is not only used to put bread on the table, but also as a form of identity, thereby revealing the social and cultural aspect of land grabbing as a CCH.[67] The slogan *mayibuye iAfrica*, which means African land must come back, or freedom to Africans, coined during colonial times, is still much sung by political parties across Africa. This is so despite there being no foreign political occupation on the continent. Post-colonialisation, *mayibuye iAfrica* refers to the return of ownership of African resources, including land, to Africans. There is a very strong sentiment in Africa that Africans lack economic freedom because many African natural resources are controlled by foreigners, hence there is poverty even in

[64] Weiss (n 2) 164.
[65] GRAIN (n 22).
[66] Horn, 'Globalisation, Sustainable Development' (n 14) 62.
[67] ibid 55.

countries that are rich in mineral resources, including South Africa and Nigeria,[68] and land grabs in Africa are aggravating the sentiment.[69]

IV. Multilevel Responses to Land Grabs

At the heart of the phenomenon of land grabs is lack of sound land market governance from all the players involved – communities, NGOs, corporations, governments, international organisations[70] – when land is at play in commercial transactions. This is especially true in rural Africa, where land is not only used for food security, but also forms such a strong part of communal identity.

The report of the Group of Legal Experts referred to in the introduction expresses a need to balance state sovereignty with problems of common concern, thereby calling for limits to Westphalian sovereignty and allowing multiparty stakeholders to respond to the common concern of land grabs. It is this conception that was later built on by Cottier et al, who asserted that the concept of CCH creates rights and obligations – an obligation to act and the right to act beyond national territorial jurisdictions.[71] This chapter therefore argues below that land grabs in Africa and elsewhere are a CCH that needs to trigger cooperation among states to solve this problem and to create obligations and the right for states to act against land grabs. I will therefore delineate the rights and responsibilities of different parties to curb the threat of land grabs based on a doctrine of multilevel governance, rom communities to global institutions.

A. Communities' Rights or Obligations

The CCH requires public participation and support, for it is only when the public bears responsibility that it can act in concert to address common concerns of humankind.[72] In land grabbing deals, there is hardly any public consultations – often local communities are chased away from their land, causing tensions between investors and the communities concerned.[73] The failed Daewoo–Madagascar land grab deal was characterised by secrecy, wherein the deal was hidden from the communities contrary to the principle of common concern and sustainable development.[74] Ordinarily, communities have a right to participate in issues of

[68] Magnus Ericsson, Olof Löf and Anton Löf, 'Chinese Control over African and Global Mining – Past, Present and Future' (2020) 33 *Mineral Economics* 153.

[69] Cotula (n 23).

[70] Thomas Sikor et al, 'Global Land Governance: From Territory to Flow?' (2013) 5 *Current Opinion in Environmental Sustainability* 522.

[71] Cottier et al (n 13).

[72] Horn, 'Globalisation, Sustainable Development' (n 14) 59.

[73] Byerlee et al (n 38).

[74] Vellvé and Rakotondrainibe (n 41).

governance and decision-making in their respective countries; it is only when this right is respected that land grabs can be prevented. Community consultations enhance transparency in land deals, which is in line with the FAO Voluntary Guidelines on Responsible Governance of Tenure of Land Rights.[75] In fact, the community's participation in land deals is in line with Article 21 of the African Charter of Human and Peoples' Rights, which provides that the people have a right to dispose of their land, which indicates that land alienation in Africa is a collective right.

B. Investor Obligations

Actions of companies abroad would attract common action so long as they affect common concerns abroad, which land grabs can represent. The issue of imposing obligations (and not solely conferring rights) on private investors is long overdue if the world has to attain responsible investments. Borrowing from the FAO Voluntary Guidelines on Responsible Governance of Land Tenure Rights, 'responsible investing in land should do no harm, safeguard against dispossession of legitimate tenure right holders and environmental damage and should respect human rights'.[76]

Once a matter has been classified as a common concern, it justifies states and international institutions such as the International Criminal Court (ICC) to act, which is what common concern calls for.[77] The ICC policy to prosecute land grabs must be incorporated into national, regional and global laws, regulating land purchases and land deals to ensure food security even in the host country and mutual benefit with landowners. Of course, one can expect immense resistance from governments and those interested in land acquisitions.

Further, to the extent investors can use the land, soil preservation in agricultural investments must be a condition of use. This keeps in mind the duty to preserve land for future generations, as required by both sustainable development and common concern.

C. State Rights and Obligations

When it comes to the obligations of states – three are identified as follows: (1) states must cooperate in preventing land grabs. Thus, states with land must be discouraged from disposing of land or using land in a manner that threatens sustainability while those in need of land must be discouraged from grabbing land or using land

[75] FAO, 'Voluntary Guidelines on the Responsible Governance of Tenure of Land, Fisheries and Forests in the Context of National Food Security' (2022) 1.

[76] ibid para 12.4.

[77] Cottier et al (n 13).

in foreign countries in a manner that is at loggerheads with sustainability. The Saudi Arabian example depicted above is a case in point – if Saudi Arabia is of the opinion that growing wheat is bad for the environment, resulting in a domestic production ban, should it be purchasing foreign land for wheat production? (2) This overlaps with the responsibility of states at home and abroad – an action cannot be acceptable if done abroad if it cannot be done at home for reasons that it threatens the environment in like circumstances. As land grab is a common concern, 'States should, with appropriate consultation and participation, provide transparent rules on the scale, scope and nature of allowable transactions in tenure rights and should define what constitutes large-scale transactions in tenure rights in their national context'.[78] While large-scale land transactions should generally be avoided, in the event that such large-scale land transfers to investors are made, they should be approved by higher bodies, such as Parliament, for public scrutiny and to avoid corruption.[79] Cotula notes that other countries have already taken measures to suspend large-scale land deals and/or are tightening the rules on these types of transactions, and this must be a template to other countries facing land grabs.[80] (3) States must also impose obligations on investors, whether local or foreign, regarding land preservation and good agricultural practices to ensure that future generations can still use the land.

D. International Institutions' Obligations

Treaties do not always work to solve global problems because during their negotiations there can be lobbying, especially from transnational corporations (TNCs), against the adoption of measures that could otherwise prove effective and not all countries ratify such treaties, or they are simply ignored or unenforced, just like environmental protection treaties often continue to be weakly implemented.[81] Meanwhile, global problems persist; however, with the invocation of concepts such as CCH, there may be hope for addressing these global problems. Common concern is viewed as an ethical concept that can develop into an international norm,[82] but it can also be invoked as a principle by international organisations to control land grabs. The proposals herein are that the United Nations needs to start conversations for the return of land that has been grabbed and this must further be reinforced by the ICC's 2016 policy position to prosecute land grabs. Thus, a remedy for any land grab deal that has been successfully prosecuted must be the

[78] FAO (n 75) para 12.5.

[79] ibid para 12.6.

[80] Lorenzo Cotula, 'The New Enclosures? Polanyi, International Investment Law and the Global Land Rush' (2013) 34 *Third World Quarterly* 1605, 1612.

[81] United Nations, 'Report of the World Summit on Sustainable Development', Resolution 1, Annex, 'Johannesburg Declaration on Sustainable Development' 1, para 13, UN Doc A/CONF 199/20 (2002).

[82] Horn, 'Globalisation, Sustainable Development' (n 14) 53–54.

return of such land to its rightful owners plus compensation. Insurance bodies such as the World Bank's Multilateral Investment Guarantee Agency (MIGA) could be called upon to require proof of ownership, including history of ownership, before investments can be insured.

V. Conclusion

Common concern of humankind is gaining traction in international relations among states, though it continues to appear mainly in the preambles of various treaties and in scholarly work. It is nonetheless emerging as an important principle guiding states in responding to global problems. While its prominence has so far chiefly concerned international environmental issues such as climate change, its flexibility allows it to be applied to other areas beyond the environment. In this chapter, the concept of CCH is extended to land grabs.

In applying salient features of CCH to land grabs, largely occurring in Africa, I posit that land grabs are indeed a CCH. Specifically, this chapter shows that there is an international or global consensus that land grabs are a common concern based on the fact that they have caught the attention of the G7, G20, FAO and World Bank, among others, as well as civil society organisations such as GRAIN and farmlandgrab.org. Although land grabs happen within specific jurisdictions, thereby questioning whether they are a matter of national competence or require global cooperation, this chapter shows that through the approach taken with the Convention on Biological Diversity, common concern applies even to issues that occur within national jurisdictions as long as other countries are experiencing similar problems. Accordingly, land grabs are a common concern, as many countries (estimated at more than 78) are experiencing the phenomenon. In addition, the consequences of land grabs affect the rights of future generations, thereby falling within the ambit of common concern and therefore warranting international action. Furthermore, the likely consequences of land grabs – heightened poverty and forced migration – are on their own right issues of CCH.

This chapter concludes by identifying the role of different actors in addressing the problem of land grab. While scratching the surface in the recommendations provided, the chapter suggests the various roles that communities, investors, states and international bodies can play in curbing land grabs. Starting with communities, this chapter recommends consultation and participation in the decision-making process, as reinforced by Article 21 of African Charter on Human and Peoples' Rights, which recognises that land in Africa is a collective right, warranting collective decision-making in alienating it. States are enjoined to take responsibility both at home and abroad, and to cooperate in preventing land grabs, while investors are expected to undertake responsible agricultural investments, which not only respect the rights of the communities and governments to land, but also preserve the soil for future generations. Lastly, international bodies, especially the ICC, are further expected to prevent land grabs, and to prosecute them and return 'stolen' land to its rightful owners as a remedy after successful prosecution, while MIGA is expected to require proof of land ownership, including its historical ownership.

16

From William Rappard to Thomas Cottier: Ordoliberal Market Integration and the Rules-Based International Trade Order

ERNST-ULRICH PETERSMANN

I. Introduction: Swiss Federalism and Trade Diplomacy

Switzerland has a long tradition of diplomacy for international trade liberalisation inspired by the Confederation's domestic experiences with creating a common market among the 26 cantons. When I studied international law at the University of Geneva in 1965/66 and attended Wilhelm Röpke's classes on international economic order at the Geneva Graduate Institute of International Studies, the books and articles by William Rappard were often referred to. Rappard was the Swiss founder of the Graduate Institute and the Swiss representative in many inter-war conferences organised by the League of Nations on (i) international order and collective security (as represented by the League of Nations); (ii) free trade and private commerce to depoliticise economic relations by mutually beneficial cooperation; and (iii) respect for the dignity of the individual and protection of equal rights to liberty and labour rights to assure a free and just society.

When I returned to Geneva in 1981 to work as legal officer in the Secretariat of the General Agreement on Tariffs and Trade (GATT 1947), the former GATT Director-General Olivier Long asked me to comment on the draft of his book on Law and Its Limitation in the GATT Multilateral Trade System (1985). Just as Rappard had complained about the cantonal trade protectionism impeding equal freedoms and the progressive establishment of a common market inside Switzerland, Long emphasised the need for pragmatic realism in accommodating the domestic political constraints inside many GATT contracting parties. At the time, these were impeding, for instance, liberalisation of cotton, textiles and agricultural trade, full compliance of customs unions and free trade agreements (FTAs) with GATT rules, and operation of the GATT dispute settlement system.[1] Even though the first GATT Director-General (Eric Wyndham White) and Long had both been lawyers, it was only the third GATT Director-General, Arthur Dunkel – like Long a former Swiss trade diplomat and part-time professor – who decided to establish a GATT Office of Legal Affairs. He did this in 1983, following his appointment of a long-standing GATT official, Hielke van Tuinen, as *ad personam* legal adviser in 1981. The establishment of the GATT Office of Legal Affairs responded to the widespread criticism of the legal inconsistencies of previous GATT dispute settlement reports and the legal uncertainties created by the 1979 Tokyo Round Agreements complementing GATT rules and dispute settlement procedures.[2]

It was in the context of my work as GATT legal counsellor that I first met Thomas Cottier as a member of the Swiss GATT delegation in the Centre William Rappard, the official seat of the GATT Secretariat. During the Uruguay Round negotiations (1986–93) and my work for the Uruguay Round Negotiating Group elaborating the World Trade Organization (WTO) Dispute Settlement Understanding (DSU), as well as for the Working Group finalising the text of the 1994 WTO Agreement, I was grateful for Thomas's advice, friendship and academic cooperation.

II. National Constitutions and International Economic Law

My 1976 dissertation on Economic Integration and Investment Laws of Developing Countries, had concluded that the diverse legal design of regional economic integration in Europe, Africa and Latin-America had been largely due to the diverse constitutional laws, policies and colonial legacies of the countries concerned. My 1991 monograph on Constitutional Functions and Constitutional Problems of International Economic Law, examined these complex interactions between internal and external trade laws and policies from the comparative perspectives of the eighteenth-century US Constitution, the nineteenth-century Swiss Constitution, the 1949 German Basic Law and European integration law. My book concluded that the neoliberal common market law of the US Constitution, the communitarian common market law made possible by Switzerland's constitutional reforms

[1] *cf* O Long, *Law and its Limitations in the GATT Multilateral Trade System* (Nijhoff, 1985) 108: 'GATT's pragmatism and flexibility, without undue regard to legal technicalities, have been much commended'. Yet, Long embraced some of my criticism of the original French text of his book by paying greater attention to international law in the book's revised English translation.

[2] *cf* EU Petersmann, 'The Establishment of a GATT Office of Legal Affairs and the Limited Public Reason in the GATT/WTO Dispute Settlement System' in G Marceau (ed), *A History of Law and Lawyers in the GATT/WTO. The Development of the Rule of Law in the Multilateral Trading System* (Cambridge University Press, 2015) 182–207. On Dunkel's legacy, see J Bhagwati and M Hirsch (eds), *The Uruguay Round and Beyond: Essays in Honor of Arthur Dunkel* (Cambridge University Press, 1986), notably the contribution by Robert Hudec on the history of the GATT Office of Legal Affairs.

of 1874 and the multilevel democratic and economic 'ordoliberal constitutionalism' underlying the German and European 'social market economies' established diverse constitutional frameworks for market- and business-driven US trade policies, Switzerland's trade protectionism and the European Economic Community's common commercial policies. When I prepared a 1993 conference book on National Constitutions and International Economic Law, exploring the future implementation of Uruguay Round agreements in domestic legal systems, I asked Thomas Cottier to contribute a chapter on the perspective of a Swiss trade negotiator and constitutional lawyer involved in Swiss, European and global trade governance.

A. Structure–Substance Pairings in European Economic Integration Law

Thomas's contribution[3] proceeded from the 'constitutional approach' elaborated by the Geneva school of law and economics, explaining why legal protection of freedom to trade, non-discriminatory conditions of competition, the rule of law and individual rights can improve the substantive quality of domestic constitutional norms ('material Constitution') for multilevel governance of public goods (PGs). For instance, the legal ranking in GATT law of trade policy instruments according to their transparency, democratic and judicial accountability and economic efficiency (eg tariffs rather than non-tariff trade barriers), and the procedural and substantive GATT requirements for justifying trade restrictions and subsidies, promote rules-based, non-discriminatory conditions of competition.[4] Based on his dissertation on The Constitution and the Requirement of a Legislative Basis (1983/1991), Thomas explained why the application of substantive constitutional law disciplines to trade regulation and policies, such as rule-of-law requirements, public interest justifications, necessity and proportionality, had to be accompanied by procedural and structural guarantees so that, for instance, 'decisions are taken on an appropriate level with appropriate procedures which foster, and do not undermine, the basic equations of democratic rule'.[5] Thomas's research explored 'adequate structure-substance pairings with a view to promoting *structural justice* or *structural due process*' in the evolution of GATT practices, the 1960 European Free Trade Association (EFTA), the 1972 EFTA–European Community FTAs and the 1992 Agreement on the European Economic Area (EEA). His case studies

[3] T Cottier, 'Constitutional Trade Regulation in National and International Trade Law: Structure-Substance Pairings in the EFTA Experience' in M Hilf and EU Petersmann (eds), *National Constitutions and International Economic Law* (Kluwer, 1993) 409–42.

[4] *cf* the contributions by M Hilf, R Hudec, J Jackson, EU Petersmann and F Roessler, and their references to economists (like J Tumlir and H Hauser) and political scientists like V Curzon, in Hilf and Petersmann (n 3).

[5] Cottier (n 3) 411.

confirmed the need 'for a constitutional approach and for an overall regulatory theory covering both domestic and international law': 'substance, complexity and intensity of regulation of international economic relations are inherently dependent on adequate constitutional structures through which such regulation is formed and implemented' through legislation and administrative and judicial protection of the rule of law.[6] For instance, Articles 29–31 of the Swiss Constitution protecting freedom of trade and industry could be rendered more effective if construed in conformity with Switzerland's international trade commitments and supplemented by more effective judicial protection of the rule of law. As EFTA and Switzerland's other FTAs include more precise trade liberalisation commitments than can be found in Swiss national laws, Thomas found it 'somewhat paradoxical' that the Swiss constitutional traditions of '*Rousseauean* ideas of unfettered sovereignty of democratic representation and the electorate (referendum)' prompt Swiss citizens to oppose stronger judicial protection of transnational market freedoms (eg as recognised in EEA and EU common market law), and that the EFTA and FTA dispute settlement provisions remained less developed than those in GATT and WTO law. '[J]udicial policies', he noted, 'need better coordination among Member States and institutions engaged in a process of integration.'[7] The Swiss traditions of direct and representative democracy invoking outdated legal 'neutrality principles' explain the Swiss opposition against joining the EEA or EU.

B. Structure–Substance Pairings in WTO Dispute Settlement Reforms

The dispute settlement provisions in GATT Article XXIII – and their confusingly vague distinction between violation complaints, non-violation complaints and 'situation complaints', without clear indication of the relevant legal standards, dispute settlement procedures and legal remedies – gave rise to the progressive 'judicialisation' of GATT/WTO dispute settlement practices since 1948:

- Initially, in 1948/49, some disputes submitted to the GATT contracting parties (usually the GATT Council), were settled based on 'rulings' given by the chairman or recommendations prepared by a GATT working party that included the parties to the dispute and other interested GATT contracting parties.[8]
- From 1949 up to the establishment of the GATT Office of Legal Affairs in 1983, dispute settlement findings were regularly elaborated by panels composed of three or, exceptionally, five trade experts from countries other than the parties to the dispute, with support for 'diplomatic trade jurisprudence' from the

[6] ibid 412–13.
[7] ibid 421.
[8] See the examples cited in EU Petersmann, *The GATT/WTO Dispute Settlement System. International Law, International Organizations and Dispute Settlement* (Kluwer, 1997) 248.

operational divisions in the GATT Secretariat in charge of the relevant trade matter (eg the Division for Agricultural Trade assisting in disputes over agricultural trade restrictions).

- Starting in 1983, a lawyer from the GATT Office of Legal Affairs complemented the Secretariat representative from the relevant operational division in assisting GATT panels in drafting the legal findings, thus prompting panel reports to increasingly justify their legal findings also by reference to the customary methods of treaty interpretation as codified in the 1969 Vienna Convention on the Law of Treaties.
- In 1989, the Legal Affairs Division replaced the previous GATT Office of Legal Affairs (which had been part of the Conference and General Affairs Division) in order to enhance consistency in panel proceedings, panel jurisprudence and GATT institutional matters, thereby responding to an increasing number of procedural delays, dissenting opinions among panellists, opposition by GATT contracting parties against the adoption of panel reports and additional demands for legal advice in the Uruguay Round negotiations.
- Since 1991, the Rules Division has provided specialist legal advice to panels dealing with trade remedy disputes (such as dumping, subsidies and safeguards issues), which account for almost half of WTO disputes.
- Between1995 and 2020, the Appellate Body (AB) Secretariat provided legal advice and assistance to the seven AB members appointed to decide appeals of panel cases.
- Following the US refusal to consent to the appointment of AB members, rendering the WTO AB dysfunctional since December 2019, and US pressures to dissolve the AB Secretariat, plurilateral agreements among more than 50 WTO members introduced a 'multi-party interim appeal arbitration' (MPIA arbitration) based on Article 25 DSU, which became a voluntarily agreed substitute for AB proceedings.

Thomas Cottier was part of the 'judicialisation journey' depicted above. He served on numerous GATT and WTO dispute settlement panels. He is also on the list of 10 arbitrators available for MPIA arbitration based on Article 25 DSU. His unique GATT/WTO dispute settlement experience and his personal commitment to due process of law also prompted Thomas to get involved in WTO deliberations on reforming WTO panel and appellate proceedings.

Yet, like other academics interested in protecting the WTO's rule-of-law system and in limiting the damage of mounting US trade protectionism, Thomas shared my own experience that proposing policy reforms from outside government was much less influential than our previous advice as lawyers working inside GATT and the WTO.

Thomas's suggestion to introduce a more deferential standard of reasonableness in appellate review of panel findings – while securing a continued leading AB role on what he called 'constitutional issues and fundamental principles' of the

WTO legal system[9] – reflected his search for adjusting dispute settlement procedures to the particular context of rule systems (such as the difficulties of amending WTO rules, the exceptionally short deadlines for AB proceedings).

C. Human and Constitutional Rights in International Economic Law

During my chairmanship of the International Trade Law Committee of the International Law Association, Thomas supported initiatives aimed at clarifying the relevance of human rights for interpreting and developing international economic law (IEL). The domestic political, legal and economic systems of the – now 166 – WTO members differ depending on whether they prioritise democratic constitutional nationalism (as in most democracies outside Europe), authoritarianism (as in China and Russia) or, as in the 27 EU Member States and four EFTA states, accept multilevel democratic and judicial protection of human rights by the different European democratic and judicial governance institutions. Analysing the different kinds of market, constitutional and governance failures in policy fields characterised by collective action dilemmas (such as international rule of law, division of labour through international trade and investments, climate change mitigation) is influenced by the reality of *constitutional pluralism*, with diverse governance types for protecting PGs:

- Anglo-Saxon democracies continue to prioritise civil, political and economic rights in their pursuit of liberalisation, deregulation, privatisation and financialisation of international trade and investments based on neoliberal trust in market competition, business-driven self-regulation and military power, complemented by increasing resort to nationalist industrial policies (eg the 2022 US Inflation Reduction Act, with trade discrimination against third countries);
- EU and EEA Member States prioritise 'social market economies' with multilevel democratic, executive and judicial institutions (like European parliaments, EU regulatory agencies, European courts, EU citizenship) protecting civil, political, economic, social and cultural rights more comprehensively (eg as codified in the EU Charter of Fundamental Rights (EUCFR)), complemented by common market, monetary, competition, environmental, commercial and foreign policy rules and institutions of a higher legal rank, comprehensive protection of human rights and judicial remedies, all of which offer a restraint

[9] *cf* T Cottier, 'Recalibrating the WTO Dispute Settlement System: Towards New Standards of Appellate Review' (2021) 24 *Journal of International Economic Law* 515, 517–18: 'While constitutional issues of systemic importance should be subject to full and de novo review by the AB, other issues could be reviewed under a rule of reason, along the lines of the WTO standard developed for reviewing factual determinations by domestic authorities: neither de novo review nor total deference.'

on the 'accountability gaps' of neoliberal abuses of power (such as the maximisation of shareholder interests in corporate governance);

- states with authoritarian power monopolies (like China, Iran, North Korea, Russia) disregard the 'embedded liberalism' underlying UN human rights law (HRL) and the WTO legal guarantees of non-discriminatory conditions of market competition; and
- 'emerging economies' (such as BRICS members Brazil, India and South Africa) prioritise their national development interests over collective countermeasures against violations of UN law (eg in Russia's wars against Ukraine, China's military extension in the South China Sea).

Each of these diverse 'value priorities' (like neoliberalism, ordoliberalism, authoritarian power monopolies, national industrialisation) and diverse constitutional contexts favours diverse 'international legal policies'. In the WTO, for instance,

- the business-driven US insistence on its own interpretations of WTO trade remedy rules, safeguard measures and security exceptions led to its blocking of the AB system, disrupting the compulsory WTO third-party adjudication and international rule of law;
- the EU's constitutional commitment to protecting the rule of law also in international relations prompted the EU Commission to initiate voluntary 'interim appellate arbitration' based on Article 25 DSU among now more than 50 WTO members;
- authoritarian WTO members (like China and Russia) started unprovoked military aggression against other WTO members (like Ukraine, the Philippines, Taiwan); and
- less-developed WTO members insist on 'special and differential treatment' and 'WTO waivers' (eg from the WTO Agreement on Trade-Related Intellectual Property Rights) responding to their development needs (eg non-reciprocal preferential treatment).

In 2001, my publications on making multilevel governance of PGs more democratically accountable by 'mainstreaming human rights into the law of international organizations' were attacked by the Australian lawyer Philip Alston on the ground that governments should implement the recommendations of UN human rights bodies in international economic institutions rather than interpret human rights in different governance contexts (eg of WTO law and institutions).[10] Thomas Cottier and Fred M Abbott organised two conferences on human rights and international

[10] *cf* EU Petersmann, 'Time for a United Nations "Global Compact" for Integrating Human Rights into the Law of Worldwide Organizations: Lessons from European Integration' (2002) 13 *European Journal of International Law* 621; EU Petersmann, 'Taking Human Dignity, Poverty and Empowerment of Individuals More Seriously: Rejoinder to Alston' (2002) 13 *European Journal of International Law* 845.

trade to explore the contested interrelationships between HRL and IEL.[11] As a member of UN and European human rights conventions, Switzerland accepts individual and state access to the European Court of Human Rights (ECtHR) and the legally binding force of ECtHR judgments also inside Swiss law. But the Swiss constitutional traditions of direct democracy (eg by means of referenda) and of 'consensus-based' federal governments limit 'normative individualism', legal primacy and the 'direct applicability' of European integration rules inside Switzerland. Cottier's case studies on the contextual relevance of the *Hertel Case* in the ECtHR for clarifying trade and unfair competition law[12] and of governmental human rights justifications for legitimising trade governance[13] illustrate how due process of law and mutually coherent interpretations in economic and human rights jurisprudence promoted rules-based dispute settlements more convincingly than Alston's prioritisation of politicised UN human rights recommendations, notwithstanding contestation of their legal relevance in GATT institutions.

Cottier perceives multilevel trade regulation as a five-storey house based on private and public, national, international and transnational regulation. Just as the EUCFR prescribes interpreting EU law consistent with the European Convention of Human Rights (ECHR), the human rights jurisprudence of the Court of Justice of the European Union (CJEU) enhanced the democratic input- and republican output-legitimacy of EU common market law with due respect for the ECHR and the diverse constitutional rights traditions in EU Member States. It remains to be seen whether the – so far few – references to human rights in WTO practice and jurisprudence will increase due to the references to human rights in European economic, environmental and social law and governance (like 'human rights clauses' in FTAs concluded by the EU with third WTO members).[14]

III. Europe's Ordoliberal Constitutionalism in a Multipolar World

Ordoliberalism as an interdisciplinary research methodology and political project emerged in Germany in response to the market, governance and constitutional failures disrupting the social, economic, political and legal order in Germany's 'Weimar Republic' since 1919. Following WWII, ordoliberal methodologies

[11] See T Cottier, J Pauwelyn and E Bürgi (eds), *Human Rights and International Trade* (Oxford University Press, 2005); FM Abbott, C Breining and T Cottier (eds), *International Trade and Human Rights* (Michigan University Press, 2006).

[12] See T Cottier, 'Linkages between Freedom of Expression and Unfair Competition Rules in International Trade: The *Hertel Case* and Beyond' in Abbott et al (n 11) 245–72.

[13] See T Cottier, 'Governance, Trade and Human Rights' in Cottier et al (n 11) 93–120.

[14] See EU Petersmann, 'The World Trading System, Human Rights and Sustainable Development' in J Hossain, Bhuiyan and M Rafiqul Islam (eds), *Business, Human Rights and Sustainable Development* (Brill, forthcoming) 169–91.

were extended to the task of constructing European integration law protecting a common market and democratic peace among the 27 EU Member States, four EFTA states and associated third states in Europe and beyond. Ordoliberal arguments were also frequent in the WTO (notably in the WTO Working Group on Trade and Competition and in WTO jurisprudence on interpreting WTO rules protecting non-discriminatory conditions of competition and prohibiting market distortions based on price-fixing cartel practices).[15] Thomas Cottier welcomed my proposal to publish a conference book on Constitutionalism and Transnational Governance Failures in his book series of the World Trade Institute, notably the book's method of 'ordoliberal constitutionalism' for enhancing the input- and output-legitimacy of multilevel governance of PGs.[16]

The answers offered by German ordoliberals after WWI and WWII from constitutional and human rights perspectives to the question of how to respond to constitutional, governance and market failures were elaborated in the unique *national* context of post-war Germany. The national post-war contexts of the 1920s and 1940s no longer exist in the global context of European integration and world trade in the twenty-first century. Hence, explicit references to the idiosyncrasies of German ordoliberalism (as proposed by the Freiburg school of law and economics and the Cologne school of social market economy) are rightly avoided in European and WTO decision-making processes.[17] Yet, ordoliberal principles and research methods – as applied not only by German ordoliberals,[18] but also by ordoliberals in France and other EU countries[19] – are still practised in many areas of European integration law and policies (notably common market rights, competition and 'social market economy' policies). Europe's humanist ordoliberal culture protecting a peaceful 'European society' (Article 2 of the Lisbon Treaty on European Union (TEU)) has been one of Europe's most important 'political inventions' different from liberalism outside Europe (eg in the Americas).

In Voltaire's novel *Candide*, Dr Pangloss explains the difference between poesy and prose. Candide acknowledges that he was not aware of having spoken prose throughout his life. Similarly, European policy-makers and academics often

[15] See EU Petersmann, 'Competition-oriented Reforms of the WTO World Trade System – Proposals and Policy Options' in R Zäch (ed), *Towards WTO Competition Rules* (Kluwer, 1999) 43–71.

[16] *cf* T Cottier. 'Preface' in EU Petersmann and A Steinbach (eds), *Constitutionalism and Transnational Governance Failures* (Brill, 2024) https://brill.com/display/title/69434. This book defines (eg on p 30) ordoliberalism by its emphasis on protecting normative and methodological individualism and non-discriminatory market competition by legal limitations of market failures, governance and constitutional failures, as discussed below.

[17] On the Brussels and Geneva schools of ordoliberalism, see EU Petersmann, *Transforming World Trade and Investment Law for Sustainable Development* (Oxford University Press, 2022) ch 4.

[18] See T Biebricher, W Bonefeld and P Nedergaard (eds), *The Oxford Handbook of Ordoliberalism* (Oxford University Press, 2022); see also my criticism of its neglect of European ordoliberalism in EU Petersmann, 'Neoliberalism, Ordoliberalism and the Future of Economic Governance' (2023) 26 *Journal of International Economic Law* 836.

[19] For a summary in English language of French ordoliberal views, see G Grégoire and X Miny (eds), *The Ideal of Economic Constitution in Europe. Genealogy and Overview* (Brill, 2022).

neglect the differences between rights-based ordoliberalism and utilitarian neoliberalism. Just as Socrates compared his discourses (aimed at provoking people to discover themselves) with the labours of a midwife assisting in the birth of new reasoning, greater awareness of Europe's ordoliberal traditions – as promoted by trade diplomats (like William Rappard and Franz Blankart) and professors (like Jan Tumlir and myself) at Geneva's Graduate Institute of International Studies – could reinvigorate the value premises of European integration, related research (also at Cottier's World Trade Institute) and what Article 2 Lisbon Treaty calls a 'European society' in which human rights, democracy and the rule of law prevail.

A. Principles and Methodologies of European Ordoliberalism

EU law prescribes a 'competitive social market economy' (eg in Article 3 TEU) and 'sustainable development' (eg in the same Article 3) as integral parts of a European 'society, in which pluralism, nondiscrimination, tolerance, justice, solidarity and equality between women and men prevail', and which is characterised by 'respect for human dignity, freedom, democracy, equality, the rule of law and respect for human rights, including the rights of persons belonging to minorities' (Article 2 TEU). This peaceful creation of a rules-based, pluralist and democratic 'European society' has been the most successful 'democratic revolution' in human history, avoiding the human rights violations following the eighteenth-century democratic American revolution (eg slavery and genocide of indigenous tribes) and French revolution (with its subsequent terror, eg vis-à-vis dissenters in the French National Assembly). EU law clarifies (eg in the EUCFR and the 2024 EU Corporate Sustainability Due Diligence Directive) that the EU legal concepts of 'market economy' and 'sustainable development' exclude neoliberal conceptions of business-driven (self-)regulation without comprehensive protection of human rights and judicial remedies (as inside the USA), as well as authoritarian conceptions of a 'socialist market economy' (eg in China). European ordoliberalism proceeds from 'constitutive principles' like (i) multilevel constitutional regulation of the interdependencies of social, economic, political and legal orders (as acknowledged in Article 2 TEU) by (ii) legally constructing a social market economy based on (iii) transnational rule of law (eg as prescribed in Articles 3 and 19 TEU) protecting (iv) human and constitutional rights of citizens (eg as codified in the EUCFR). Similar 'constitutive principles' and complementary 'regulative principles' (like monetary stability, competition and social policies) were already advocated by postwar German ordoliberals. As globalisation has rendered 'national constitutionalism 1.0' an incomplete governance system, the EU's multilevel democratic, economic, environmental and foreign policy constitutionalism limits the ubiquity of market failures, governance failures and constitutional failures in protecting PGs beyond state borders as demanded by EU citizens.[20]

The methodologies underlying these 'ordoliberal principles' recognised in EU law can be described as normative individualism, methodological individualism and multilevel democratic constitutionalism requiring active 'constitutional politics' and 'constitutional economics' aimed at promoting 'citizen sovereignty' in democratic markets and 'consumer sovereignty' in economic markets:

1. *Normative individualism* rejects authoritarianism and business-driven (self-) regulation of economic and democratic markets by acknowledging that respect for equal freedoms of citizens (like the human and constitutional rights codified in the EUCFR) requires social and democratic legitimacy based on protecting informed, individual consent by citizens in both economic and democratic markets.
2. *Methodological individualism* argues that decentralised economic and democratic markets with undistorted competition offer more efficient, citizen-driven information and sanctioning mechanisms for decentralised coordination of decision-making by free and equal individuals than authoritarian and business-driven coordination methods, which risk being more manipulated by abuses of public and private power.
3. *Multilevel democratic, republican and cosmopolitan constitutionalism* are considered necessary and mutually complementary for limiting the ubiquity of market failures, governance failures and constitutional failures in order to protect democratic and rights-based input-legitimacy, republican output-legitimacy and cosmopolitan rule of law in the multilevel ordering of societies and protection of PGs in a globally interdependent world. The EU mandate for a 'social market economy' protecting human and social rights must stabilise the social support for EU law in Europe's transnational society, economy and democratic polity.

[20] *cf* EU Petersmann, *Multilevel Constitutionalism for Multilevel Governance of Public Goods* (Hart Publishing, 2017), arguing for integrating the successive developments of 'national constitutionalism 1.0', 'international constitutionalism 2.0' and transnational 'cosmopolitan constitutionalism 3.0' as progressively done in European constitutional law. A Somek, *The Cosmopolitan Constitution* (Oxford University Press, 2014) focuses, by contrast, on successive, emancipatory changes of liberal, national 'We the people Constitutions' (like the US Constitution, focusing on negative freedoms, and the US common market as sources of freedom) to post-war 'human dignity Constitutions' (like Germany's 1949 Basic Law, protecting civil, political, economic and social rights, democratic self-government and rule-of-law) and national 'cosmopolitan Constitutions' in EU Member States (eg promoting multilevel administrative, democratic and judicial protection of common markets, common policies, human rights and the rule of law beyond national borders). On the EU's 'regulatory soft power' and global 'Brussels effects' of EU common market law, see EU Petersmann, 'European Economic and Environmental Constitutionalism as Driver for UN and WTO Sustainable Development Reforms' (2023) EUI Law Working Paper 2023-5.

B. The Future of Ordoliberal Market Regulation in Europe and Beyond

The EU legal approach to regulating the 'competitive social market economy' reflects ordoliberal – rather than neoliberal or authoritarian – values and methodologies. Ordoliberal strategies – such as protecting common market law and EU democracy by individual rights and judicial remedies[21] – promoted the realisation of a European society as social and legal realities. As many arguments developed in the national context of 'German ordoliberalism' may not be relevant in the very different European economic, democratic and legal contexts of the EU, references to national idiosyncrasies are rightly avoided. Ordoliberal methodologies for regulating market, governance and constitutional failures distinguish EU law from neoliberal and authoritarian market regulations. By defining the European society and 'social market economy' as a community of liberal values which the EU is required to defend against internal and external threats, the CJEU acknowledged the need for adopting EU 'crisis responses' (eg in the fields of health and environmental regulation) if social and economic interactions in the private realm ('market failures') or political 'governance' and/or 'constitutional failures' undermine European integration.[22] As illustrated by the widespread opposition from business to the ongoing UN negotiations on an international treaty on business and human rights, many business actors find ordoliberal principles easier to support than politicised human and labour rights compromises in UN bodies.

Conceptions of liberty, democracy, society, economy and foreign policy inside and outside the EU – notably in the UK and the USA – diverge. The multilevel democratic, economic, environmental, legal and judicial constitutionalism inside the EU is rejected by the nationalist constitutionalism inside the UK and the USA, as illustrated by Martin Loughlin's recent book, *Against Constitutionalism*.[23] Likewise, many developing country democracies – like India, South Africa and Indonesia – prioritise constitutional nationalism and reject the transnational constitutionalism which European citizens demand inside the EU.

[21] *cf* EU Commission, *70 Years of EU Law. A Union for its Citizens* (EU Commission, 2023).

[22] *cf* Loic Azoulay, 'The Law of European Society' (2022) 59 *CML Rev* 203.

[23] *cf* M Loughlin, *Against Constitutionalism* (Oxford University Press, 2022), who criticises the European 'rights revolution', 'judicial revolution' and 'invisible constitutions' for protecting a new 'constitutional legality' undermining his conception of Anglo-Saxon democracy (represented by 'the Crown, the Lords and the Commons'). Loughlin claims that the people and their elected representatives, rather than citizens and courts of justice invoking and defending human and constitutional rights, should define the nation's political identity and make its most important policy decisions (124–35). His focus on nation states neglects the democratic demand of citizens for protecting transnational PGs as a task of 'living democratic constitutionalism'; he also ignores the collective action problems of transnational rule of law, which require multilevel protection of human and constitutional rights and transnational constitutional, parliamentary, participatory and deliberative democracy as prescribed in EU law (eg Arts 9–12 TEU).

'Sovereign equality' of states and related legal freedoms foster 'regulatory competition', with frequent distortions by subsidies and extraterritorial power politics by stronger actors, for example if state-capitalist countries distort competition by state subsidies; or when the US Trump administration welcomed the adoption in the WTO Dispute Settlement Body of 'constructive WTO dispute settlement rulings' supporting its legal complaints vis-à-vis other WTO members, but rejected similar WTO dispute settlement findings against it on the ground that the rulings create 'new obligations' not consented to by their government.[24] Switzerland's constitutional traditions of direct and representative democracy and consensus-based federal governance render EU membership of Switzerland unlikely. The regulatory competition among authoritarian, neoliberal and ordoliberal policies also impedes 'constitutional reforms' of the WTO legal and trading system.

C. Europe's Economic and Environmental Constitutionalism as a Driver for Plurilateral Sustainable Development Reforms

The creation of a peaceful 'European society' respecting human rights, democracy and the rule of law transformed EU law into the most effective peace treaty ever concluded in Europe. This 'constitutional transformation' was made possible by the democratic and judicial transformations of the EU treaties into multilevel democratic, economic and environmental constitutionalism enabling multilevel democratic legislation, administration and judicial protection of transnational rule of law progressively implementing the constitutional principles codified in the TEU and the EUCFR. A 'constitutional approach' also underlies the UN Secretary-General's 'Common Agenda' for responding to the 'triple crisis of climate disruption, biodiversity loss and pollution destroying our planet', for instance its emphasis on the need 'to renew the social contract between Governments and their people and within societies' and to view 'human rights as a problem-solving measure' for a 'renewed social contract anchored in a comprehensive approach to human rights';[25] without such a social contract at the national level anchored in human rights, transnational cooperation across countries cannot remain effective.[26] Yet, just as national democratic and republican constitutionalism depend on successive constitutional and democratic legislation and administrative and judicial protection of the rule of law, so too does multilevel governance of PGs depend on transnational legislative, administrative and judicial implementation of agreed constitutional principles in domestic, international and transnational legal

[24] On the illegal blocking and contradictory criticism by the USA of the WTO dispute settlement system, see Petersmann, *Transforming World Trade* (n 17) ch 3.

[25] 'Our Common Agenda', Report of the Secretary-General (UN 2021) 3, 6 and 22.

[26] ibid para 10.

systems. Multilevel UN governance of PGs remains much less effectively implemented than EU governance, notably in UN Member States with authoritarian and neoliberal policies.

Europe's multilevel democratic and republican constitutionalism enabled the EU to respond to UN and WTO governance failures by initiating reforms such as the plurilateral MPIA arbitration system as a temporary substitute for the dysfunctional WTO AB system and the EU's carbon emission trading system (ETS). The transitional application of the ETS-related Carbon Border Adjustment Mechanism (CBAM) since 2024 prompts ever more third states to introduce, often with assistance from the EU, their own ETS and CBAMs to avoid paying, as of 2026, carbon border duties to the EU. Europe's dynamically evolving 'human rights constitutionalism', and economic and environmental constitutionalism – including 'digital constitutionalism' protecting data privacy and other fundamental rights in the EU's digital platform regulations in the EU Digital Services Act and Digital Market Act[27] – remain contested by third countries with diverse constitutional priorities (like censorship and data localisation requirements in China and business-driven self-regulation by US tech companies). Some EU common market regulations have global 'Brussels effects' if access of foreign goods, services and investments to the EU market is made conditional on compliance with EU fundamental rights and common market regulations (like EU product and production standards).[28] Yet, the EU's 'soft power of attraction' (eg through successive EU enlargements, conditional association policies and FTAs with third countries) is no substitute for its underdeveloped 'hard power' (eg in terms of military and fiscal capacities) to protect European values and PGs. Europe's costly 'social model', underdeveloped capital markets and protection of EU welfare standards entail competitive disadvantages.

IV. Constitutional Pluralism and the Need for Institutionalising Public Reason

The reality and legitimacy of 'constitutional pluralism' – as illustrated by Switzerland's *sui generis* approach to European integration – entails that countries

[27] For details, see A Bradford, *Digital Empires: The Global Battle to Regulate Technology* (Cambridge University Press, 2023).

[28] *cf* A Bradford, *The Brussels Effect: How the European Union Rules the World* (Cambridge University Press, 2020), according to whom it is wrong to cast the EU 'as an aging and declining power' (xiii) beset by slow growth (267). The most fundamental constraint on EU power – its lack of autonomous capacity to mobilise fiscal and military power to project power in a traditional sense – compelled the EU to mobilise 'regulatory power' based on an extensive apparatus of rules to govern the Union's large internal market (16, 36). In order to access that market, external actors must meet the EU's often stringent regulatory demands; this generates a broader compliance pull, with strong extraterritorial ramifications. The global impact of this regime demonstrates how the Union is 'an influential superpower that shapes the world in its image' (xiii).

with diverse constitutional traditions respond in diverse ways to the task of constituting, limiting, regulating and justifying governance institutions and rules of a higher legal rank protecting democratic support for collective protection of the SDGs. For instance, state-trading enterprises from China and other authoritarian countries criticise EU state subsidy regulations and the EU Corporate Sustainability Due Diligence Directive requiring business compliance with EU human rights and environmental regulations not only inside the EU, but also in their transnational supply chains. Constitutional lawyers like Thomas Cottier know that law is a response to the 'bounded rationality' of human beings: as famously stated by James Madison, law and governance would be unnecessary if people were angels. Diverse national constitutions lead to diverse ways of popular self-government, for example if social contracts are inspired by JJ Rousseau (as in Switzerland), or by the libertarian human rights conceptions of J Locke (as in the USA), rather than by Kantian 'cosmopolitan constitutionalism' (as, arguably, inside the EU) or by communist power monopolies (as inside China).

Authoritarian rulers suppressing democratic liberties illustrate the 'paradox of liberty', as discussed by Plato in his book *The Laws*, and more recently in Karl Popper's book *The Open Society and Its Enemies*. Equal freedoms among people with unequal capacities, resources and political priorities risk being destroyed by abuses of public and private power, as illustrated by the authoritarian suppression of human and democratic rights in many UN Member States. Exploring and answering the question of why a transnational society could successfully be created inside the EU over the past 75 years requires understanding the 'political psychology' justifying pre-commitment theories for 'constitutional hand-tying'.

Thomas Cottier's foundation of the World Trade Institute in Berne, like William Rappard's foundation of the Graduate Institute of International Studies in Geneva, institutionalised public reason through interdisciplinary research on the governance of public goods. Like Rappard, Cottier acknowledges the political importance of continuing the ordoliberal search, since the 1920s, to place coherent legal restraints on market failures (such as restraints on anti-competitive conduct, harmful externalities, social injustices, information asymmetries or PGs) and related governance failures (eg to protect PGs like human and social rights, monetary and price stability, the rule of law) and constitutional failures. Swiss traditions of direct and representative democracy may limit respect for ordoliberal 'normative individualism' (ie values should be derived from informed, individual consent to be protected by human and democratic rights of citizens) and multilevel democratic constitutionalism.

Yet, Switzerland's respect for judgments of the ECtHR and for compulsory WTO adjudication reflects recognition of the need for constitutional rules and institutions of a higher legal rank limiting abuses of power by protecting human rights and transnational rule of law. Cottier's insistence on 'structure–substance pairing' reflects the need for justifying due process of law and 'balancing' democratic and legal conceptions of the rule of law. While the 'constitutional trio' of individualism, liberty and equality underlying classical liberalism might have justified neutrality vis-à-vis legitimately diverse conceptions of a good life, Europe's prioritisation of the multilevel human, constitutional and democratic rights of citizens challenges such 'neutrality'; it excludes authoritarian power monopolies suppressing human and democratic rights, and limits neoliberal, constitutional nationalism (eg relying on business- and market-driven self-regulation, with greater social inequalities and less protection of economic, social and cultural rights).

The increasing inability of UN and WTO governance to protect PGs (like human rights and transnational rule of law) renders the future evolution of ordoliberal principles in European integration and IEL uncertain. Will global health, environmental and social crises prompt WTO reforms limiting market failures (like environmental degradation and social injustices) and governance failure (like insufficient protection of human rights and related PGs)? How can Europe's 'competitive social market economy' be protected against neoliberal and state-capitalist market distortions and help workers, consumers and producers adjust to social disruptions? Can functionally limited 'republican constitutionalism' be extended to multilevel environmental governance and de-carbonisation of economies notwithstanding disagreements on democratic constitutionalism (as revealed by Brexit and by Switzerland's *Sonderweg*)? Can UN human rights law and international judicial protection of the rule of law be made more effective in a multipolar world dominated by power politics? Can 'constitutional politics' and 'constitutional economics' be maintained in UN and WTO governance of PGs if authoritarian and neoliberal governments disregard UN and WTO law? Will Europe's ordoliberal order increasingly diverge from Anglo-Saxon neoliberalism (eg prioritising business-driven liberalisation, deregulation, privatisation and financialisation of economies without effective regulation of market failures, related governance failures and constitutional failures) and from authoritarian orders (eg characterised by concentration rather than separation of powers)? Can transnational 'regulatory competition' (eg as illustrated by Brexit, China's state subsidies for 'greening its economy') protect global PGs by distorting international competition?

The more democratic voters remain 'rationally ignorant' towards complex, multilevel governance of global PGs, the more important becomes Europe's ordoliberal constitutionalism for limiting abuses of power and decarbonising and digitalising Europe's common market by protecting rights and judicial remedies of European citizens to hold governments and business actors legally more accountable. Thomas Cottier supports constructing democratic constitutionalism as a 'five-storey house', committing citizens to multilevel 'institutionalization of public reason'. The democratic revolutions in America and in France during the 1780s illustrated how even democracies may neglect human rights (eg of slaves and indigenous tribes in the USA) and 'democratic terror' (eg in France). Since WWII, decolonisation, universal franchise, public education, the welfare-enhancing trading system and social policies have promoted an increasing number of democracies. Why is it that, during the past decades of geopolitical rivalries and 'polycrises', authoritarian strongmen and populism have succeeded, once again, in undermining democratic support in 'illiberal democracies' and authoritarian states like China and Russia?

The transformative constitutionalism in Switzerland and in the EU proceeded more peacefully than the violent, anti-feudal French and American democratic revolutions and communist revolutions. Yet, the 'bounded rationality' of human beings renders the process of limiting market, governance and constitutional failures a perennial challenge also within democracies, as illustrated by social injustices and other neoliberal governance failures inside the USA. Europe's citizen-driven common market law was interpreted by ordoliberal Europeans (like EJ Mestmäcker and myself) as 'cosmopolitan international law' in terms of Kantian legal theory. Europe's multilevel democratic constitutionalism also justifies (eg in terms of Rawls's theory of democracy) implementing rights-based constitutional contracts among citizens through multilevel democratic legislation, administration, adjudication and an international 'law of peoples' institutionalising 'cosmopolitan public reason'. As Europe's multilevel democracy remains imperfect, republican constitutionalism and 'common law constitutionalism' offer additional justifications and reform strategies.[29]

'Democratic constitutional pluralism' may justify Switzerland's *Sonderweg* in European integration as long as it does not undermine UN law (eg by Swiss invocations of outdated 'neutrality' concepts neglecting the *erga omnes* UN prohibitions of use of force) and EU law (eg by claiming unreasonable 'Swiss exceptions'). Switzerland's federal 'bottom-up constitutionalism' confirms the EU's experience that respect for individual rights, participatory democracy and judicial remedies remains the indispensable foundation for collective protection of PGs. Yet normative and methodological individualism must be reconciled with the fact that globalisation has transformed *national* into *transnational* PGs requiring multilevel governance by governmental and non-governmental organisations supported by citizens. Swiss leadership for the needed governance reforms depends on people like William Rappard and Thomas Cottier promoting construction of 'multilevel constitutional houses' for peaceful cooperation among citizens across national frontiers.

[29] See EU Petersmann, 'Strengthening Multilevel Governance of Public Goods through Democratic and Republican Constitutionalism' (2022) 11 *Cambridge Journal of International Law* 180.

PART IV

The Living Legacy of Thomas Cottier

17

The World Trade Institute – Swiss Soft Power at its Best

ARTHUR APPLETON

My contribution to Professor Cottier's Festschrift comes from a privileged vantage point. Since 2004, I have taught at the World Trade Institute (WTI, the Institute), which he established. I have served on the Institute's Advisory Board for more than 10 years and engaged in numerous Swiss government-sponsored consulting projects around the world on behalf of the WTI. My involvement has permitted me to observe the Institute's evolution and to witness firsthand the effect that the WTI has had on its students, alumni, staff, Switzerland and governments and officials near and far. My involvement has also permitted me to befriend many unique and talented individuals, in particular Professor Cottier.

When Professor Cottier founded the WTI in 1999, he had a clear and progressive vision – to develop a world-class academic and research institute that would train future government officials and trade practitioners. He was riding what was then a large wave. The World Trade Organization (WTO) was in its infancy. Globalisation was gaining momentum. There was broadly shared optimism that trade could unite countries, bridge differences, help maintain peace and further economic development. This optimism was not misplaced. Trade has had many salubrious effects, despite globalisation's current retrenchment.

During Professor Cottier's tenure as the WTI's Managing Director, he developed a challenging curriculum characterised by several very un-Swiss innovations: (i) he recruited many foreign visiting professors – often leaders in their field – who would travel to Bern to teach weekly modules; (ii) he decided that all modules would be taught solely in English; (iii) he insisted that law be combined with economics and political science/political economy – a fundamental factor, as competence in trade requires an understanding of both law and economics, as well as an appreciation of political ramifications; (iv) he organised weekly take-home examinations that were due in 24 hours – which, when combined with the required readings, ruined the weekends of bright student cohorts but accustomed them to the rigours of the working world; and finally (v) he decided that students would pay significant fees to attend – which meant that WTI students had to make a financial investment in their education and subsequent professional trajectories.

Thomas's vision resulted in a very intensive and highly original programme that has left its mark on the world. Thomas made the WTI into a pre-eminent centre of education, emphasising the legal, political and economic aspects of international trade. As a result, the Institute has produced more than 600 graduates from approximately 110 different countries. WTI alumni have gone on to successful careers as trade ministers, ambassadors, academics, international civil servants, law firm partners, international consultants and in-house legal counsel. They work as attorneys, economists, political scientists, trade advisors, consultants and activists, and in many other fields. It is seldom that I visit a country and do not run into a WTI alumnus in a senior role in government, industry, international organisations, academia or civil society.

The success of WTI graduates and of the many experts trained in the WTI's tailor-made programmes speaks for itself. But this success obscures another of Professor Cottier's remarkable achievements – one that many Swiss citizens may not appreciate. Whether intentional or not, Professor Cottier greatly expanded Swiss soft power globally – by this, I mean Thomas helped to expand Switzerland's political, economic, social and cultural influence and prestige internationally in a friendly and non-coercive manner. By spending one year in Switzerland, WTI students from around the world are exposed to 'all the good' that Switzerland offers, and even more importantly they carry Swiss ideals back to their homelands.

This reflection requires some elaboration. What does Switzerland gain when foreign students spend a year in Bern? The benefits are abundant. In addition to exposing students to some of the best professors in the trade field (a topic I will return to later), one year in Switzerland exposes students to daily life in a highly developed and well-governed country that has benefitted greatly from international rules governing the cross-border exchange of goods, services, people and ideas.

Switzerland is indeed a model of good governance. It is safe, prosperous and environmentally conscious, and has been largely peaceful for more than 700 years. Its infrastructure, in particular public transportation, is superb. Its healthcare is excellent, and its education is world class and affordable. Swiss citizens are law-abiding. Switzerland takes care of its poor, accepts its fair share of refugees and offers opportunities for all socio-economic classes, from financial and industrial executives to tradesmen and farmers. Students leave Bern with the knowledge that even a small country of only nine million, with different languages, religions and ethnic groups, and no appreciable natural resources other than its human capital, can thrive. WTI students inevitably leave Bern as unofficial Swiss ambassadors. They take their knowledge and appreciation of 'Swissness' to all corners of the world. Many even return later with their families to visit. This is soft power at its very best.

We should not underestimate the importance of Swiss soft power and the role the WTI has played in its advancement. Switzerland survives in its present form based on its reputation worldwide. Just as the *Swiss* Federal Institute of Technology in Lausanne (EPFL) and its German-speaking brethren in Zurich – ETHZ – serve as academic beacons for the promotion of science, so too does the WTI serve as an academic beacon for the promotion of international trade law, economics and political science. Swiss politicians from the 26 cantons would gain from a visit to the WTI. They would be impressed by what Thomas and the Institute have done to advance Swiss academic, commercial and political interests worldwide.

Thomas was also instrumental in developing links with some of the best and brightest trade experts worldwide. He brought in prominent trade academics and professionals from around the world to teach week-long modules. They came from universities, international organisations and law firms. These experts not only promoted the WTI, but upon returning from the beautiful city of Bern, they would also promote Switzerland. The fame of the WTI's early faculty, who came to the WTI out of friendship and respect for Thomas, served as a powerful magnet to attract many talented international students and faculty members. While the teaching styles of faculty members could differ markedly, their cutting-edge expertise was truly exceptional and a key point of attraction. I still remember the frustration of students when, only occasionally, a faculty luminary had to cancel an appearance due to sickness or scheduling conflicts. The fame of the WTI's faculty helped make the WTI distinctive and an academic success.

When one works with Thomas, one realises that he is unique in many ways. His openness to European and North American points of view meant not only that WTI students benefitted from a broad spectrum of ideas and different teaching styles, but that Swiss interests were also represented on the foreign agendas of some of the most important WTO members. This helped advance Swiss positions related to intellectual property, trade in services, foreign investment and agriculture – all important to Swiss political stability and economic prosperity. Thomas's experience as a Swiss negotiator, a WTO panellist and a trade law consultant also provided students with a unique perspective – an insider's understanding of the WTO and other international organisations.

Thomas also accomplished a great deal by working closely with established Swiss officials and institutions. By forging close links with the Swiss State Secretariat for Economic Affairs (SECO), Thomas was able to match well-deserving WTI students from developing countries with Swiss scholarships and to build lasting academic partnerships with trade policy programmes in a host of emerging countries. He also forged strong working relationships between the WTI, the Swiss National Centre of Competence in Research and the Swiss National Science Foundation. These links allowed talented PhD students to contribute to important economic, political and legal projects that advanced their careers, academia and Swiss interests. Such contributions also played an important part in the reputation and success of the WTI in its formative years and left an important mark on generations of WTI researchers as well as on Swiss policy.

Lastly, Thomas created a strong link between the WTI and the WTO, the World Bank and the United Nations Conference on Trade and Development. Senior staff from these organisations have long taught at the Institute. They give guest lectures and they hire WTI graduates as interns, many of whom have gone on to become professionals in the trade field. These organisations, along with prominent law firms, multinational companies and non-governmental organisations, have all gained from the knowledge and rigorous training of WTI graduates.

As we all know, Switzerland is a small country. It has few national resources. It is dependent on market access (low tariffs) for its exports, and tariff protection for its politically powerful agricultural sector, which must cope with a lack of arable land. Switzerland is also dependent on intellectual property protection for its important pharmaceutical and chemical industries – exemplified by Roche and Novartis – and trademark protection to shield its luxury watch industry and other important brands such as Richemont and Nestlé. Lastly, Switzerland requires market access for its vital service sector, including its international banking and financial services industry, its commodity traders and its engineering firms. In short, Switzerland is trade dependent. Thomas recognised this early, and his genius was linking this knowledge with the emergence of the WTO and the protection WTO rules offer for the above sectors.

It goes without saying that Thomas did not accomplish all of the above on his own. From the beginning, he was aided by devoted staff members and colleagues who deserve mention. For many years, Margrit Vetter, who headed Institute administration, was the unofficial mother and guidance counsellor to foreign students. She was also the repository of WTI's history and served as a mentor on what worked and what could be improved. Her loyalty to the WTI and to Thomas was important to the Institute's success. Likewise, Simon Evenett, Roberto Rios, Nicole Pohl and Pierre Sauvé, each of whom served as Director of Studies, made important contributions to WTI's success and expanded its many partnerships, as did many other present and past staff members, too numerous to name here. Lastly, I would be remiss if I did not mention the important role played by Ambassador Luzius Wasescha, who is missed by all of us. Luzius made many contributions to the WTI, and while serving as the Chair of the Institute's Advisory Board made everyone realise that diplomacy is largely about understanding the needs of others before you can successfully pursue one's own. Thomas learned this lesson well – the WTI is a testament to his understanding of the needs of others, sometimes at the cost of his own interests.

Credit must also be given to the WTI staff and faculty, led by Pierre Sauvé, who engaged in tremendous outreach efforts under SECO's auspices – often in SECO priority countries. They taught and consulted on trade issues in Asia, Africa and Latin America, and mentored a generation of trade scholars and practitioners from developing countries. Again, the value to Switzerland in doing this is incalculable. These academic efforts, largely staffed by Swiss citizens and residents, continue to generate good will and to cast Switzerland in a very positive light. This work abroad also helped to attract students to the WTI and to other Swiss educational institutions, and continues to attract tourism, which is vital to the Swiss economy.

Having said many important things about Thomas and what he produced at the WTI, I am the first to recognise that to preserve and promote his legacy, and that of the Institute, there is still much to be done in the trade field in general, and at the WTI in particular. Thomas's academic and institutional endeavours were largely focused on government institutions, including the role that international organisations and government negotiators play in the creation and implementation of the trade-related legal framework. As a result, WTI students now staff international organisations and government offices worldwide. However, globalisation's retrenchment, and the failure of recent WTO Ministerial Conferences due in part to the WTO's increasingly untenable consensus system, have meant that preferential trade agreements are assuming greater importance. Switzerland is dependent on its network of preferential trade ties with the EU, EFTA, India and China, among others, and is actively negotiating new agreements – for example with the UK. Looking forward, the WTI will need to increase its focus on bilateral and regional trade agreements in general, and the EU in particular, to stay relevant.

In the same vein, the WTI should sharpen its focus on the relationship between trade rules and the business community – the ultimate beneficiary of many trade agreements and a source of career opportunities for students. Often academics focus on trade and development but forget that this development comes through the work of the business community, where many WTI graduates will eventually find employment. This does not mean abandoning the study of trade and development, or other trade-related fields such as trade and environment, labour and human rights. But it entails building on Thomas's legacy by focusing more on the bigger picture – the role of the business community in trade matters.

As business school professors and graduates know, multinational enterprises are not only a fertile source of jobs and potential benefactors; such enterprises are also ripe for academic study. Of course, WTI students must understand trade agreements before they can focus on business issues, but there are many trade-related business issues that are ready for examination. For example, more attention should be given to rules affecting the construction and management of global supply chains, and the role that supply chain resilience plays in economic success. Greater focus should also be placed on the commercial aspects of trade, such as trade finance, customs, taxation and trade documentation, as well as on the general trade-related regulations that affect businesses, such as the EU Carbon Border Adjustment Mechanism and its Corporate Sustainability Due Diligence Directive.

Just as the IMD Business School has become a beacon for the better understanding of the financial and management issues that affect multinational businesses, so should the WTI equip its students with a better understanding of how trade and investment rules affect international companies, including important Swiss companies active in banking, financial services, reinsurance, food production, pharmaceutical, biotech, mining, engineering, luxury goods and logistics. Efforts are needed to reach out to these companies to study how their businesses are shaped by the existing and emerging trade architecture, including the EU rules mentioned above. These areas are the new dimensions of trade studies – they are legal in nature – but have financial implications suitable for economists to study, and important social and environmental effects for political scientists to examine. While one should applaud and show appreciation for how the WTI has influenced and staffed governments and international organisations worldwide, the time has come to focus attention on the private sector and the job opportunities that WTI students are likely to find there. If such outreach is properly developed and managed, private sector firms with trade interests may even become the WTI's natural allies, partners and benefactors.

In closing, perhaps the greatest complement that I can offer to Thomas is to let him know that every time I attend one of his lectures, I learn something new and important. He continues to be an inspiring teacher and confidant whose approach to trade and political issues is global in nature. While a strong advocate for Swiss interests, Thomas sees many issues from a broader, cosmopolitan and multilayered perspective, knowing and caring what political, economic and trade decisions mean for people from all walks of life and at all levels of development. It is an honour to contribute to Thomas's Festschrift, even if I believe that the mandatory Swiss retirement age is set too young, and that I should have been able to delay writing this chapter by 10 more years!

18

Thomas Cottier and the Development of International Trade Law

GARY HORLICK[1]

I. Introduction

Thomas's scholarship and writings, and the lengthy research and discussions they demonstrate, are one of his obvious sources of influence on the development of international trade law. The other essays in this book discuss that impact at length, so this appreciation (among the lines of those I wrote for Bob Hudec[2] and John Jackson[3]) will focus on other important ways he has influenced the development of international trade law.

II. GATT and WTO Activities

Professor Cottier to date has served on four General Agreement on Tariffs and Trade (GATT) and nine World Trade Organization (WTO) dispute panels:

GATT:

EEC – Apples (1989), L6513;
USA – Magnesium (1993), SCM174;

[1] I first met Thomas when we were members of the International Law Association's Committee on International Trade Law, which included, in addition to Thomas, other giants in the field, including Debra Steger, John Jackson, Mitsuo Matsushita, Amy Porges, Georgio Sacerdoti, Ernst-Ulrich Petersmann, Fred Abbott, Petros Mavroidis, Mary Footer, Peter Tobias Stoll, Markus Krajewski and Meredith Kolsky Lewis, as well as many, many others. Bizarrely, the International Law Association (ILA) decided to terminate the Committee in 2023, just as interest in the field, and pressing developments, made participation by the ILA more important.

[2] Professor Robert Hudec, my law school contracts professor; see the long first footnote in Gary N Horlick, *Problems in the Compliance Structure of the WTO Dispute Resolution Process, in The Political Economy of International Law: Essays in Honor of Robert E Hudec* (D Kennedy and J Southwick eds, Cambridge University Press, 2002).

[3] Gary N Horlick, 'John Jackson as a Resource for Scholars and Others' (2016) 19 *Journal of International Economic Law* 401.

USA – Taxes on Autos (1994), DS 31/4;
EEC – Bananas II (1994), DS 38/R;

WTO:

USA – Underwear (Panel) (1996), DS 24;
EC – Hormones (Panel/USA) (1997), DS 26;
EC – Hormones (Panel/Canada) (1997), DS 48;
India – Patents (Panel) (1998), DS 50;
Canada – Renewable Energy/Canada – Feed-In Tariff (Panel) (2012), DS 412, 426;
China – Cellulose Pulp (2017), DS 483;
Thailand – Cigarettes (Philippines), Article 21.5 (2019), DS 371;
Thailand – Cigarettes (Philippines), Article 21.5 II (2019), DS 371;
India – Sugar and Sugarcane (2021), DS 579, 580, 581.

In this regard, he exemplifies the respect WTO members have for the Swiss tradition of mutuality.[4] Many of those reports are crucial to understanding WTO law and practice, including panels dealing with sanitary and phytosanitary standards (SPS), the Agreement on Trade-Related Aspects of Intellectual Property Rights, national treatment and taxation, quota allocation, antidumping and countervailing duties, and renewable energy. Panel reports are the product (and responsibility) of all three panel members, and when adopted by the Dispute Settlement Body, they became part of the WTO's legal record. So, it is a safe guess that a fair amount of that record reflects Thomas's analysis and drafting.

In addition, as discussed in greater detail below, Professor Cottier was the founder of the World Trade Institute (WTI) at the University of Bern, and partly inspired the creation of the Academy of International Economic Law and Policy at the University of Barcelona. After only 25 years of the WTI, its graduates are almost certainly the largest number of graduates of any programme working in the WTO Secretariat.

It is worth noting here that Professor Cottier is generous with his time, talking with staff at the missions of WTO members, the WTO Secretariat, academics and others focused on international economic law (IEL). Those informal conversations may influence the developments in that field as much as or more than his impressive published output.

[4] Switzerland has supplied 59 WTO panel members, third only to New Zealand and Australia (by contrast, the EU Member States have had 68, but that includes some before joining the EU; China, a relatively recent entrant, has had two; and the USA has had 17, of which at least three were the author, presumably because he could read and listen in Spanish, thus triggering enormous savings by not translating the voluminous record in many of these cases).

III. The World Trade Institute of the University of Bern

Thomas founded the WTI in 1999. He, along with many talented colleagues, secured the funding and staff that built it into what it is now. His vision that IEL goes much deeper and is much broader than some thought has helped expand the view of what it is today. The result in only 25 years is that there are about 600 graduates of WTI programmes. These alumnae form a vibrant presence in the ministries, international organisations, universities, businesses, non-governmental organisations and bars of the world. Many other high-level programmes within other universities provide a menu of excellent IEL courses, but the WTI's focus on the broadest curriculum of IEL, including all of WTO law, means the WTI's year-long master's programmes are among the few places where one can mention to students the acronyms GPA and PSI and see a very wide understanding of the content of those terms.

In addition, the WTI is a centre of scholarship, with 20–25 PhD candidates at any one time working on expanding their knowledge in the IEL context. Dissertation topics have included:

- 'Exceptions that Protect National Security and Public Order in IIAS: Challenges and Prospects for Latin American States' (2014)
- 'SPS in Eurasian Economic Union, Comparison with WTO SPS and EU law' (2017)
- 'The Balance between Foreign Investor Protection and State Regulation under New Treaties: China as a Host State' (2016)
- 'The Role of Law Reform Programs for Economic Growth' (2016)
- 'The BRICS: A New Source of International Intellectual Property Standards?' (2016)
- 'Impact of Trade Liberalisation on Economic Growth in Landlocked Low-Income Countries' (2016)
- 'The Effects of Investment and Trade Agreements on Foreign Direct Investment, Technology Transfer and Global Value Chains Participation' (2015)
- 'Non-tariff Measures in International Trade – Perspectives on Costs and Benefits' (2016)
- 'Essays in Computational Econometrics' (2021)
- 'Empirical Essays in International Trade' (2018)
- 'Essays on the International Trade of Services' (2023)

And more are on the way.

It is also worth noting that the WTI has no 'majority' group of students, as happens in some programmes. The geographic diversity leads to vigorous debate but without national blocs. It helps that students encounter each other frequently in Bern, although the WTI has also been a noted innovator in the use of several different forms of distance learning.

IV. World Trade Forums (WTF)

Linked to the WTI's study programme was its role as the convener of major international discussions of important issues in IEL under the title 'World Trade Forum' (WTF). These, under Professor Cottier's leadership, were often very far-sighted: the first WTF in 1998, for example, dealt with the status and activity of state enterprises, which are discussed even more now than in 1998. Note, too, the event on International Trade and Human Rights in 2005. Further Forum topics were:

2006	'International Trade in Services: New Perspectives on Liberalization, Regulation and Development'
2007	'International Trade on a Warming Globe'
2008	'Food Crisis and the World Trading System'
2009	'Making Decisions at the World Trade Organization: Past, Present and Beyond Doha'
2010	'Trade Governance in the Digital Age'
2011	'New Directions and Emerging Challenges in International Investment Law and Policy'
2012	'The Rule of Law in Monetary Affairs: Lessons from the Trade Field'
2013	'Trade Cooperation: The Purpose, Design and Effects of Preferential Trade Agreements'
2014	'International Trade in Electricity and the Greening Economy
2015	'20 Years of the World Trade Organization'
2016	'Behind-the-Border Policies and Global Trade'
2017	'Trade Policy in Turbulent Times'
2018	'Trade, Development and Sustainability'
2019	'Multilateralism at Risk'
2020	'The Future of Trade Policy and External Cooperation: Is Soft Power Passé?'
2021	'Digital, Green and Open? Global Trade Policy at a Crossroads'.
2022	'What Does the Future Hold for Trade Policy?'
2023	'Non-economic Objectives and International Trade'

Finally, it should be noted that Thomas and his family have been genial hosts over decades to literally hundreds of members of the ILA International Trade Committee, GATT and WTO Secretariat people, and national missions and people in Geneva for meetings on IEL themes, all of which have gone better with Thomas's warm hospitality.

19

Thomas Cottier, the Myth of Ulysses and the Evolution of International Economic Law

ROBERTO ECHANDI

A long time ago, I heard an especially useful analogy summarising the political economy of international economic law (IEL). It referred to Ulysses' plight in Greek mythology. Ulysses (or Odysseus) faced numerous challenges during his journey back from the Trojan War. One of these was navigating past the sirens, mythical creatures whose enchanting songs lured sailors to their doom. Once the sirens started to sing, anyone who heard their song was bewitched by its sweetness, and they are drawn to where they were like iron to a magnet. Thus, ships would smash upon rocks as sharp as spears, and the sailors would join the many victims of the sirens in a meadow filled with skeletons.

Understanding the peril, Ulysses devised a plan: his crew plugged their ears with beeswax, and he had himself tied to the ship's mast to resist the sirens' chant. The crew, unaffected by the song, could then row the ship to safety.

The reader may ponder the relevance of this story to the political economy of IEL. In fact, the analogy is quite relevant, illustrating, like the myth, the critical importance of Thomas Cottier's contribution to IEL and, with it, to international economic governance.

In this analogy, the ships represent national economies led by politicians – the ships' crews. The sirens represent vested interest groups – corporations, lobbying factions or political constituencies – that tempt politicians to maintain or gain popularity (as well as political and financial support for their electoral campaigns) in exchange for protecting their rents. Like crews being drawn to the sirens, politicians often fall prey to the spell of short-term popularity. Such behaviour typically occurs at the expense of sound, long-term trade and investment policies pursuing an economy's greater good through the greater stability and predictability of policy regimes. Just as Ulysses bound himself to avoid yielding to temptation, IEL aims to 'tie governments to the mast' by creating a rules-based system that helps to shield the governments from the temptation of short-term impulses in favour of longer-term stability. The crew (governments) must navigate these dangerous waters without succumbing to the alluring but perilous calls of the sirens, lest the ship (the national economy) sink because of poor, short-sighted policies.

Thus, the art and science of IEL rule-making requires not only far-sighted vision, but also the skilful management of a given historical context that makes it viable for politicians to accept the disciplines of rules constraining their policy sovereignty. This is where Thomas's contribution has been so invaluable. The 1990s and early 2000s represented a 'golden age' for international trade and investment rule-making. During this period, not only did the World Trade Organization see the light of day, so too did a multilayered framework of trade and investment agreements at the bilateral and regional levels. Growing cohorts of developing and transition economies – alongside the industrialised economies – came to embrace the case for the freer cross-border trade and investment flows that this new framework embodied.

Among his many contributions, Thomas's scholarship on multilayered governance contributed to shaping discussions on how best to erect a 'multistorey international regulatory house'. He did so by applying the principle of subsidiarity to differing levels of policy interventions with a view to efficiently articulating social, political and economic interactions in an increasingly globalised world. In short, Thomas was part of the small community of Ulysses thinking, helping to design rules and negotiating processes to enable crews and ships to reach their desired destinations and to prevent them from being sunk by sirens along the way.

Recent years have seen the global international trade and investment landscape undergo profound changes, with an increasing number of governments attempting to 'cut the ropes' that once tied them to a stable global system of rules. Several chapters of this book illustrate the different dimensions and impacts of such a shift in the various areas of IEL dear to Thomas's work. In the name of affording governments more 'policy space', the world is witnessing not only a marked rise in recourse to unilateral and protectionist trade and investment measures, but also equally profound mutations in the very setting in which rules used to apply.

In the past, states used to negotiate rules among themselves to incentivise the private sector to embark on trade and investment negotiations. More often than not, such talks aimed at promoting cross-border transactions. Today, unilateralism is increasingly prompting policy responses exerting de facto extraterritorial effects. Devolving from rule-oriented towards power-oriented diplomacy, various governments are leveraging their economic dominance to enact domestic regulations no longer aimed at trading partners but rather at individual firms trading and investing across borders. Domestic regulations relating to a large swath of policy areas, such as environmental standards, data protection, labour standards and subsidies – often guided by geopolitical and national security considerations – are being unilaterally imposed as conditions governing access to major trade and investment markets, generating potentially significant adverse policy spillovers all too likely to prompt retaliatory responses.

Regardless of their merit, the unilateral nature of these measures introduces new challenges for the global trade and investment regime. The predictability that once characterised the multilateral trading system is being steadily eroded, leading to increased power-oriented dynamics and greater unpredictability, higher transaction costs and heightened uncertainty for traders and investors alike. The ropes that once tied opportunistic government behaviour to the mast are being cut.

Thomas's work remains relevant in helping us rethink how the international trade and investment system can and should adapt to such changed global circumstances. It is urgent to think about how to devise a new strategy to allow governments to renew their cooperative efforts and mutually agree on a minimum degree of discipline in restraining destructive unilateralism. More than ever, the world needs Ulysses-like thinking from experts to consider new ways to leverage IEL and adjust it to the exigencies and realities of a new reality. It is an urgent task indeed to design the types of ropes that could prove acceptable to governments currently blinded by today's fractured geopolitical context. Thomas and the students he trained are among those trying to do this, keeping in mind the lesson of Ulysses: that by adhering to agreed international norms and resisting calls for ill-informed short-term policies, governments can ensure the long-term stability of their national economies and the improved welfare of their citizenry.

The challenge for the future will be to find the right balance between the pursuit of increasingly vocal domestic interests and the benefits of a coordinated, rules-based system that fosters sustainable trade and investment growth. In navigating this challenge, the multilayered governance framework devised by Thomas Cottier will without doubt come in handy.

INDEX

www.ingramcontent.com/pod-product-compliance
Ingram Content Group UK Ltd.
Pitfield, Milton Keynes, MK11 3LW, UK
UKHW020239290926
15470UKWH00002B/618

9 781509 980789